RECOVERY FROM CULTS

Help for Victims of Psychological and Spiritual Abuse

Edited by

MICHAEL D. LANGONE, PH.D.

W. W. Norton & Company · New York · London

A NORTON PROFESSIONAL BOOK

Printed in the United States of America

First Edition

The text of this book was composed in 10/12 Century Textbook, with display type set in Korinna. Composition by Bytheway Typesetting Services, Inc. Manufacturing by Haddon Craftsmen. Book design by Justine Burkat Trubey

Library of Congress Cataloging-in-Publication Data

Recovery from cults : help for victims of psychological and spiritual abuse / edited by Michael D. Langone.
    p.   cm.
    Includes bibliographical references and index.
    ISBN 0-393-70164-6
    1. Cults – Psychology.   I. Langone, Michael D.
BP603.R43 1994   93-1923 CIP
616.89′1 – dc20

W. W. Norton & Company, Inc., 500 Fifth Avenue, New York, NY 10110
W. W. Norton & Company, Ltd., 10 Coptic Street, London WC1A 1PU

1 2 3 4 5 6 7 8 9 0

I dedicate this book to John G. Clark, M.D., who, though a private practitioner without institutional legal protection behind him, had the courage to proclaim the truth about cults in the face of years of relentless attack on his professionalism and character. Those of us who have known and admired Dr. Clark were gratified when he received the 1991 Psychiatrist of the Year Award of the U.S. Psychiatric Mental Health Congress for his "extraordinary courage in standing up to terrorist attacks against our patients, our profession, and our society." Dr. Clark has been a mentor, a friend, and an inspiration to me and to many others.

CONTENTS

ACKNOWLEDGMENTS

SO MANY PERSONS HAVE HELPED bring this book about that it is impossible to name them all. In addition to the contributors to the book, I want to thank those who participated in the American Family Foundation's (AFF) Project Recovery study groups, the directors of AFF, and the generous individuals who contributed financially to Project Recovery.

I am also indebted to Herbert Rosedale, Dr. Margaret Singer, and Dr. Arthur Dole for their reviews of the manuscript; Susan Barrows Munro, Norton's patient and helpful editor; and my son, Jose, who brought joy to my life while I was struggling with this project. I am especially grateful to Janja Lalich, whose discerning comments, encouragement, and expert copyediting skills were vital in bringing this book to completion.

ABOUT THE EDITOR

Michael D. Langone, Ph.D., is the Executive Director of the American Family Foundation and editor of its *Cultic Studies Journal,* published since 1984. He received his Ph.D. in Counseling Psychology from the University of California, Santa Barbara, where he was a Regents Fellow for three years. Dr. Langone has been studying cults since 1978 and has worked with more than 150 former cultists and family members. He is the coauthor (with Joan C. Ross) of *Cults: What Parents Should Know* (Lyle Stuart) and (with Linda O. Blood) of *Satanism and Occult-Related Violence: What You Should Know* (American Family Foundation).

Dr. Langone has written many papers on the subject of cults, including articles for *Psychiatric Annals: The Journal of Continuing Psychiatric Education* and other scholarly and professional journals, and chapters for a number of books, including the *Handbook of Psychiatric Consultation with Children and Youth, Innovations in Clinical Practice, Vol. 10,* and *Scientific Research and New Religions: Divergent Perspectives.*

From 1984 to 1987 Dr. Langone served on the American Psychological Association Task Force on Deceptive and Indirect Techniques of Persuasion and Control.

ABOUT THE CONTRIBUTORS

Susan Andersen, Ph.D., is Associate Professor of Psychology at New York University. The author of "Resisting Mind Control," Ms. Andersen's research focuses on developing a social-cognitive model of transference, on the link between self and social knowledge, and on the cognitive processes underlying depression.

David Clark has been an exit counselor for more than 10 years and has worked with over 300 cult members since 1975. Mr. Clark has spoken widely on the subject of cults to lay and professional audiences.

Richard L. Dowhower, D.D., a Lutheran pastor in Bowie, Maryland, has been addressing the cult issue for more than 15 years and is the author of several articles on cults. Rev. Dowhower has spoken widely on the subject, especially to religious audiences.

Gary Eisenberg, M.A., is in the real-estate business. He is a former Hebrew high school principal who has been involved in cult education for more than 17 years. Mr. Eisenberg is the editor of *Smashing the Idols: A Jewish Inquiry into the Cult Phenomenon* (Jason Aronson).

Geri-Ann Galanti, Ph.D., is on the faculty of the Statewide Nursing Program at California State University, Dominguez Hills, and the Anthropology Department at California State University, Los Angeles. Ms. Galanti has done research on cults and deprogramming, and is the author of "Brainwashing and the Moonies" and the book *Caring for Patients from Different Cultures* (University of Pennsylvania Press).

Kevin Garvey has been an exit counselor for more than 10 years and is the author of several articles, including a series in *Our Town* on Erhard Seminar Training (est). Mr. Garvey has spoken widely to lay and professional audiences.

Carol Giambalvo, an exit counselor since 1984, is a former Director of FOCUS, a nationwide support group for ex-cultists. Ms. Giambalvo is the author of *Exit Counseling: A Family Intervention* (American Family Foundation).

Noel Giambalvo, M.S., has been an exit counselor since 1984. Now retired, Mr. Giambalvo was an elementary school counselor for 34 years.

Lorna Goldberg, M.S.W., A.C.S.W., is a faculty member at the New Jersey Institute for Psychoanalysis. With her husband, William, Ms. Goldberg has conducted a support group for ex-cultists for 16 years, and has also worked with dozens of ex-cult members in psychotherapy. She is the author of several papers on the subject.

William Goldberg, M.S.W., A.C.S.W., is Director of the Community Support Center in Pomona, New York. With his wife, Lorna, Mr. Goldberg has conducted an ex-cultists' support group for 16 years. He has also worked with dozens of former cult members and is the author of several papers on the subject.

David Halperin, M.D., is Associate Clinical Professor of Psychiatry at Mt. Sinai School of Medicine in New York City. Dr. Halperin is the editor of *Religion, Sect, and Cult: Psychodynamic Perspectives* (John Wright PSG) and the author of many papers on the subject. Dr. Halperin has extensive clinical experience with cultists and ex-cultists and is a member of the Task Force on Cults of the American Academy of Psychiatry and the Law.

Susan J. Kelley, Ph.D., R.N., is Associate Professor of Nursing at Boston College. Dr. Kelley is the editor of *Pediatric Emergency Nursing* (Appleton & Lange), for which she received the American Journal of Nursing Book of the Year Award. Dr. Kelley also received the John G. Clark Award for Distinguished Scholarship in Cultic Studies for her research comparing ritually abused and sexually abused children in day care.

Janja Lalich, a former member of a political cult, is an editor and publishing consultant in Alameda, California. She is the author of

"The Cadre Ideal: Origins and Development of a Political Cult," and coauthor with Madeleine Landau Tobias of *Captive Hearts, Captive Minds: Healing the Damage of Cults and Other Abusive Relationships* (Hunter House). Ms. Lalich is currently writing a book about her 10-year cult experience.

Arnold Markowitz, M.S.W., C.S.W., is Director of the Cult Hotline and Clinic and Director of Adolescent Services for the Jewish Board of Family and Children's Services in New York City, which has worked with over 4,000 cult victims and family members during the past 12 years. Mr. Markowitz has been a clinical social worker for more than 17 years and is the author of several articles on the subject of treating cultists and their families.

Paul R. Martin, Ph.D., is Director of Wellspring Retreat and Resource Center in Albany, Ohio. Dr. Martin, a psychologist with extensive teaching and research background, has worked with over 200 former cult members at Wellspring, a rehabilitation center for ex-cultists. Dr. Martin is the author of several articles and the book, *Cult-Proofing Your Kids* (Zondervan).

Herbert L. Rosedale, Esq., is Senior Partner at Parker Chapin Flattau & Klimpl in New York City and President of the American Family Foundation, a nonprofit institute focusing on cult research and education. Mr. Rosedale, who has been involved in the cult education field for more than 12 years, is the author of several articles on the subject.

Patrick L. Ryan has been an exit counselor since 1986. A former member of Transcendental Meditation (TM), in 1991 Mr. Ryan settled a suit against TM for fraud and negligence. He has spoken widely about his experiences and is cofounder of TM-Ex, a support and education group (and newsletter) for former members of TM.

Margaret Thaler Singer, Ph.D., is Adjunct Professor of Psychology at the University of California, Berkeley. Dr. Singer is the world's leading expert on cults and thought reform and is the author of many scholarly papers on the subject. Dr. Singer has been a contributor to many edited volumes on cults and related subjects, including *The Family Therapist as Systems Consultant* (Guilford Press).

Madeleine Landau Tobias, M.S., R.N., C.S., formerly the Director of the Downtown Counseling Center in East Hartford, Connecticut, is currently in private practice in northern New England. Ms. Tobias has worked with over 200 former cultists in psychotherapy, support groups, and exit counseling, and she lectures on aspects of the cult phenomenon. She is coauthor with Janja Lalich of *Captive Hearts,*

Captive Minds: Healing the Damage of Cults and Other Abusive Relationships (Hunter House), a book on specific recovery guidelines for former cult members.

Mark Trahan, a former member of the NYC Church of Christ (the NYC branch of the Boston Church of Christ Movement), is an exit counselor. Mr. Trahan, who lectures on college campuses and for civic organizations on the cult problem, is also the associate editor of *Thresholds,* a newsletter for ex-members of the Discipling Ministries.

Rob Tucker, M.Ed., is a school counselor in British Columbia. Mr. Tucker is the author of several papers on the subject of cults and is currently working on a book about destructive organizations. While he was Director of the Council on Mind Abuse in Toronto, Canada, Mr. Tucker spoke widely to lay and professional audiences.

Philip Zimbardo, Ph.D., is Professor of Psychology at Stanford University. A leading social psychologist, Dr. Zimbardo has written several articles on mind control and cults, and is coauthor of *The Psychology of Attitude Change and Social Influence* (McGraw-Hill).

PREFACE

FOR NEARLY THREE DECADES I have been involved in some form of work with individuals and families who have been impacted by one or another of the several thousand cults that exist in the United States today. Fourteen years ago, in 1979, I wrote the first article that appeared in the popular press designed to help those leaving cults. It was called "Coming Out of the Cults" and appeared in *Psychology Today*. Having counseled so many ex-members by that point in time, I hoped such an article would be of use to cult veterans who had exited from groups and had no one nearby with whom they could talk over their time in the cult and the multitude of problems they faced on leaving the group. Hundreds of former cultists told me how useful the article had been when they were given copies by exit counselors or friends.

Ex-members told me of their dismal contacts with clergy and mental health professionals who did not know about cults, social influence programs, psychological adaptations to the stresses of life inside closed, intense, mind-control groups, and the pains of life after leaving the cult. When I began helping ex-cultists, there were only a few mental health professionals—Dr. John Clark and Mrs. Jean Merritt in Boston were among the most experienced and knowledgeable—who knew about the social and psychological processes that resulted from life in cults. Jean Merritt remonstrated in 1981 that "mental health professionals and clergy are generally the worst people to talk to about cults." She was struggling to get professionals and clergy to learn what was occurring in cults and the recovery process.

The present volume is intended to serve the needs of those wanting to know about cults: cult victims, parents, families, clergy, mental health professionals, lawyers, writers, and law enforcement personnel.

For all too long a small, loud group of cult apologists, primarily sociologists of religion, untrained in the effects of intense indoctrination, thought reform, coercive persuasion, classical social influence, and coordinated programs of coercive influence and behavior control, wrote and spoke of ex-cult members as if they were creating lies about their life in the groups they left. These academics tried to equate what was being reported by ex-members as reflections of exaggerations, witch hunts, or the work of vigilante parents. These academics seemed to choose not to listen to what was being reported by ex-members, labeling them apostates and acting as if they were a special brand of sinners and liars.

Time has turned the tide and evidence supporting the reports of ex-members has accrued. Jim Jones had 914 followers who committed suicide or were murdered along with United States Representative Leo J. Ryan and four journalists in the jungles of Guyana. Two hundred seventy-six of these were children and teenagers.

Since then investigative journalists have studied the reports of ex-members chronicling the deaths of at least 103 children and mothers in the infamous Indiana Faith Assembly, which had maternal death rates 100 times that of the state average and a perinatal death rate nearly three times the average. These are but a few examples of the more blatant cult harms which had occurred during the period between Jonestown and the Waco, Texas cult's fiery ending at the command of its leader. To me, Waco was a replay of Jonestown. Both illustrate to an alarming degree the control that a cult leader can exert over followers, and how difficult it is for relatives and families to help members. Waco illustrated that the world does not yet understand the psychological and social influence programs that cult leaders use and the destruction these programs can cause. While, fortunately, few cults end as disastrously as Jonestown and Waco, every year cults adversely affect thousands of individuals.

This volume has been written in recognition of the needs of former cult members now in the process of recovery, which is both grueling and joyful. Their readaptation to mainstream society, which is complicated by the heavy guilt, fear, and denigration imposed by life in the cult, is a hard, lonely, and bewildering road. This volume is intended as a resource book to assist the former member, the family, and helping professionals understand the not-so-simple recovery from mind-control influences and the social and psychological pummelings and dilemmas with which the ex-member wrestles.

Sometimes the treatment afforded cult members leads them to seek legal redress after leaving the group. I have appeared on behalf of a number of former cultists whose lives were so damaged by their time in a cult that they eventually sued the group, usually for fraud and deception, as well as for an array of egregious conduct put upon them by the group. Five of these cases went to the United States Supreme Court, and in each instance the court supported the original verdicts in favor of the former cult members. The time spent on those cases was sparse, however, compared to the time I have put in counseling more than three thousand women and men after they left cults. Often I met with groups of ex-members from a particular cult who learned of my work and wanted some time to discuss what happened in their cult and the kinds of reentry problems they were having.

I got involved in this work not because any family member was in a cult. Rather, my interest began during the Korean War era when I worked at the Walter Reed Army Institute of Research and studied thought-reform, influence, and intense indoctrination programs. Since then I have continued the study of group influence.

In the 1960s I began to heed the appearance of cults and heard the descriptions of hundreds of parents who noticed certain changes in the personality, demeanor, and attitudes of their young-adult offspring who had become involved in cults. From those descriptions, and from working with many who were among the first to exit the cults, I concluded that cultic groups were not using mysterious, esoteric methods, but they had refined the "folk art of human manipulation and influence." They had combined ages-old manipulative and persuasive techniques known to social psychologists, influence professionals, salesmen, and other "compliance professionals." The cults created programs of social and psychological influence that were effective for their goals. And I noticed especially that what had been added to the basic thought-reform programs seen in the world in the 1950s was the new cultic groups' use of pop psychology techniques for further manipulating guilt, fear, and defenses.

The appearance of this book is based on three decades of observations, work, and dedication by a number of people. It is a monument to the strength of family ties and the pursuit of good research by professionals, be they mental health practitioners, investigative journalists, clergy, law enforcement personnel, lawyers, or educators. The best traditions of each of those professions rests upon accurate observations and correct reasoning. The sequence of efforts is roughly the following:

When parents lost their offspring into a burgeoning array of new cults in the 1960s, they began to call attention to the cult phenomenon and to seek help. Their descriptions of the changes in their cult-involved loved ones intrigued the professionals they consulted. Fortunately, these parents found a few mental health professionals, lawyers, and clergy who understood something of what the parents were describing.

These "pioneer" families began grass-roots groups to collect information, to offer solace and assistance to one another, and to see what could be done to help their offspring exit from these groups. The parents' concerns were not that their young-adult children had taken up a new religion, nor were they concerned that their loved ones had left school and home or had completely redirected the course of their lives to help mankind by joining truly altruistic groups. They were concerned that these young adults were doing none of the above but seemed to have closed their minds to their past, their families and friends and were simply helping a band of itinerant gurus, pied pipers, and self-proclaimed messiahs become wealthy and powerful.

The first wave of cults recruited 18- to 25-year-olds. These early groups were often based on Eastern philosophies. Since then the world has come to see that cults can be formed around any philosophy. There are political, religious, psychological, and life-style cults. Cults now recruit the elderly, single mothers, young couples. Today's cults are no longer youth cults, and no longer based primarily on religious themes. Many groups do incorporate as religious entities because of the many tax and other advantages, but close inspection often reveals that the religious properties are sparse compared to the other aspects of these groups. Each cult is a reflection of the personal interests, persuasion, and choices of the leader.

In reading this volume, remember that none of us is beyond being manipulated by an intense, dedicated, and persistent persuader who meets us at a time when we are vulnerable, needy, and lonely. We must also remember the 914 who died in Jonestown, Guyana, at the whim of Jim Jones, and that Charles Manson was a cult leader. Cults are not all simple, odd little groups doing "their own thing." Nor are those who join aliens in our midst. The potential cult victim is you and I.

This volume is a monument to the contributions of the "pioneer" parents and families who called attention to the phenomenon, and to the former members who provided the basic descriptions that a series of professionals over the years have now come to understand. Good observations underlie all science, and this volume indicates that the science of understanding cult growth, cult recruiting, and maintenance tactics is on solid ground.

Above all this book is dedicated to those coming out of cults now, as well as to those who have been out for some time and have never had the opportunity to read and discover what some of the effects of cults can be. It is also for those yet to emerge from abusive groups who need a book to study and to see that they are not alone, and that what is happening to them is understandable. This book is a giant step both in validating the anguish felt by former cult members, their friends, and families and in acknowledging the special recovery needs of ex-cultists.

Margaret Thaler Singer
Berkeley, California

RECOVERY FROM CULTS

INTRODUCTION

Michael D. Langone, Ph.D.

THE FUNDAMENTAL GOAL of this book is to help former members of cults and related groups, their families, and helping professionals increase their understanding of the post-cult recovery process. The book does not aim to be an overview of the cult phenomenon. Nor does it seek to be a "Good Housekeeping Seal of Disapproval" detailing the dubious practices of individual groups. Instead, the book tries to illuminate general principles pertinent to understanding cult conversion, post-cult problems, and post-cult recovery. It also describes practical techniques for facilitating recovery from cultic involvements.

This book is a product of the American Family Foundation's (AFF) Project Recovery, a multiyear project to improve the quality and quantity of professional services for ex-cult members. AFF is a tax-exempt research and educational organization founded in 1979 to assist ex-cult members and their families. AFF's staff, which includes myself, work with more than 100 professionals who volunteer time to a variety of committees and study groups. Certain study groups were established in 1990 in order to examine post-cult recovery in a comprehensive and coordinated manner. In large part, the chapters of this book reflect the findings and conclusions of these study groups. Most of this book's contributors served on these study groups or are otherwise associated with AFF.

The point of view advanced in this book rests on a variety of information sources:

1. Psychological literature that illustrates how and the degree to which human beings can be manipulated and exploited, including the literature on thought reform, popularly called "brainwashing" (Chen, 1960; Farber, Harlow, & West, 1956; Group for the Advancement of Psychiatry, 1956, 1957; Lifton, 1961; Mindszenty, 1974; Schein, Schneier, & Barker, 1961); the psychology of social influence (Asch, 1952; Cialdini, 1984; Milgram, 1974; Zimbardo, Ebbesen, & Maslach, 1977); and a growing body of research on cults (Conway, Siegelman, Carmichael, & Coggins, 1986; Dubrow-Eichel, 1989; Langone, Chambers, Dole, & Grice, in press; MacDonald, 1988; Martin, Langone, Dole, & Wiltrout, 1992; Yeakley, 1988)
2. Clinical reports by psychotherapists and pastoral counselors (Ash, 1985; Clark, 1979; Clark & Langone, 1984; Dubrow-Eichel & Dubrow-Eichel, 1988; Goldberg & Goldberg, 1982; Halperin, 1990; Hassan, 1988; Hochman, 1984; Langone, 1985, 1990; Ross & Langone, 1988; Singer, 1978, 1986; Singer & Ofshe, 1990; Singer, Temerlin, & Langone, 1990; Temerlin & Temerlin, 1982)
3. The clinical experience of the book's contributors, who collectively have worked with at least 9,000 cultists and their families, with the cult clinic of the New York Jewish Board of Family and Children's Services alone having helped more than four thousand individuals (Markowitz, 1989; A. Markowitz, personal communication, December 11, 1992).

OVERVIEW OF THE CULT PHENOMENON

Before outlining the structure of this book, I believe it is important that I provide an overview of certain basic concepts and findings that must be understood before one can appreciate the uniqueness of the recovery issues facing former cult members.

Definitional Issues

Although the term cult is vague and controversial, it has firmly implanted itself in popular discourse. The term is often associated with "thought reform" (popularly called "mind control"), which, according to Lifton (1961), describes certain processes of behavior change used on civilians in mainland China and on Korean POWs. Ofshe and Singer (1986) distinguish influence and control programs as either first or second generation of interest. By "first generation of interest" they are referring to

> Soviet and Chinese thought reform and behavior control practices studied twenty to thirty years ago. Second generation examples are of programs which are either currently operating or have been in existence during the last decade. . . . In older programs, attacks on the stability and acceptability of existing self-evaluations were typically focused on elements of self we classify as peripheral. Newer programs tend to focus on elements of self we classify as central.
>
> Peripheral elements of self are defined as self-evaluations of the adequacy or correctness of public and judgmental aspects of a person's life (e.g., social status, role performance, conformity to societal norms, political and social opinions, taste, etc.). We define as central elements of self, self-evaluation of the adequacy or correctness of a person's intimate life and confidence in perception of reality (e.g., relations with family, personal aspirations, sexual experience, traumatic life events, religious beliefs, estimates of the motivations of others, etc.). (pp. 3–4)

In a later paper Singer and Ofshe (1990) define a thought-reform program as "a behavioral change technology applied to cause the learning and adoption of an ideology or set of behaviors under certain conditions" (p. 189). They note that the following conditions distinguish a thought-reform program from other forms of social learning:

- Obtaining substantial control over an individual's time and thought content, typically by gaining control over major elements of the person's social and physical environment
- Systematically creating a sense of powerlessness in the person
- Manipulating a system of rewards, punishment, and experiences in such a way as to promote new learning of an ideology or belief system [or behavior] advocated by management [i.e., leadership]
- Manipulating a system of rewards, punishments, and experiences in such a way as to inhibit observable behavior that reflects the values and routines of life organization the individual displayed prior to contact with the group
- Maintaining a closed system of logic and an authoritarian structure in the organization
- Maintaining a noninformed state existing in the subject (pp. 189–190)

Examples of first-generation thought-reform programs include, in addition to those used on Korean War POWs, the "revolutionary universities" in Mao's China, other programs to influence civilians in China, and the Russian purge trials of the 1930s (Mindszenty, 1974). Examples of second-generation thought-reform programs include certain large group awareness trainings (sometimes called "transformational trainings") and certain contemporary groups commonly called "cults."

The term "cult" is applied to a wide range of groups, including historical cults (e.g., the cult of Isis), non-Western cults studied by anthropologists (e.g., Melanesian cargo cults), and a myriad of unorthodox groups—religious, psychotherapeutic, political, and commercial—that have caught the public's attention during the past two decades.

Thought-reform programs are the methods often used by cults to produce the behavioral and attitude changes the groups desire. A thought-reform program is a particular type of social learning, which may be of short duration (e.g., as in certain large group awareness trainings) or of long duration (e.g., as in programs used on Korean War POWs [Singer, 1987], or in current cults).

A cult is a particular type of social system, that is, it is a group of people with a particular and enduring pattern of relationships, beliefs, values, and practices that give the group a unique identity.

Until recently the term "cult" in a general sense referred to groups that exhibit "great or excessive devotion or dedication to some person, idea, or thing," and in a more specific sense referred to "a religion regarded as unorthodox or spurious" (*Webster's Third New International Dictionary*, Unabridged, 1966). The public concern of the past two decades, however, has demanded additional clarification of the concept. One attempt at such clarification resulted from a conference on cults sponsored by the American Family Foundation, the UCLA Neuropsychiatric Institute, and the Johnson Foundation:

Cult (totalist type): a group or movement exhibiting a great or excessive devotion or dedication to some person, idea, or thing and employing unethically manipulative techniques of persuasion and control (e.g., isolation from former friends and family, debilitation, use of special methods to heighten suggestibility and subservience, powerful group pressures, information management, suspension of individuality or critical judgment, promotion of total dependency on the group and fear of leaving it, etc.), designed to advance the goals of the group's leaders to the actual or possible detriment of members, their families, or the community. (West & Langone, 1986, pp. 119–120)

By relating this definition to Singer and Ofshe's description of the two generations of interest thought-reform programs. The following definition emerges:

> A cult is a group or movement that, to a significant degree, (a) exhibits great or excessive devotion or dedication to some person, idea, or thing, (b) uses a thought-reform program to persuade, control, and socialize members (i.e., to integrate them into the group's unique pattern of relationships, beliefs, values, and practices), (c) systematically induces states of psychological dependency in members, (d) exploits members to advance the leadership's goals, and (e) causes psychological harm to members, their families, and the community.

This definition does not refer to beliefs because a group's belief system, although sometimes related to and supportive of the features that make the group a cult, is not necessarily nor directly related to its status as a cult. Thus, cults may be religious (with seemingly orthodox or bizarre beliefs), psychotherapeutic, political, or commercial.

The characteristics of a cult tend to produce conflict between the group and society. In order to manage this conflict, cultic groups tend to become isolated, psychologically if not physically, governed by hidden agendas, and totalistic, that is, they will dictate, sometimes with excruciating specificity, how members should think, feel, and act.

As defined here, cults differ from "new religions," "new political movements," "innovative psychotherapies," and other "new" groups in that cults make extensive use of unethically manipulative techniques of persuasion and control to advance the leader's goals. Of course, some groups that cause concern do not meet all of the definitional criteria, while others become more or less cultic over time.

Cults differ from merely authoritarian groups, such as boot camp or certain monastic orders, in that the latter are explicit about their goals, are contractual rather than seductive, and usually are accountable to authorities outside the group.

Satanic activity, which has received a great deal of media attention during the past few years, may be cultic, but is not necessarily so. A small group of teenagers who meet together to practice occult rituals, for example, do not necessarily constitute a cult as defined here, even if they engage in destructive acts such as sacrificing animals. Whether or not a group is a cult depends upon its structure and psychological dynamics. The group may, nevertheless, be destructive for other reasons. Not all destructive groups are cults, although all cults, as defined here, will tend to be destructive.

Why Do People Join Cults?

Laypersons and professionals tend to have a fundamental misconception about why people join cults. Laypersons tend to think that cults are weird groups that attract crazy people. Professionals, especially those with some knowledge of psychoanalysis, are more sophisticated but basically say the same thing, akin to the following: People join cults because cults fulfill their members' need for believing and belonging and help their members resolve unconscious conflicts regarding their relationship with their parents.

This view is incorrect for several reasons. First, it assumes that people actively seek to join cults, when in fact most cult members, to the degree they were seeking anything, were not seeking anything so controlling and deceptive as the cult they joined. Second, it assumes that cults actually fulfill members' needs, when in reality they exploit needs in order to promote compliance with the leadership's wishes. Third, it assumes that people who join cults do so because of some fundamental personality deficiency such as unconscious conflicts. Although there is some truth in this statement for some cultists, it greatly overstates the actual situation. Most cultists were relatively normal persons experiencing an unusual level of stress when they encountered a cult. Those that had enduring psychological problems were not necessarily attracted to the cult because of their problems, although their problems may have made them more vulnerable to the cult's "sales pitch" and control tactics.

Consider an analogy. A depressed young woman enters a dating bar seeking companionship. A charming, smooth-talking man persuades her to go for a ride in his convertible. If he takes her to a lonely place and rapes her, or if he seduces her by playing on her loneliness and trusting nature, does one conclude that the young woman unconsciously *wanted* to be raped or seduced? Obviously, no. People are not always *motivated* to seek that which they get. Sometimes they are fooled and get what they didn't bargain for. People join cults, not because they make a rational, informed choice. They join because they are duped. The process is a seduction, not a mutually beneficial agreement or the choice of an informed "consumer."

The process of joining cults can be briefly described by adapting the DDD syndrome (Farber et al., 1956), which was one of the explanations of what is popularly called "brainwashing." Farber and his colleagues maintained that during the Korean War the Chinese were able to gain a high degree of control over American POWs through a process of debility, dependency, and dread. Contemporary cults, which operate in an open society and do not have the power of the state at their disposal, cannot forcibly restrain prospects and run them through a debilitating regimen. Instead, they must fool them. They must persuade prospects that the group is beneficial in some way that appeals to the targeted individuals. As a result of this deception and the systematic use of highly manipulative techniques of influence, recruits come to commit themselves to the group's prescribed ways of thinking, feeling, and acting; in other words, they become members, or converts. By gradually isolating members from outside influences, establishing unrealistically high, guilt-inducing expectations, punishing any expressions of "negativity," and denigrating independent critical thinking, the group causes members to become extremely dependent on its compliance-oriented expressions of love and support. Once a state of dependency is firmly established, the group's control over members' thoughts, feelings, and behavior is strengthened by the members' growing dread of losing the group's psychological support (physical threat also occurs in some groups), however much that support may aim at ensuring their compliance with leadership's often debilitating demands. Thus, the new DDD syndrome is one of deception, dependency, and dread.

Although the process just outlined is very complex and subtle, let me provide here somewhat more detail about the prototypical cult conversion, acknowledging at the outset that real life provides countless variations on and departures from this conceptual simplification.

During the early stages of the cult recruitment process, when the group tries to present itself as benevolent and capable of fulfilling recruits' needs, recruiters shower much attention and other positive reinforcement on prospects. Moonies, for example, have used the term "love bombing" to describe this phase (Edwards, 1979). As recruits lower their defenses in this "loving" climate, intimate and seemingly caring conversations enable recruiters to assess the psychological and social status of prospects, to learn about their needs, fears, dependency potential, and actual and possible resistances. Meanwhile, testimonies from group members (who are not averse to lying for the "cause"), credentials (whether valid or bogus) of leaders, attacks on the group's competitors, and prospects' favorable reaction to members' seemingly warm and caring attentiveness tend to support the group's claim of benevolence and superiority, and to convince prospects that they will benefit by joining the group.

Those who do make the commitment to join are rarely aware of the subtle techniques of persuasion and control shaping their behavior, thoughts, and feelings. The apparently loving unanimity of the group masks, and in some cases bolsters, strict rules against private as well as public dissent. Questions are deflected. Critical comments are met with smiling pleas of "no negativity," or some other "thought-terminating cliche." If prospects or new members persist in "negativity," they may be reminded of personal problems or guilty memories they have revealed to leaders, or they may be subjected to subtle ad hominem attacks that short-circuit their questions. Examples of such personal attacks might be, "You're intellectualizing" or "You're being divisive." Doubt and dissent are thus interpreted as symptoms of personal deficiency.

Once the dominance of the group is established, once it is permanently "one-up," new members slide down a spiral of increasing dependence on the group. They are often encouraged or ordered to live with other group members. People outside the group are viewed as spiritually, psychologically, politically, or socially inferior, or as impediments to the members' development. In order to "advance" at a satisfactory pace, members must avoid outsiders and spend long hours involved in various tasks or practices the leadership deems necessary. In short, members spend more and more time with and under the direction of the group.

To ensure continuation of the group's rewards (praise, attention, promise of future benefits, social contact, and so on), members must implicitly, if not explicitly, acknowledge the group's authority in defining what is real, good, and true. The group challenges and tests the sincerity of members' subservience by establishing extremely high, if not impossible, expectations regarding activities (e.g., fund-raising quotas) and personal development (e.g., to be free of "negative" thoughts and doubts). Because dissent, doubt, and negativity are forbidden, members must project a facade of "happiness," acceptance, and agreement while struggling to achieve the impossible. Those who fail to project the requisite facade are attacked and punished. The dependency described earlier makes members dread the loss of the group's support thereby causing them to cave in to the pressure and "reform" themselves. Those who do not reform will be ejected, thereby reminding others that "rebellion" can have dreadful consequences.

Adaptation to the group, then, requires a capacity, much like trance logic in hypnosis, to deceive oneself and others in order to believe that the group is always right, even if it contradicts itself. Increasing isolation from the outside world, exhausting activity in service to the group, and hours spent in practices that induce dissociative states (e.g., meditation, chanting, speaking in tongues, "criticism sessions") facilitate a psychological splitting that permits adaptation to the group's contradictory agendas and demand for subservience. Members who are tempted to object to or disagree with elements of the group's agenda may find themselves in a "loyalty/betrayal funnel" (MacDonald, 1988). If they remain loyal to their own perceptions about self and world, they betray the group on which they have become inordinately dependent; if they remain loyal to the group, they betray their own perception of what is real, good, and true. Dissent thus places members in a "funnel" from which there is no escape and which inevitably leads to betrayal, either of themselves or the group.

The result of this process, when carried to its consummation, is a pseudopersonality (West, 1992), a state of dissociation in which members are "split" but not "multiple," in which they proclaim great happiness yet hide great suffering.

Why Do People Leave Cults?

Obviously, the control cult leaders achieve is not absolute because ultimately most people leave cultic groups (Barker, 1984), although a sizeable number remain for many years. In one of the few studies that investigated why people leave cults, in structured interviews of 90 subjects, Wright (1983a, 1983b) identified four main reasons for defection. The first reason is a break in the cult's social insulation. Only 4 of 12 persons separated from the group for three or more weeks (for example, on an extended visit to family) returned to the group. The second reason is unregulated interpersonal intimacy, which can permit members to share doubts that they would normally suppress. In "every case where one spouse or mate defected the other also left the movement" (Wright, 1983b, p. 112). Third, cult members will often leave their groups when they become disillusioned with the group's achievements or repeated errors in "prediction," for example, when the world doesn't end – again. Lastly, members may depart in disillusionment when they learn about the hypocrisy or immoral behavior of the cult's leaders.

That members felt considerable pressure to remain in the group is further supported by Wright's finding that 42% of cult defectors left covertly (e.g., by sneaking out in the middle of the night), while 47% made an overt withdrawal "without fanfare or public 'announcements' to the group" (Wright, 1983a, p. 186), although only 11% made "an open announcement or declaration to the group that one is leaving" (Wright 1983a, p. 187). In a more recent analysis of his data, Wright (1987) found that members who were in the group less than one year were much more likely to leave covertly than members in one to three years (92% vs. 22%) or more than three years (92% vs. 21%).

Wright's study provides abundant evidence, including some fasci-

nating anecdotes, of the degree to which cult members' group affiliation results from the social and psychological controls of the cult environment. His results are consistent with the findings of Korean War
studies of thought reform (Lifton, 1961; Schein et al., 1961) in that
these apparent "conversions" to a very different way of thinking tend
not to hold when the "convert" leaves the highly controlled environment. Wright's results are also consistent with the observations of
exit counselors (Giambalvo, 1992; Hassan, 1988; see Chapter 8), who
have found that the patient presentation of information unavailable in
the cult (basically the same kind of information that impelled Wright's
subjects to leave because of disillusionment over the group or its
leader) will cause a large majority of cultists to renounce their affiliation.

The marked difference in frequency of covert departure between
short-term and long-term members is an interesting finding that does
not have an obvious interpretation. Perhaps longer-term members do
indeed regain a measure of autonomy within the group and exercise
this autonomy by leaving publicly. Perhaps their decision to leave
merely reflects a newly found and short-lived autonomy that results
from a long, painful, and very private reevaluation of the group. Or
perhaps the unrepresentativeness of Wright's sample resulted in an
overrepresentation of overt leavers. Skonovd (1983) reported that in
his interviews of 60 former cultists, in a sample that was "a good
mix between those sympathetic and nonsympathetic with the anti-cult
movement" (p. 91), "only one person interviewed attempted to leave
publicly" (p. 101).

Post-cult Needs and Problems

The contributors to this book discuss this issue at length, so I will
make only a few general remarks.

People who are seduced into cults have markedly different backgrounds. Some appear to be models of psychological health, others are
severely disturbed. When they join a cult, a number of significant
changes occur. They will be exploited and abused, some terribly so,
others only mildly so. They usually miss out on important life experiences; for example, many drop out of college when they join or give
up vocational or artistic pursuits or remain celibate contrary to their
pre-cult intentions. They are indoctrinated to believe that disagreement with or doubt about the group's teachings or practices is always
their fault, as are any personal problems (e.g., "You are depressed not
because the meditation we prescribe is inadequate but because you
are not meditating enough"). The very core of their sense of self is

attacked as deficient (Ofshe & Singer, 1986). They become extremely dependent on the group's leadership for sometimes ridiculously minor decisions. They are subjected to high and sometimes impossible and contradictory demands, which tend to leave them feeling like failures. Yet they are commanded not to express any negativity that may reflect badly on the group.

When they leave, for whatever reason, they will tend, as do victims of other forms of abuse (Boulette & Andersen, 1986), to believe that they left because something was wrong with *them*. They do not usually view the group as a cult – at least not initially. Holding the layperson's view of cults, they think that cults are weird groups for crazy people, and since they are not crazy and their group isn't weird, it isn't a cult. Hence, they will tend not to seek help from educational organizations such as the American Family Foundation. In a recent survey of 308 ex-cult members a sizeable minority had had very little contact with cult educational organizations; further, these subjects reported that they collectively knew an estimated 5,000 ex-cultists who had had no contact with such organizations, even though the majority were viewed as needing help (Langone et al., in press). Therefore, ex-cultists must be educated about the dynamics of cult control and exploitation, not only so they can recover from the adverse effects of their cult experience, but also so they will know what kind of help they require. Otherwise they may waste much time, effort, money, and unnecessary suffering pursuing false explanations of their problems, for example, with a psychotherapist who doesn't appreciate the power and influence of cultic environments.

In addition to blaming themselves, former cultists will also tend to have difficulty adequately pinning down who they really are. They had a certain personality before the cult. They developed an adaptive pseudopersonality while in the cult. Aspects of the pre-cult personality may have been pathological. Aspects of the cult pseudopersonality may have been beneficial and genuine. Their cult indoctrination led them to believe that their pre-cult personality was virtually all bad and the cult personality all good. A substantial residue of the cult indoctrination remains even after they leave the group. Thus they often feel as though they have two personalities. How do they put it all together?

While trying to develop an internal integration and sense of coherence, former cultists must simultaneously contend with a myriad of life challenges for which they may be very unprepared: employment, housing, making friends, repairing old relationships with friends and family, school, and even learning how to behave appropriately in social situations. Is it any wonder that many former cultists describe their post-cult experience as an emotional roller coaster?

Life's challenge to ex-cult members is daunting. It is not surprising that many make a partial adaptation by denying the cult experience, by weaving a web of revisionism or forgetfulness around the pseudo-personality of the cult. However, whether they "pocket" the cult experience or confront it, it inexorably permeates their lives. There is no escaping its effects. Consequently, if it is not properly understood, it cannot be effectively managed.

Hundreds of thousands of former cult members struggle alone. Many are undoubtedly pursuing psychotherapy or seeking pastoral counseling to help with their emotional turmoil and confusion. I fear that in too many instances these helpers either ignore the cult experience or reinforce the cultic indoctrination by searching for "unconscious motivations," or "dysfunctional family dynamics," or whatever — searching for some explanation of why the person "wanted" to join such a terrible group. Ex-cultists are not merely misguided or troubled seekers. They are victims. Overlooking or minimizing the noxious role of the cultic environment, regardless of the degree and nature of pre-cult psychopathology, will lead to victim blaming, not to victim assistance.

STRUCTURE OF THE BOOK

This book is divided into four sections: mind control, leaving cults, facilitating recovery, and special issues.

Chapter 1, which stands outside the four sections, focuses on certain historical issues that should be understood if one is to help cult victims. This chapter examines the development of cult educational organizations, the social context that gave rise to contemporary cultism, prevalence data, the pro-cult/anti-cult polarization within professional circles, the deprogramming controversy, clinical and research reports on cult-related harm, and recent changes in the cult scene.

Mind Control

This section provides several perspectives on how cults gain control over recruits. Chapter 2, by Janja Lalich, describes the formation, operation, and dissolution of a political cult with which she was once affiliated. Her account, which contains many illuminating anecdotes, communicates the subtlety and complexity of cultic environments. Because it deals with a political cult, her chapter also underlines the fact that the cult phenomenon is not fundamentally a religious issue, at least in an organizational sense. Groups earn the label "cult" because of what they do, not because of what they believe.

Chapter 3, by anthropologist Geri-Ann Galanti, describes her experiences as a participant observer at a Unification Church (the "Moonies") training weekend. She also analyzes this experience in light of Robert J. Lifton's (1961) eight themes of thought reform, the most influential conceptualization within this field. Lifton's approach is structural, providing a cross-sectional view of the cult environment, and consequently complements the process-oriented DDD syndrome (deception, dependency, dread) discussed earlier.

Chapter 4, by social psychologists Philip Zimbardo and Susan Andersen, attempts to demystify the notion of mind control by relating it to a body of research concerning the psychology of social influence. They accomplish this task by focusing on how we can *resist* mind control. In following this approach, they also contribute to the post-cult recovery process. Many ex-cult members are liable to be recruited into another cult, in large part because of the exaggerated dependency needs induced by their first cult. Zimbardo and Andersen's advice on resisting mind control can help former cultists avoid getting seduced again.

Leaving Cults

This section has two objectives. First, it describes the problems former cultists face when they return to mainstream society. Chapters 5 and 6, by former group members Patrick L. Ryan and Mark Trahan, respectively, are autobiographical accounts that not only illustrate post-cult problems but also provide some insight into joining and living in a cultic group. Chapter 7, by exit counselor Carol Giambalvo, expands the scope of the personal accounts by briefly describing the types of problems she has observed other ex-members struggling with. Her observations also help to orient the reader for the next section on facilitating recovery.

The second objective of this section is to increase the reader's understanding of exit counseling. Exit counselors (to be distinguished from deprogrammers, see Chapter 8) have helped hundreds of cultists make informed decisions to leave their cults. Their success underlines one of the fundamental themes of this book, namely, that cult affiliation is in large part sustained through manipulation and information control. When cultists, through exit counseling, receive information unavailable in the cult and learn about how cults manipulate members, they will, in the large majority of cases, decide to leave their groups. If individuals join and stay in cults because the cult provides something

the members genuinely need, they would not permanently and relatively quickly give up their membership simply because they listened
to someone talk for a few days. Cultists leave their groups because
they realize they have been duped and manipulated.

Chapter 8, by exit counselors Dave Clark, Carol Giambalvo, Noel
Giambalvo, Kevin Garvey and myself, describes information-focused
exit counseling, which the first four coauthors practice. Chapter 9, by
Kevin Garvey, is a composite case study of a bizarre and dangerous
New Age cult. This case is intentionally an extreme example; most
exit counseling cases are routine by comparison, mainly because much
is already known about the group in question. The example here was
chosen in order to accentuate the importance of information – and of
information collection when little information is available – in attempts to help a person reevaluate a cult involvement. Garvey's chapter also sheds light on the control techniques of certain New Age cults.

Facilitating Recovery

This section is the "meat and potatoes" of this book because it provides
concrete recovery guidelines for helping professionals, families, and
ex-cultists. Chapter 10, by psychologist Paul Martin, provides an overview of the recovery process, with a particular focus on psychological
assessment. Dr. Martin also describes the unique post-cult rehabilitation program he and his colleagues have developed at the Wellspring
Retreat and Resource Center.

In Chapter 11 social worker Lorna Goldberg describes the psychotherapeutic process with former cult members. Using a number of case
examples, she explains why it is vital to teach ex-cultists about how
the cult experience influences their current problems. She also gives
some practical advice on details of the therapeutic process, such as
the need to take an active, rather than a passive, stance and why long
silences can be counterproductive.

Chapter 12, by the Reverend Richard L. Dowhower, examines recovery issues from the standpoint of the pastoral counselor. Reorienting
themselves spiritually is one of the most compelling and persistent
problems ex-cultists face. Their resolution of spiritual issues is hampered, however, by the clergy's sharing in the common misconception
that cults fill unmet needs and their resulting tendency to avoid examining cultic experiences with a critical eye. Rev. Dowhower explains
why it is important to "raise, develop, and heighten the spiritual gift
of discernment." He also provides concrete advice for pastoral counselors, such as a section on how to distinguish religions from cults.

Psychiatrist David Halperin, in Chapter 13, uses case studies to illustrate the special treatment needs of former cultists requiring psychiatric hospitalization. He describes in particular the differences in treatment for ex-members who had significant pre-cult psychopathology and those who did not have any significant pre-cult psychiatric illness. He also briefly describes a case of a young man whose psychiatric hospitalization was influenced in part by his satanic activities.

Social worker William Goldberg, in Chapter 14, offers practical suggestions on organizing and conducting support groups for ex-cult members. The role of the group leader, frequency of meetings, advantages and disadvantages of professional leaders and peer leaders, and screening members are some of the issues addressed here. Support groups can play a vital role in helping ex-cultists understand their cult experience, regain the capacity to trust others, and increase their self-confidence.

Chapter 15, by social worker Arnold Markowitz, tries to help families better understand what they can do to facilitate a loved one's post-cult recovery. Markowitz explains that families should respond to a loved one's departure from a cult as the beginning of a series of problems, which he organizes into three phases of recovery. The family's support during the recovery process can be vital.

In Chapter 16 psychotherapist and former cult member Madeleine Tobias gives practical advice and encouragement to ex-members, who, whether in psychotherapy or not, must take primary responsibility for their own recovery. Ms. Tobias addresses issues relating to separating from the cult self, the emotional turmoil encountered when returning to mainstream society, the often-neglected physical needs of cultists, the vocational challenges that are especially troubling to those who spent many years in an isolated group, learning how to trust again, and reorienting oneself spiritually.

Special Issues

This section addresses areas of concern that relate to post-cult recovery but are not appropriate for the previous section. In Chapter 17 Gary Eisenberg and I describe the abuse and neglect often associated with children in cultic groups. Unlike youth or adults, children, especially those who were born into cults, do not have mature pre-cult personalities that can be "awakened" through exit counseling. For this reason, successfully treating adults raised in cults or children who come out of cults, for example, because their parents defect, requires changes in approach from the model expounded throughout much of this book. Because there has been so little clinical work with such children, the suggestions we offer are based on reasoned extrapolations from what we know, rather than actual experience. This is an area that cries out for research.

Chapter 18, by psychologist and nurse Susan Kelley, reports on the results of a study of children in day care who had been ritualistically and/or sexually abused. Dr. Kelley found that ritualistically abused children suffered more severe and more enduring psychopathology than children who had been sexually abused. Eighty percent of her subjects were associated with legal cases in which convictions for abuse were obtained, frequently with confessions. Ritualistic abuse is often associated with satanic cults that employ occult rituals during ceremonial abuses of children, although child molesters may use ritual merely to intimidate children. Kelley's study does not comment on the extent to which the ritual abuse of her subjects was "religiously" motivated. Her study is important, however, because it demonstrates the reality of ritualistic abuse and the apparent added destructiveness of ritual elements in child sexual abuse.

Kelley's study is also relevant to a topic intentionally left out of this book, that is, the claims of adult survivors of ritual abuse. During the past few years, thousands of persons (usually, though not always, women) claim to have been ritualistically abused as children, often in the ceremonies of satanic cults (Sakheim & Devine, 1992). These claims have generated considerable controversy because so many of the memories are "recovered" in psychotherapy. Psychotherapists generally accept that events from childhood can be repressed for many years and recovered in psychotherapy. However, the recovery of dissociated memories of trauma occurring after early childhood (which is the case with many ritualistic abuse survivors) tend to come in a flood (Nemiah, 1985), rather than a little at a time, as seems to be the case for most ritualistic abuse survivors.

Moreover, experts in the field of hypnosis and dissociation (M. T. Singer, personal communication, November 19, 1992) suspect that the apparent epidemic in recovered memories may be due in part to many psychotherapists' lack of appreciation for the suggestibility of many troubled persons or certain psychotherapists' tendency to make diagnostic decisions based on insufficient evidence. The improper use of hypnosis to recover memories is especially controversial. Indeed, the American Medical Association concluded that "recollections obtained during hypnosis can involve confabulations and pseudomemories and not only fail to be more accurate, but actually appear to be less reliable than nonhypnotic recall" (Council on Scientific Affairs, 1985, p. 30).

The recovery of ritualistic-abuse memories by adult survivors is part of a broader controversy regarding the recovery of sexual-abuse memories in general. Many support groups have formed throughout the country around the themes of sexual abuse, ritualistic abuse, and incest. In March 1992 parents accused of sexual abuse by their adult children formed the False Memory Foundation, which had been contacted by nearly 2,000 people by the end of 1992. Where this controversy will lead is not clear.

In my view evidence supports the existence of both of these colliding phenomena: false memories induced by psychotherapists and valid memories of ritualistic abuse, whether recovered in psychotherapy or not. If, as Kelley's study shows, some children are ritualistically abused today, it seems reasonable that some were so abused 20 or 30 years ago. On the other hand, compelling cases indicate that false memories can indeed be "induced." One of the most striking examples was a false memory that an expert witness intentionally induced in a ritual-abuse suspect in order to determine experimentally if the man were as suggestible as the expert suspected (Ofshe, 1992).

The central, still-unanswered question is what percentage of recovered memories are valid. This is an important question because if, as some claim, only a very small percentage are valid, then the psychotherapy profession has a serious problem on its hands, namely, educating therapists so that they will not mistakenly induce memories of abuse in their clients. If, on the other hand, most memories are valid, society has a serious problem, namely, helping this population of victims and stopping the perpetrators. If both phenomena are common (i.e., 50% valid and 50% false memories), then it will be absolutely vital to develop effective procedures for avoiding the induction of false memories and detecting true memories, and to train therapists.

Within the network of professionals associated with the American Family Foundation, there is disagreement about the degree to which memories of ritualistic abuse are based on events that really happened. Some are inclined to believe that most recollections are based on fact. Others contend that in the large majority of cases, the memories are an artifact of the psychotherapeutic process or are fantasies having some other origin. One's position on the credibility of ritualistic-abuse memories will affect one's treatment approach. If one is inclined to be skeptical, one may not be as alert to indicators of repressed memories of abuse, and one may tend to probe for indicators of fantasizing processes if a client reports such memories. If one is inclined to believe the reports, one may run a greater risk of unintentionally suggesting memories, and one may be less likely to probe for indicators of fantasizing because such probing may interfere with the clinical relationship.

Because one of this book's major goals is to provide useful and generally well-accepted suggestions for facilitating the recovery process of former cultists, I have not included a chapter on the treatment of ritualistic-abuse survivors. This issue is simply too problematic at present. I recommend that interested readers consult Greaves (1992) for a more detailed analysis of the controversy.

There is, however, one aspect of the occult about which our knowledge is more reliable, that is, teen Satanism. Educator Rob Tucker, in Chapter 19, describes in detail the types of teenage satanic involvement, what attracts teens to Satanism, how it affects them, and what can be done to help them break the destructive bonds to Satanism. He also briefly discusses some of the social implications of this problem.

I want to remind the reader that much activity falling under the category of Satanism is not cultic in the sense used in this book, although it is cultic in the lay sense of "weird groups for crazy people." As Tucker explains, satanically involved teens tend to be troubled, and sometimes extremely disturbed. Satanism can give such youth a sense of meaning, belonging, and power. In a perverse way it does meet needs and does not necessarily exploit needs, as is the case with the "traditional" cults that are the primary object of this book. When the bonds to Satanism have been broken, the adolescent's next task isn't only "recovery" from Satanism. It is the resolution of the psychological problems that attracted the youth to Satanism in the first place.

Chapter 20, by Attorney Herbert Rosedale, is the first written material to comprehensively address practical legal problems confronted by former cultists. Rosedale explains how a cult involvement may affect legal aspects of marriage, divorce, custody, contracts, fraud, and emotional distress. He urges ex-members not to become discouraged or intimidated by legal questions, at the same time warning against unrealistic expectations. He also provides a useful checklist of post-cult legal issues to consider.

The chapters in this book in a sense are different windows looking out on the same landscape. Their common object is the intriguing and sometimes devastating post-cult recovery phenomenon. Each window sees a different part of the landscape. Thus the pastoral counselor may be particularly attracted to Rev. Dowhower's chapter, while the parent of an ex-cultist may want to study Markowitz's chapter. Taken as a group, I believe that the chapters in this book provide a well-rounded and comprehensive perspective on post-cult recovery. I am deeply grateful to the contributors for their hard work and dedication to the victims of cults. I absolve all contributors, however, of any responsibility for the thoughts I have expressed in this introduction or in other chapters. This book is a collaborative effort by a group of people who, although generally agreeing on the major issues relating to cults and related groups, do make independent judgments on various aspects of the cult phenomenon. I hope that the reader will benefit from their collective wisdom concerning this subject.

REFERENCES

Asch, S. E. (1952). *Effects of group pressure upon the modification and distortion of judgments.* New York: Holt, Rinehart & Winston.

Ash, S. (1985). Cult-induced psychopathology, part 1: Clinical picture. *Cultic Studies Journal, 2*(1), 31–91.

Barker, E. (1984). *The making of a Moonie.* New York: Basil Blackwell.

Boulette, T. R., & Andersen, S. (1986). "Mind control" and the battering of women. *Cultic Studies Journal, 3*(1), 25–35.

Chen, T. E. H. (1960). *Thought reform of the Chinese intellectuals.* New York: Oxford University Press for Hong Kong University Press.

Cialdini, R. B. (1984). *Influence: How and why people agree to things.* New York: William Morrow.

Clark, J. G. (1979). Cults. *Journal of the American Medical Association, 242,* 279–281.

Clark, J. G., & Langone, M. D. (1984). The treatment of cult victims. In N. R. Bernstein & J. Sussex (Eds.), *Handbook of child psychiatry consultation.* New York: SP Medical and Scientific Books.

Conway, F., Siegelman, J. H., Carmichael, C. W., & Coggins, J. (1986). Information disease: Effects of covert induction and deprogramming. *Update: A Journal of New Religious Movements, 10,* 45–57.

Council on Scientific Affairs. (1985, April 5). Scientific status of refreshing recollection by the use of hypnosis. *Journal of the American Medical Association, 253,* 30–35.

Dubrow-Eichel, S. K. (1989). Deprogramming: A case study. *Cultic Studies Journal, 6*(2), 1–117.

Dubrow-Eichel, S. K., & Dubrow-Eichel, L. (1988). Trouble in paradise: Some observations on psychotherapy with New Agers. *Cultic Studies Journal, 5*(2), 177–192.

Edwards, C. (1979). *Crazy for God: The nightmare of cult life.* Englewood Cliffs, NJ: Prentice-Hall.

Farber, I. E., Harlow, H. F., & West, L. J. (1956). Brainwashing, conditioning, and DDD (debility, dependency, and dread). *Sociometry, 20,* 271–285.

Giambalvo, C. (1992). *Exit counseling: A family intervention.* Bonita Springs, FL: American Family Foundation.

Goldberg, L., & Goldberg, W. (1982). Group work with former cultists. *Social Work, 27,* 165–170.

Greaves, G. B. (1992). Alternative hypotheses regarding claims of satanic cult activity: A critical analysis. In D. K. Sakheim & S. E. Devine (Eds.), *Out of darkness: Exploring satanism and ritual abuse* (pp. 45–72). New York: Lexington Books.

Group for the Advancement of Psychiatry. (1956). *Factors used to increase the susceptibility of individuals to forceful indoctrination: Observations and experiment.* Washington, DC: American Psychiatric Association.

Group for the Advancement of Psychiatry. (1957). *Methods of forceful indoctrination: Observations and interviews.* Washington, DC: American Psychiatric Association.

Halperin, D. A. (1990). Psychiatric perspectives on cult affiliation. *Psychiatric Annals, 20,* 204–218.

Hassan, S. (1988). *Combatting cult mind control.* Rochester, VT: Park Street Press.

Hochman, M. (1984). Iatrogenic symptoms associated with a therapy cult: Examination of an extinct "new psychotherapy" with respect to psychiatric deterioration and "brainwashing." *Psychiatry, 47,* 366–377.

Langone, M. D. (1985). Cult involvement: Suggestions for concerned parents and professionals. *Cultic Studies Journal, 2*(2), 148–169.

Langone, M. D. (1990). Working with cult-affected families. *Psychiatric Annals, 20,* 194–198.

Langone, M. D., Chambers, R., Dole, A., & Grice, J. (in press). Results of a survey of ex-cult members. *Cultic Studies Journal.*

Lifton, R. J. (1961). *Thought reform and the psychology of totalism.* New York: W. W. Norton.

MacDonald, J. P. (1988). "Reject the wicked man"—Coercive persuasion and deviance production: A study of conflict management. *Cultic Studies Journal, 5*(1), 59–121.

Markowitz, A. (1989). A cult hotline and clinic. *Journal of Jewish Communal Service, 66*(1), 56–61.

Martin, P., Langone, M. D., Dole, A., & Wiltrout, J. (1992). Post-cult symptoms as measured by the MCMI Before and After Residential Treatment. *Cultic Studies Journal, 9*(2), 219–250.

Milgram, S. (1974). *Obedience to authority: An experimental view.* New York: Harper & Row.

Mindszenty, J. (1974). *Memoirs.* New York: Macmillan.

Nemiah, J. (1985). Dissociative disorder. In H. I. Kaplan & B. J. Saddock (Eds.), *Comprehensive textbook of psychiatry/IV* (pp. 942–957). Baltimore, MD: Williams & Wilkins.

Ofshe, R. (1992). Inadvertent hypnosis during interrogation: False confession due to dissociative state; mis-identified multiple personality and the satanic cult hypothesis. *International Journal of Clinical and Experimental Hypnosis, XI*(3), 125–156.

Ofshe, R., & Singer, M. T. (1986). Attacks on peripheral versus central elements of self and the impact of thought reforming techniques. *Cultic Studies Journal, 3*(1), 3–24.

Ross, J. C., & Langone, M. D. (1988). *Cults: What parents should know.* New York: Lyle Stuart.

Sakheim, D. K., & Devine, S. E. (1992). *Out of darkness: Exploring satanism and ritual abuse.* New York: Lexington Books.

Schein, E., Schneier, I., & Barker, C. H. (1961). *Coercive persuasion.* New York: W. W. Norton.

Singer, M. T. (1978). Therapy with ex-cult members. *Journal of the National Association of Private Psychiatric Hospitals, 9,* 15–18.

Singer, M. T. (1986). Consultation with families of cultists. In L. I. Wynne, S. H. McDavid, & T. T. Weber (Eds.), *The family therapist as systems consultant.* New York: Guilford Press.

Singer, M. T. (1987). Group psychodynamics. In R. Berkow (Ed.), *The Merck manual of diagnosis and therapy* (15th ed.) (pp. 1467–1471). Rahway, NJ: Merck.

Singer, M. T., & Ofshe, R. (1990). Thought reform programs and the production of psychiatric casualties. *Psychiatric Annals, 20,* 188–193.

Singer, M. T., Temerlin, M., & Langone, M. D. (1990). Psychotherapy cults. *Cultic Studies Journal, 7*(2), 101–125.

Skonovd, N. (1983). Leaving the cultic religious milieu. In D. G. Bromley & J. T. Richardson (Eds.), *The brainwashing/deprogramming controversy: Sociological, psychological, legal and historical perspectives* (pp. 91–105). Lewiston, NY: Edwin Mellen Press.

Temerlin, M. K., & Temerlin, J.W. (1982). Psychotherapy cults: An iatrogenic perversion. *Psychotherapy: Theory, Research, and Practice, 19,* 131–141.

West, L. J. (1992, May). Presentation at American Family Foundation Conference, Arlington, VA.

West, L. J., & Langone, M. D. (1986). Cultism: A conference for scholars and policy makers. *Cultic Studies Journal, 3,* 117–134.

Wright, S. A. (1983a). *A sociological study of defection from controversial new religious movements* (Doctoral dissertation, University of Connecticut, 1983). Ann Arbor, MI: U.M.I. Dissertation Information Service, University Microfilms International.

Wright, S. A. (1983b). Defection from new religious movements: A test of some theoretical propositions. In D. G. Bromley & J. T. Richardson (Eds.), *The brainwashing/deprogramming controversy: Sociological, psychological, legal and historical perspectives* (pp. 106–121). Lewiston, NY: Edwin Mellen Press.

Wright, S. A. (1987). Leaving cults: The dynamics of defection. *Society for the Scientific Study of Religion Monograph Series, Number 7.*

Yeakley, F. (Ed.). (1988). *The discipling dilemma.* Nashville, TN: Gospel Advocate.

Zimbardo, P. G., Ebbesen, E. B., & Maslach, C. (1977). *Influencing attitudes and changing behavior: An introduction to method, theory, and applications of social control and personal power.* Reading, MA: Addison-Wesley.

1

HELPING CULT VICTIMS:
HISTORICAL BACKGROUND

Michael D. Langone, Ph.D.

THE WORK ON WHICH THIS BOOK IS BASED has its roots in the early 1970s, when parents of young adults who had joined cultic groups began to speak up about alarming changes they had observed in their children. Although some sociologists, warning about a "great American cult scare," claimed that these parents were upset merely because their children had chosen unorthodox paths (Bromley & Shupe, 1981), the reality was very much different. Most of these parents, who themselves were often caught up in the "new-is-good" intoxication of the times, did not object to the newness of the groups, even if some of the beliefs mystified them. Indeed, many initially welcomed their children's unorthodox choices because of the immediate positive effects: "Thank God he doesn't look like a dirty, smelly hippie anymore!" "I don't understand this guru stuff, but at least she isn't doing drugs." These parents of cult members became concerned not because of the groups' offbeat nature, but because of striking behavioral and personality changes that their young adult children began to exhibit. Clark, one of the first mental health professionals to criticize cults, described the types of changes that alarmed parents:

> Personality changes drastically—a fact that often brings terrified parents into the physician's office. Converts often seem drab and dreamy outside the group, stereotyped, and somewhat expressionless when discussing any-

thing other than their new experience. They lack mirth and richness of vocabulary. The devices of expression – irony, metaphor, and delight in the use of abstraction – are gone. Many converts report hallucinations, even olfactory ones, and experience group-validated delusions as well as nightmares. The sense of current history is quickly lost. If challenged they may become excited or even violent but at best answer difficult questions with memorized cliches. (1979, p. 280)

Clark also articulated the belief, held by many parents and former cult members, that cult joiners had been subjected to an unusual and powerful program of behavior control and change, what was popularly called "brainwashing" or "mind control." Clark's view emphasized the capacity of cult environments to induce dissociative states, a position many still emphasize, although others (see, for example, Chapter 4) stress sociopsychological manipulation.

The unique capacity of these absolutist groups to cause harm stems from . . . the sudden conversion through aggressive and skillful manipulation of a naive or deceived subject who is passing through or has been caused to enter a susceptible state of mind. Through highly programmed behavioral control techniques and in a controlled environment, the subject's attention is narrowed and focused to the point of becoming a trance. Within the totally controlled atmosphere provided by each group, this state is maintained during several sleep periods until it becomes an independent structure. The loss of privacy and sleep in a bizarre new atmosphere, change of language, and continuous control of excitement level amount to an onslaught of information that sustains the continued state of dissociation; throughout this period of focused attention, new information is absorbed at an accelerated rate and rapidly becomes integral to the available mechanisms of the mind. As a result, the convert becomes dependent on this new environment for definitions of reality. From this stage the group controls not only the forms of action but also the content of thought through confessions, training, and conditioning. To think for oneself is suspect in many groups; to think wrongly is satanic. (Clark, 1979, p. 280)

Singer (1979), another one of a handful of psychotherapists who spoke out against cult abuses in the 1970s, wrote about the problems cultists experienced after leaving their groups. These problems included depression, loneliness, indecisiveness, slipping into altered states, blurring of mental acuity, uncritical passivity, guilt, fear of cult reprisals and supernatural personal catastrophes, an acute sensitivity to the "watchfulness" of parents and friends, difficulty explaining how they could have joined such a group, apprehension about their own idealism and altruism (which the cult had manipulated), a loss of the feeling of being a member of an elite, and financial difficulties.

Many parents and former cultists were convinced that they had been victimized (the young adults directly and the parents indirectly) by unscrupulous groups that employed powerful techniques of persuasion and control. These individuals were often eager to tell their stories. Unfortunately, the overwhelming majority of clergy and helping professionals whom they consulted were either uninterested or unsympathetic. Politicians were of very limited help. But journalists, who know deep in their bones that the world has an abundance of scoundrels, perked up their ears. Within a matter of a few years, dozens of newspaper and magazine stories told about innocent youth being seduced and exploited by cults. After the Jonestown murders/suicides in 1978 there was an explosion of media stories.

As a result of the publicity accorded the cult issue during the 1970s, parents of cultists began to discover one another. Their typical response upon finding others who shared their concern was: "I thought I was all alone!" Initially, ad hoc groups formed in various parts of the country – and in Europe, which was experiencing a similar problem. Most of these groups were oblivious at first to the existence of the others. In time, however, they began to communicate and organize on a national scale. In 1979 the Citizens Freedom Foundation (CFF, now called the Cult Awareness Network) was chartered and served as a unifying force for more than a dozen grass-roots groups across the country. The Citizens Freedom Foundation's primary objectives were public education (accomplished through speaking engagements and by providing information to the media) and helping parents. In the same year the American Family Foundation (AFF) was formed; its focus, however, was on research and professional outreach.

WHY NOW?

Cults have always existed, and probably always will exist so long as some people are willing to abuse and exploit others. But why are they so much more conspicuous and apparently more numerous than at any time in recent memory? Although any answer to this question is bound to be speculative, reflecting upon the question may help readers see the cult phenomenon within a broader context and better understand the deeper recovery needs of ex-cultists. I hope that my speculations will stimulate readers to think more about the context and cultural implications of the cult phenomenon.

In my opinion, the recent growth spurt of cults began with the 1960s, an era of major social change. In 1959 we were complacently secure in "motherhood and apple pie." In 1969 we were rattled by chants of "off the pig!" In 10 years the nation changed course suddenly, markedly, and decisively.

West and Allen (1968) described three "rebellions" that together defined the areas in which America was changing. (I am talking here about cultural movements, not cults.) The Red Rebellion of the New Left was, in the words of M. Stanton Evans, "American liberalism writ large, demanding that the regnant abstractions be enforced *instanter* and across the board, with no exceptions" (Evans, 1966, cited in West & Allen, 1968, p. 102). The New Left institutionalized political activism and drastically changed government, politics, and the law, in part through the galvanization of its opponents as well as through its own achievements. The Black Rebellion aspired to social and economic equality. Although its goals were only partly achieved, it succeeded in making America more tolerant—of much more than racial differences—than would have been dreamed possible 50 years ago. The Green Rebellion (not to be confused with the ecology movement of today), which began with the hippies of San Francisco, was "cultural, religious, mystical, and passively pharmacological" (West & Allen, 1968, p. 103).

In my opinion, the Green Rebellion has most profoundly influenced American culture. It championed sexual liberation, challenged traditional religion with an Eastern mysticism (Cox, 1977) that seemed to make sense of hallucinogenic experiences, and defied an "uptight" world to be "mellow." The Green Rebellion complemented the Black Rebellion by helping to make America conspicuously more tolerant. It also spiritualized hedonism and relativism and set the stage for the New Age movement, which has gained prominence in recent years. "Do your own thing" was not meant as a call to selfishness; it was a call to a new, nonjudgmental, anti-intellectual spirituality of simplicity and pleasure—"If it feels good, do it."

Aagaard (1991) distinguishes between religious change and religious conversion. Religious conversions happen to individuals; religious change to societies. Religion, in a social sense, is the "code," the interpretive schema that underlies the worldview of a cultural group. Religious change in a culture is "a very complex process, and on a large scale it is not carried out consciously. This does not mean that it happens without awareness, but it is not necessarily understood as religious change, for its simple elements are not seen as part of the whole to which they belong" (Aagaard, 1991, p. 92). According to this view, one could interpret the Red, Black, and Green Rebellions as initiating a religious change in the United States (indeed, in all of Western culture) that has not yet played itself out. Paradoxically, these rebellions helped make America simultaneously more secular and more religious (usually rephrased as "spiritual"), but less Judeo-Christian.

The Red Rebellion was blatantly secular and pushed for an absolute separation of church and state. The Green Rebellion, though apolitical, undermined the credibility of traditional religion, which was secularism's major rival. The Black Rebellion, helped by the Green, increased tolerance for the nontraditional, in part by stimulating America's collective guilt about its long history of racial, ethnic, and religious intolerance. Together, these rebellions made American culture doubt itself.

As a result, the importance of religion declined. The Gallup organization, for example, found that the percentage of people who say religion is "very important" in their lives decreased from 75% in 1952 to 52% in 1978, and increased to only 58% by 1991 ("Final 1991 data," 1992). By the 1960s many intellectuals had come to see religion as an unnecessary, even destructive, anachronism that would pass away as science and technology progressed. Sociologists wrote about the "secularization thesis," which "denotes *more people becoming less religious or ceasing to need religion*" (Robbins, 1988, p. 56). Following the secularization trend, some influential elements of the religious mainstream challenged various elements of orthodoxy. There were theologians who said that "God is dead," priests who wore dungarees and T-shirts, nuns who left their cloisters in droves, and ministers and rabbis who were practically indistinguishable from social workers. Many welcomed such changes as signs of religionists' attempts to stay "relevant" and to join the largely secular movements for social justice that swept over the country in the 1960s.

Religion's predilection for the supernatural, considered by many secularists to be irrationalism at best and superstition at worst, appeared to be giving way to at least a semisecularized social ethics centered on individual freedom. Society seemed to be moving in the direction advocated by the Humanist Manifesto II (American Humanist Association, 1973). This manifesto affirmed individual liberty, equality, internationalism, autonomous and situational ethics, and the capacity of reason and science to solve mankind's problems. It condemned traditional religions explicitly: "Traditional dogmatic or authoritarian religions that place revelation, God, ritual, or creed above human needs and experience do a disservice to the human species." "Promises of immortal salvation or fear of eternal damnation are both illusory and harmful."

As the 1960s gave way to the 1970s and 1980s, some surprising things began to happen in this secular climate of expanding individual liberty. Instead of becoming even more secularized, society appeared to be turning back toward religion, even if unorthodox. Hundreds of thousands, if not millions, of young people, many influenced by psychedelic drug experiences, began to study Eastern religions and follow "gurus," whose numbers increased steadily (Cox, 1977). "Jesus people" formed communes (Richardson, Simmonds, & Harder, 1972) and gained enough attention to merit a rock musical, "Jesus Christ Superstar." Radical political groups that were fanatically "religious" in their commitment to an ideal—for example, the Symbionese Liberation Army—sprang up as disillusionment with mainstream politics and values spread (Lalich, 1992). Fundamentalists attempted to convert the "unsaved" with a new vigor and confidence, finding televangelism to be especially appealing (Hadden & Shupe, 1987). Humanistic psychologists began talking more and more about the necessity of spiritual development (Marin, 1973), and quasi-spiritual "psychotechnologies" such as est became a growth industry (Behar & King, 1985). Gallup's findings, cited above, on the importance of religion probably understate the backlash of the 1970s and 1980s against secularism because the Green mind-set viewed "religion" in a negative light, seeing it as judgmental, rigid, and intellectually demanding, while seeing "spiritual" as nonjudgmental, tolerant, and reassuringly vague.

Some sociologists have tried to explain these changes by hypothesizing that the level of religiosity in society is more or less stable, although its nature changes (Stark & Bainbridge, 1981). As mainstream religions decline, unorthodox religious groups gain adherents, and vice versa. The 1920s, for example, like the 1970s, was a time of decline for mainstream churches and growth for various spiritualist and other unorthodox groups. Other theories "identify cultic effervescence as a prerevolutionary condition," for example, Dickens's depiction of an "exotic occultism flourishing among the degenerate and demoralized upper class of the Ancien Régime" (Robbins, 1988, p. 27).

Although seeing merit in these explanations, I am most intrigued by Wilson's contention that "it is the *system* that becomes secularized" (Wilson, 1985, p. 19, cited in Robbins, 1988, p. 56). Wilson suggests that the religious ("spiritual") impulse may achieve full expression in a free, secular society. Religions, however, become fragmented and marginalized relative to the increasingly secularized institutions of education, media, and government, from which religions, or traditional religions anyway, are essentially banished (Neuhaus, 1984). The profusion of cults and quasi-religious psychotherapeutic and political groups may be the price a tolerant, pluralistic society with a secular social system must pay in order to prevent more powerful traditional religions from threatening the secular authority. Thus, a secular system can defend itself against a strong religious impulse among its members by fostering—however unintentionally or nondeliberately—a dynamic religious marketplace in which exotic and innovative groups vigorously compete with and weaken established religions. This is a simple strategy for strengthening secularism: divide and conquer, or to be more precise, divide and contain. Not surprisingly, the competing religions will tend to support the secular authorities in order to prevent other religions from becoming dominant.

Some observers welcome the diversification of the religious "marketplace," in which "entrepreneurs of experience" provide more choices to "consumers" (Kilbourne & Richardson, 1984). Others, including myself, see a wild and unrestrained bazaar in which serious and responsible innovators are likely to play second-fiddle to market-wise and unscrupulous frauds, charlatans, and self-proclaimed "prophets," who prosper at the expense of their followers.

Religion is an especially appealing arena for such manipulators, many of whom engage in blatantly criminal activities, for two reasons. First, one can more completely and predictably control individuals by changing their fundamental religious beliefs because in so doing one alters their fundamental assumptions about what makes the world work. This approach can be much more effective and efficient than a frontal assault on peripheral values, attitudes, and behavioral predispositions. Second, in the United States religion is protected by the First Amendment, which can bring benefits that even the most expensive public relations and legal experts couldn't provide to a business client.

Thus, the growth of cultic groups is a natural consequence of a secular free market that treats religion as a consumer item, as a matter of personal "taste" or preference, rather than a fundamental and necessary unifying factor in the human psyche and society at large. Cult leaders and would-be cult leaders can easily disguise themselves in the confusing and unrestrained religious marketplace. Simultaneously, they can take advantage of the potential power that religion has within the psyches of individuals who no longer see their fundamental beliefs reflected in and reaffirmed by the institutions of the society in which they live. That which is most vital becomes an exchangeable commodity in an unrestrained marketplace in which hucksters prosper, while their "spin doctors" label cult critics (who would be called "consumer advocates" in the economic sphere) religious bigots.

PREVALENCE

In 1984 the Cult Awareness Network (CAN) compiled a list of more than 2,000 groups about which they had received inquiries (Hulet, 1984). The frequency with which CAN and the American Family Foundation have encountered previously unheard-of groups – at least 6 to 12 a week – suggests that 2,000 is a low estimate for the number of cultic groups in the United States today, even given the fact that many about which inquiries are made are probably not cults.

Most cults appear to be small, having no more than a few hundred members. Some, however, have tens of thousands of members and formidable financial power.

Zimbardo and Hartley (1985), who surveyed a random sample of 1,000 San Francisco Bay area high school students, found that 3% reported being members of cultic groups and that 54% had had at least one contact with a cult recruiter. Bloomgarden and Langone (1984) reported that 3% and 1.5% of high school students in two suburbs of Boston said they were cult members. Bird and Reimer (1982), in surveys of the adult populations of San Francisco and Montreal, found that approximately 20% of adults had participated in new religious or parareligious movements (including groups such as Kung Fu), although more than 70% of the involvements were transient. Other data in this study, and Lottick (1993), suggest that approximately 2% of the population have participated in groups that are frequently thought to be cultic. It seems reasonable, therefore, to make a conservative estimate that at least four million Americans have been involved with cultic groups.

However, as West says, "cults are able to operate successfully because at any given time most of their members are either not yet aware that they are being exploited, or cannot express such an awareness because of uncertainty, shame, or fear" (1990, p. 137). Therefore, in any survey, however random, the actual number of cultists is likely to be much *greater* than the number of persons who identify themselves as members of cultic groups or even of groups that other people might deem cultic. Because the victims do not identify themselves as such, they are not likely to be identified as cult-affected by psychotherapists or other helpers unless the helpers inquire into the possibility that there might be a cult involvement.

PRO-CULTISTS AND ANTI-CULTISTS

When contemporary cults first began to arouse parental concern in the late 1960s and early 1970s, it was sometimes possible for parents to persuade their adult children to talk to former cult members who knew about the group's hidden agendas and deceitful practices. Frequently, the offspring would leave as a result of these extended conversations. The term *deprogramming* was applied to this process because the parents believed that the cult had "programmed" their children through the use of very powerful psychological and social forces. These successes, however, apparently motivated cultic groups to become even more closed and hostile to families, and it became more and more difficult for parents to persuade their adult children to listen to "the other side of the story."

The Evolution of Deprogramming

Thus frustrated by the cults' insulation, parents began, usually with the aid of former cult members, to take their adult children away from the cult—for example, by meeting them on the street and forcing them into a car—and confine them in houses, mountain cabins, or hotel rooms. There they were "deprogrammed," that is, they were talked to for three to five days in a safe environment where they had adequate nutrition and opportunity to rest. In nearly two-thirds of the cases (Bromley, n.d.; Langone, 1984), the information presented was sufficient to "awaken" the cultists and cause them to leave their groups. (Bromley, however, found that with regard to the Unification Church, the "success" rate of deprogramming declined to 40% for members who had been in the church four years or more.) During the late 1970s and early 1980s, several hundred such involuntary deprogrammings occurred, and the term "deprogramming" came to take on the negative connotation of "coercive" that is now one of its distinguishing features (although many persons still protest against making coercion a defining feature of "deprogramming").

Parents did not pursue deprogramming gleefully. It was a frightful decision made only as a last resort. When it worked, parents tended to be relieved that the ordeal was over, overjoyed to have their offspring back, and angry that no authorities had been willing to spare them this ordeal by legally rescuing their adult children from the exploitative and harmful environments of cults. Many of them channeled their anger into social activism, much of which was pursued under the CFF umbrella. In addition to public education and helping other parents, many activists lobbied politicians to pass "guardianship" bills that would permit parents to extract their young adult children from cults legally, place them under psychiatric observation, and have them legally "deprogrammed." Aronin (1982) favorably discussed guardianship proposals in the *Columbia Journal of Law and Social Problems,* although others (e.g., Shapiro, 1983) wrote in opposition. A number of state legislatures debated such bills, and some almost became law.

Larger and wealthier groups have fought activists and critics through well-financed public relations campaigns (e.g., "Scientology Ad," 1990), through cult-financed media (e.g., Rotheimer, 1984), and by training their members to sabotage deprogrammings. The Unification Church (the "Moonies"), for example, taught members how to force their parents to take them to a hospital (for example, they would break a bathroom mirror and use the glass to cut their wrists) so that the member could call their leadership, who would come to the hospital with a lawyer (Freed, 1980). Many groups also had members who successfully escaped deprogramming sue their parents and the deprogrammers and/or file charges for kidnapping (Langone, 1984). Few deprogrammers and even fewer parents lost these cases. As with the media, judges and juries tended to sympathize with the parents, who often used the necessity defense – that is, the "snatching" and confinement were necessary to end the greater harm of cultic exploitation. Those cases that did result in legal punishment or fines, however, caused many persons to look for alternatives to (involuntary) deprogramming.

This tendency was strengthened by the fact that the support for guardianship legislation and deprogramming was not unanimous, even among activists and the professionals who criticized cults. Many feared that the existence of guardianship laws might diminish the motivation to develop noncoercive means of helping cultists and might lead to a new set of abuses. Most professionals avoided getting involved in deprogrammings, even indirectly, and viewed deprogramming as a last resort of desperate parents. Because of these ethical and legal concerns, many persons tried to help cultists leave their groups through voluntary means, that is, without "snatching" or confinement. Although initially called voluntary deprogrammings, these interventions came to be called exit counselings, because the term "deprogramming," even with the qualifying adjective "voluntary," still conjured up images of "snatching." The exit counseling process is described in detail in Chapter 8. Langone and Martin (1993) discuss the ethical dimension of deprogramming and exit counseling.

Cult Sympathizers in Academia

Cults' efforts to discredit deprogramming and cult critics were supported – wittingly or unwittingly – by a handful of academicians, mostly sociologists (see Robbins, 1988, for a review of sociological analyses). These scholars came to call cult critics, including those with scholarly credentials, "the anti-cult movement." Some scholars critical of cults returned the favor by calling their detractors "pro-cultists," or "cult apologists." Here I will use "critics" and "sympathizers" to refer to these two groups (see Kilbourne, 1985, for the proceedings of a symposium that included representatives from both camps).

Although I am simplifying this dispute for the sake of brevity, I believe that it is accurate to say that disagreement on the following important points fueled the pro-cult/anti-cult debate. Sympathizers viewed cultists as "seekers" who freely and rationally chose to join their groups. Critics viewed cult joining as a process dependent upon deception and manipulation, that is, as an illusory or an uninformed choice, as a more intense and enduring form of the psychosocial influence studied by social psychologists. Sympathizers, nevertheless, often misrepresented the critics' position by portraying them as advocates of a robotization theory of cult conversion based on *The Manchurian Candidate*. Sympathizers saw cultists' families as threatened by cults and desirous of gaining control over their cultist children. Critics saw families as worried and anxious to save their loved ones from cult harm. Sympathizers considered cults to be "innovative" groups and cult leaders to be "entrepreneurial." Critics viewed cults as destructive and their leaders as deceitful and hypocritical. Sympathizers tended to accept at face value cultists' reports while doubting the accuracy of ex-cultists and their reports, sometimes pejoratively referring to them as "apostates" (Lewis, 1989; Shupe & Bromley, 1981) and "atrocity tales" (Bromley, Shupe, & Ventimiglia, 1979), respectively. Critics tended to doubt the accuracy of the reports of cultists, whom they considered to be deceived and manipulated, and looked favorably on ex-cultists' reports. Lastly, sympathizers condemned deprogramming and guardianship proposals, sometimes with a level of passion inconsistent with their official persona of "dispassionate scientists." Critics, although not usually in favor of deprogramming, tended to sympathize with parents who attempted to deprogram their loved one and to at least be open to considering guardianship proposals.

Obviously, I align myself with the critics. Although space limitations preclude a complete review of the sympathizers' position, the following critique of an influential book in the sympathizer camp (*Strange Gods: The Great American Cult Scare* by D. Bromley & A. Shupe, 1981) summarizes the heart of the critics' quarrel with the sympathizers:

> [Bromley and Shupe's] notion of coercion doesn't go much further than the use of torture and threats of violence, so it is rare that anyone ever is guilty of unjustified manipulation of human behavior. They construct a straw man argument which they attribute to the critics of the cults that is

easily refuted. For unwarranted coercion to exist, one would seem to need to develop a metallic sheen, walk with a gimp, smile on cue, and not exhibit fear of death. Under their subtle touch, brainwashing appears literally as a washed-out cranium with wind whistling through the brain cavity. Short of physical violence, they presume that "free will" is operating intact . . . Overall, their method is most dubious because of the double standard of interpretation. Throughout the book, they systematically *doubt* the assertions made by parents and ex-cult members about their experiences (unless the statements are sufficiently outrageous and then they are allowed to stand) since these parties have a vested interest in rewriting history. This scrupulous caution doesn't extend to the current cult members' statements about the camaraderie, idealism, moral vision, and purpose of their lives. These statements are accepted at face value and even underscored as one of the positive contributions of the cults. In short, cult members *mean* what they say, while ex-cult members do not . . . If we look more closely at the traditional liberal values which influence this book, we find that John Stewart Mill never suggests that the protection of individual liberty entails the loss of our critical faculties. We can oppose the legalization of deprogramming without needing to believe that cults are as benign as depicted here. A case for the civil liberties of new religious movements does not need to entail this flight from objectivity. (Schuller, 1983, pp. 9–11)

Schuller's critique suggests that the sympathizers' civil-libertarian distaste for deprogramming motivates them to create an easily assailable straw-man view of cult critics. Sympathizers repeatedly and incorrectly imply that critics see "brainwashing" as a sinister, virtually irresistible force that turns human beings into automatons. They frequently point to a study (Barker, 1983) which found that "only" 10% of those who attend an introductory Unification Church workshop end up joining the group, and that after two years only about 50% of these new converts remain. They say, "Where's the brainwashing?!" (The sympathizers rarely cite Taylor's study of the Unification Church in which he states, "Slightly more than half of the prospects chose to stay beyond the first week. Nearly all those who remain experience a gradual conversion and become members of the Family after three more weeks of indoctrination" [1982, pp. 202–203].) I look at even the more conservative results of Barker and say: "Imagine! The Moonies approach total strangers on the street, persuade some to come to a free lecture and get a free meal, and then within a matter of two to three weeks persuade 10% of those persons to radically alter their lives and become full-time missionaries and fund-raisers for the Unification Church!"

As a comparison, consider the reactions of nonbelievers who attend Billy Graham crusades: "2%–5% of the attendees 'make a decision for Christ' and only about half of these converts are active a year later.

About 15% [of the 2%–5%, or about .30%–.75%] remain permanently converted" (Frank, 1974, p. 82). Bear in mind that converts at Billy Graham crusades, unlike Moonie converts, return to their families, their jobs, their friends, their plans, and their goals, in short, to autonomous lives. Thus, I conclude that cult environments, although certainly not "robot factories," are compellingly powerful. They are, as my colleague John Clark has called them, "impermissible experiments" on changing human behavior, "impermissible" because no ethical psychological researcher would ever do what cults do routinely.

In addition to propagating the robot straw man, cult sympathizers have made ad hominem attacks on critics by implicitly impugning their motives and tagging labels on them (while criticizing their opponents for "labeling" cults), rather than dealing with the substance of their opponents' arguments. In a tongue-in-cheek essay, "On Dialogue Between the Two Tribes of Cultic Researchers," in reaction to sociological articles that tended to implicitly impugn the integrity of scholars associated with the so-called "anti-cult movement" (Bromley & Richardson, 1983; Bromley & Shupe, 1981; Bromley, Shupe, & Ventimiglia, 1979; Kilbourne & Richardson, 1986; Robbins & Anthony, 1982; Shupe & Bromley, 1980; Shupe, Spielman, & Stigal, 1977), I wrote:

> Thus, through my association with the anti-cult tribe, I have been indirectly accused of being a "witch-hunter," a modern-day "demonologist," sadly misinformed (the ultimate "tut tut"), ruled by the impulse to expand the regulatory power of psychiatrists, insensitive to the religious strivings of the young, in league with evil deprogrammers, a "medicalizer," an inveterate "labeler," and on and on. (Langone, 1983, pp. 11–12)

If sympathizers attributed unkind motivations to cult leaders as readily as they apparently attribute them to cult critics, they might find themselves agreeing with the critics. They seem to fear, however, that fully admitting to cult harms would necessarily lead to restrictions on civil liberties, such as the legalization of involuntary deprogramming. Some sympathizers fortunately acknowledge this tendency:

> The linkage of cult/mind control debates to intense and emotional controversy over the "counter-technology" of "deprogramming" has probably distorted scholarly discourse and pushed scholars (reacting against coercive deprogramming or speculative psychophysiological models) into downplaying manipulative and coercive elements in some movements. (Robbins, 1988, p. 73)

When I first returned from the UFO cult, I gave several talks about the group where I tried to dispel certain misconceptions fostered by the media, especially those alleging mind control. My descriptions focused on the voluntary aspects of membership and almost completely ignored the ways that Bo and Peep used group dynamics to promote conformity. It was not until later, after interviewing defectors and reflecting on the patterns recorded in my field notes, that I began to appreciate the subtleties of social pressure in the group. With greater detachment I realized that my efforts to defend the cult against unfounded charges had led me to bias my descriptions by selective reporting. (Balch, 1985, p. 33)

Such honest self-disclosure is commendable. But it is time for the remaining ideologically driven scholarship in this area to end. That which sympathizers apparently most feared — guardianship legislation and deprogramming — is either dead (guardianship legislation) or dying (deprogramming). Whatever validity their fear might have had 10 or 15 years ago is gone. In the cult arena today, cults' unethical exploitation of members is the only real threat to civil liberties.

I have described the critic-sympathizer debate at length for two reasons. First, I want to alert readers so that they will be better prepared to evaluate literature that is sympathetic to cults. But also, by calling for an end to ideologically driven scholarship, I put forth the hope that the academic resources that have been squandered on tendentious and often ad hominem attacks on a "brainwashing" straw man will be directed toward the study of issues that will enhance therapeutic and preventive educational efforts aimed at reducing cult-related harm.

HARM

If cult involvements did not harm people, this book would have no purpose. Later chapters will describe post-cult distress and offer suggestions on helping former cult members. In this section, I will provide additional background by briefly reviewing the literature on harm associated with the cult experience.

It is important to note that research on cult members is fraught with methodological problems. Studies are often based on different definitions of what constitutes a cult or "new religious movement." Subject samples are nearly always biased in some way. Self-reports from members of groups whose willingness to deceive is well documented can be untrustworthy. "Pen-and-pencil" personality tests and surveys do not effectively measure certain psychological states such as dissociation. Interview data are readily influenced by the fundamental conceptual assumptions of the interviewer. Those who observe cults may not be sensitive to the psychological subtleties that clinicians detect. Conversely, clinicians working with one cultist at a time may not fully appreciate social factors in cults. Statistical analyses are sometimes inappropriate to the problem at hand. And tendencies to overgeneralize and make unwarranted causal inferences are common.

These technical difficulties are compounded by the fact that cultic groups are reluctant to cooperate with critics. Therefore, with a few exceptions, most of the nonclinical studies have surveyed ex-cultists or have been conducted by researchers whom cult leaders viewed as sympathetic. Indeed, influencing academicians is a major goal of some groups, especially the Unification Church (Dole & Dubrow-Eichel, 1981).

As noted earlier, clinical reports tend to see dissociation as central to a cultist's adaptation to a demanding and contradictory environment. Because self-report instruments do not effectively detect dissociation, critics view studies that use instruments such as the Minnesota Multiphasic Personality Inventory (MMPI) with considerable skepticism. Indeed, in studies using the MMPI there is evidence that cult members are not honest in their responses, that is, their Lie Scales tend to be elevated (Ungerleider & Wellisch, 1979) and there appears to be a "moderate attempt for both men and women to 'look good'" (Ross, 1983, p. 418).

Given these methodological caveats, what does the literature tell us?

Levine and Salter (1976) and Levine (1984a) found little evidence of impairment in structured interviews of over 100 cultists, although Levine and Salter did note some reservation about "the suddenness and sharpness of the change" (p. 415) that was reported to them. In his book, Levine (1984b) reported on a study of 800 cult members, stating that "more than fifty percent of former members of radical groups show signs of emotional upheaval severe enough to warrant treatment during the first few months after their return" (p. 151). Ross (1983), who gave a battery of tests, including the MMPI, to 42 Hare Krishna members in Melbourne, Australia, reported that all "scores and findings were within the normal range, although members showed a slight decline in mental health (as measured on the MMPI) after 1.5 years in the movement and a slight increase in mental health after 3 years in the movement" (p. 416). Ungerleider and Wellisch (1979), who interviewed and tested 50 members or former members of cults, found "no evidence of insanity or mental illness in the legal sense" (p. 279), although, as noted earlier, members showed elevated Lie Scales on the MMPI. In studies of the Unification Church (Galanter, Rabkin, Rabkin, & Deutsch, 1979; Galanter, 1983), the investigators found improvement in well-being as reported by members, approximately one-third of whom had received mental health treatment before joining the group.

Otis (1985) examined data from a survey of 2,000 members of Transcendental Meditation (TM) in 1971. Dropouts reported significantly fewer adverse effects than experienced meditators, and "the number and severity of complaints were positively related to duration of meditation" (p. 41). There was a consistent pattern of adverse effects, including anxiety, confusion, frustration, and depression. The "data raise serious doubts about the innocuous nature of TM" (p. 46).

The Institute for Youth and Society (1980) in Bensheim, Germany reported that TM members tended to be withdrawn from their families (57% of subjects), isolated in social relations (51%), anxious (52%), depressed (45%), tired (63%), and exhibited a variety of physical problems, such as headaches and menstrual disorders.

Former members of a psychotherapy cult (Knight, 1986) reported that they had had sex with a therapist (25% of subjects), had been assigned love mates (32%), had fewer than six hours sleep a night (59%), and in therapy sessions were shoved at least occasionally (82%), were hit at least occasionally (78%), and were verbally abused (97%). These subjects, 86% of whom felt harmed by the experience, also reported depression (50%) and menses cessation (32%).

In Conway et al. (1986) ex-members reported the following experiences during their time in the cult: sex with leaders (5%; 60% in the Children of God), menstrual dysfunction (22%), and physical punishment (20%). Conway and Siegelman (1982) reported that ex-members experienced floating (52% of subjects), nightmares (40%), amnesia (21%), hallucinations and delusions (14%), inability to break mental rhythms of chanting (35%), violent outbursts (14%), and suicidal or self-destructive tendencies (21%).

Galanter, who studied 66 former Moonies, reports that "the large majority (89%) felt that they 'got some positive things' out of membership, although somewhat fewer (61%) did feel that 'Reverend Moon had a negative impact on members,' and only a bare majority (53%) felt that 'current members should leave the Unification Church'" (1983, p. 985). Galanter also found that "36% of the respondents indicated the emergence of 'serious emotional problems' at some time after leaving the church; 24% had 'sought out professional help for emotional problems' after leaving; and 3% (i.e., two respondents) had been hospitalized for such problems during this interval" (p. 985). These findings were consistent with clinical reports during the 1970s and early 1980s.

It is interesting, however, that Galanter was sometimes inclined to put a positive "spin" on the findings, for example, his choosing to write that "*only* (emphasis added) a bare majority (53%) felt that 'current members should leave the Unification Church.'" This is quite a large percentage given that, according to clinical investigations and countless ex-member reports, Unification Church members are indoctrinated to assume that the Church is always right and they, when dissenting, are always wrong. Indeed, Langone, Chambers, Dole, and Grice (in press) found that the suppression of dissent was one of the five most highly rated cult characteristics in a subject pool of 308 former cultists from 101 different groups. Thus, Galanter's indices of harm, though indirect and not low, are probably underestimates.

The study mentioned above (Langone et al., in press) paints an even more negative picture of the cult experience. Eighty-eight percent of the subjects saw their groups as harmful (37%) or very harmful (51%). During an average time of membership of 6.7 years, 11% of the subjects reported being sexually abused. Sixty-eight percent of the subjects each knew an average of 28 former members who had not contacted helping resources. Thus, approximately 5,500 persons known to these subjects had not sought help. Yet 30% of subjects estimated that "all or nearly all" of their friends and acquaintances had difficulty adjusting to postgroup life, 21% felt that "most" had difficulty, 4% "about half," 13% "some," 6% "hardly any," and 25% were unsure.

Martin, Langone, Dole, and Wiltrout (in press) used a variety of instruments, including the Millon Clinical Multiaxial Inventory (MCMI) to assess the psychological status of 111 former cultists. Martin says:

> This sample of ex-cultists can be characterized as having abnormal levels of distress in several of the personality and clinical symptom scales. Of those subjects completing the MCMI-I, 89% had BR's ["Base Rates"— indicates presence of a disorder] of 75 or better on at least one of the first eight scales. Furthermore, 106 out of the 111 subjects (95%) who completed the MCMI at Time I had at least one BR score on one of the MCMI scales. The contention that this population of former cultists is indeed distressed is further buttressed by the sample's mean score of 102 on the HSCL [Hopkins Symptom Checklist]. Typically, scores of over 100 are indicative of the need for professional psychiatric care. Moreover, these ex-cultists had a mean of 72 on the SBS-HP burnout scale, which is suggestive of

burnout and more than one standard deviation above the mean from Martin's (1983) sample of parachurch workers. (Martin et al., 1992, p. 234)

Yeakley (1988) gave 835 members of the Boston Church of Christ (BCC) the Myers-Briggs Type Indicator (MBTI), a psychological instrument that classifies people according to Carl Jung's type system. Individuals may differ in the way in which they tend to perceive (some being more sense oriented, others more intuition oriented), the way they judge (thinking oriented vs. feeling oriented) and their basic attitudes (extroversion vs. introversion). Isabel Myers and Katherine Briggs, the developers of the MBTI, added a dimension to Jung's typology: the person's preferred way of orienting himself to the outside world. This orientation may be judging or perceiving. The MBTI thus produces 16 personality types based on the permutations of these variables. Yeakley asked subjects to answer the questions in the MBTI as they think they would have answered before their conversion, as they felt at the time of testing, and as they think they will answer after five more years of discipling in the BCC. He found that "a great majority of the members of the Boston Church of Christ changed psychological type scores in the past, present, and future versions of the MBTI" (p. 34) and that "the observed changes in psychological type scores were not random since there was a clear convergence in a single type" (p. 35). The type toward which members converged was that of the group's leader. Comparisons with members of mainstream denominations showed no convergence, but members of other cultic groups did show convergence, although toward different types than that on which the BCC members converged. Yeakley concludes that "there is a group dynamic operating in that congregation that influences members to change their personalities to conform to the group norm" (p. 37). Although this study did not directly examine harm, it does indirectly support clinical observations, which contend that the personalities of cult members are bent, so to speak, to fit the group.

Analysis

Clinical observations (Ash, 1985; Clark, 1979; Langone, 1991) and research studies (Galanter, 1989; Langone et al., in press) suggest that people join cults during periods of stress or transition, when they are most open to what the group has to say. Approximately one third appear to have been psychologically disturbed before joining, as evidenced by having participated in pre-cult psychotherapy or counseling (with figures varying from 7% to 62% of subjects among six studies: Barker, 1984; Galanter et al., 1979; Galanter & Buckley, 1978; Knight, 1986; Sirkin & Grellong, 1988; Spero, 1982). The majority, however, appear to have been relatively normal individuals before joining a cult.

Certain studies cited earlier (Levine, 1984; Ross, 1983; Ungerleider & Wellisch, 1979) found cultists to score within the normal range on psychological tests or psychiatric interviews. Galanter (1983) found some improvement in the general well-being of cult joiners, which he attributed to a psychobiologically grounded "relief effect" of charismatic groups.

Wright (1987) and Skonovd (1983) found that leaving cultic groups was very difficult because of the psychological pressure, a finding consistent with clinical observations. There is much evidence, reviewed earlier, of psychological distress when people leave cultic groups.

And yet the majority eventually leave. Why? If they were unhappy before they joined, became happier after they joined, were pressured to remain, left anyway, and were more distressed than ever after leaving, what could have impelled them to leave and to remain apart from the group?

The inescapable conclusion seems to be that the cult experience is not what it appears to be (at least for those groups that deem it important to put on a "happy face"), either to undiscerning observers or to members under the psychological influence of the group. Clinical observers, beginning with Clark (1979) and Singer (1979), appear to be correct in their contention that dissociative defenses help cultists adapt to the contradictory and intense demands of the cult environment. So long as members are not rebelling against the group's psychological controls, they can appear to be "normal," much as a person with multiple personality disorder can sometimes appear to be "normal." However, this normal-appearing personality, as West (1992) maintains, is a pseudopersonality. When cultists leave their groups, the flood gates open up and they suffer. But they don't generally return to the cult because the suffering they experience after leaving the cult is more genuine than the "happiness" they experienced while in it. A painful truth is better than a pleasant lie.

RECENT DEVELOPMENTS

Over the years there have been a number of developments in the cult field. First, we see a change in the population of former cult members, having of course to do with a change in the types of cults that are currently prominent. There is also a greater acceptance of exit counseling as a respectful and effective means of intervention for families with a loved one in a cult. Our increase in knowledge about cults and how they work has led to greater preventive measures, as well as international outreach.

A Changing Cult Population

A much larger number of walkaways (people who have left cults on their own) and castaways (people who have been ejected by cults) have approached helping organizations in recent years. Nearly 70% of the subjects in a recent study (Langone et al., in press) were walkaways or castaways, a reversal of earlier studies in which only 27% of subjects fell into these two categories (Conway et al., 1986). Former members appear to come from a wider variety of groups, with fewer coming from Eastern groups than in the 1970s and more coming from fringe Christian or New Age groups. Whereas the overwhelming majority (76%) of Conway et al.'s (1986) 426 subjects came from only 5 of 48 groups (the Unification Church, Scientology, The Way, Divine Light Mission, and Hare Krishna), Langone et al.'s (in press) 308 subjects from 101 groups, who were selected in much the same manner as Conway and Siegelman's, were much more dispersed, with the largest five groups accounting for only 33% of the total subject population. Former Scientologists comprised Langone et al.'s largest group: 16%, compared to 11% for Conway and Siegelman. The Way, Hare Krishna, and the Divine Light Mission were barely represented in Langone et al.'s study, comprising 2%, 2%, and 1% respectively, compared to 6%, 5%, and 11% for Conway and Siegelman. Former Unification Church members accounted for 44% of Conway and Siegelman's subjects, but only 5% of Langone et al.'s. As noted in the introduction to this book, helping organizations have also witnessed a marked increase in inquiries concerning various aspects of Satanism and the occult.

The expansion of the walkaway/castaway population approaching the Cult Awareness Network (CAN) and the American Family Foundation (AFF) accounts in large part for the recent emphasis these organizations have placed on recovery issues. To a large extent this book is a result of the recent influx of walkaways and castaways needing help.

Exit Counseling

The growing professionalization of the exit counseling field (discussed in detail in Chapter 8) and AFF's and CAN's deliberate avoidance of deprogramming involvements, has caused deprogramming to become a background, even a fringe, aspect of the cult phenomenon. Although deprogrammings still occur, they are becoming more and more rare. Families have much more access to alternative means of helping their loved ones than was the case 10 or 15 years ago.

Preventive Education

Much more emphasis has been placed on preventive education. In 1987 AFF founded the International Cult Education Program (ICEP), which seeks to mobilize and assist a network of educators and clergy interested in conducting preventive education programs for youth. In addition to publishing a newsletter, *Young People and Cults,* and organizing programs, ICEP has produced (in conjunction with the National Association of Secondary School Principals Inservice Video Network) a video, *Cults: Saying "No" Under Pressure,* and a secondary school lesson plan, *Too Good to Be True: Resisting Cults and Psychological Manipulation.* ICEP also makes other educational material available.

International Issues

In 1990 the American Family Foundation organized a meeting in Paris of representatives from 17 countries, including Japan, the United States, Canada, and most of the Western European nations. All of these countries had had similar experiences with cultic groups and the resultant formation of grass-roots organizations to educate the public and help families and ex-cultists. Organizations in some countries were well established; some even had relatively adequate funding. Others were struggling to have an impact. But all were grappling with the same problems.

Although Australians did not attend the Paris meeting, several cult educational organizations have been active in Australia. Within the past two years, two cult educational organizations have formed in Argentina. AFF regularly receives inquiries from all over the world.

As a result of the Paris meeting, an international congress was planned for Barcelona. This congress, organized by the Catalan group, Asesorament i Informaciò sobre Sectes (AIS), with input from other organizations, took place in April 1993. One of the issues it addressed is that of the growth of cultic groups in Eastern Europe and the nations of the former Soviet Union. Indeed, colleagues in Europe have told me that representatives of cultic groups moved into Eastern Europe as soon as the Berlin Wall came down.

Although European governments have been hesitant to act against cults, they have not been as diffident as the U.S. government. The European Parliament (West & Langone, 1986; Wilshire, 1990), the Council of Europe (The Council of Europe's Report, 1992), the government of Israel (State of Israel Report, 1989), and the Vatican (Sects or New Religious Movements, 1986) have all published reports that have been reprinted in AFF's Cultic Studies Journal. The governments of at least seven countries – but not the United States – have contributed funds to cult educational organizations.

FUTURE TRENDS

Developments in this field during the next 10 years are likely, in my opinion, to include the following:

1. The number of qualified professionals offering assistance to cultists and their families will continue to increase and become more dispersed geographically.
2. The field of exit counseling will continue to become more professionalized.
3. The number of walkaways seeking help will continue to expand and in a few years will greatly outnumber cultists who leave through exit counseling.
4. Deprogramming will become increasingly uncommon and will fade into practical insignificance, although cult propagandists will probably continue to publicize it in order to bolster their attempts to be perceived as "persecuted new religions."
5. More academic researchers in psychology will study aspects of the cult phenomenon, including issues relating to treatment effectiveness and the recovery/constructing of memories of ritualistic abuse.
6. Significant numbers of political cults will reemerge if economic conditions deteriorate markedly.
7. Increasing numbers of bizarre New Age cults will come into being or grow in strength.
8. Pseudochristian cults will increase in number, membership levels, and political power, especially if social institutions continue the trend toward increased secularization.
9. Psychotherapy cults will markedly increase in number, if professional associations do not address the cult issue and/or if changes in the medical care system decrease the incomes of psychotherapists, and thereby provide unethical therapists with a further incentive to make clients dependent.

10. Cultic New Age groups targeting businesses and their employees will prosper, although they will probably continually alter their outward form and names in order to adapt to changing market conditions.

REFERENCES

Aagaard, J. (1991). Conversion, religious change, and the challenge of new religious movements. *Cultic Studies Journal, 8*(2), 91–103.

American Humanist Association. (1973). *Humanist Manifestos I & II.* Amherst, NY: Author.

Aronin, D. (1982). Cults, deprogramming, and guardianship: A model legislative proposal. *Columbia Journal of Law and Social Problems, 17,* 163–286.

Ash, S. (1985). Cult-induced psychopathology, part 1: Clinical picture. *Cultic Studies Journal, 2*(1), 31–91.

Balch, R. (1985). What's wrong with the study of new religions and what we can do about it. In B. Kilbourne (Ed.), *Scientific research and new religions: Divergent perspectives.* Proceedings of the annual meeting of the Pacific Division of the American Association for the Advancement of Science. San Francisco: AAAS.

Barker, E. (1983). The ones who got away: People who attend Unification Church workshops and do not become Moonies. In E. Barker (Ed.), *Of gods and men: New religious movements in the West* (pp. 309–336). Macon, GA: Mercer University Press.

Barker, E. (1984). *The making of a Moonie: Choice or brainwashing?* Oxford: Basil Blackwell.

Behar, R., & King, R., Jr. (1985, November 18). The winds of Werner. *Forbes, 42,* pp. 44, 48.

Bird, F., & Reimer, B. (1982). Participation rates in new religions and para-religious movements. *Journal for the Scientific Study of Religion, 21,* 1–14.

Bloomgarden, A., & Langone, M. D. (1984). Preventive education on cultism for high school students: A comparison of different programs' effects on potential vulnerability to cults. *Cultic Studies Journal, 1*(2), 167–177.

Bromley, D. G. (n.d.). *Deprogramming as a form of exit from new religious movements: The case of the Unificationist movement.* Unpublished paper.

Bromley, D. G., & Richardson, J. T. (1983). *The brainwashing/deprogramming controversy: Sociological, psychological, legal and historical perspectives.* Lewiston, NY: Edwin Mellen Press.

Bromley, D. G., & Shupe, A. D. (1981). *Strange gods: The great American cult scare.* Boston: Beacon.

Bromley, D. G., Shupe, A. D., & Ventimiglia, J. C. (1979). Atrocity tales, the Unification Church and the social construction of evil. *Journal of Communication, 29,* 42–53.

Clark, J. G. (1979). Cults. *Journal of the American Medical Association, 242,* 279–281.

Conway, F., & Siegelman, J. H. (1982, January). Information disease: Have cults created a new mental illness? *Science Digest,* pp. 86, 88, 90–92.

Conway, F., Siegelman, J. H., Carmichael, C.W., & Coggins, J. (1986). Information disease: Effects of covert induction and deprogramming. *Update: A Journal of New Religious Movements, 10,* 45–57.

Council of Europe's Report on Sects and New Religious Movements. (1992). *Cultic Studies Journal, 9*(1), 89–119.

Cox, H. (1977). *Turning East.* New York: Simon & Schuster.

Dole, A., & Dubrow-Eichel, S. (1981). Moon over academe. *Journal of Religion and Health, 20,* 35–40.

Evans, M. S. (1966, July 12). Orthodox rebels (A review of "The New Left"). *National Review.*

Final 1991 data show an upswing in the importance of religion in people's lives. (1992, March). *Emerging Trends, 14,* 1.

Frank, J. (1974). *Persuasion and healing.* New York: Schocken Books.

Freed, J. (1980). *Moonwebs.* Toronto: Dorset.

Galanter, M. (1983). Unification Church ("Moonie") dropouts: Psychological readjustment after leaving a charismatic religious group. *American Journal of Psychiatry, 140,* 984–989.

Galanter, M. (1989). *Cults, faith healing, and coercion.* New York: Oxford University Press.

Galanter, M., & Buckley, P. (1978). Evangelical religion and meditation: Psychological effects. *Journal of Nervous and Mental Disease, 166,* 685–691.

Galanter, M., Rabkin, R., Rabkin, I., & Deutsch, A. (1979). The "Moonies": A psychological study of conversion and membership in a contemporary religious sect. *American Journal of Psychiatry, 136,* 165–170.

Hadden, J. K., & Shupe, A. D. (1987). Televangelism in America. *Social Compass, 34,* 61–70.

Hulet, V. (1984). *Organizations in our society.* Hutchinson, KS: Virginia Hulet.

Institute for Youth and Society. (1980). *The various implications arising from the practice of Transcendental Meditation.* Bensheim, Germany: Author.

Kilbourne, B. K. (Ed.). (1985). *Scientific research of new religions: Divergent perspectives.* Proceedings of the annual meeting of the Pacific Division of the American Association for the Advancement of Science. San Francisco: AAAS.

Kilbourne, B. K., & Richardson, J. T. (1984). Psychotherapy and new religions in a pluralistic society. *American Psychologist, 39,* 237–251.

Kilbourne, B. K., & Richardson, J. T. (1986). Cultphobia. *Thought, 61,* 258–261.

Knight, K. (1986). *Long-term effects of participation in a psychological "cult" utilizing directive therapy techniques.* Unpublished master's thesis, University of California, Los Angeles.

Lalich, J. (1992). The cadre ideal: Origins and development of a political cult. *Cultic Studies Journal, 9*(1), 1–77.

Langone, M. D. (1983, March). On dialogue between the two tribes of cultic researchers. *Cultic Studies Newsletter,* pp. 11–15.

Langone, M. D. (1984). Deprogramming: An analysis of parental questionnaires. *Cultic Studies Journal, 1,* 63–78.

Langone, M. D. (1991). Assessment and treatment of cult victims and their families. In P. A. Keller & S. R. Heyman (Eds.), *Innovations in clinical practice: A source book, Volume 10.* Sarasota, FL: Professional Resource Exchange.

Langone, M. D., Chambers, R., Dole, A., & Grice, J. (in press). Results of a survey of ex-cult members. *Cultic Studies Journal.*

Langone, M. D., & Martin, P. R. (1993). Deprogramming, exit counseling, and ethics: Clarifying the confusion. *Christian Research Journal*, vol., pages. (due out in February).

Levine, S. T. (1984a, August). Radical departures. *Psychology Today, 18*, pp. 20–29.

Levine, S. (1984b). *Radical departures: Desperate detours to growing up.* New York: Harcourt Brace Jovanovich.

Levine, S. F., & Salter, N. E. (1976). Youth and contemporary religious movements: Psychosocial findings. *Canadian Psychiatric Association Journal, 21*, 411–420.

Lewis, J. (1989). Apostates and the legitimation of repression: Some historical and empirical perspectives on the cult controversy. *Sociological Analysis: A Journal in the Sociology of Religion, 49*, 386–397.

Lottick, E. A. (Feb., 1993). Survey reveals physicians' experiences with cults. *Pennsylvania Medicine, 96*, 26–28.

Marin, P. (1973). The new narcissism: The trouble with the Human Potential Movement. *Harpers, 251*, pp. 45–56.

Martin, P. (1983). *An analytical study of the Burnout Syndrome as it occurs among parachurch professionals* (Doctoral dissertation, University of Pittsburgh, 1983). Ann Arbor, MI: University Microfilms International.

Martin, P., Langone, M. D., Dole, A., & Wiltrout, J. (1992). Post-cult symptoms as measured by the MCMI Before and After Residential Treatment. *Cultic Studies Journal, 9*(2), 219–250.

Neuhaus, R. (1984, October 5). The naked public square. *Christianity Today, 28*, pp. 26–32.

Otis, L. (1985). Adverse effects of Transcendental Meditation. *Update: A Quarterly Journal of New Religious Movements, 9*, 37–50.

Richardson, J. T., Simmonds, R. B., & Harder, M. W. (1972). Thought reform and the Jesus movement. *Youth and Society, 4*, 185–200.

Robbins, T. (1988). *Cults, converts, and charisma.* London: Sage.

Robbins, T., & Anthony, D. (1982). Deprogramming, brainwashing and the medicalization of new religious movements. *Social Problems, 29*, 283–297.

Ross, M. (1983). Clinical profiles of Hare Krishna devotees. *American Journal of Psychiatry, 140*, 416–420.

Rotheimer, K. (1984, November/December). Mapping out Moon's media empire. *Columbia Journalism Review*, pp. 23–31.

Schuller, J. (1983, March). Review of *Strange Gods: The Great American Cult Scare. Cultic Studies Newsletter*, pp. 8–11.

Scientology Ad Campaign. (1990, March/April). *Cult Observer, 7*, p. 15.

Sects or new religious movements (The Vatican Report). (1986). *Cultic Studies Journal, 3*(1), 93–116.

Shapiro, R. N. (1983). Of robots, persons and the protection of religious beliefs. *Southern California Law Review, 56*, 1277–1318.

Shupe, A. D., & Bromley, D. G. (1980). *The new vigilantes: Deprogrammers, anti-cultists and the new religions.* Beverly Hills, CA: Sage.

Shupe, A. D., & Bromley, D. G. (1981). Apostates and atrocity stories: Some parameters in the dynamics of deprogramming. In B. Wilson (Ed.), *The social impact of new religious movements.* Lewiston, NY: Edwin Mellen Press.

Shupe, A. D., Spielman, R., & Stigal, S. (1977). Deprogramming: The new exorcism. *American Behavioral Scientist, 20,* 941–956.

Singer, M. T. (1979, January). Coming out of the cults. *Psychology Today, 12,* pp. 72–82.

Sirkin, M., & Grellong, B. A. (1988). Cult vs. non-cult Jewish families: Factors influencing conversion. *Cultic Studies Journal, 5,* 2–23.

Skonovd, N. (1983). Leaving the cultic religious milieu. In D.G. Bromley & J. T. Richardson (Eds.), *The brainwashing/deprogramming controversy: Sociological, psychological, legal and historical perspectives* (pp. 106–121). Lewiston, NY: Edwin Mellen Press.

Spero, M. (1982). Psychotherapeutic procedure with religious cult devotees. *The Journal of Nervous and Mental Disease, 170,* 332–344.

Stark, R., & Bainbridge, W. W. (1981). Cult membership in the roaring twenties: Assessing local receptivity. *Sociological Analysis, 42*(2), 137–161.

State of Israel Report of the Interministerial Committee Set Up to Examine Cults ("New Groups") in Israel. (1989). *Cultic Studies Journal, 6,* 32–68.

Taylor, D. (1982). Becoming new people: The recruitment of young Americans into the Unification Church. In R. Wallis (Ed.), *Millennialism and charisma.* Belfast: The Queen's University.

Ungerleider, T. J., & Wellisch, D. K. (1979). Coercive persuasion (brainwashing), religious cults and deprogramming. *American Journal of Psychiatry, 136,* 279–282.

West, L. J. (1990). Persuasive techniques in contemporary cults: A public health approach. *Cultic Studies Journal, 7,* 126–149. (Reprinted from M. Galanter (Ed.), *Cults and new religious movements,* pp. 165–192. Washington, DC: American Psychiatric Association.)

West, L. J. (1992). Presentation to the American Family Foundation Annual Meeting, Arlington, VA.

West, L. J., & Allen, J. R. (1968). Three rebellions: Red, black, and green. In J. Masserman (Ed.), *The dynamics of dissent.* New York: Grune & Stratton.

West, L. J., & Langone, M. D. (1986). Cultism: A conference for scholars and policy makers. *Cultic Studies Journal, 3,* 117–134.

Wilshire, D. (1990). Cults and the European Parliament: A practical political response to an international problem. *Cultic Studies Journal, 7,* 1–14.

Wilson, B. (1985). Secularization: The inherited model. In P. Hammond (Ed.), *The sacred in a secular age.* Berkeley: University of California Press.

Wright, S. A. (1987). Leaving cults: The dynamics of defection. *Society for the Scientific Study of Religion Monograph Series, Number 7.*

Yeakley, F. (Ed.). (1988). *The discipling dilemma.* Nashville, TN: Gospel Advocate.

Zimbardo, P. G., & Hartley, C. F. (1985). Cults go to high school: A theoretical and empirical analysis of the initial stage in the recruitment process. *Cultic Studies Journal, 2,* 91–148.

Section I

MIND CONTROL

2

A LITTLE CARROT AND A LOT OF STICK:
A CASE EXAMPLE

Janja Lalich

I guess the worst part about it
is what they did to my brain
They took my brain
and along with it my feelings
my control
my passion and my love.

They took my brain and made me something
other than I wanted to be
I lost sight of the meaning
I sunk into the madness
I lost my self-control
my self-respect
my self.

I wanted to make a better world
I was willing to fight for that
willing to sacrifice
But they took my soul
turned it inside out
made me something
other than I wanted to be.

And I guess the worst part about it
is that I did the same to others
just like me.

I WROTE THAT POEM less than one year after I got out of the political cult I had been in for more than 10 years. When I wrote it, I didn't have much understanding of cults or thought-reform processes, yet instinctively that is how I described my experience. People often ask me how I got out, to which I reply: I got out because the group fell apart, exploded, or, as I like to say now, imploded. At the time, in fact, I was secretly plotting my escape, and to this day I'll never really know if I would have had the courage to do it.

This chapter outlines the makings, workings, and eventual demise of the "Workers Democratic Union." I use pseudonyms for the name of the group, the leader, and all former members; also I use the terms *organization, group,* and *party* interchangeably throughout. Since the group was leftist in orientation, I wish to make clear that this is not a critique of political ideologies, nor an attempt to conclude that the organizational methodology of Marxism-Leninism necessarily leads to cultic formation. The Workers Democratic Union (WDU) was unique in many ways, but nonetheless a cult like so many others in the techniques used to dominate and control its members.

A feminist, Marxist-Leninist (M-L) organization, the WDU was founded in 1974 and was led by women. The members were highly dedicated, hardworking, intelligent women and men, whose ages ranged from mid 20s to early 70s. Most had some college education: There were numerous undergraduate degrees, some graduate degrees, several doctorates; there were also a few medical doctors and lawyers. Socioeconomic backgrounds varied from working poor to extremely wealthy; the racial composition was overwhelmingly white, with a handful of African-American, Latino, and Asian-American members.

At its peak the WDU claimed about 500 members, with several thousand supporters in its orbit, including influential and well-known intellectuals, professionals, and politicians. Despite sporadic periods of growth, the core group never exceeded 125 and remained more or less constant, in spite of living under a devastating system of abuse, manipulation, repression, and intrusion into every aspect of individual lives. Most of the core members (who regarded themselves as a cadre elite) joined between 1975 and 1978, years that proved to be the period of the most intense study and indoctrination. It is these same cadres who comprised the vast majority of members present for the group's dissolution in late 1985.

In late October of that year some 100 members of the WDU met in San Francisco and voted unanimously to expel their leader and dissolve their organization. This vote was taken after two weeks of intense, highly emotional, and revealing discussions. For the first time in years these political activists talked openly about the true nature of their organization, of their work together, and of the effects both on the members and on those around them.

The dissolution meetings were precipitated by frank discussions among the top leadership during the leader's absence. At a full membership meeting called by this inner circle, one by one, leadership figures presented the behind-the-scenes reality of the WDU, exposing the corrupt and abusive nature of their until-then adored leader, Doreen Baxter. Unprecedented meetings soon included all members called in from party offices around the country, as well as some former members who had been expelled over the years. Shock, dismay, disbelief, revulsion, sorrow, and anger spread throughout this group of dedicated political activists as they heard an array of chilling accounts. Overnight a dream was shattered.

Through the course of these meetings WDU members came to see that their commitment had been manipulated, abused, and distorted; their leader was alcoholic, arbitrary, and without accountability; and, as a result, their organization was politically bankrupt. Some members haltingly spoke of it as a cult experience; others saw it as an aberration of Marxism-Leninism; still others were too stunned to venture any analysis. I offer here my interpretation.

HISTORICAL BACKDROP

In the 1960s there was much political and social activism in the United States, partly due to growing economic disparity and conflict in values. Besides the unprecedented affluence of some, Americans were facing the threat of nuclear holocaust and the widespread controversy regarding U.S. participation in an unresolved war continents away. On the one hand, there was the spirit of hopefulness ("love power") of the hippie counterculture; on the other, the spirit of rebellion ("people power") of the antiwar, civil rights, women's, and Black Power movements. These radical sentiments and the resultant activism waned with the assassinations of role models John F. Kennedy, Martin Luther King, Jr., Malcolm X, and Robert Kennedy; with the horror at the student deaths at Kent State in 1970; and with the shock of the 1973 Watergate episode. By the mid-1970s disillusionment, despair, and disgust with the so-called American Dream were common emotions among an entire generation of once-idealistic youth.

The "movement" heyday seemed to be over. Yet, particularly in urban centers, there remained a flurry of leftist political activity. Participants in study groups and "liberation schools" read and discussed

political texts, and activist groups held forums to debate how to best
bring about social change. The wavering faith of some left-wing ideal-
ists was bolstered by the victory of the tiny country of Vietnam
against the strongest of world powers. This gave hope that the "little
man" could win! These students of revolution worshipped and romanti-
cized the working class. Extrapolating from their study of Karl Marx's
writings, they saw the working class as the oppressed sector of society, which would heroically throw off its shackles and lead the way to
a better world, a world of equality.

Countless activists felt that the "revolution" they envisioned during
the 1960s and early 1970s had failed to materialize because of the
Left's lack of organizational structure, discipline, theoretical development, and accountable leadership. Thus arose the New Communist
Movement, or the "party-building movement," whose adherents believed in the need for a Marxist-Leninist, disciplined party that would
lead the U.S. working class to revolution. Members of "preparty formations," as these groups were called, spent a great deal of energy trying
to recruit to their cause, each grouplet being convinced of having
found the "correct line." The WDU, with Doreen Baxter as its leader,
arose from this contentious milieu – from what turned out to be fertile
soil for a soul-crushing political cult led by a woman highly skilled in
psychological manipulation.

THE FOUNDING

Thirteen women met together in San Francisco in the summer of 1974
to found a new organization, another preparty formation. Twelve of
these women were in various San Francisco Bay Area study groups;
the thirteenth was Doreen Baxter, a Marxist professor at a university
thousands of miles away. These women were white and primarily from
middle-class backgrounds (although party lore always described the
"founders" as being of the working class). Eight had some college education; six had degrees (four B.A.s, one M.S.W., and Baxter with a
Ph.D.). Baxter was 39 years old, while most of the others were in their
mid 20s, which meant that they (with one exception) were 7 to 20 years
younger than Baxter. Other than Baxter, they held working-class or
"alternative" jobs. Some did traditional women's work as clerical, library, and hospital workers; others performed nontraditional work as
carpenters, a printing press operator, and a phone company techni-
cian.

Having been activists since the 1960s – in their communities, in the
antiwar movement, in the women's movement, or at their work-

places – each of these women now felt an acute dissatisfaction with previous political experiences and was looking for a better way to channel her energies. They self-identified as radical lesbians (with the exception of Baxter and one other person) and/or anti-imperialists (opposed to the political and economic exploitation of one country by another). They considered themselves to be serious political women intent on working for social change in America – or, in their words, "to bring about revolution."

Deeply influenced by the prevalent party-building atmosphere, they were eager to make a dedicated commitment to some form of revolutionary struggle. The fact that 11 of them were lesbians provided an additional focus: to find a group with an outlook that was feminist as well as Marxist *and* that would allow them their sexuality, for a number of groups would not accept homosexuals as "true" Marxist-Leninists. Since groups with such advanced thinking were apparently nonexistent within the M-L movement, these women were talking about starting their own group. Their agreed-upon goal was to build an alternative to existing preparty formations, to be free of what they saw as the ills rampant in the movement – in particular, racism, sexism, and lack of direction.

The Leader Arrives

Doreen Baxter was a minor figure in the progressive movements of the time. In describing her political past (which she did repeatedly and often, particularly in the WDU's formative years), she spoke with flourish and embellishment (and, according to some of her contemporaries, with great exaggeration) about her years in the civil rights movement, community organizing efforts, the antiwar movement, the New Left, the women's movement, the New Communist Movement, and on and on. Baxter boldly proclaimed that she saw herself brandishing impeccable credentials to be anybody's spokesperson and leader.

During her years in academia, Baxter became very interested in mass social psychology and group behavior modification. She studied Robert Jay Lifton's work on thought reform; she studied and admired "total" communities, such as Synanon, and directed methods of change, such as Alcoholics Anonymous. She spoke of these techniques as positive ways to change people. Although generally popular with the students, whose rights she supported, Baxter's academic reputation was marred with in-fighting and threats of dismissal, from one university post to the next.

In 1974 Baxter went to San Francisco to look up a former student,

Miriam. Miriam hadn't heard from Baxter since the summer of 1969. On that visit Baxter had been drinking and there was a big blow-up, with Baxter berating Miriam for being politically naive and stupid. Since they had not parted amicably, Miriam was quite surprised to see Baxter at her door five years later; Miriam was even more struck by the actual person standing before her. Baxter said she had given up drinking; obviously she had lost a lot of weight, she looked good, healthy. She attributed all of this to having found Marxism. Miriam, herself entrenched in leftist study groups, saw her former professor as a living testament to Marxism-Leninism. Here was truly a way to change your life. Excited, Miriam brought Baxter to her study group to meet her political friends—and so began the year of forming what was to become the WDU.

When Doreen Baxter started attending their meetings, the discussions took on a new dimension. She spoke with conviction and dynamism. Not only was she well-versed in Marxist theory but also she had a minor reputation for her theories on the role of women in capitalist society. She spoke with the assurance of a known figure in the women's and radical movements, with published articles and public speeches.

Finding herself with others enamored with "the people's struggle" and equally fed up with the system, Baxter called the question: She urged the formation of a serious, radical women's group that would evolve into a disciplined Marxist party. According to the recollections of some, this process happened almost overnight. At one meeting they were a group; by the next they were a real preparty formation. One founder remembered both the thrill and the tension of these days: "I woke up one morning thinking, my god, I'm in a party now. I was in a panic, feeling totally responsible for the class struggle. I knew that if I messed up now it was another nail in the coffin of the working class."

A Cult in the Making

At Baxter's urging, and with her suggestions of who should serve, a Central Committee was elected by secret ballot in the summer of 1974. She assured the others that despite their small size a leadership body was needed. To bolster her position she informed them that Mao Tsetung's party began with only six people and had a Central Committee right from the start. Baxter left San Francisco in the fall to return to her teaching post; meanwhile, the others continued to read and study, keeping their newly formed group very secret.

The Central Committee assigned itself, also at Baxter's suggestion, the task of writing a position paper, "On the World Situation," a title that suggests the grandiosity of their vision. During one of Baxter's subsequent visits the women made the decision to let men into the group because they did not see men as the enemy and did not want to be part of a separatist movement. During this time some very cautious recruitment was going on, bringing in a small number of close friends, spouses, and relatives.

From the start Baxter insisted on setting up various units. She began a process of dividing up the group, small as it was. Some were put in leadership over others. Already there were separate meetings of this newly formed "leadership" before and after meetings with the rest of the group. Immediately there was a recognition that some were being favored and pushed into leadership, that there was going to be a lot of hierarchy and structure, and that there was a right or wrong way, according to Baxter.

Baxter instilled a sense of discipline, as well as an aura of secrecy. She described the group as a "paramilitary formation." She impressed upon the others that what they were creating was so potent that the State would immediately infiltrate if it knew what they were doing. They were decidedly clandestine, an "underground" organization. One founder described walking into a room to find Baxter playing with and cleaning a gun: "Baxter threw the loaded gun across the room for me to catch. She said it was to make me stronger, harder, and get my reflexes in shape. Baxter talked me into buying a rifle. As usual, instinct told me that something was not right about this, and, as usual, I was afraid to say anything." (Over the years Baxter amassed a cache of guns, which very few members knew about. She would sometimes refer to the guns in inner-circle meetings, saying we'd never know when we may need them. Occasionally she would brandish a gun at a public meeting.)

One year after the founding meetings the group had about 25 members and a growing recruitment pool. Doreen Baxter was firmly established as the theoretical and organizational leader. It had become standard practice in this first year while she was away to check in with her before proceeding with any activity. One founder explained: "We would go to several different phone booths and make these convoluted long-distance calls to her because of all the security we felt was needed. We would talk with her for an hour or so to get direction on what we were doing or should do next. I don't think a single decision was made without consulting her and getting her approval from the very beginning. We learned to do that very early on—so she wouldn't blow up about something."

Returning on each of her university breaks, Baxter always took charge, "reclaimed the crown," said one of the founders. Invariably she was highly critical of what they had been doing, proving once again that her leadership and guidance was something they couldn't do without. Indeed, she always found something or someone to "blow up about." Baxter was big, loud, good at slamming down her things and making a scene, expert at making the other person look stupid. She commonly used ridicule combined with stern criticism to attack any decisions she didn't have the final say in. Since her political analysis was always much more sophisticated than that of any of the others, time and again her view was accepted, with a mixture of awe, shame, and guilt.

When she was in town, 18-hour meetings were not uncommon. Since she always found something amiss, she insisted on lengthy discussions and much merciless and humiliating criticism to set the group back on the right path. Despite these persistent upheavals, the other women, eager not to lose what they had begun, were willing to go along. Doreen Baxter was charismatic, intelligent, impressive, and serious. She was calling on them to live out their own political beliefs with the same commitment and seriousness that she herself avowed. It became apparent now to the women in this founding group that they were destined to be "professional revolutionaries" and that this at last was "the real thing."

The Importance of the Second-in-Command

Shortly after Baxter's permanent relocation to San Francisco in the summer of 1975, she moved into a small house, which the others painted and got ready for her. She did not get a job; instead, she set to work at building the organization: She wrote, studied, led criticisms, and conducted political education. Initially her financial support came from some of her own savings, but very quickly it came primarily from members' monthly dues. When others came to visit her, they were ordered around, told to clean up, empty her ashtrays, open her sodas. Often it was obvious that she had been lying around in bed for days reading spy novels. Through long babbling conversations, she would convince her visitor that she "learned about the enemy by reading spy novels." One founder said, "I thought all this was pretty bizarre, but I went along with it. I didn't want her screaming at me."

From the time of their first meetings one of the founders, Sandra, was drawn to Baxter's leadership style. Sandra very quickly became Baxter's staunchest supporter. This relationship was key to the smooth functioning of the organization and to the members' devoted adherence to Baxter's leadership. Sandra, who had a history of alcoholism and codependency, became the classic enabler and classic second-in-command/enforcer.

Sandra did not have an outside job; hence, she was able to spend most of her time at Baxter's side. Trained as a counselor, Sandra had a great deal of insight into people and was herself a charismatic personality. In the years to come, Sandra, more so than Baxter, conducted almost every major criticism, denunciation, and disciplinary action. She headed recruitment, training of new members, discipline, security, and finances. She, along with Baxter, had final say in all promotions, demotions, assignments, punishments, and expulsions.

Sandra learned every detail about every member's life, both before and after a person joined the organization; she used this knowledge with skill. She had the capacity to be the harshest critic or the most ardent supporter. She made sure that every whim uttered by Doreen Baxter was carried out. Without Sandra, Doreen Baxter could not have pulled it off. Baxter often spoke about the party as her "human experiment" and Sandra was her most loyal surgical assistant.

During the first summer several of the founders had uncomfortable encounters with Baxter, who obviously was not as reformed in her alcoholism as she had attested to Miriam one year before. Invariably, Sandra's intervention alleviated the negative impact of these encounters on the others (quotes are reconstructed from notes).

Penny: I had mentioned to someone else, one of the others in the group, about Doreen's drinking, that she seemed to have a problem with drinking. Shortly afterward I was at Sandra's house one day, and she sat me down for a very serious talk. She said it wasn't good to talk to *anyone* about Doreen's drinking problem. She said the State could use it against Doreen, against us. She brought up some example from the Black Panthers or something. The gist was to keep my mouth shut – this was not to be talked about.

Miriam: I knew Doreen had a long history of alcoholism, but she had convinced me she was now squeaky clean. Then one time at her house she got very drunk. I went along with it like I did in college, as a codependent. When I mentioned it to Sandra, I got severely criticized. She said I should just let her pour the booze down, let her do what she wants. So I shut it out of my mind and lived in a fantasy. I never saw her drunk again after that. You have to understand, I held her as a god. I was terrified because she had an evil side to her, but there was also a level of brilliance that kept me from questioning these things.

The Expulsion of Baxter's Rival

There was one woman among the founders, Helene, who from the beginning was prone to voicing her doubts and objections. Whenever Baxter was in town, she was quick to launch attacks upon Helene.

Helene presented the strongest opposition to Baxter. Because she did not worship Baxter, she didn't let Baxter ride on her laurels, and she wasn't afraid to let this be known. Helene was not only raising theoretical questions but also she was asking who Doreen Baxter was and why the group always had to follow her lead. One of the group's debates, for example, centered around what Baxter would do to support herself when she moved to San Francisco: Would she get a job or be supported by the others? Helene promoted the view that Baxter should work like the rest, "proletarianize herself," as she put it.

Within hours of Baxter's relocation to San Francisco in the summer of 1975, she moved against Helene with a vengeance, challenging her to open warfare. She began with criticisms that were of a political nature. She knew that, besides herself, Helene was the most studied in Marxism. Baxter immediately labeled Helene's influence as Stalinist and dogmatic – very serious and very negative charges in this new group that was aspiring to be exactly the opposite and so different from the rest of the Marxist-Leninist Left. With a mimeo machine in one of their apartments, members spent much energy typing, reproducing, distributing, and discussing opposing documents.

Two Founders Discredited

Doreen Baxter won the battle. Helene, although domineering, was clearly less skilled as an organizer of people, while Baxter was a genius at using a combination of flattery and emotional terrorism. Helene quickly found herself isolated. Baxter mobilized the others against Helene, whipping them into a frenzy. She called Helene a dogmatist, a class traitor, an enemy of the people. Miriam, a Central Committee member at the time, remembered it like this: "The charges laid out against Helene were beyond anything I could have conceived of. I thought to myself, if I were brighter I would have spotted Helene as this corrupt influence in our midst, but clearly I didn't understand the ramifications. The complexity of Baxter's criticisms and her political analysis somehow made the severity of her accusations easier to accept."

Soon enough Miriam herself was being blamed by Baxter for having allowed a renegade to worm into their group. Thanks to Baxter's constant reminders in the months and years to come, Miriam was never able to outlive this derogatory image. Despite having been Baxter's original connection to the group, a founder, well read, and a hardworking activist, Miriam was never again given a position of responsibility in the organization. This negative stereotyping of Miriam was the beginning of many moves by Baxter over the years to discredit, denounce, humiliate, demote, and, in some cases, expel the 12 other founders. In fact, eight were expelled. Three others were relegated to low-level, nonleadership positions; their images were that of the incompetent but loyal follower.

Baxter's attacks on Helene and Miriam were also typical of the kind of power and intimidation tactics used throughout the years. Soon it was known throughout the organization, and remained known over the years, that one mistake could cause the kind of fall and/or disgrace experienced by these two early comrades. Anyone could become a Helene or a Miriam.

At Baxter's instigation, Sandra led an "investigation" of Helene. Sandra called on Lucie, previously Helene's best friend, to carry out this task. Using Lucie ensured her silence by forcing her to suppress any doubts she might have had, thereby binding her into going along with leadership's decision. At the same time, making Lucie the chief investigator would intimidate Helene, who would soon realize that even her best friend was against her. The use of a best friend, or in some cases a spouse, as a key player in an investigation, denunciation, trial, or expulsion became a standard technique. Not only did it serve to separate people from one another, instilling a distrust for any and all comrades, but also it taught the lesson of organizational allegiance above and beyond any personal loyalty.

Finally, Baxter determined that Helene was to be expelled as an enemy. This meant that for all intents and purposes Helene no longer existed and was to be completely shunned. If party members saw her on the street, they were to look straight through her as though she wasn't there. This, too, became a standard party method for dealing with adversaries (real or otherwise), expelled members, defectors, anyone who spoke out against the organization, anyone Baxter decided she didn't like.

The First Goon Squad

Besides Helene's formal expulsion, as a finishing touch, a small squad (of female members from the founding group) was sent to physically intimidate her. One evening Helene was stalked at her job and chased home by women who were her comrades just days before. They stormed her house, pushed her around, ransacked her belongings, threatened her. They knew that Helene was recovering from recent major surgery; yet this did not prevent them from carrying out their orders to intimidate her into silence about the organization. This was the first use of goon squad tactics – to be used both inside and outside the party – which the WDU came to be known for in ensuing years.

The Experiment Works

In the day-to-day process of the WDU's formation, everything that was happening took on a seriousness heretofore unknown. The members spent more and more time together, bound by a shared political commitment and a vision of the future. Their energies in every waking hour were spent on perfecting themselves in the image of the cadre ideal. They knew that this was not an easy calling. They worked feverishly toward building a party that would be new and different, Marxist and feminist, nondogmatic and American.

Just a year after Baxter was introduced to the original group of women, she was in complete control of an organization that exhibited the most extreme sort of cultic behavior. Behavioral norms of the core group had been firmly established. The foundations of Baxter's control had been laid: dominance through hierarchy, secrecy, segmentation into cells, devastating criticism, turning friend against friend, paramilitary activities, goon squads, members' terror of making mistakes, expulsion, physical and mental abuse, and the capricious and arbitrary exercise of power.

These tactics were accepted and internalized by these hardworking, dedicated, driven activists in their quest to change the world for the better. Their fervent political commitment fostered a seeming willingness to go along with what very early on was recognized by many outsiders as cultic behavior. In a sense, each member had become a little Doreen Baxter, looking to her as a revolutionary role model.

By mid-1975 the course of the WDU's next decade had been set. Dozens more well-intentioned political activists would be inducted and trained in the WDU's brutal methodology, with extreme, often irreparable personal sacrifice. In the name of beneficent social goals, activists became part of a duplicitous machine that impoverished its members, stripped them of their individuality, turned them into organizational spies, exhausted them with 24-hour-a-day demands, and attempted to destroy their pasts and connections with friends and family.

THE CIRCLE WIDENS

In the early years many new members were recruited from the women's community, through a front group called "Women and the State." (I was recruited at this time.) Like all WDU activity, the recruitment plan was methodical, strictly supervised, well-rehearsed, and focused. A member would engage a targeted friend in a seemingly spontaneous political discussion. If the potential recruit gave the right answers, she was asked, in a tone of extreme seriousness, to join Women and the State—and she was sworn to secrecy.

Secrecy fit in with the times. FBI agents were knocking on activists' doors, looking for newspaper heiress Patty Hearst, recently kidnapped in the Bay Area by the Symbionese Liberation Army. Radical groups such as the Weather Underground were known to be operating clandestinely. Paranoia was rampant in leftist circles and in the women's community.

The aura of secrecy around Women and the State heightened both the intensity of the decision and the honor of being asked to join a "secret cell." It was implied that there was something bigger and even more serious behind Women and the State, although a new recruit quickly learned that questions about the organization were not allowed. Security measures generated a feeling that both the individual and the group would be well cared for. There was a "need-to-know" policy, explained as a protective measure for all involved, which set the stage for countless future demands for total acceptance and blind faith.

Several study groups of 10 or 12 people, formed around various themes, met weekly in the evenings, reading the simpler texts of Marx, Engels, Mao, and others. Discussions were led by two teachers, usually one of them was known to a participant as his or her original recruiter. It was silently understood that the study group leaders were getting their know-how from somewhere. But where? It was vague, mysterious—and very exciting. No one ever mentioned Doreen Baxter.

Study group members had the sense that they were being observed, watched; participation was encouraged, praised. All of this added to a growing sense of being special, of being part of an elite, of being "chosen." Suddenly each recruit had a new circle of very serious friends . . . and something to be kept secret from other friends or family who weren't in the circle.

Recruitment to the Next Level

Within four to eight weeks many of the study group participants were individually approached by the teachers about joining the group behind all this. Once again recruits were told that these meetings were to be kept confidential. A recruit was led to understand that her seriousness in the study group made her stand out as ready for this next step. This was not for everyone, they said; this would be a full-time revolutionary commitment to something much "heavier" than the study group. A recruit would be asked, "Isn't this what you've been waiting for?"

Deceptions were used to entice someone to join. Most of the recruits coming out of Women and the State, for example, were told that they were joining a national organization with "cells" around the country and in Canada, and that it was solely a women's organization. In reality, at the time, the group was barely larger than the original 13 founders, it existed only in San Francisco, and it included both women and men. Similarly, African-American and Latino recruits were commonly led to believe that the WDU had a large multinational membership when in fact it did not. In the end, recruiters said whatever would work.

In my case the deception began when I thought I was joining a national women's group; yet, at my first meeting, I found myself in a mixed group of women and men. During a break I made a comment to a friend, who had also just joined, that I was surprised and somewhat upset that this wasn't what I'd been told. When the meeting reconvened, I was suddenly the target of a harsh criticism led by my initial recruiter (Sandra) for having a "backward and antirevolutionary attitude." Everyone joined in, and I was incredibly embarrassed. I was told to come back to the next meeting with a written self-criticism. The deception issue remained unacknowledged by everyone. I was both angry and taken aback, but I wrote the self-criticism and continued to go to meetings. (On some level the seriousness with which a person's every comment was taken put a new member off balance. The idea was to "unite" with the criticism, we were told, not to make trouble — after all, there was so much work to be done in the life of a revolutionary.) The following week my self-criticism was held up as an example of someone who really "took to heart" what was said. Once again I was treated well, while my friend was denounced once more and told to write another self-criticism. I felt relieved that mine had "passed" and that the anger was no longer focused at me.

It was made clear to recruits that acceptance into the group was not a given. As an intimidation tactic, a recruit was told that she would undergo an investigation to ensure that she was not a police agent. Financial forms were filled out; legal documents, such as birth certificates and passports, were given over for examination to verify identities; family, education, and employment background was requested. A recruit might be questioned about a friend who was going through a similar process in order to verify and cross-check information.

This scrutiny was very one-sided. It was supposed to be enough of an honor to be considered for membership in this elite group. It was very uncool to want to know too much. Details about size of membership, racial or sexual composition, geographic location, who else were members, or exactly what kind of work a new member might be doing were not to be discussed. It was implied that older, more experienced women were calling the shots, making the decisions, and that they knew best how to protect the organization in such risky times. Often a recruit's apprehension was relieved because she or he usually had a friend who was already a member or who was also being recruited. One former member described it like this:

> I thought to myself that this was all pretty weird and I probably would not have joined except I knew that two of my best friends were going through the same investigation and were expecting and hoping to join. They were both mature and level-headed individuals whom I respected, so I thought it must be all right and worth a try. At the same time I was being treated with a lot of favor: praised in meetings for my "great" presentations, held up as someone from the working class who managed to get a college education and yet was about to give up "easy living" for the life of a dedicated political activist. The words of praise overshadowed my inner doubts and fears.

Acceptance into the Group

When finally admitted, recruits were told they were in Trial Member status: They had no rights. If they passed this stage (based on study, level of participation, and good behavior), they would be advanced to Candidate Member, with partial voting rights. The security precautions emphasized during the final intake interviews brought to the fore the realization that the recruit was about to join a secret, clandestine organization. A jumble of emotions—fear, anticipation, confusion, excitement, relief—overwhelmed the new recruit upon being told that he or she had been accepted.

From that moment on life took on new meaning and a new reality. A rush of instructions, a wealth of study materials, a list of security guidelines, a seemingly endless series of meetings, all wrapped up with new responsibilities and new obligations—new things to remember and old things to forget. Life became long hours of work, criticism, and study sessions with new comrades; recruits experienced a shared sense of commitment, a growing feeling of solidarity and togetherness. Within a matter of weeks a new member's entire world revolved around the internal life of the organization. It happened almost imperceptibly. Being asked to do more was a sign of greater acceptance and trust on the part of the leadership; agreeing to do more was a show of willingness to make the commitment on the part of the new member. Any resistance was met with criticism, signaling a weak link. Soon all personal activities fell by the wayside – sports, evening classes, visits with family or friends.

THE CONVERSION

Once Doreen Baxter was asked how she was able to build such a strong and mindful organization. "How do you get all those people to abide by the discipline, to follow orders all the time?" Baxter leaned over in her chair, stared the questioner in the eye, and replied, "With a little carrot and a lot of stick."

Reeducation and Remolding

New members began an intensive indoctrination process referred to as "reeducation and remolding," using the techniques of struggle sessions and class histories. Deemed tainted by life in a competitive, individualistic, capitalist society, recruits were ordered to analyze their lives and socioeconomic ("class") backgrounds to extinguish all "incorrect" ideas. What comprised a good or bad class stand was defined by Baxter and changed as her goals and need to manipulate members changed. One of the worst criticisms that could be leveled was that a person was a "bourgeois individualist," one who refused to accept the group's views without question.

Collective critiques of a new member's class history often lasted 8 to 10 hours. These badgering, grueling interrogations became the initiation rite of party membership in which a written report about a member's family background and personal history was rigorously evaluated. These tortuous political autopsies did not finish until the person adopted the "correct class analysis" of his or her life. As a new member and throughout the years, members were subjected to relentless, vicious group "criticism/self-criticism," or struggle sessions, a process by which a person was made to account for some statement or action that was seen as politically incorrect, or antiparty.

Self-denial was glorified as the only road to purification – that is, the ideal must always come before the individual. The message was:

Be harsh to find goodness. Suffer to find happiness. Work hard to find freedom. Ruthlessness is kindness. Change yourself to fit the mold or be banished to the selfish fate of the rest of the world.

Baxter's teachings include the following principles:

> Those who do not change should be expelled. We are sincere cadres with time only for those who are equally sincere, honest, and devoted to the cause of the people's liberation first and foremost. Never lose sight of the fact that the bourgeois individualist is dangerous. We know from hard experience that if there is any hope for the bourgeois individualist it is we who must be positively unrelenting in our criticism and in our attitude toward that person.

* * *

> Each comrade is to constantly remind herself or himself of this guiding principle: The whole is greater than the sum of its parts; the organization always and forever comes before the individual. There is *only* the organization. We are nothing without it.

* * *

> We do not indulge faults, we rectify them; we do not justify errors, we overcome them. Ours is a hard calling and a stern discipline: It is also liberation.

LOSS OF IDENTITY

Upon acceptance, a new member was instructed to choose a "party name," just a first name. From this point on, identification was by this name only. Members (now referred to as "militants") were told never to reveal their real name to other members, not even to roommates. Party names were used in all party gatherings and in all houses where party members lived. Militants who mistakenly used their own or another member's real name were severely reprimanded for committing a security breach. For the new member, taking on a party name was the first stage in losing his or her preparty identity and taking on a party-molded one.

A new member was also told (1) to get a post office or rental mail box for receiving all mail, (2) to change the name on household utility bills to an alias, (3) to use an alias when subscribing to any publications, particularly leftist publications, and (4) to change car registrations and driver's licenses to either a "safe" address (such as the home of an apolitical friend) or the mail box address. Making these changes comprised another step in the personal burial process.

A Tidal Wave of Meetings

At a minimum, a new member was expected to attend a Branch meeting, New Members class, a one-on-one ("one-help") meeting, a work unit meeting, and, in certain years, a Party School meeting. Each of these met weekly.

New Members Classes were held with six to eight new members and two specially trained teachers. The goal: to "break" new members—that is, to move each new member from the shaky, uncertain commitment normal upon joining to a firm, unwavering devotion to the party.

All members (except Baxter and Sandra) were assigned to a Branch of 10 to 12 members. Branches initially met each Saturday from 1–10 p.m. Later they met on Fridays from 6–11 p.m. or later.

Party School classes of about 20 members were led by one highly trained leader. Party School was touted as elite training. The criticism was more intense than in the Branch, going to the core of the member's commitment. Criticism here focused on thoughts and feelings rather than actual mistakes or actions. All members (except Baxter and Sandra) attended Party School.

The "One-help"

Every new member was assigned a "one-help," or buddy. The new member and the one-help met weekly; the one-help was to assist the new member's integration into party life. The new member was supposed to tell everything to the one-help—all thoughts, questions, or feelings about the organization. One-helps were to help new members "see things from a party point of view" and coach them in scheduling their time and figuring out how they could do even more for the organization.

The one-help wrote detailed reports on everything the new member said and did. These reports were used to monitor development and to pick out something that could serve as the basis of a group criticism in future meetings. It didn't take long for a new member to realize that his one-help reported on him in great detail. A new member's acceptance of this fact was another boost for the party, reinforcing the institutionalization of an important control mechanism: the incessant reporting on one another and the fear of fellow comrades.

Surrender to the Party

Very quickly it became clear that submission to the organization was the ruling principle. There was intense pressure to conform. The written class history and detailed membership application were key in providing the party with complete information about each new member. Submitting that degree of personal information was a crucial step in the process of turning over one's entire life to the party.

New members were also required to write a summary of all "external contacts," that is, absolutely everyone they knew who was not already in the party. These reports could be very long, taking a great deal of time to write. The new member was to identify who was recruitable among the friends, relatives, and co-workers listed. New members were taught that previous acquaintances — no matter how intimate — were to be treated as potential recruits. If someone wasn't a potential recruit, there was no reason to maintain the relationship.

One former member recalled a high-level meeting where they were boasting about a prized new member (a woman of color with great leadership potential) who had just decided to break her engagement to a man who was never likely to join the party. This act was regarded as a sign of her increasing commitment to the party. "Hah, we own her now!" Baxter exclaimed triumphantly. The others nodded in agreement, laughing along with her.

A New World

These techniques created the most loyal, rigid followership. Shortly after the Jonestown massacre a Central Committee member dared to question what we were creating. "I'm afraid we're a cult," he said. "How are we different from the Moonies?" he rather painfully asked. "We are not a cult," Baxter professed, "and we're not brainwashed. Why? Because we willingly and consciously submit to cadre transformation. Transformation is our goal!"

Members came to participate in activities that would have been unimaginable before their conversion — one example being the violence. Goon squads were used against other groups on the Left, against groups within the local labor, peace, and antinuclear movements, and against certain former members. Cars were spray-painted. Houses and offices were ransacked. Documents were stolen. Political meetings and conventions were disrupted. "Enemies" were surveilled, threatened, and beaten up. In one case, two recently expelled members were beaten up in front of their child. Jobs were put in jeopardy, for example, by anonymously calling an employer to identify a certain employee (someone the party was after) as a child molester or thief.

Baxter set up an elite group called the Eagles whose job was to carry out these orders. Eagles received special training in security and physical fitness from an ex-Marine member. Eagles served as Baxter's

personal bodyguards, as monitors during demonstrations, as disrupt-
ers, goons, and rabble-rousers whenever needed. Baxter rarely went
anywhere without her huge Rottweiler guard dog, plus an attendant
or bodyguard.

CONTROL MECHANISMS

From the beginning recruits were instilled with an utter and absolute
respect for Doreen Baxter. Baxter was revered as the ultimate working-class heroine, lauded for knowing more about Marxism, world politics, revolution, and life than anyone else. She was praised as a genius
and a revolutionary leader, in the tradition of Lenin and Mao.

Members were taught that they would be nothing without Doreen
Baxter, that there would be no party without her. She was to be de-
fended at all costs. She was, members were told, overworked and over-
burdened. Soon it was understood as part of this logic that the undue
stress on her was caused by the "incompetence" of the members. Because of this, members were to do anything, make any sacrifice to
make her life better, more comfortable so that, for once, she could do
the work that a revolutionary leader should do.

As the party grew, fewer and fewer members actually saw or met
Baxter, which made her even more mysterious and awesome. She shut-
tled between her country and city residences, the whereabouts known
only by a small circle of trusted militants. In latter years Baxter made
perhaps one, or at most two, appearances before the entire membership. At the last all-party Assembly in 1985, Baxter sent her communi-
que by modem: It was an unintelligible poem.

Group Pressure

Group meetings provided a key venue for forcefully teaching militants
to conform. For example, leaders would start a meeting by denouncing
a comrade for some error. Once leadership finished, each militant
would be expected to say how much he or she agreed. Ideally each
person was to say something different from what had already been
said; questions, should there be any, had to be couched within an
overall agreement. After years of this process, party members became
incapable of any kind of critical thinking. They could only parrot one
another and had shrunken vocabularies riddled with arcane internal
phraseology.

If someone was too silent during a meeting, didn't speak heartily
enough, or dared to express any doubt, that person would be singled
out for criticism. This would give license to a verbal attack by the rest

of the group, with lots of derogatory name-calling (supposedly in a political context). At a moment's notice the entire direction of *any* meeting could be turned into a group denunciation of someone. When finally given a chance to respond, the comrade was usually criticized again – and this could go on for hours! "It was like chickens pecking at blood. You had to, or you'd get pecked," said one former member.

The criticized militant was not to be let off the hook. This process was often carried into future meetings – the next day, the next week, or the next several weeks. In the meantime the militant's behavior was monitored more than usual, and he or she was generally shunned by the others. This comrade walked on eggs, with a biting, clenching pit in the stomach, a gnawing pressure in the chest, waiting for the tension to be released, for reacceptance into the group, to no longer be the focal point of angry criticism, unbridled moralism, and pent-up emotions. Over time, living with this unsettling internal anxiety and feeling of impending doom was the way militants faced every waking hour.

The Trap

Why did the members put up with this treatment? Why didn't they object? Why didn't they leave? I can offer only the beginnings of an explanation. First, when we initially came into contact with the group, we were idealistically disposed toward Communism, or at least toward left-wing politics. Because of our idealism we were willing to sacrifice for the "revolution."

Second, the party had convinced us – first through its sophisticated recruitment meetings and then by means of directed study – that it had intellectual substance, integrity, and the potential to bring about the changes we believed were needed. Consequently, we saw the party – and Baxter – as "authorities." The roles were defined fairly quickly: Baxter, usually via other leadership figures, would teach; and we, the militants, were there to learn.

Third, and possibly most important, we were taught early on that the party is always right, that there is a kernel of truth in every criticism, and that criticism is the "life" of the party, the meat and potatoes, so to speak, that keeps the cadre going. Once we accepted this rationale and the fundamental assumption it supported, criticism became simultaneously our raison d'être and our cross to bear.

In the WDU we came to understand (and accept) that revolutionary theory = the party = Doreen Baxter. That kind of ruling principle covers a lot of territory. Moreover, that equation linked our idealism to Baxter's demands for obedience. Our highest aspirations became subservient to her whims. In day-to-day practice this meant that we had to either accept the rules or leave; the latter, of course, meant abandoning the revolutionary struggle, the ideal that animated us. Because the rules were so demanding, contradictory, and sometimes out-and-out senseless, at times a person recoiled, spoke or acted out of turn, or just plain made a mistake. And that person would be criticized. At other times the criticisms were completely trumped up to make a lesson or prove a point. Since integral to each militant's commitment was an acceptance of the discipline and the rigid obedience, in the end we "took it [the criticism] like a cadre man (or woman) and didn't talk back."

Talking back meant punishment at best, getting kicked out at worst. Once in this world, as awful as it was, being thrown to the outside became an unthinkable alternative: It meant failure to meet the test; even worse, it meant failing the working class, betraying the ideals that first attracted us to the party's pitch. It also meant acknowledging that we had bought into a horrible lie and, in so doing, had hurt our comrades as they had hurt us. Once caught in such a trap, decent human beings, which we were, don't easily say, "Sorry, friends, I'm getting out of here." Rather, they look for ways to rationalize their subservience and exploitation.

In that sense we were *required* to relinquish our selves in order to "cut the mustard." And we did just that—perhaps not consciously— because we desperately wanted to believe. Over time the cadre militant repressed or rejected every shred of independent and critical thinking, "submitting" to the criticism and to the party's standards of denunciation, humiliation, and punishment, as well as to any other party decision. Whatever internal battles may have gone on when a party member instinctively felt that something was amiss were invariably won by the party's voice in each person's head. Preparty norms or values were made to seem "antirevolutionary" in the face of our training, which taught us to dismiss such individualistic thinking. Thus, each person quietly squelched any dissenting thoughts, turning them inward, thinking to herself or himself how long was the road to the cadre ideal.

Instilling this extreme level of obedience and loyalty in each militant was a primary function of the party's top leadership. Immediately upon joining, members were subjected to test after test to prove their commitment and willingness to serve and to sacrifice. For the party these tests were a way to weed out the "weak." Cadre recruitment targeted achievement-oriented personalities who could serve the party well; the tests were meant to teach these high achievers how to fulfill the authority figures' expectations. The party's goal in setting up an environment of constant criticism was not so much to ensure that work was being done correctly as to create an atmosphere of tension and lack of certainty that kept militants on edge.

Additional factors not to be discounted are the positive reinforcement members got (or thought they got) from the organization, the influence of peer pressure, vestiges of self-esteem, and the consequences of a continued personal investment in the party.

First, the party employed a version of the pleasure/pain, or carrot/stick, principle. There were times, and mostly this was early on in a person's membership, when the party showered "love" upon a militant. This could take the form of praise for a job well done, a special stipend to buy some new clothes, a day or two off, or some other personal attention meant to make the militant feel as though the party really cared. During the times when someone was under criticism or exhausted to the bones and wondering whether this life made sense, those moments of "love" came into play to reassure the militant that the party's intentions were honorable.

Second, not a moment of a militant's life went unobserved – either by leadership or fellow comrades. In a sense, a commitment to join the party was a collective commitment; part of each person's role was to bolster others in carrying out their cadre commitment. This peer pressure created an environment where our mutual respect for the commitment we each had made served as the vise grip that kept each of us in line. If everyone else was going along with it, then I must too, I thought to myself on countless occasions. It was fruitless to think of contesting a criticism – it would be regarded as self-centeredness or cowardice. The harsh life-style was accepted as part of the commitment; no, even more than that, it was seen as *key* to the purity of the cadre fighter. Certainly within such a circle no one wants to be regarded as a whiner or a wimp. This manipulation was woven deeply into the third factor – a person's sense of self-esteem: Simply put, an honorable person keeps a commitment. Reneging meant leaving with your tail between your legs.

And lastly, the price to be paid went higher and higher. The longer a person was in, the greater the fear of leaving: fear of trying to make it in the outside world, fear of the party's retribution, and fear of nowhere to go. Too many bridges had been burned on every level for a long-term party member to consider leaving the party as a viable option. This was the ultimate trap.

Purges

Just after Christmas 1976 Doreen Baxter ordered the party's first purge, or mass expulsion of members, called the "Campaign Against

Lesbian Chauvinism and Bourgeois Feminism." A number of women were expelled on a moment's notice. Even though the party's membership was always mixed (in both gender and sexual preference), in the early years there were still quite a few lesbian members. The purge was carried out under a political pretext, with Baxter providing a new theoretical "line" on homosexuality to support her actions. This purge, which came out of the blue, served many purposes.

First and foremost, it highlighted that the party was always right and had unmitigated power over members' lives. In addition, it struck terror into people's hearts: Someone could be here one day, gone tomorrow—including a mate or spouse. The investigation surrounding the campaign, with probing interviews and search-and-seizure tactics, left nothing sacred. Afterward, carrying around a fear that terror lurked at every turn became an accepted way to live.

The purge also helped to institute one of the party's main control mechanisms: the method of pitting members against each other to breed mistrust and foster loyalty only to Baxter. This precedent was set with the lesbians in the party, but eventually there were campaigns against and purges of men, parents, intellectuals, those with a political past, those from middle-class ("petit-bourgeois") background—it simply had no boundaries. This divisive tactic went on and on over the years ensuring that no one would trust anyone else.

In the Lesbian Chauvinism Campaign militants were identified, their so-called "crimes" described, their punishments highlighted. A pamphlet outlining all this was produced overnight for partywide study. Other than those who were expelled without trial and never heard from again, each accused militant was ordered to come before a body of members to face criticism and denunciation. Many were suspended, unable to participate in any party activity and cut off from everyone else for anywhere from three to six weeks. People's lives (and minds) were shattered. Many women lost their loved ones; good friends were afraid to be close again; those who were readmitted were beaten down and turned their entire lives around. Some never had relationships again; some became heterosexual in preference.

And last but not least, the Lesbian Chauvinism Campaign served to break up a key friendship network. Those who were "named" in this campaign were either founders or part of the first ring of members to join soon after the party's founding. They were some of the hardest workers, most politically dedicated, and fervently loyal followers. Many were in middle-level leadership positions. Many were people who in some way posed a threat to Baxter.

As one of those charged with "crimes against the party," I lost friends and a lover in this purge. I was put on trial, suspended for four weeks, and demoted. My new assignment was to be the party's typesetter working 12-hour shifts, 7 days a week. I remember that experience—the investigations, the interrogations, the judgments, the trials—as completely devastating. During and afterward I felt such repulsion at the things that had been said to me at my trial, where I had to stand for four hours before a group of 20 members, that I no longer wanted to be "that person" who had committed such sins against the party. One symbol of my rejection was that I took off the jacket I had on at the trial and never wore it again. I could barely touch it. Months later I found it in the back of a closet and threw it in the garbage.

"Cadre Crises"

"Cadre tests" were contrived, planned, and forced to happen. Episodes were provoked to induce a "cadre crisis" as a means of thought reform. These tests chipped away at the person, at one's thoughts, beliefs, self-image, and core being—until the "party woman" or "party man" emerged. For example, I was in the party about six months when I was assigned to help Baxter move. She seemed relaxed and friendly; she started talking about her past and showing me photo albums and news clippings in which she was mentioned. Out of natural curiosity and a desire to be polite and make conversation, I asked a few questions, such as what year something took place or where a certain snapshot was taken. The next day I was called into a meeting before four high-level members. In a dark room with the curtains drawn, I was informed that on Baxter's orders I was under security investigation. I was suspected of being an agent, they said. I was grilled and regrilled about my background, my personal life, my friends, how I earned my money, and about the questions I asked the day before. I was told that others in the party, including my friends, were also being questioned about me. (And they were.) I was completely shocked, and I was terrified by this experience.

Not long after that incident I was named secretary to the Central Committee and assigned to work with Baxter on organizing her writing. This meant more access to "party secrets" and more exposure to Baxter. I found this rather confusing, but I took it as a sign that I was now trusted. I suppose I had passed a cadre test.

Discipline

Members were punished for all sorts of real or fabricated charges. Those being punished or awaiting organizational trial were suspended (removed from party life), put on punitive suspension (could not be talked to by another member, that is, lived in total silence, sometimes for as long as six weeks), put under house arrest, and sometimes guarded round the clock. A member returning from a party assignment was met at the airport by a "goon" and escorted home in silence, given orders where to report the next day. A female militant sat for hours while Baxter, drunk, held a gun to the young woman's head. An expelled founder was whisked from her house, everything taken from her, and put on a plane to her parents' home across the country. An expelled militant was thrown out of his house, his clothes and belongings discarded onto the street. An expelled foreign-born inner-circle militant was put on a plane to Europe without a penny in her pocket. Others were threatened, extorted, given a schedule to repay the party for the "training" they received. This "debt" was sometimes set in thousands of dollars.

Some members were expelled "with prejudice," that is, shunned and declared nonexistent. Generally by means of criticism, staged trials, threats, and at times acts of violence, the person would be intimidated into years of silence and would not imagine speaking about his or her party experience, much less taking any action against the group. Others were expelled "without prejudice," that is, could be spoken to if seen, could sometimes work with one of the party's front groups, would often be expected to give a regular monthly "donation," and, in some cases, after a certain amount of time determined by the party, could apply to rejoin the organization. These isolationist techniques were used to create a feeling of superiority among members, as well as a sense of paranoia and hostility, as though these "enemies" truly posed a threat.

Destruction of Personal Mementos and Documents

It is almost unfathomable to ponder the amount of paper that existed in the WDU. Whenever Baxter decided there was too much information on paper, or when some freak incident sounded a security alert, a cleansing would be ordered, with assigned militants serving lengthy shifts at the party's great shredders.

On one occasion in early 1976 all members were ordered to destroy any piece of paper that could in any way be "revealing" (which meant any trace of information about the person's background, likes or dislikes, political leanings, sexual preference, family origin, and so forth). This era predated the shredder; thus, one by one militants brought great bundles and suitcases jammed with personal items to be turned over to the party for disposal. Three of us were assigned to burn these precious documents and mementos. We sat for three days and three nights, throwing the lives of our comrades into the fire: passports, photographs, diaries, poetry, artwork, treasured writings and notes, packets of correspondence, health records, marriage certificates, and on and on. The excuse in this case was a "security breach that threatened the safety of the party." The effect was the destruction of identities and memories—another step in the remolding process.

Impoverishment

Dues were based on members' salary or income. Dues increased once the initial stage of membership was passed, which often came as a great surprise to advancing Trial Members and was invariably cause for "class-stand struggle." Each militant was to give over all monies received above the party's standard living amount, which was set at poverty level. Any monetary or substantial gifts, job bonuses, legal settlements, and inheritances belonged to the party, to be reported immediately in order to arrange payment or transfer of ownership. Meanwhile Baxter, with two well-furnished homes, a new sports car, all the latest electronic equipment, money in IRA's, and so forth, easily lived on the equivalent of several hundred thousand dollars per year. Her lavish life-style was known only to the inner circle and a handful of trusted lower-level militants.

Militants were poor, with no money to spare, no chance to save. They dressed shabbily, drove broken-down cars, rarely attended to medical or dental needs, lived in sparsely furnished places usually in the poorer neighborhoods. If they didn't meet fund-raising or paper-selling quotas, they often made up the difference out of their own pockets, making a bad situation even worse. At times militants sold their blood to get money for food. They had no financial means to escape, should the thought come to mind.

Housing

Although the entire membership did not live communally, everyone was encouraged to live in a house with other members (a "party house"). This quickly became a necessity given the poverty-level incomes. Anywhere from three to eight members shared a house or an apartment. Each house had a code name and a house captain, whose job was to ensure that party regulations were being followed.

The individual had no privacy whatsoever. Militants learned very quickly that a good friend, even a spouse, would report them. There was a constant sense of being watched. Paranoia, mistrust, and defensiveness were spawned in an organization that proclaimed itself as honest, caring, and humane.

Reports and Spying

For years everyone turned in weekly discipline and security reports. A discipline report was a written record of all errors (of thought or deed) committed during the past week. A security report was a written record of any security violations committed by a militant, or observed in any other militant, during the past week. These reports would be used by the leadership to monitor behavior and ferret out criticisms. They were also used to evaluate a militant's progress and willingness to conform.

Members rigidly followed party rules and reported on one another. For example, a longtime friend and I became housemates when she was still a relatively new member. After a visit by her mother, my friend was harshly denounced for having called me by my real name during the time her mother was with us, even though her mother already knew me. Certainly it would have seemed bizarre to her if suddenly I had a different name. Yet, I was the one who reported my friend for the security violation.

Ultimately, no one, except Baxter herself, was safe from minute-by-minute observation and potential denunciation.

Complicity

In the WDU Baxter and Sandra became role models for perverse behavior, while the rest of the membership provided the support mechanism for the implementation of a cruel, violent, and unjust life-style. A kind of mob mentality set in, not unlike what's seen in the mafia, the Ku Klux Klan, or even neighborhood gangs. Acknowledging each person's participation in this conduct is by no means meant to undermine the exploitation of the membership by the cult. Instead, it helps to explain how decent people can end up playing into the brutality of cults.

One former member wrote about "the near glee with which each one of us pounded upon the other." On some level WDU militants had a great deal of power over one another. Indeed, there was active participation of all the membership. At one time or another, almost every militant had the opportunity, for example, to lead a criticism session. Certainly everyone participated in daily denunciations. The same former member wrote, "The reward was this: inside the party we were little potentates, comrade kings, lording it over one another."

Yet this complicity must be seen within the context of the overall conversion. The WDU's control worked not simply because each person who joined had a desire for power, or even a desire to be mistreated or punished. Rather, the extent to which the system worked highlights the success of the transformation process. Over time strong-willed individuals and independent thinkers became "willing" participants in a vicious and harmful closed society – all in the name of "serving the working class."

WORK

Work varied from internal administration, running party businesses, political organizing, and academic research, to menial work performed for top leaders.

Internal administration included maintaining membership records, developing recruitment plans, planning disciplinary actions, carrying out investigations, overseeing finances, and doing guard duty. There were party-owned businesses to be run: a graphics, type, and print shop, a publishing house, a medical clinic, and a research institute. Thousands and thousands of leaflets, a biweekly bilingual newspaper, academic journals, and books were written, produced, and distributed by the party. Through numerous front groups, the WDU ran electoral, labor, and community campaigns. At one point the WDU led a grass-roots (front) organization of nearly one thousand members who worked on local issues. And of course, Baxter and Sandra were served by those who cleaned their homes, cooked, shopped and ran their errands, paid their bills, walked their dogs, chauffeured them, repaired their cars, or did anything else requested.

Each member also had numerous quotas: fund-raising, newspaper sales, recruitment, petition signatures, and volunteer activation. Beginning with the electoral organizing (1978), fund-raising became and remained an obsession. Militants were required to sell a vast array of things: buttons with political slogans or the party's name, political posters, party literature, raffle tickets, tickets to party-sponsored film series, even candy bars.

Facilities

Work was always done in collective situations. At first, work went on at selected members' homes, those places that the party considered to be "secure." Later, houses and commercial spaces were rented to be set up as "party facilities." Everyone worked at one or another of these locations, depending on his or her assignment. For example, one place housed the staff headquarters for all internal administrative work. A warehouse space served as the production headquarters and printing and publishing plant. Another building housed the data bank and research institute. Yet another was a labor organizing center or the public office for electoral efforts. Baxter's city home and Sandra's apartment were also considered to be party facilities, with certain militants assigned there to perform maid and clerical work.

Knowing the existence of or being allowed to go to any one of these locations depended on the party's degree of trust in a particular member. Most often a militant worked only at one location and knew only of that location. All locations had code names. Militants were never to tell anyone (in or out of the party) which location they worked at or what they did there.

All of the facilities (even those with public faces, such as the party-run businesses) were supposed to be secret locations. In some years cars had to be parked at least two and one-half blocks, around corners, from any party house or location. Security regulations ensured that no one could make or receive phone calls so that the State would not be able to trace calls to these locations. For many years no calls could be made from one party house to another. Public telephones, at least two blocks away, were to be used for any party-related call.

Schedules

Controlling the daily environment was a major means of enforcement. Members were expected to be at their assigned facility at all times, except when at an outside job or some other preapproved assignment. When reporting to a facility, militants signed in on a log; they signed out when they left; they had to account for each moment. Militants arrived either early in the morning or immediately after an outside job, and stayed until late into the night. Those with outside jobs were not to go home first to change clothes or eat dinner; they were not to stop anywhere else along the way. Generally militants bought fast-food on the way in, or ate junk food, or didn't eat at all.

Full-time functionaries were expected to be at their facility *all* the time. They reported for work at 9 a.m. (and often earlier) and generally stayed until 11 p.m. (and often later). Because there was a seven-day work week, full-time functionaries rarely saw the light of day, much less the changing of seasons.

More often than not, the party was in the midst of some activity which meant working anywhere from 16 to 20 hours a day, sometimes for days on end without sleep or even going home. Reading, study, and writing self-criticisms and other reports were not to be done at the work facility. That meant doing these things somewhere between midnight and 6 a.m., before the next day started the cycle all over again.

At some point it was decided that Sundays should be a day off, for personal errands, laundry, food shopping, paying bills, and calling parents. Even with this understanding, most years most militants never had a Sunday off, including those party members who had children.

Assignments

Work assignments often had little to do with a person's skills, training, or preferences. Doctors could be given production work, intellectuals put in typing pools. This was supposed to teach humility. In later years, however, such assigning was used only for punishment—for example, a party intellectual under criticism might be assigned to work in the bindery to be taught a lesson. Over time there came to be an obvious distinction between mental and manual labor, resulting in a somewhat privileged group of intellectuals and administrative leadership and another somewhat disregarded group of lower-level workers. This rather glaring class division would never have been admitted to since the party thought of itself as a microcosm of a perfect socialist society—with equality and justice for all members.

THE EFFECTS

WDU members thought of the party as a family, although that word would not have been used—"family" would have been considered too touchy-feely. Rather, militants looked upon one another as comrades—at home, at work, at meetings, at the party facility. Within a brief period of time after joining a member had no other life but the party. Anything that wasn't party-related was regarded as an intrusion on this very special existence, the life of a dedicated cadre.

As time went on, for most members, there was less and less contact with the outside world. Since militants could never explain to anyone outside the party what they were doing, where they lived, much less why they were never home, why they were never available for socializing, how they earned a living, and so forth, they found it simply easier not to see family or former friends. WDU members' lives became dominated by the daily task, the daily criticism, and whatever political campaign (internal or external) was in focus at the time. Cut off from all external support systems, they lost their sense of self and their pasts. Expulsion or trying to leave would have meant ridicule, debasement, and being cut off from all remaining social and economic support.

A harsh and unusual life-style was accepted as the sacrifice necessary for the political cause, for the achievements the party supposedly was making. Over and over militants were taught that this kind of sacrifice was difficult but do-able. It was explained that cadre life was not meant for everyone; militants were told that they should feel honored to be part of the revolutionary cadre tradition. It was also emphasized that being in the WDU carried a double responsibility, because the WDU was the only principled, genuinely communist group remaining in the North American Left. WDU militants truly believed that there would be no leftist movement if it weren't for them and their efforts. We compared ourselves to the fighters against fascism in WWII, never for a moment considering that in fact we were not living in a country at war, nor were we a people under siege. We behaved absolutely as though we were, and we held ourselves to those standards.

If a militant was on a personal errand (such as a doctor's appointment) and the wait was too long, he or she became anxious, angry, hostile because of the guilt and dread at being away from the facility. Times away from party work were dominated by the fear of getting criticized or reported. Going out into the world became a frightful and unpleasant experience, fraught with anxiety. Militants felt that there was something wrong with them if they had these other, nonparty things to do. They began not to do them. Militants canceled, missed, or put off countless medical and dental appointments, car repairs, family gatherings, driver's license renewals, legal matters, even seeing their children. Militants canceled their own weddings and failed to show up for their own parents' funerals.

THE DEMISE

In 1983 Baxter decided to expand the party nationally, and teams of three to seven members were sent out from San Francisco to set up "stations" in five cities in the south, midwest, and east. To maintain control over party members thousands of miles away, Baxter and Sandra used computers. The party purchased over 50 computers and modems and set up its own Bulletin Board; all reports and communications were done by computer. Militants and party facilities were given code names: Baxter was "Mean Dog Alpha"; others had names like "Mad Max" and "Bulldog."

Also in these later years Baxter's theoretical interests were becoming more obscure; party organizing was becoming more abstract; in effect, everything was becoming even more alienating. Occasionally there would be outbursts of rage from Baxter sensing that she was losing control. Sandra was sent around to the stations to expel "rotten apples." A similar purge was going on at party central. A climate of irrationality and despair prevailed. Many of the founders and original members were gone or demoted, having been kicked out or reduced to low-level functionaries with shattered self-images. Longtime members were getting expelled left and right, or disappearing into the night. Sandra's right-hand assistant, for example, was expelled for staying home to study on her assigned "study night." Leading cadres were put on trial over and over again, subjected to merciless denunciations; some were demoted, some were expelled. There was an atmosphere of terror and instability, even more so than members had become accustomed to.

The effects of years of endless work and punitive criticism were taking their toll. The majority of the membership at this point were those who joined in the early years. They were supposed to be the hearty, the loyal, the tireless; they were, however, losing what little grasp on reality they had left. They were too tired or too confused to read (much less understand) even the daily newspaper; they had little or no contact with the outside world. "Productive work" consisted of hours of criticism sessions and primarily menial work necessary to get Baxter ready for her next international trip, or just plain cleaning up after her and her increasing alcoholism. Sometimes upper-level leadership spent hours trying to decipher one of Baxter's incomprehensible computer messages.

By 1985 Baxter was exhibiting even more paranoia, cynicism, and hostility. In discussions with the inner circle she began to talk about splitting from the bulk of the party. She said she was tired of the burden, of dragging all these militants around, of having to explain everything all the time and put up with the militants' stupid mistakes. She wanted out. Her idea was to take a handful of cadres: those she called the "intellectuals" and those with money. The plan was to go to Washington, D.C., and start a think tank, to be around the nation's policymakers. She began to have one-on-one meetings with certain cadres, putting out her idea and getting their commitment to follow her. "The rest be damned," she would say. "They can fend for themselves."

Baxter also turned on Sandra, who was suddenly persona non grata. Banished to her house, Sandra was to have no visitors unless approved by Baxter; her party mail was re-routed. Baxter called Sandra daily, screamed and screamed at her over the phone, blaming her for messing up everything. Baxter was not including Sandra in her plan to leave.

In return, Sandra turned on Baxter. And this created an opening for the pent-up militants to burst through, like roaring water breaking through a dam. Sandra was having secret conversations with her favored few, giving certain militants literature on adult children of alcoholics. She was outwardly saying that the problem with the party was Doreen Baxter. She was talking privately about planning a sort of coup, suggesting to her cronies that they begin to raise criticisms of Baxter in their meetings with other militants.

The channel for this was to be the current party campaign, ironically called "Quality of Life" discussions. Baxter wanted her life to change and she wanted this talked about in the Branches. These discussions were the first real crack in the structure, allowing people for the first time in years to talk about their feelings.

In a sense the Quality of Life meetings turned into group therapy sessions. Still bound by party discipline and riddled with guilt and self-critical attitudes, militants tiptoed into the unknown. They spoke with anguish about losing friends and family. One woman described how she felt when her husband was put under house arrest and eventually expelled; at the time she had been told not to think or ever talk about it. She never saw him again and her distress at this event remained bundled up inside her for years. Parents shed tears over never having time to see their children. Some said they knew they weren't supposed to but they felt incredibly lonely; others said they felt lost and hopeless about our accomplishments in the movement. A well-respected doctor and party theoretician in his 50s said he was so tired he prayed daily for a heart attack to give him some release. A number of others said they secretly wished they would get killed in a car accident because they couldn't think of any other way of getting out.

In the middle of these discussions Baxter left for a trip to Eastern Europe (her obsession at the time). Without Baxter's threatening presence and without Sandra playing her crucial role of whipping everyone back into line, and with sufficient cracks in the structure, in late 1985 the Workers Democratic Union blew wide open. The doors to the outside world opened to a disoriented, exhilarated, frightened, hopeful group of people who blinked as they once again saw the light of day.

3

REFLECTIONS ON "BRAINWASHING"

Geri-Ann Galanti, Ph.D.

ONE OF THE AREAS OF GREATEST CONTROVERSY surrounding the cult issue is that of "brainwashing," or mind control. For the purposes of this chapter, I will use the two terms interchangeably. What exactly is mind control, and what role does it play in cult conversion? Because popular models of brainwashing are derived from the thought-reform processes used by the Chinese communists on prisoners during the Korean War, anything not involving extreme physical abuse or deprivation is not thought of as brainwashing. This outdated and inaccurate stereotype remains as one of the barriers to recognizing and understanding brainwashing in the context of cults. Contrary to this stereotype, the techniques used by cults are also used to socialize individuals as members of society. Although the process is much more intense and manipulative during cult indoctrination, it is not outside our sphere of comfortable recognition.

What brainwashing, or mind control, is really about is *influence*: the ability of certain individuals and environments to cause us to change our beliefs, attitudes, and/or behavior. We are constantly encountering the influence process—in advertising, in schools, in military basic training, in the media.

All forms of influence are not the same. Langone (1989), for example, discusses a continuum of influence, ranging from choice-respecting influence (educative, advisory, and certain types of persuasion) to com-

85

pliance-gaining influence (persuasion and controlling). According to Langone's formulation, therapeutic influences would fall in the choice-respecting part of the continuum, while the destructive influence observed in certain cults would fall in the compliance-gaining part of the continuum. Although definitions of what is therapeutic vs. what is destructive will vary according to personal biases—for example, cult members would surely argue that what they do is for the benefit of the members—a strong case can be made that cults largely utilize indirect and deceptive techniques of persuasion and control to serve the interests of the leaders rather than those of the members.

A further impediment to our understanding of mind control is that our society does not recognize the full range of altered states of consciousness available to human beings. When the average American thinks of altered states, he or she usually acknowledges dream states, drug-induced states, and psychopathological states. Social scientists, on the other hand, recognize many more (see Tart, 1969). Although we generally do not think of driving as an altered state of consciousness, most people have had the experience of traveling some distance on the freeway and suddenly realizing they have no memory of the last few miles. That is because they were in a different state of consciousness. If people could get past the idea that a person must feel "stoned" or at least "high" to be in an altered state of consciousness, they would accept the reality of brainwashing far more easily.

The cult experience creates a state of consciousness similar to what is experienced during hypnosis. Contrary to popular belief, hypnosis is nothing more than a state of focused attention. It is a testament to the learning potential of a focused mind that hypnosis can be so effective in influencing behavior. An individual going through "training" in a cult is put in an environment where all attention is focused on the cult's beliefs and behaviors. There are no conflicting messages, no non-cult distractions. Given this condition of focused attention, "learning" occurs much more rapidly and thus indoctrination takes place. In this way, individuals are "brainwashed," or influenced, to take on the behavior and then the beliefs of the group.

The preceding points will be illustrated with examples based on a three-day participant-observation field experience undertaken in the course of my own anthropological research on cults and deprogramming. What follows is an analysis of brainwashing as it occurred during a weekend in 1983 at Camp K, a Unification Church (Moonie) training camp in Northern California. It is my hope that the principles and analysis put forth here can be generalized to experiences in other cultic groups.

BACKGROUND

I made the decision to go "undercover" because I was certain that if the Moonies knew I was a researcher I might not have the same experience as the average recruit off the street. Prior to this, I had done a fair amount of research on the Unification Church. I had read several books by former members, I had interviewed a number of former members, and I had seen a docudrama on the training-camp experience. I had even read some "pro-cult" literature in order to gain a more balanced perspective than I would have gotten solely from ex-members.

I also carried in my baggage of assumptions a lot of notions about the process of brainwashing. Having watched too many movies during the 1950s, I visualized evil torturers in rooms lit by a single bare lightbulb dangling from the ceiling, casting shadows upon a few instruments of unspeakable torture. Accounts by several ex-members led me to expect long nights without sleep, protein deprivation, and constant badgering. I felt certain that I would recognize that I was being brainwashed at the point when the Moonie doctrine began to make sense. It certainly made no sense prior to my field experience, so if it did later, that would be evidence that my mind, which I equated with my intellect, was indeed being "controlled."

What I found was completely contrary to my expectations and served to underscore both the power and subtlety of mind control. Unfortunately, our stereotypical misconceptions about the nature of brainwashing prevent us from recognizing it. Also, from this experience I conclude that—contrary to what I once believed—it is *not* the mind that is first affected by the influence. Rather, if there is any time lag between changes in our beliefs and behavior, our behavior changes first and then our beliefs follow; in that way, we maintain a consistency between the two.

THE EXPERIENCE

All the accounts I had read by former Moonies described how members went to great lengths to hide from new recruits the fact that they were Moonies. Apparently there were a lot of changes in the recruiting process between the 1970s and 1980s, for when I walked into the Unification Church on Bush Street in San Francisco on a Friday evening, the first thing said to me was, "You understand that this is the Unification Church and that we're followers of the Reverend Moon?" Also a clearly visible sign stating their affiliation was attached to the front of their building. That same evening, after professing ignorance about the church and an interest in learning more, I was shown a videotape about both the church and the Reverend Moon. In order to go to their camp for the weekend, I had to sign a release that clearly stated that I was going with the Unification Church. In the face of my previous expectations, all of this apparent straightforwardness conspired to weaken my defenses.

Another obvious Unification Church response to years of negative press was the way in which members now met the accusations head on—though in an indirect manner. During the first night I heard the word *brainwashing* four or five times, always used in a joking context. Finally I asked "John," my "spiritual father" for the weekend, why that word cropped up so often. He said it was because people often accuse them of being brainwashed. "People are so cynical. They can't believe that we can be happy and want to help other people and love each other, so they think that we must be brainwashed to feel this way," he explained, with a good-natured laugh afterward to underscore the ridiculousness of the charge. Also, two different Moonies told me about a recent psychological study comparing Moonies with young adults from mainstream religious groups. Moonies came out much better, they said, in terms of independence, aggressiveness, assertiveness, and other positive characteristics. The Moonies' statements about brainwashing, repeated several times throughout the weekend, brought to mind the old cliché, "The best defense is a good offense." On some level, their explanations seemed quite reasonable; and my answer to their frequent query, "We don't *look* brainwashed, do we?" was always no.

Not taking into account the subtlety of different phases of consciousness, I was looking for glassy-eyed zombies as an indication of brainwashing. I didn't find any. The closest approximation to that false stereotype was one new member of less than two months whose gaze wandered constantly. Everyone else acted perfectly normal. They were able to laugh and joke as well as talk seriously about things. The only trait that struck me as strange was a kind of false overenthusiasm: There were many opportunities to perform that weekend and whenever anyone did, they were treated with the kind of cheers and applause usually reserved only for the most talented of artists. One sign of my own "brainwashing" was that by the end of the weekend I began to see this response as more charming than odd.

One by one, my expectations of the appearance of overt mind control crumbled. Not only did they present themselves openly as Moonies and look "normal," but also once we were up at the camp I experienced no lack of sleep, protein deprivation, or badgering. Both mornings I arose around 8:30 or 9:00—when I got tired of lying around; there was no one telling me to get up early. We were fed eggs, fish, tuna, cheese, and other protein-rich foods during the three daily meals, plus there were three snacks each day. I was "allowed" to talk privately—if only briefly—with other new recruits; I even had occasional moments to myself. Where was all this so-called brainwashing?

THE "EDUCATIONAL" EXPERIENCE

As an educator in the elementary and university systems, I took an interest in their methods of transmitting doctrine. I also anticipated that the real "brainwashing" would occur during these lecture periods. I was constantly monitoring my mental state. During the three doctrinal lectures per day, each lasting about an hour to an hour and a half, I sat smugly critiquing the lecture to myself. Seven years in graduate school, plus a year in the School of Education, prepared me well for this task. I amused (and most likely insulated) myself by noting the kinds of techniques they utilized.

Immediately before and after each lecture, the instructor led us in songs from their songbook to the accompaniment of a guitar. The songs were very beautiful, with upbeat lyrics. Most of them were about love and happiness and God and family. Singing is a right-brain function; critical analysis is largely the work of the left hemisphere. Thus, the singing not only served to surround the lectures with an aura of "goodness," but also managed to stimulate the nonanalytical portions of the brain.

The Lecture

Lectures were presented in a rapid-fire manner, with little opportunity to think. The instructors wrote a lot on a blackboard while they spoke. We were all given paper and pencil to use for notes; as I looked at the papers of those around me, I observed that the other listeners were simply copying what was written on the board: words and phrases that by themselves were meaningless. There was no time to write down the major points in their entirety.

In order for real learning to take place, it is necessary for the learner to actively participate in the learning process. I am a firm believer in the Socratic question-answer method; the Moonies, however, are not. They do not allow questions during lectures. (Traditional Asian teachers generally do not allow questions either. Students are taught to just write down what the teacher says.) When I later asked why questions weren't allowed, I was told that the purpose of the primary lectures is to give an overview; they want to cover everything and stopping for questions would interrupt the flow. (Former members have reported that they don't allow questions during advanced lectures either.) They explained that we would be allowed to ask questions in the small discussion groups which followed the lectures. In the meantime, we could use the paper and pencils provided to write down our questions for later.

So I wrote down my questions and objections as the lecture progressed. I found, however, that by the end of the lecture many of my questions would have sounded stupid and picky, so I didn't ask them. If an argument is based on 15 points, and point 2 is fallacious, the whole argument falls apart. But if you cannot question point 2 until after the final conclusion has been arrived at, the objection becomes meaningless and the conclusion stands. What makes it even more difficult is that the conclusions are very general and idealistic. Who wants to argue that the world *doesn't* need love?

I spent at least eight hours in lecture during the weekend; afterward I remembered almost nothing, other than that the world is filled with hate and what it needs is God and love, and how we need a God-centered family — one that is rooted in God's love. That's not very much for eight hours, especially for someone who has spent 25 years in school and is trained to learn. The Moonies listen to the same lectures over and over. I asked a few if they didn't get tired of hearing them so many times. They told me no; they said they hear new things in them every time. Looking back, I'm not surprised. The methods they use are not designed to teach, so one does not really learn. Phrases stick, but that's all. The ultimate goal becomes "learning" the lecture, which distracts the listener from the task of understanding and analyzing what is said.

Discussion Group

There was very little critical analysis during discussion groups. Most comments by members involved questions of clarification or praise for certain ideas. Since no one else was raising arguments over content, I took on that job. During the weekend, I earned the reputation in my group as a "discussion hog." I asked what I thought were penetrating questions about the nature of God and reality, the role of evolution, the Church's position on the "saved" vs. the "damned" (which differed from descriptions of the church's position given by former members), the possibility of acting purely unselfishly given natural selection, and so forth. They responded to my queries with a lot of double-talk, but they did it so nicely and sincerely that it was difficult to debate them.

On the whole it was never communicated that these issues were open for discussion; discussion leaders acted as though their role was merely to clarify for us novices what had been said.

Summary Conclusions

There are two points I wish to make regarding the "educational" experience. First, the approach and techniques are highly manipulative and designed to create in the "learner" the idea that this information is to be accepted and memorized rather than challenged and analyzed. The Moonie instructors actively discourage the use of higher critical-thinking skills. Instead, their manner is one that is more appropriately used with a small elementary school child. I constantly felt that I was being talked down to, which is in fact consistent with the whole approach of the weekend: We were continually made to feel like children rather than adults. Lecturers take on a position of authority because they are the ones in possession of the knowledge; until we've learned it all, we must remain unquestioning children/students.

Second, because of my education and background, I was far more prepared than the average recruit to deal with the influence process. Psychologically I was protected by a very strong belief system of my own, as well as by my self-imposed role as observer. At no time did I feel that my beliefs were being influenced; my intellect appeared intact. I was actively monitoring myself the entire weekend. The fact that despite all this I *was* influenced underscores the power of the techniques of persuasion.

ROBERT JAY LIFTON AND MIND CONTROL

Anyone who has studied mind control is familiar with Lifton's (1961) seminal work, in which he outlines the eight conditions that result in *ideological totalism*. Here I will describe how these conditions were applicable to the Moonie experience.

Milieu Control

The first condition described by Lifton (1961) is milieu control, or the limiting of all forms of communication with the outside world. The environment is a closed one. This was certainly true at Camp K, which was physically isolated in the woods, far from any town. There were no televisions, radios, newspapers, or other outside influences. As a result, the group became the only reality.

This in itself is not very sinister. It is something that occurs naturally during the process of socialization. Every culture has its own "description of reality," as Castaneda (1972) says. A growing child learns this reality easily enough. In moving to another culture, people go through a process of acculturation during which they take on the beliefs, values, and behaviors of the new culture. The speed at which this occurs depends upon many factors, including the amount of time spent with "outside" influences, that is, members of the person's native culture. The more time spent exclusively within the new culture, the more rapid and complete acculturation is likely to be.

The ability to adapt is built into the human biogram. It is one reason we are so successful as a species. Socialization and acculturation processes are natural; they occur all the time and we are "programmed" to respond to them. We've all experienced them. So when it happens during the cult conversion process, no warning signal sounds; it's nothing new. What is different in the cult context, perhaps, is that it is done with the specific intent of acculturating someone who may or may not at that point *want* to be acculturated. When someone moves from one country to another, he or she knows what to expect; the average recruit attending a weekend "camp" does not.

Mystical Manipulation

The second characteristic Lifton discusses is mystical manipulation. The potential convert is convinced that the group is working toward a "higher purpose" and that he will be instrumental in the attainment of that goal. From the very beginning, Moonies let me know that they were working to bring the world back to God. In doing so, they would wipe out all evil, hunger, poverty, and crime. They were different from other religions and organizations, they said, because they didn't just *have* ideals, they *lived* them. You can do good works on your own, but by joining with the group and working with them, the effect of your efforts will be much greater. I was struck more than anything by the apparent sincerity of their belief that they were really going to save the world—and that God was depending on each and every one of them to do it.

This is related to another factor, which is not as deceptively manipulative but which is part of the appeal of cults: The group provides a meaning for existence. People who join are convinced that they can make a difference in the world. The existentialist position is a difficult one to take; humans need meaning in their lives. In the 1960s we could turn our energies toward the Vietnam War. Though I was not a politically oriented person in my undergraduate years, some of my most memorable recollections of college include my participation in antiwar protests. The sense of community I felt during the candlelight moratorium, the sense of being involved in something much larger than myself was an incredible feeling that I've rarely had since. Young people today have few causes to inspire them. Cults provide a cause.

Sacred Science

Lifton also discusses the acceptance of basic group dogmas as sacred: An aura of sacred science surrounds the belief system. As intimated earlier, church dogma was presented in lectures as though it were scientific truth. At one point, the lecturer mentioned that it was simply a "theory," but the rest of the weekend it was presented as "Truth." One of the questions I raised in discussion was whether they were presenting the Divine Principle (the bible of the Unification Church) as absolute Truth or as one truth among many. The answer I got was essentially this: All religions have elements of the truth. We believe that we have the Greater Truth. We've tried it. It works. Recruits are invited to try it for themselves and see.

Note the emphasis on the traditional scientific method of hypothesis and testing. It is, however, only the veneer of science. What is lacking is falsifiability. The basic tenets of their beliefs must be accepted on faith; there is no way to prove them false. The corruption that exists in the world is evidence to them that Satan controls us. There is no way to scientifically prove or disprove the existence of Satan. All discussion starts from the basic assumption that the Divine Principle is true. Its veracity is not a point of discussion.

The presentation of dogma as Truth is, in my opinion, another point that appeals to young people. One of the courses I teach is human evolution. What I like best about the subject is what most students like least: the fact that we know so little about the past and that our ideas are constantly changing with each new fossil discovery. Intelligent scholars debate competing theories. Rather than delight in the mystery, most students are frustrated by the lack of solid facts; they want to know whose theory is right.

Perhaps because there is so much uncertainty in the world today, young people are searching for ultimate answers, for something stable to believe in. Traditionally, cultures changed very slowly. Since the advent of industrialization, this is no longer true. Technology has grown at such a rapid rate, culture must leapfrog to keep up with it. Truth is constantly changing, and many young people don't like that.

Therefore, when someone tells them that this is the way things really are, that Truth exists and we've found it, they can breathe a sigh of relief and relax in the false security.

Subordination of Person to Doctrine

According to this characteristic, group doctrine is made to take precedence over everything a person has previously learned. The value of the individual is subordinated to the value of the group, its work, and its doctrine. In the context of the Unification Church, you're made to see how selfish it is to place yourself and your individual needs and wants first. We must think of others and of God before we think of ourselves. Individuality becomes linked with the notion of selfishness, the group with the concept of unselfishness. Our culture has taught us to believe that being selfish is bad and being unselfish is good; therefore, it is natural to learn to subjugate yourself for the good of the group in the name of being a "good" person. (This, too, is characteristic of many Asian cultures.)

Dispensing of Existence

Here, a sharp line is drawn between those who will be "saved" and those who will be "damned" (nonmembers). In response to my question, the Moonies openly denied this as one of their beliefs, although ex-members report that this view is taught later on. This tenet forms the basis for much of the fear and guilt that some former members say kept them in the group for so long. Although it could be argued that ex-members are biased, dispensing of existence is a part of many, if not most, major religions and is likely to also be part of the Unification Church's thought.

Personal Confession

Requiring personal confession of one's innermost fears and anxieties is another technique used in achieving thought control. I experienced a very mild version of this during my weekend at camp. Confession consisted mainly of being asked questions about myself and my feelings. I presented myself as a psychologically healthy person, and they didn't push.

I witnessed something, however, that may be related. My "spiritual mother" showed me a letter written and hand-delivered to her by one of her "spiritual sisters," a young woman with whom I had spent a great deal of time talking. My "mother" explained that they exchanged letters once a month. She read it to me to mark the contrast between the types of letters she gets from her "real" sister (her birth sister) and her "sisters" in the church. Her birth sister writes to her about the events in her life. "Susan" (my spiritual mother) said she was not interested in that. Her church sisters write to her about their feelings, about what is going on inside them spiritually. In the letter she read to me, her sister Jane confessed that the previous day she had been feeling really down and depressed and she had to work hard to overcome those feelings. She wrote about her constant inner struggles and challenges – a major theme in much of what I heard that weekend.

The issue of sister Jane's letter is significant for two reasons. First, it illustrates a form of confession that goes on in the group, although I'm not sure how widespread it is. Second, it exemplifies some of the emotional deceptiveness that occurs. I had, in fact, spent a lot of time with Jane on the day she was referring to in her letter to Susan. I pride myself on being sensitive to other people's moods and feelings, yet I did not pick up on Jane's mood of "feeling down," as she described in the letter. To me, she appeared happy – just as everyone there seemed happy. Nevertheless, here was Jane, admitting that she was not. Whether the happy facade was for the benefit of the new recruits, or was something the Moonies are trained to do (à la "gray skies are gonna clear up, put on a happy face . . . "), or was a combination of the two, I'm not really sure. Also, I'm not clear on why they allowed me to see the discrepancy. It does indicate, however, that what we see on the surface does not always reflect what is underneath. This is highly significant and part of how they "hook" people. Levine (1984) has commented:

> As much as I have looked at beatific faces and witnessed gushes of joy, something has always prevented me from being swept up. Again and again, with hundreds of committed group members, I have felt that theirs is a performance, a case of bad acting in which the actor is himself carried away by the ringing truth of his role yet fails to convince the audience. . . . They are not brainwashed or weird, but neither are they quite whole. The happy face that joiners wear is uncontagious precisely because it does not accurately represent their inner dynamics. (pp. 25–26)

Susan also made a "confession" to me. She frequently talked about her work at Project Volunteer, a government program to give free food to the poor. She is white; most of the Project's recipients are black and many are hostile to her because of her skin color and her affiliation with the Moonies. She confessed that this was very hurtful and difficult for her but added that she viewed it as a challenge, something to help her grow and become a better person.

Psychologically, confession has the effect of drawing people closer together and influencing them to share their own innermost thoughts and feelings. We tend to feel stronger ties with those to whom we have revealed ourselves. Perhaps this was their reason for allowing me to see some of their unhappiness. Perhaps the message that *it is good to share what you think and feel* was such an important part of the psychological hook, that it didn't matter that they allowed me to see beyond their "happy" facade.

The Need for Purity and
Loading the Language

The need for purity is the need to constantly strive for perfection in order to achieve the higher goal. Jane's letter and Susan's conversations with me attest to the fact that they are always aware of trying to be better people.

Loading the language involves creating a lingo that assigns new meanings to familiar words. This assists in further separating members from nonmembers. One major example of this is the use of the terms *mother, father, sister,* and *brother*. Rather than referring to blood relationships, they reflect church ties. "Brother" refers to all male Moonies, "sister" to all female Moonies; your spiritual "mother" and "father" are those who take care of you (and almost never leave your side) from the moment you enter the church. "Father" by itself refers to the Reverend Moon and "Mother" to his wife. They are your "true parents."

Assigning new meaning to emotionally loaded terms also serves, in this instance, to separate individuals from their natural families. In addition, the use of these particular terms de facto turns the recruit into the "child." The Moonies never call you that outright, but if they are your spiritual mother and father, what else can you be but their child? The implication is that you are someone who does not know very much, someone who needs to be taught. Along with the childlike nature of other activities (discussed in the next section), it serves to psychologically transport you to the time when socialization first occurred, thus facilitating the resocialization process.

Summary Conclusions

As stated earlier, none of the conditions defined by Lifton is particularly sinister as manifested within the context of the camp weekend;

many of them are aspects of ordinary life. The major objection to their use in cults in that they are all used at once with the intention of converting potential recruits, without fully informing them about what's going on. Caught up in a whirlwind of experience and allowed little free time in which to analyze what is happening, recruits become "hooked" almost without their knowledge or consent.

The process of resocialization – or acculturation to the new subculture – takes place over a period of time; it doesn't all happen in just one weekend. The process of changing beliefs occurs more slowly. The trick is to get the recruit to stay long enough for this to occur. This is where many of the manipulative and deceptive practices come in. In the next section, I will address the issue of how the Moonies influence new recruits to remain.

TECHNIQUES OF INFLUENCE

An important area of study in business management is the study of power – or the ability to influence and/or control the behavior of others. Johnson and Johnson (1975) describe six bases of power: reward, coercive, legitimate, reference, expert, and informational. Four of these are of particular relevance here:

1. Legitimate: Group members believe the person ought to have power because of his or her position or responsibilities.
2. Reference: Group members do what the person wants out of respect, liking, or wanting to be liked.
3. Expert: Group members believe the person has a special knowledge or skill and is trustworthy.
4. Informational: Group members believe the person has useful knowledge not available elsewhere.

The aura of legitimate power is conferred upon those individuals who are in the role of lecturer. They wouldn't be given the position of teacher if they didn't have the knowledge and abilities, right? Thus, expert power is attributed to them as well. Legitimate power is also given to the group members – as opposed to recruits – since they are now in the position of being spiritual parents, and we all know that parents have the same legitimate power over children that teachers have over students.

The Moonies presented an alternative life-style which was very appealing: community, love, idealism. They presented a picture of true happiness, though one I learned was false. Most young people strive toward goals like these, goals that are shared by many of the people attracted to cults. These goals are all valued by our culture. The Moonies presented themselves as people who have found a way *that works* to achieve these goals. Not only that, but they also want to share their way with us so that we too can attain these worthwhile goals. Thus, they work from both expert and informational bases of power.

I experienced a direct example of a display of reference power on Saturday evening when we gathered in our small groups to discuss "what we liked best about the day"—not what we *thought* about the day, but what we *liked best*. As we went around the circle, people mentioned things like the lecture on the Reverend Moon, the movie about the Unification Church, or a point made in a lecture. Personally, what I liked best about the day was the volleyball game. But I realized if I said that I would sound quite shallow. I liked these people and I didn't want them to think I was shallow, so I searched for something that would make me look better in their eyes, yet would still be true. When my turn came, I said, "I really enjoyed meeting a lot of really nice people." Already, in this small way, my behavior was being influenced.

"Love Bombing"

A basic human need is for self-esteem. The Moonies utilize a technique known as love bombing to capitalize upon this need. Basically it consists of giving someone a lot of positive attention. For example, one morning Jane said to me, "You know, you're really one of the most open people I've ever met. You don't put up any defenses. You're really open, I think that's so great." Besides reinforcing the behavior of openness to new ideas, which would clearly serve their goal of having me become a member, it made me feel good about myself. Of course I was prepared for this; immediately part of my mind flashed, "Love bombing, love bombing." The other part of my mind, however, said, "Yes, but it's really true. I *am* an open person." Even though I knew it was a manipulative technique, I *wanted* to believe she meant it, and I decided that she really did. After all, it matched my own perception of myself.

During one of the initial group sessions when we were first introducing ourselves, I mentioned that I liked to dance. That night while we were making up our group's presentation for the "Saturday Night Live Talent Show," everyone kept encouraging me to choreograph our musical number. (The musical number involved writing new words to an old song. After much nondiscussion, we finally chose "On Broadway."

I suggested a number of humorous lyrics poking very mild fun at Camp K; none were accepted. I was told to be more "up." I quickly learned that you don't make jokes about the Moonies or their way of life. Resocialization continued.) As for my choreographing, I felt a bit shy but figured, why not? I had never seen a more supportive group in my life. The only way to fail was to not take part. I had about five minutes to make up and teach the number to a group of 15 people. Needless to say, my "dance" was quite simple and rather silly, but it was all in fun and didn't really matter. It made me feel part of the group (another technique for creating emotional ties: get people to actively participate in group activities); it also gave the Moonies ample opportunity for more love bombing. After the show and all the next day, at least a dozen people came up to me to tell me what a "great" dance I choreographed. Despite the fact that I knew it wasn't, it still felt good to have people compliment me on something that is important to me. Thus, I was made to feel good by being recognized for taking an active part in the group.

Influence through Identification and Example

Another effective technique for enticing members to join is to make you identify with the individuals in the group. Part of my "cover" was saying that I was a third-grade school teacher, something I actually did once for 10 weeks. When I mentioned this to my spiritual father, he replied, "I used to be a school teacher, too." He kept emphasizing how much alike we were when in fact we're not. He also told me how much I reminded him of a close friend of his. Someone else told me how much I reminded her of her sister-in-law. Other people told me that I looked "so familiar." It was rather transparent to me that this was merely a technique to make me feel that we were not so different and that I could be a part of their group; I really don't look that much like so many other people!

They also practiced the technique of shaping behavior through example. One way they did this was to constantly serve me. One of my secret desires is to have someone follow me around, picking up after me. That's exactly what happened that weekend. After the volleyball game, I went to take a shower and commented on the odor of my T-shirt. Instantly, one of the Moonies picked it up and proceeded to wash it for me! The next morning, I found it neatly folded on top of my suitcase.

If I got hungry, it seemed I only needed to think of eating something and someone would bring me a plate of food. They were constantly serving me, getting things for me, trying to carry my things for me. At first, I liked it. Soon, however, it made me feel uncomfortable. The only way I could get over this discomfort was to model their behavior: I began doing things for them. Again, resocialization, while at the same time teaching subordination of person to doctrine.

Influence through Emotion, Not Intellect

My overwhelming response to my experience that weekend was that I was having fun. It was like being a child again. Most of the time not spent in lectures was passed by eating, playing games, and singing songs. No wonder it is called *Camp* K. At first I held back in the singing; I have a terrible voice and can't carry a tune. But soon I decided, "Why not get into it like everyone else? After all, I want to see what they're experiencing." (Good rationalization.) So I did. I sang with all the energy and enthusiasm I could muster, because it felt good. It was nice to be a child again, with no responsibilities except to have a good time and learn a little. Children tend to experience things more on an emotional level rather than on an intellectual one. Certainly that particular approach was stressed during the weekend; it places the recruit in a vulnerable position and helps strip him or her of the power to resist those in authority, those who are trying to influence him or her.

DISCUSSION

In the preceding section, I described several of the techniques I experienced. The effects were to shape my behavior in a way that was consistent with the group's goals, to cause me to identify with the members and thus the group, and to create emotional/psychological ties with them. These are the first steps in the "brainwashing" process. I was beginning to act like them: cheering wildly at mediocre performances, reporting attitudes that I felt would meet with their approval, actively participating in games and songs from childhood. My attitudes were also changing. Most telling was a remark I made to the friend I had arranged to pick me up from Camp K: "I had a great time. Remind me again what's so bad about the Moonies."

The day after the camp experience I was interviewing a former deprogrammer who had spent several years in the Moonies. About halfway through the interview I asked her to describe exactly what she did during a deprogramming. She looked me straight in the eye and said, "Exactly what I've been doing with you."

I was shocked; I didn't need deprogramming; I didn't buy their doctrine; they didn't brainwash me. Despite my protestations, I came to realize that they *had* influenced me: "Remind me again what's so bad about the Moonies." I knew very well the reported abuses of members by the Unification Church—the long hours of fund-raising, late at night, often in dangerous areas; the lack of proper nutrition; the suicide training; the fear and guilt; the relative poverty in which the members live, while the leaders dwell in splendor; the munitions factory owned by a church that is supposedly striving for world peace; the divisions created between family members; the deceptions—all of the horrors. But that knowledge no longer seemed important. I had a great time, the people seemed good, so by association, the group did as well. While I was with them I was unable to reconcile the emotional truth with the intellectual one, and the more immediate emotional reality won out. It was only later, when I was outside the environmental influence of the group, that what I knew began to sink in. Then, free of the gentle pressure to react on the basis of feeling rather than thought, I could begin to analyze what had occurred.

Mind control is a heavily loaded term, evoking images of men reaching long fingers into our brains, controlling us like helpless puppets. In reality, it refers to the use of manipulative techniques that are for the most part extremely effective in influencing the behavior of others. They are not easily recognized because they are techniques utilized by all cultures—directly and indirectly—to socialize children and acculturate immigrants. Socialization occurs with an unformed human being; thus, its influence is usually much stronger than that of acculturation. As suggested earlier, the experience of being a child again during the training weekend serves to intensify the experience by psychologically bringing the person back to the period in his or her life when socialization first occurred. At the same time, the fact that individuals can be deprogrammed—that is, brought back to their original personality and level of functioning—is a by-product of the fact that a cult's "resocialization" is but an overlay on something deeper and stronger.

Human societies function in an orderly way only because there is a general human tendency toward conformity. This is especially strong during adolescence, the period of time when many people join cults. It is not easy to persist in seeing something as blue that everyone else keeps saying is red. Cult members present a unified, consistent worldview. They seem sure and confident. It is a natural human response to be influenced by such a view if that is the only one presented to you. The longer you spend with them, the more of their beliefs you acquire. Through the use of techniques such as peer pressure, reward and punishment, modeling, and relying on the basic human need to be loved and admired, they influence you to stay with them until you become completely acculturated. You are now a Moonie, so it's safe to let you outside the camp.

The perspective on brainwashing presented here is based on my personal experience at a Moonie training camp. I have suggested that brainwashing be viewed as a form of indirect and manipulative influence that utilizes familiar techniques found in the normal societal process of socialization. These techniques are used in socialization precisely because they are extremely powerful. They appear innocent, but when put to deceptive ends, they are no less potent.

The confusion surrounding the brainwashing process stems from the fact that most people are looking for something overt and foreign – akin to sensationalized media accounts of brainwashing done by the Chinese (in fact, the Chinese didn't do what those accounts led people to think) – when it most surely is not. I went to Camp K looking for something big and evil; what I found was very subtle and friendly, thus I didn't recognize its power.

Furthermore, although the terms *brainwashing* and *mind control* place emphasis on their effect on the intellect, what I found was that the process works first on an *emotional* level and a *behavioral* one. Since the emotional brain (limbic system) is phylogenetically older than the analytical neocortex, its power is very strong. The need for love and approval – upon which cult members play – leads to psychological and behavioral identification with the group. Over time, beliefs change as well, but more through the repression of the intellect than the changing of the intellect. Thus, deprogramming, exit counseling, and post-cult rehabilitation are geared toward restimulating the analytical faculties.

Brainwashing is even harder to recognize when it happens to us because, in addition to all the points mentioned, it involves a lot of ego issues. "If they were actually brainwashing me, does that mean I am a bad judge of character? Am I not as good as they said I am? Did they care about me as an individual, or was I just another potential member?" And so on.

The cult issue is exceedingly complex. I came to my field experience with a definite anti-cult bias based on my own experiences and my personal belief in the importance of individuality; nevertheless, I still saw the people I met at Camp K as good people. If their primary motive was to get me to join the Unification Church, it was because they (the members) believed that by doing so they were helping to save the world and my soul. Is that so dishonest? Yet how honest is it to use such manipulative techniques? I left the camp regarding the Moonies I met as simultaneous victims and victimizers.

My weekend with the Moonies was intended to answer some questions I had. Instead, it raised many more. The most solid thing I came away with, however, is a new understanding of brainwashing. If we are to avoid it, first we must learn to recognize it.

REFERENCES

Castaneda, C. (1972). *Journey to Ixtlan*. New York: Simon & Schuster.

Johnson, D. W., & Johnson, F. P. (1975). *Joining together*. Englewood Cliffs, NJ: Prentice-Hall.

Langone, M. D. (1989). Social influence: Ethical considerations. *Cultic Studies Journal 6*(1), 16–31.

Levine, S. (1984, August). Radical departures. *Psychology Today*, pp. 20–27.

Lifton, R. J. (1961). *Thought reform and the psychology of totalism: A study of "brainwashing" in China*. New York: W. W. Norton.

Tart, C. T. (Ed.). (1969). *Altered states of consciousness*. New York: John Wiley.

4

UNDERSTANDING MIND CONTROL: EXOTIC AND MUNDANE MENTAL MANIPULATIONS

Philip Zimbardo, Ph.D.
Susan Andersen, Ph.D.

THE GOAL OF "MIND-CONTROL STRATEGIES" is to manipulate others' thoughts, feelings, and behavior within a given context over a period of time, resulting in relatively greater gain for the manipulator than for those influenced. The changes produced may be narrowly focused or affect a broad realm of human reactions. They can become manifest suddenly or develop gradually, may be induced with or without awareness of any manipulative or persuasive intent of the change-agent, and they may result in temporary or enduring changes. Although some types of mind control utilize what we will term "exotic" technologies, such as hypnosis, drugs, and intrusive assaults directly on the brain, most forms of mind control that we will consider are more mundane (Schwitzgebel & Schwitzgebel, 1973; Varela, 1971; Weinstein, 1990). They rely on exploiting fundamental human needs in order to elicit compliance or conformity to the change-agent's desired rules and behavioral directions (Deikman, 1990; Milgram, 1992). While some change-agents are "compliance professionals" working within institutional settings, notably governmental, religious, military, or business, many others are "intuitive persuaders" who regularly utilize "rule-of-thumb," home-remedy-type compliance tactics and heuristics for personal gain and control of others, often their associates, friends, and relatives (Cialdini, 1993; Zimbardo & Leippe, 1991).

This chapter outlines some uses of mind-control strategies and tactics that achieve their effects using both exotic and mundane approaches; our primary focus, however, lies in suggesting means of enhancing the reader's *resistance* to mind control. The context for those suggestions to minimize one's vulnerability to such forms of social influence enmeshes us in the basic, yet non-obvious, dialectic of detachment/disengagement and involvement/saturation – with life.

While total obedience to cult leaders can result in dramatic instances of mind control, lesser forms of control rely on the same basic principles: the manipulation of motives, the creation of social rewards, and the meting out of social punishments, such as nonacceptance, ridicule, and rejection. Even in simple social situations, often we are subjected to choreographed confidence games. At a number of Broadway theaters, for example, concessionaires are trained to hand glossy programs to escorted women, saying with a smile, "Your personal souvenir of the show, madam." "Thank you," she replies and walks on, as the concessionaire whispers firmly and formally to her companion, "The lady's program is one dollar fifty, sir." With obviously restrained resentment, the escort pays the dollar fifty. Rarely are programs returned. The language of flattery – "madam," "sir," "your personal souvenir" – sets the stage for acquiescence to rules that uphold a public image of civilized, generous behavior.

A wheeler-dealer clothing store owner may use a "hard of hearing" script to ensnare price-conscious customers into spending extra money. After evoking someone's interest in new merchandise, not yet price-tagged, he calls out to his partner for the selling price. From the back room the associate shouts, "Eighty-six fifty," just as the owner's hearing aid comes loose. Tinkering momentarily with the device, the owner curiously examines the merchandise and says, "Only fifty dollars, huh? Okay, if that's the price, that's what you get it for." Then, looking the customer straight in the eye, he emphasizes, "But no free alterations for that kind of money." Thinking they're leaving with a "real deal," customers tend to pay cash on the spot – for a garment worth somewhat less than what they paid.

Most of us realize – after the fact – that we can be taken when, in a convincing context, a manipulator is willing to exert the time, effort, and ingenuity to deceive us. In fact, each year millions of Americans pay thousands of dollars to automobile mechanics for labor and supplies that aren't delivered. In 1978 it was documented (Renberger, 1978) that over two million Americans underwent surgical operations they didn't need – at a cost of over four billion dollars. Even more Americans start smoking cigarettes or maintain this lethal habit because of the expensive promotional campaigns of cigarette companies directed toward women, youth, and minorities (Blum, 1989).

BASIC TRAINING IN COMPLIANCE

John Marks's (1979) exposé of the CIA's secret mind-control program made it clear that no foolproof way of "brainwashing" another person has ever been found. (The word *brainwashing* is used here in its popular connotation, which came out of movies and sensationalized press accounts—that is, absolute control over another. This was not what the leading researchers [Lifton, 1961; Schein, Schneier, & Barker, 1961] of Korean War-era "brainwashing" meant by their terms, *thought reform* and *coercive persuasion*, respectively.) Electroshock therapy, hypnosis, exquisite torture devices, and psychoactive drugs have not proved adequate for the task of reliably directing behavior through specific scenarios designated by would-be manipulators. It is a person (or various persons) in a convincing social situation—not gadgets or gimmicks—who control the minds of others. The more worried we are about being regarded as ignorant, uncultured, untalented, or boring, and the more ambiguous the events that must be evaluated, the more likely we are to take on the beliefs of those around us to avoid being rejected by them (Haney & Zimbardo, 1977).

Components of effective mind control exist in the most mundane aspects of human existence: the inner pressures to be bonded to other people, the power of group norms to influence behavior, the force of social rewards such as a smile, a compliment, a gentle touch (Asch, 1951; Barker, 1984; Cialdini, 1993; Franks, 1961; Zimbardo, 1972). What ensures the success of undesirable social influences—whether they involve buying new products, entering new relationships, or simply maintaining the status quo in a contrary environment—is our blindness to the potency of certain situations. Etiquette and protocol are powerful inhibitors of unconventional action. When people around us behave alike and in ways they are expected to, it becomes difficult for us to evaluate their actions critically or to deviate from what is also expected of us in the situation.

This phenomenon is not limited to "ignorant" or "evil" personalities. The kinds of social programming we are all subjected to in childhood circumscribe our perception of such behavioral possibilities with a neat cleave. The "good child" learns his or her place in all social settings, stays put, is polite, speaks only when spoken to, is cooperative, does not make trouble, and never makes a scene. As children we are rewarded for going along with the group, for not insisting on getting our own way. It is the wiser course of action, we are taught, to go with power than to challenge it (Deikman, 1990; Haney & Zimbardo, 1973).

By assuming situational social roles in a setting, we can be led unwittingly to take on companion roles in the various scenarios being enacted: if she wants to play "guest," we become "host"; if he is quick to assume responsibility, we passively surrender some of our own; if they are a couple in conflict, we become mediator. Once we become ensconced in some social role, our behavioral freedom is compromised in subtle ways. Interviewees answer but don't ask questions; guests don't demand better food; prisoners don't give commands; audiences listen; "true believers" believe; rescuers sacrifice; tough guys intimidate, others recoil (Goffman, 1971; Hochman, 1990; Milgram, 1992).

Expectations about what behaviors are appropriate and permissible within the structure of a role can come to control us more effectively than the most talented persuader. As a nation we saw in the Watergate cover-up how the "best and brightest" caved in to the pressures that required "team players" to win this one for the President. Unquestioned protocol persuaded them to betray their public offices (Dean, 1978; Kadish & Kadish, 1973).

SATURATION AND DETACHMENT

While most of us feel immune to being sucked into any group with an even mildly cultic appearance, most of us can be deeply inspired by a social cause or by people who seem to share our sense of values. At Scientology's introductory meeting and during the first stages of est training, for example, people are sincere and open, even inspiring; however, our interviews indicate that the control techniques used later on to suppress dissent within the ranks are precisely those used by other cults. Synanon, est, Scientology, Krishna Consciousness, the People's Temple, and Moon's Unification Church, to name a few, have all asked prospective members to "open their minds" to exciting new identities, to saturate themselves with new meaning and a sense of belonging, and to refrain from being judgmental (Barker, 1984; Butterworth, 1981; Conway & Siegelman, 1978; Galanter, 1989; Mills, 1979; Reston, 1981).

It helps to remember that when any of us are faced with complex problems, we often yearn for simple answers and rules of thumb for how best to proceed. It can be comforting to become immersed in the teachings of a powerful leader, or in the total ideology of any highly cohesive group. But losing the desire to formulate unique, creative ideas in any situation is tantamount to giving up one's sense of self. Thorough, unquestioned saturation hinders our ability to evaluate our actions critically, when it is in our best interests to do so.

To counteract this possibility, we could refuse to play social roles, seek social rewards, join organized groups, or notice modeled behaviors — but only if also we are prepared to withdraw entirely from society. Alternatively we could choose to detach ourselves emotionally from certain aspects of social life, but usually this has the drawback of leaving us without social support, friends, lovers, or anything in which to believe. Although being detached enough to observe and analyze is intimately tied to survival, utter detachment can lead to withdrawal or paranoia (Pilisuk & Parks, 1986). A prisoner at a federal penitentiary, who was held in solitary confinement for several years, said he "beat the system" by turning off his emotions before they could get to him. Now he feels nothing (personal communication to PGZ, June, 1975).

Herein lies the paradox. Detaching ourselves from social life to avoid "being taken" is obviously absurd; yet the more open we are to other people's thoughts, the more likely we are to be swayed by them. At the same time, open, passionate involvement is essential to some of the richest forms of human experience. We want to feel strongly, trust completely, act on impulse, and feel connected to others in the community. We want to be "saturated" with living and feel we can suspend, at least for periods of time, our evaluative faculties, our innate cautiousness. Yet we must be able to pull back and monitor our experiences, reflect upon the choices we've made, and assess the "goodness" of our involvements. Oscillating between these poles, immersing and distancing again at appropriate intervals is the challenge.

Knowing when to be involved, when to support and be loyal to a cause or a relationship rather than exiting or rebelling against it is a delicate question each of us faces in a world where some people would use us to further their own needs for control, while others genuinely want us to share what they believe are mutually positive goals (Brehm, 1992). Although deception is often difficult to detect, interactions or social situations that are likely to proceed unerringly toward one predictable end — passivity and acquiescence — can usually be identified in time to regain some modicum of control. By recognizing the social pressures that exist in a particular situation, choosing to discount them becomes possible (Johnson & Raye, 1981).

STRATEGIES FOR RESISTANCE

Our concern has been to demystify mind control by confronting the processes by which it is enhanced and those by which it is disabled. The following strategies for resisting unwanted control have been derived from a diverse body of information gained through our research and experience.

Perceiving Discontinuities

Many notable politicians gave their support to pastor Jim Jones without questioning why he was surrounded by a half-dozen guards, why his church had locked doors, and why newcomers were searched before being approved by the Welcoming Committee. Members of the People's Temple admired "Dad" because he cared for them and because he said he cared most of all about the children. Meanwhile they failed to critically appraise or even to acknowledge the reality that he punished them severely (at times with electric shock) and subjected them to public ridicule for minor transgressions (Kilduff & Javers, 1978; Reiterman, 1982; Reston, 1981).

Often the biggest lies are hidden by a compelling context. Later these lies are "discovered" on the basis of discontinuities that are obvious in hindsight. The slave-labor camp created in Guyana by Jim Jones revealed an unanticipated nightmare that thrived on his systematic distortion of every detail of the reality of Jonestown: There was mild weather, he said, an abundance of food, no mosquitoes, easy work days, no sickness, no death. The discontinuities were there to be perceived: "The moment I got off that plane I knew somethin' was wrong," said Richard Clark, who led an escape party out of Jonestown through the jungle the morning of the massacre (Clark & Louie, 1979). Jonestown was in fact the opposite of what had been promised: a jungle hell where people worked long hours on menial jobs in sweltering heat, often hungry and sick. But denial en masse of these obvious discrepancies kept Jones's system of total mind control going until the very end. According to Margaret Singer's (1979) extensive studies of former cult members, those who left cults on their own—that is, without the aid of deprogrammers—did so because they had "grown bitter about discrepancies between cult words and practices" (see also Adler, 1978).

To participate successfully in the social world while retaining a critical eye takes some practice (Chaffee, 1991). By sensitizing ourselves to the power dynamics in our social surroundings, we are in a better position to recognize potent influence tactics when they arise and to postpone making decisions in relation to them. Knowing when and what to resist requires being vigilant to *discontinuities* between the ideals people espouse and their concrete actions. Separating the preacher from the practice, the promise from the outcome, the perceived intention from the consequence is at the crux of resistance— precisely because it is so easy to mistake labels for the things being described, to deal in symbols and concepts instead of people and their behavior (Lutz, 1983; Schrag, 1978).

To assert the freedom to choose options that are not apparent in a situation we must be simultaneously committed to our social worlds and sufficiently disengaged from them to maintain a critical analysis (Janis, 1982). While a low-level analysis murmuring in the background need not lead to a preoccupying, full-time compulsion, experimenting with various ways of allocating attention to social interactions is part of acquiring the kind of sensitive skepticism and critical eye that enables undesirable influences to be detected when they arise.

Normal Appearances

Most persuaders recognize the importance of standard operating procedures—form and style—which serve to undercut our ability to apprehend "unexpected" events or influences. According to sociologist Erving Goffman (1971), these persuaders conceal their intent amid "normal appearances." They know we are more likely to be caught off guard when we find ourselves in situations that appear normal (Zimbardo & Hartley, 1985).

Information from rape prevention centers reflects the precision with which we allow social etiquette to control our behavior. Entering dangerous situations with potential rapists can seem like part of a standard routine, tantamount to being polite, friendly, or helpful for women who have been trained to be ladylike. Feeling compelled to answer all questions put to them with a friendly, gracious smile, to defer habitually, when in doubt, to the protection and judgment of men, and to be courteous and open with service personnel at the expense of requesting proper identification are frequent responses reported after-the-fact by rape victims. Customarily, simple situational rules were treated with too much sanctity (see Basow, 1986).

When reliable information is subtly hidden or methodically withheld, we are led to believe that we are "freely" choosing to act, when we are not really. At those times we are especially susceptible to making commitments, generating our own justifications, and feeling convinced of them. This is true of deception on all levels of social interaction. When government officials refused to warn the public about the risks of radioactive fallout during the atomic-bomb tests in Nevada in the 1950s, perhaps merely disguising their ignorance in order to prevent alarm, most residents stayed in the area—for a very long time (Ball, 1986). Only recently have imputations been voiced; but the damage is already done. Similarly, when a Kerr-McGee plutonium plant in Oklahoma misled its employees about the hazards of its operation, even amid flagrant safety violations, several years passed before workers began to complain (Rashke, 1981).

Because effective manipulators provide as coherent a scenario as possible in which to gain our compliance, detecting discrepant or ulterior motives is difficult. But unfailing adherence to simple, unquestioned protocol can have dangerous consequences whenever people continue to accept information at face value (Marks, 1979; Weinstein, 1990). Uncovering oppression or deception for what it is requires learning to question the rules others lay down in a situation and it requires being alert to the role-based constraints of one's own actions. Testing for the presence of stated and unstated rules that unnecessarily restrict freedom of speech, action, and association can be done by subtly violating some of the rules and then observing the consequences. How much latitude is allowed for idiosyncracy, for creative or eccentric self-expression? Breaking rules unobtrusively is not only an exercise in social know-how and grace, but also it facilitates one's ability to step back periodically in an effort to monitor ongoing communications and to examine situations from other perspectives.

Assumed Similarity

Effective persuaders not only influence people but also win friends in the bargain. After intensive interrogation for the murder of two socialites, George Whitmore, Jr., "broke" and gave a 61-page confession of guilt. He went on to express his admiration for his interrogator, a detective Whitmore now claimed to respect more than his own father. Subsequent events established that Whitmore was persuaded to confess to a capital crime he did not commit (Zimbardo, 1967; see also Ofshe, 1990; and Inbau, Reid, & Buckley, 1986).

When someone appears to share our concerns, that person becomes a colleague, an ally, someone we can trust and give the benefit of the doubt. Now, the conversation is led slowly into areas where our disagreement would otherwise be obvious, while the persuader's credibility leads us gently over each successive hurdle as we change our attitudes through small, continuous modifications. In the end, we perceive that we have brought about change on our own (Zimbardo & Leippe, 1991).

Because attitude change, like all socialization, is most effective when it goes unnoticed, it is crucial to check for signs of ingratiation, an overemphasis on mutual interest, and requests for just one small commitment now. How deep do the stated similarities go? How well does the persuader really know the common ground you supposedly share?

Apparent Competence

Regardless of someone's "real" credibility, what we end up responding to is how competent, confident, and stable he or she appears. Powerful people express confidence and self-assuredness across all channels of communication – through body language, through words, and paralinguistically. Someone who looks us straight in the eye, stands very close, and speaks forcefully is not intimidated but intimidating; that person is perfectly in control of the encounter.

In reaction, those who get persuaded express doubt, as much by what they say as by what they don't say. Minor hesitations like "uh," "ah," "er," or even a pause can be capitalized on and manipulated because they convey momentary lapses of thought, momentary vulnerabilities. Training manuals for sales personnel in bargaining situations are filled with tactics for skillfully manipulating the choices people make by first "reading" their body language (see Professional Salesman's Desk Manual, 1976).

Learning to see through programmed responses to authority is the first step in transcending the social and psychological processes that ensure transient feelings of intimidation in persuasive situations. Here it is important to be assertive. Refusing to accept the initial premise from someone that he or she is more powerful, more competent, more in control than we are can be accomplished by creating an appearance of confidence and calm equal to the sense of control conveyed by the other person through voice and actions.

Carry with you a powerful, concrete image, replete with tactile sensations, sights, and sounds; it can remind you of your own competence. Remember a time when some person or group of people thought you were the best thing to hit the planet. Remember a photograph, person, or place. Think of whatever makes you feel exhilarated and alive. By not revealing that special image to others, you will retain it as an inner core that cannot be violated. Focus attention on what you are doing rather than on thoughts about yourself; stymie your interlocutor from taking hold with a barrage of negative internal dialogues. As the interaction unfolds, the need for the image fades. If you can get your questions asked, your bargaining done, your experiences had, you will have more control over your actions and over the choice others try to make on your behalf.

Cognitive Confusion

In coming to accept a new reality, the errors of our old ways of looking at the world are exposed and a new reality is embedded in their place. This transformation is often aided by false analogies, elaborate explanations, semantic distortion, and convenient rhetorical labels. We are often dissuaded from probing beyond surface illusions of meaningfulness by letting symbols substitute for reality, abstract maps for concrete territories. John Dean (1978) reminds us that the entire Watergate cover-up was shrouded in cute euphemisms, jargon, and rhetoric. Instead of referring explicitly to the money involved in the scandal, they spoke only of the "bites of the apple." At the extreme, it is easier to talk in jargon, referring to "wasting an enemy" or engaging in "revolutionary protest" than to come right out and say you are going to murder other human beings (Lutz, 1983).

Recognizing vague generalities and inadequate explanations for what they are means learning to distinguish messages that are actually confused or ambiguous — perhaps intentionally so — from those that are confusing due to one's own inability to reason effectively. If someone suggests that "you're too stupid to understand" or that "women get too emotional to think logically," calmly interrogate yourself about the meaning of what has been said and paraphrase it for yourself to see if the conclusions espoused follow from the arguments.

Emotional Confusion

A "60 Minutes" documentary (Wallace, 1979) reported that sellers of industrial insurance have their working-class clients nearly paralyzed with fear over spiraling medical and burial costs. Relief is at hand, however, as the salesperson unfolds insurance policies that will resolve any uncertainties the future may hold. If the client owns other policies, they go unmentioned or are dismissed as inadequate. All that is clear is the imminence of death and an eight-inch replica of a satin-lined mahogany coffin in the hands of a credible-looking businessman who adds in a deep clear voice, "Wouldn't you prefer your loved one to rest in a beautiful casket like this than to be buried in an old pine box?"

The most potent persuasive appeals get their wallop by reaching beyond reason to emotions, beyond awareness to unspoken desires and fears, beyond trivial attitudes to basic concerns about self-integrity and survival. Clever persuaders are adept at detecting what we want from a situation, what our fears and anxieties are, and what areas of supposed mutual interest will best gain our attention. Once someone has our trust, that person can change our attitudes by inducing emotion-laden conflict requiring immediate resolution. By making us feel fearful, guilty, or awkward, the manipulator is in a position to ease our discomfort by providing reasonable explanations and soothing solutions. Much advertising is based on this principle; so are many social interactions (Franks, 1961; Hinkle & Wolff, 1956; Riles & Trout, 1986).

Professional beggars, for example, make it their business to make passersby feel guilty for being well dressed and well fed. Often organizations that support themselves through door-to-door canvassing thrive on the proceeds collected by mildly handicapped solicitors. More broadly, the pivotal contingency in Patty Hearst's psychological transformation at the hands of the Symbionese Liberation Army was the guilt she was led to feel over her family's privileged position – the disparity between her family's wealth and the poverty of so many – and her life of noninvolvement in the struggle of oppressed peoples. Uneasiness was relieved slowly with each step she took in the direction of accepting her captors' definition of reality (Szasz, 1976).

Indebtedness and guilt can arise also from allowing someone to make sacrifices on your behalf. Diane Louie, who escaped Jonestown with Richard Clark the morning of the massacre, recounted for us her experience in the hospital there (Clark & Louie, 1979). She was suffering from a severe intestinal virus, feeling duped and dissatisfied, when Jim Jones came to her bedside. "How are your living conditions?" he asked. She shifted uncomfortably in her cot trying not to raise her eyes to him. "Is there any special food you would like?" She thought of her stifling crowded bungalow, the maggots in her rice, her exhaustion, the broken promises. "No," she replied, "Everything is fine; I'm quite comfortable." To us she said, "I knew once he gave me those privileges, he'd have me. I didn't want to owe him nothin'." She was one of a handful able to escape the mass murder and suicide.

The crucial issue here is if, when, and how to reveal our needs and vulnerabilities. No matter what the relationship, unwanted confessions may later become substantive manipulative tools. Many cults and mind-control systems utilize public confessions, self-exposure "games" (used by Synanon, see Anson, 1978), and similar techniques to catalogue the weaknesses of their followers for possible later exploitation. To the degree that we are personally aware of the guilt and anxiety reactions we typically experience, we are in a better position to circumvent their illicit use by skillful manipulators. Learning to confront frustrations and fears is the most effective way to prevent their being exploited unknowingly.

Plays on "Choice"

When the opposition is about to yield, successful persuaders employ tactics of ingratiation to build bonds of fondness and respect that will extend past the initial sale. Once aware that their prey is bagged, the slickest operators then emphasize the victim's freedom of choice – after tactfully putting constraints on the alternatives. "Of course, the choice is yours," they remind us once we're considering *what* to buy rather than *whether* to buy. Properly executed persuasion never appears to be designed to induce change but rather ends in a natural resolution of "mutually generated" concerns – perhaps ones you didn't even know you had. New attitudes and behaviors that are accompanied by the feeling that they have been chosen without extrinsic pressures or justifications are enduring and resistant to change.

Skillful persuaders may deny apparent freedom in order to control behavior with the help of the *reactance principle*. The work of psychologists Jack and Sharon Brehm (Brehm & Brehm, 1981) suggests that when we perceive severe limitations on our behavioral freedom, we sometimes move to reassert it by advocating the opposite position – perhaps just what the opposition wanted. "So, you're gonna let that guy – or nation – get away with treating you in that shameful way!" "No salesman could possibly sell more of this product in such hard times!" "Excuse me for saying so, sir, but this is quite an exclusive line; you may not be able to afford it."

Reacting against someone's dogmatic assertions about who you are or what you should do is not the sole avenue to freedom of action. Sometimes it is best to test someone else's intentions by giving the impression that you may comply with the stated demands, if only to observe the reaction. If suddenly he or she starts pushing in the opposite direction or simply looks befuddled, you may have uncovered a hidden agenda.

Also it is wise to recognize an overemphasis on how free you are to choose among the options someone else has prescribed. Test the limits of those options by selecting "none of the above" or by tentatively proposing unexpected alternatives that you believe to be better. Electing Anacin over Bayer is not the same as deciding whether you want any aspirin. Nor is the question, "How many bombs should we drop? Two? Three? Ten?" the same as, "Should we drop any bombs?"

"Groupthink"

Large-scale systems of social persuasion depend on controls that impart a sense of belonging to a broad movement. Persuaders bring us to their place of power and separate the "we" who are righteous and good from the "they" who are ignorant and evil. By limiting our access to ideas that they find heretical or traitorous, they phase out other versions of reality.

This process can occur in two-person relationships just as it can in impersonal social institutions or large organizations (Janis, 1982; Milburn, 1991). When tightly knit groups are insulated from outside sources of information and expertise and the leader endorses prospective policies before members have a chance to air their views, decision-making processes deteriorate. People become more preoccupied with seeking and maintaining unanimity of thought than with carefully weighing the pros and cons of alternative actions, raising moral issues, and critically appraising decisions. Often, unanimous resolutions are reached prematurely and members are led to support them for better or for worse, even though in reality there is only an "impression" that *we* are part of the decision-making process that binds us to its product.

It is impossible to make unbiased decisions when we are isolated from outside information. Police interrogators question suspects at their station not at the suspects' homes (Inbau et al., 1986; Zimbardo, 1967). Synanon rehabilitates alcoholics and drug addicts – and keeps its other members in line – by removing them from their usual haunts and restricting their liberty (Anson, 1978). Jim Jones carried the isolation principle to the extreme when he led his People's Temple members into the jungle of a strange land (Reiterman, 1982). When we come to believe so thoroughly in our favorite concepts that we begin to hate those who don't share our views, to develop rehearsed programmatic responses to discrediting arguments, and to acknowledge only ideas stated within our terminology, it may be time to start making our belief systems a little more permeable. While we/they dichotomies cut us off from others and suggest we think of them in terms of dehumanizing labels, such as animals, sinners, queers, rednecks, women's libbers, the teaming masses, and so forth, nothing is so simple as the labels "good" and "evil" suggest. They foster utter vulnerability to whatever system is the "good" one – naturally the one that wants our support.

To establish whether you can actually have an impact on decision-making processes in a relationship or group, or whether you are simply part of the clean-up crew for decisions that have already been made, monitor premature closure and initial consensus in ongoing discussions. What arbitrary constraints are placed on the consideration of alternatives? Do rigid procedural devices limit discussion and suppress unusual suggestions? Any worthwhile association should tolerate dissent, or it should be abandoned. Continued commitment in the face of contrary evidence is usually not an expression of loyalty but a sign of rigidity, delusion, or prejudice.

The bottom line for preventing utter usurpation by any system is maintaining outside interests and sources of social support. Battered wives, some religious converts, undercover agents, mafia informants, inmates of prisons and mental hospitals all suffer from impoverished connections to outside systems. Severing all outside ties for the sake of any social contract increases one's powerlessness within it.

Friends and relatives can be of help to those who have strayed by leaving open the path back home and making explicit an unconditional accessibility. Disowning loved ones after disapproving of their decisions is much less effective in the long run than a gentle hand and some warm words. "Love-bombing" is the favorite tactic of most cults because it works best with the love-deprived (Barker, 1984; Hassan, 1988).

Impersonal Structures

The tighter a system is, the more likely minor challenges will be met with retaliation. In prisons, mental hospitals, religious or political cults, military establishments, and concentration camps, the "authorities" have virtually total control over the existence of others, and minor deviations or threats to that power are intolerable (Lifton, 1961; Zimbardo, 1975).

When maintaining the status quo within a system becomes unbearable, the question remains whether or not rebellion and subsequent change are feasible. Some systems have time on their sides: They can wait out the opposition and have their officers paid for doing so. Supporters are employed while those who oppose do so as outsiders and struggle to make ends meet. This notwithstanding, often it is more practical to challenge systems from without – if getting out is possible. First, however, it must be determined what change is possible within the system, and, alternatively, what avenues of escape are available.

In any potentially destructive system, it is best not to let perfect silence pass for agreement. When talking to others, you can subtly imply discontent in areas of mutual concern, making sure to stop short of incriminating yourself in the face of their utter resolve. Learn to intuit their responses as the interaction unfolds; overstep only those rules that are of least concern to the system.

Once comfortable with a group of allies, band together so that there is a *group position* that will get acknowledged rather than individual *dispositions* that tend to get "dealt with." This will create the possibility of a consistent minority, firm in its conviction to undo a majority. The contributions you make to the system, which are significant to its functioning, are the resources that can be withheld, providing an impetus to the power holders to reassess the stability of the power balance. By assessing the power base of those who hold the reins, it becomes possible to seek substitutes for the resources *they* now threaten to withhold. Do you really need the attention, respect, security, approval, money, or whatever it is that these particular people have to offer?

Organized labor and civil rights coalitions of blacks, women, and other minorities have become adept at operationalizing these strategies. Collective resistance by a group that states its problems concisely and specifies clear and concrete goals, resources, and strategies is infinitely more likely to succeed than are disorganized spit-and-run tactics.

ESCAPING A
MIND-CONTROL SYSTEM

Escape plans, if they are made, must be carefully thought through in concrete terms, not wished about vaguely; once out of the system, the veil of secrecy that conceals its mind-control practices will be lifted only through public exposes. Jeannie Mills (1979), defector from the People's Temple and cofounder of the Human Freedom Center in Berkeley, California, was unable to get people to believe her horrendous tales of Jim Jones's brutality and deceit until she convinced several reporters to check out the discontinuities between his preaching and his practice. It takes a firm sense of social commitment to escape a system of mind control, and then to persist in challenging it from without so others can hear the message.

When trapped in a system without opportunity to exit, often people still show the stuff of humanity by striving to maintain some kind of human empathy and hope amid conditions that by definition demand psychological distance and detachment. Bettelheim's (1979) studies of mental and spiritual survival in the Nazi death camps point to this tenuous balance between cool, rational observation and human compassion, to being at once detached and yet capable of saturation.

It is because we can exercise our cognitive ability to evaluate critically ideas, institutions, and our own behavior that we can perceive options beyond those provided by convenient dogma and ostensibly inescapable circumstances (Chaffee, 1991; Langer, 1989). As thinking beings, we can resist the lure of engaging in the "cardiac comprehension" proposed by cultic leaders, of listening and evaluating with one's heart, not one's mind (Adler, 1978; Barker, 1984; Bowers, 1984; Johnson & Raye, 1981). It is only by understanding our own vulnerabilities and the persistent tendency to believe that our inner traits are more powerful than situational forces that we can come to see that there are indeed potent situational forces working on us. But with this awareness of the operation of the fundamental attribution error (overestimating dispositional power while underestimating situational power) we can avoid unwanted forms of social control by exercising our freedom to choose what we will do and become (Ross & Nisbett, 1991; Zimbardo, 1978). It is not by self-deception but self-awareness and reality monitoring that we can begin to level the playing field in the struggle against would-be mind manipulators (Johnson & Raye, 1981; Lattin, 1992; Nisbett & Wilson, 1977; Sarbin, 1981).

Nevertheless, we must be aware that the world is full of people who are engaged in full-time careers of persuading us to say "Yes" to their requests, suggestions, advertisements, and commands (Cialdini, 1993; Galanter, 1989; Riles & Trout, 1986). They make a living by changing their ineffective marketing tactics to fit changing circumstances and new, more vulnerable audiences. We can witness this phenomena in America with the expensive, extensive promotion of cigarette smoking to youth, women, and minorities, and overseas to peoples in developing nations (American Cancer Society, 1981; Blum, 1989). Less deadly, but no less sophisticated are attempts to recruit adolescents into cults (Zimbardo & Hartley, 1985), to manipulate the reality of children's desires for hundreds of products through televised commercials (Roberts, 1982), or to shape the political reality of adults (Lutz, 1983; Milburn, 1991; Zimbardo, 1984).

Although we cannot provide remedial advice for guarding against all of the many guises that mind-control systems may assume, we hope that the general knowledge provided here at least creates an intellectual context for appreciating the host of paths such influence takes. Knowledge is the most important ingredient in the solution of lessening one's vulnerability to mind control, but while necessary, it is not sufficient. It must be put into practice, tested, tried out, role-played, and the emotional-motivational component personally experienced before you can rely on your knowledge and good intentions being translated into effective counteractions.

Below is a set of guidelines for resisting mind control, culled from

literature on persuasion, compliance, and attitude change, supplemented by our personal and professional experience (Chaiken, 1987;
Cialdini, 1993; Flacks, 1973; Hart, Friedrich, & Brooks, 1975; Hassan,
1988; Kadish & Kadish, 1973; Milgram, 1992; Vohs & Garrett, 1968;
Zimbardo & Leippe, 1991). Think about them, learn them, practice
them, teach them to others, improve on them, fit them into your situation — or ignore them; it's your choice.

Checklist of 20 Ways to Resist Unwanted Social Influence

1. Practice being a deviant at times; violate your usual role/self-image; learn to accept rejection; play with viewing yourself differently.
2. Practice saying: "I made a mistake." "I'm sorry." "I was wrong." " . . . and I have learned from that error."
3. Be aware of the general perspective that others use to *frame* the problem, situation, or issue at hand, because accepting their frame on their terms gives them a powerful advantage. Be willing to step back and reject the entire framework, and propose your alternative before debating the specifics.
4. Be willing to suffer short-term losses in money, self-esteem, time, and effort, rather than suffer from dissonance about a wrong commitment which keeps you locked in. Accept "sunk costs," cut bait, and move on with the vital knowledge of having learned from your mistake, or wrong decision, not to repeat it.
5. Be willing to step back from any interpersonal situation and say to yourself and to that significant (overcontrolling) other: "I can survive without your love, friendship, liking, abuse, even though it may hurt now to give it up — unless you stop doing X and start doing Y."
6. Always avoid taking uncertain actions that the change-agent insists must be made immediately; move out of the situation, take time to think, get unbiased second opinions, never rush to sign on the dotted line.
7. Insist on an understandable explanation, without double speak; paraphrase your view of it. Don't let change-agents make *you* feel stupid; poor explanations are signs of deceptions or lack of adequate knowledge by the allegedly informed.
8. Be sensitive to situational demands however trivial they may seem: role relationships, uniforms, symbols of authority, signs, titles, group pressures, rules, apparent consensus, scarcity slogans, obligations, and commitments.

9. Be especially tuned into the establishment of host-guest relationships in which you are made to feel and act as the guest, thereby compromising your freedom of choice and action.

10. Don't believe in simple solutions to complex personal, social, and political problems.

11. Remember there is no such thing as instant, unconditional love from strangers; Love, friendship, and trust must be developed over time and usually involve reciprocity, negotiation, and sharing—some work and commitment on your part.

12. When caught up in an impersonal influence setting, individuate yourself and the agent of influence to establish mutual humanity, identity, shared concerns; break through role constraints by using eye contact, personal names, flattery; manage personal identities, yours and theirs.

13. Avoid "total situations" that are unfamiliar and in which you have little control and freedom; immediately test the limits of your autonomy; check out psychological and physical exits: Accept small hassles as reasonable exit costs from what could be a bigger loss if carried to conclusion.

14. Practice "detached concern," engage your mind in critical evaluation, disengage your emotions in confrontations with those who are Machiavellian power manipulators.

15. Greed and ego-inflating flattery will get mind-control manipulators and con agents far, but only if you allow yourself to be seduced by these spurious motives; resist their lure by taking the perspective of the most honest, self-assured person you know.

16. Recognize your symptoms of guilt and the guilt inductions others use on you; never act from guilty motives. Tolerate guilt as part of your human nature, don't rush to ameliorate it via paths others lay out for you.

17. Be mindful of what you are doing in a given situation, not allowing habit and standard operating procedure to make you react mindlessly in what is a subtly different situation.

18. It is not necessary to maintain consistency between your actions at different times; you can change and not be held to the false standard of being "reliable" and maintaining the status quo.

19. Legitimate authority deserves respect and sometimes our obedience, but illegitimate authority must always be rejected, disobeyed, and exposed.

20. It is not enough to dissent vocally, or to be emotionally distressed at the operation of injustice, or a change in the rules of

the game, as you understood them—you must be willing to openly disobey, to defy, to challenge, and to suffer any consequences of doing so.

REFERENCES

Adler, W. (1978, June 6). Rescuing David from the Moonies. *Esquire*, pp. 22–30.

American Cancer Society. (1981). *Smoking and genocide.* New York: Author.

Anson, R. S. (1978, November 27). The Synanon horrors. *New Times*, p. 28ff.

Asch, S. E. (1951). Effects of group pressure upon the modification and distortion of judgments. In H. Guetzkow (Ed.), *Groups, leadership, and men.* Pittsburgh, PA: Carnegie Press.

Ball, H. (1986). *Justice downwind: America's atomic testing program in the 1950s.* New York: Oxford University Press.

Barker, E. (1984). *The making of a Moonie: Choice or brainwashing.* Oxford, England: Basil Blackwell.

Basow, S. A. (1986). *Gender stereotypes: Traditions and alternatives* (2nd ed.). Belmont, CA: Brooks/Cole.

Bettelheim, B. (1979). *Surviving, and other essays.* New York: Knopf.

Blum, A. (1989). The targeting of minority groups by the tobacco industry. In L. A. Jones (Ed.), *Minorities and cancer* (pp. 153–162). New York: Springer-Verlag.

Bowers, K. S. (1984). On being unconsciously influenced and informed. In K. S. Bowers & D. Meichenbaum (Eds.), *The unconscious reconsidered.* New York: Wiley.

Brehm, J. W., & Brehm, S. A. (1981). *Psychological reactance: A theory of freedom and control.* New York: Academic Press.

Brehm, S. A. (1992). *Intimate relationships* (2nd ed.). New York: McGraw-Hill.

Butterworth, J. (1981). *Beliefs: Cults and new faiths.* Elgin, IL: David Cook.

Caplan, G.A. (1969, November). A psychiatrist's casebook. *McCall's*, p. 65.

Chaffee, J. (1991). *Thinking critically.* Boston: Houghton Mifflin.

Chaiken, S. (1987). The heuristic model of persuasion. In M. P. Zanna, J. M. Olson, & C. P. Herman (Eds.), *Social influence: The Ontario symposium* (vol. 5, pp. 3–39). Hillsdale, NJ: Erlbaum.

Cialdini, R. B. (1993). *Influence: Science and practice* (3rd ed.). New York: HarperCollins.

Clark, R., & Louie, D. (1979, March 9). Quoted in "Jonestown survivors tell their story," by D. Sullivan & P. G. Zimbardo. *Los Angeles Times*, Part 4, pp. 1, 10–12.

Conway, F., & Siegelman, J. (1978). *Snapping: America's epidemic of sudden personality change.* Philadelphia: Lippincott.

Dean, J. (1978, January). Quoted in "Comparing notes on obedience to authority: Dean and Milgram. *APA Monitor,* p. 5.

Deikman, A. (1990). *The wrong way home: Cults in everyday life.* Boston: Beacon Press.

Enroth, R. (1977). *Youth, brainwashing, and the extremist cults.* Exeter, England: Potemaster Press.

Flacks, R. (1973). *Conformity, resistance, and self-determination: The individual and authority*. Boston: Little, Brown.

Franks, J. D. (1961). *Persuasion and healing*. Baltimore, MD: Johns Hopkins University Press.

Galanter, H. (1989). *Cults: Faith, healing, and coercion*. New York: Oxford University Press.

Goffman, E. (1971). *Relations in public: Microstudies of the public order*. New York: Harper & Row.

Haney, C., & Zimbardo, P. G. (1973). Social roles, role-playing and education: On the high school as prison. *The Behavioral Science Teacher, 1,* 24–45.

Haney, C., & Zimbardo, P. G. (1977). The socialization into criminality: On becoming a prisoner and a guard. In J. L. Tapp & F. J. Levine (Eds.), *Law, justice and the individual in society: Psychological and legal issues* (pp. 198–223). New York: Holt, Rinehart & Winston.

Hart, R., Friedrich, G., & Brooks, W. (1975). *Overcoming resistance to persuasion*. New York: Harper & Row.

Hassan, S. (1988). *Combatting cult mind control*. Rochester, VT: Park Street Press.

Hinkle, L. E., & Wolff, H. G. (1956). Communist interrogation and indoctrination of "enemies of the state." *American Medical Association Archives of Neurology and Psychiatry, 76,* 115–174.

Hochman, J. (1990, April). Miracle, mystery, and authority: The triangle of cult indoctrination. *Psychiatric Annals,* 179–197.

Inbau, F., Reid, J. E., & Buckley. (1986). *Criminal interrogation and confessions*. Baltimore, MD: Williams & Wilkins.

Janis, I. (1982). *Groupthink*. Boston: Houghton Mifflin.

Johnson, M., & Raye, C. L. (1981). Reality monitoring. *Psychological Review, 88,* 67–85.

Kadish, M. R., & Kadish, S. H. (1973). *Discretion to disobey: A study of lawful departures from legal rules*. Stanford, CA: Stanford University Press.

Kilduff, M., & Javers, R. (1978). *The suicide cult*. New York: Bantam Books.

Langer, E. (1989). *Mindfulness*. Reading, MA: Addison-Wesley.

Lattin, D. (1992, May 15). Robertson gives mixed signals about religion's role at UPI. *San Francisco Chronicle,* p. A9.

Lifton, R. J. (1961). *Thought reform and the psychology of totalism*. New York: W. W. Norton.

Lutz, W. (1983). *Double-speak: From "revenue enhancement" to "terminal living."* New York: Harper & Row.

Marks, J. (1979). *The search for the "Manchurian Candidate": The CIA and mind control*. New York: Times Books.

Milburn, M. A. (1991). *Persuasion and politics: The social psychology of public opinion*. Pacific Grove, CA: Brooks/Cole.

Milgram, S. (1992). *The individual in a social world: Essays and experiments* (2nd ed.) (Edited by J. Sabini & M. Silver). New York: McGraw-Hill.

Mills, J. (1979). *Six years with God: Life inside Reverend Jones' Peoples Temple*. New York: A & W Publishers.

Nisbett, R. E., & Wilson, T. D. (1977). Telling more than we know: Verbal reports on mental processes. *Psychological Review, 84,* 231–259.

Ofshe, R. (1990). Coerced confessions: The logic of seemingly irrational acts. *Cultic Studies Journal, 3*(3), 37–41.

Patrick, T. (1979, March). Interview with a deprogrammer. *Playboy*, p. 53ff.

Pilisuk, M., & Parks, S. H. (1986). *The healing web: Social networks and human survival.* Hanover, NH: University Press of New England.

Professional salesman's desk manual. (1976). Waterford, CT: National Sales Development Institute, Division of BBP.

Rashke, R. (1981). *The killing of Karen Silkwood: The story behind the Kerr-McGee plutonium case.* Boston: Houghton Mifflin.

Reiterman, T. (1982). *Raven: The untold story of the Rev. Jim Jones and his people.* New York: Dutton.

Renberger, B. (1978, April 2). Rate for operations fell slightly in 1976. *New York Times.*

Reston, J., Jr. (1981) *Our father who are in hell: The life and death of Jim Jones.* New York: Times Books.

Riles, A., & Trout, J. (1986). *Positioning: The battle for your mind.* New York: Warner Books.

Roberts, D. F. (1982). Children and commercials: Issues, evidence, interventions. *Prevention in Human Services, 2,* 19–36.

Ross, L., & Nisbett, R. E. (1991). *The person and the situation: Perspectives of social psychology.* New York: McGraw-Hill.

Sarbin, T. R. (1981). On self-deception. *Annals of the New York Academy of Sciences, 364,* 220–235.

Schein, E. H., Schneier, I., & Barker, C. H. (1961). *Coercive persuasion.* New York: W. W. Norton.

Schrag, P. (1978). *Mind control.* New York: Pantheon Books.

Schwitzgebel, R. L., & Schwitzgebel, R. K. (Eds.). (1973). *Psychotechnology: Electronic control of mind and behavior.* New York: Holt.

Singer, M.T. (1979, January). Coming out of the cults. *Psychology Today*, pp. 72–82.

Szasz, T. (1976). Patty Hearst's conversion: Some call it brainwashing. *The New Republic, 174,* pp. 10–12.

Varela, J. (1971). *Psychological solutions to social problems: An introduction to social technology.* New York: Academic Press.

Vohs, J. L., & Garrett, R. L. (1968). Resistance to persuasion: An integrative framework. *Public Opinion Quarterly, 32,* 445–452.

Wallace, M. (1979, January 28). Soak the poor. *60 Minutes.*

Weinstein, H. (1990). *Psychiatry and the CIA: Victims of mind control.* Washington, DC: American Psychiatric Press.

Zimbardo, P. G. (1967, June). The psychology of police confessions. *Psychology Today, 1,* pp. 17–27.

Zimbardo, P. G. (1972). The tactics and ethics of persuasion. In E. McGinnies & B. King (Eds.), *Attitudes, conflict, and social change* (pp. 81–99). New York: Academic Press.

Zimbardo, P. G. (1975). On transforming experimental research into advocacy for social change. In M. Deutsch & R. Hornstein (Eds.), *Applying social psychology: Implications for research, practice, and training* (pp. 33–66). Hillsdale, NJ: Erlbaum.

Zimbardo, P. G. (1978). Psychology of evil: On the perversion of human potential. In L. Frames, P. Pliner, & T. Alloway (Eds.), *Advances in the study of communication and affect, Vol. 4, Aggression, dominance, and individual spacing* (pp. 115–169). New York: Plenum.

Zimbardo, P. G. (1984). Mind control: Political fiction and psychological reality. In P. Stansky (Ed.), *On nineteen eighty-four* (pp. 197–215). New York: Freeman Press.

Zimbardo, P. G., & Hartley, C. F. (1985). Cults go to high school: A theoretical and empirical analysis of the initial stage in the recruitment process. *Cultic Studies Journal 2*(1), 41–47.

Zimbardo, P. G., & Leippe, M. R. (1991). *The psychology of attitude change and social influence.* New York: McGraw-Hill.

Section II

LEAVING CULTS

5

A PERSONAL ACCOUNT:
EASTERN MEDITATION GROUP

Patrick L. Ryan

IN THIS CHAPTER I EXAMINE PERTINENT AREAS that relate to my involvement in and subsequent departure from the Transcendental Meditation (TM) movement. My involvement, departure, and recovery span approximately 18 years of my life. In the space of this chapter I can only touch on key aspects: my background, the group recruitment process (attraction), the nature of the group, my process of leaving, and recovery.

BACKGROUND

I was born in St. Petersburg, Florida, the youngest of five children in a middle-class Irish-Catholic family.

The year was 1975. Maharishi Mahesh Yogi was on the cover of *Time* magazine. He had appeared on "The Merv Griffin Show." The book *Transcendental Meditation*, by Harold Bloomfield, M.D., was on *The New York Times* Best Sellers list. Courses on Transcendental Meditation (TM) were offered as part of the New Jersey and California public school systems. TM was a household word.

During my senior year in high school, recruiters from Maharishi International University (MIU) came to my public school. We learned that MIU is an accredited university in Fairfield, Iowa. Presentations were made to students on the benefits of this "scientifically validated

129

program," the basis for the innovative educational system offered at their university.

RECRUITMENT

First, I attended an introductory lecture where well-dressed TM teachers ("initiators") presented TM as the "IBM of the human-potential movement." Scientific-sounding research, testimonials, and homey analogies supported the points of their presentation. They spoke of personal growth, social change, environmental progress, and world peace. The recruiters ardently represented the TM technique as not a religion, life-style, or philosophy.

I was shown the TM "vision of possibilities." My future was laid out. There were to be follow-up programs: advanced lectures, weekly and monthly meditation check-ups, residence courses, the Science of Creative Intelligence course (SCI), MIU education, and an introduction to the worldwide scope of the "movement." All of this led me to MIU.

I bought the bait and went to learn TM. I was seventeen. I received my mantra, attended the suggested follow-up lectures, weekly meditation checks, advanced lectures, and the 10-day check. At each step I was assured by the serenely smiling faces of my TM teachers that I too would experience enlightenment.

Next came the residence course, where twice-daily meditation is replaced by "rounding." This is the process of more frequent meditations, breathing techniques, yogic postures, and repetitive videos of Maharishi. To ensure the residence course participant remains "one-pointed" on "Maharishi's teaching," we were instructed to never be alone. We were assigned "buddies" to accompany us everywhere. We were told not to read newspapers, watch television, listen to radio, or make phone calls. They claimed this would give maximum benefit to the course.

One of the fundamental concepts presented during residence courses is stress release. As a meditator progresses, "stress" from actions in this and previous lives (karma) is released. In the TM vernacular this is called "unstressing." We were taught that the release of stress can "cloud the thinking process" and lead to "doubts" about the teachings of the TM movement. Our buddies were to remind us that any doubts we had about the weirdness of the movement were just "unstressing."

During my first rounding, I experienced states of euphoria punctuated by periods of dissociation, depersonalization, confusion, irritability, and memory difficulties. Lectures extolling the virtues of prolonged rounding for personal growth were supplemented with talks on the importance of increasing the membership in the TM movement in order to save the world.

One of the lecturers who was portrayed as having already gained enlightenment was a celebrity's sister, "Mary." Mary acted as a recruiter for MIU, extolling the virtues of MIU as a university that would deliver not only the world's finest education but also would produce an individual who used his or her full potential. I would be an enlightened man like the Maharishi.

Mary gave heartwarming speeches about her time with the Maharishi in India. She spoke of the universal qualities that he imbibed: kindness, charity, ceaseless concern for world peace, and his ability to always perform "spontaneous right action." The movement taught that the enlightened man does not have to use critical thought, he lives in tune with the "unbounded universal consciousness." He makes no mistakes, his life is error free. His desires are automatically fulfilled.

As my commitment to the movement deepened and strengthened, I began breaking away from my family's traditions. I stopped attending Mass, missed family holidays, explored vegetarianism, stopped wearing blue jeans. I refused my parents' desire that I attend college in Florida. I went to MIU.

MAHARISHI INTERNATIONAL UNIVERSITY

The goal of MIU is to have the student see how Maharishi's theories are connected to everything through the Science of Creative Intelligence (SCI), Maharishi's science of life. At MIU every discipline is taught through "the light of the SCI." Courses were titled Mathematics and SCI, Music and SCI, Accounting and SCI, Psychology and SCI, Maharishi's Absolute Theory of Government, Maharishi's Absolute Theory of Defense, Maharishi's Absolute Theory of Agriculture.

MIU is structured on a block system. Students study one class at a time. Course length ranges from one week to one month. The academic courses listed above are supplemented by monthlong rounding courses ("Forest Academies"). The buddy system was strictly enforced and now we had dress codes, a special diet, and curfews. Our behavior was carefully monitored by our instructors, most of whom were TM teachers.

As exposure to the TM movement's layers of teaching unfolded, commitment to the movement solidified. Extreme secrecy was required. We were given color-coded badges to determine our "movement status." The status titles – Citizen, Governor, Minister – indicated what level of doctrine we had been exposed to. Our loyalty to the movement was questioned weekly during private interviews.

In 1976 Maharishi introduced advanced forms of meditation called TM-Sidhis. The TM-Sidhi program promised to develop supernormal powers such as levitation (flying), omniscience, and invisibility. From Switzerland Maharishi directed that a new three-month academic course be structured to teach TM-Sidhis to the MIU students. I paid for the $1400 course with federally insured student loans.

The structure and content of the course was shrouded in secrecy. Maharishi's apparent fear of infiltration by U.S. and foreign government agencies led to increased internal security. The standard advance course requirements of buddies, increased meditations, prohibitions of television, radio, and newspapers were supplemented with required agreements to refrain from conversation with the opposite sex and the need for lifelong celibacy.

One example of the Maharishi paranoia occurred the day we learned the TM-Sidhis flying technique. We were told to report to a meeting hall in our finest attire, security badge in hand. Familiar guards met us at the door, checking our "World Government of the Age of Enlightenment" sealed picture badges. Our badges were checked again as we passed the inner door. We were then instructed to check our buddy's badge. Then our Group Leader was instructed to check the badges of each group member. The Dean of Students and school psychologist reverified our badges, and the TM-Sidhi Course Administrators checked our badges. There were eight security checks in all. Then they laid out an elaborate earphone system. Indian ceremonies, known as pujas, were offered to a picture of Maharishi's dead Master. There was another security check, and then the instruction began.

Maharishi on videotape connected to our earphones said, "You are seated on the foam?" [we were seated at desks] "So you want to learn to fly?" He whispered the phrase "relationship of body and akasha – lightness of cotton fiber" and told us to repeat it in 15-second intervals. This he said would make us fly.

We were sent to the flying hall, a room covered with foam rubber mattresses. A few in our group began to hop like rabbits. Those of us who remained grounded began to reflect on our transgressions of movement rules. I thought of the time I ate popcorn after 10:00 p.m. – that must be the reason I was not flying.

As the days progressed, the group pressure to fly increased. The flying rooms were punctuated by endless hyperventilation, nonstop screams, involuntary body jerking, laughter, out-of-body experiences, and ballistic hopping: "the first stage of flying!"

We students were given academic credit for this. We were required to assemble twice a day to practice this two-hour program of meditation, breathing, flying, and reading Hindu scriptures. The chairman of the physics department explained that Maharishi had "discovered" that groups of TM-Sidhi practitioners flying together could create world peace.

Maharishi then sent teams of flyers to "hot spots" — war-torn areas of the world like Nicaragua, Iran, El Salvador — to calm the fighting. He then pronounced "World peace has been achieved." The boldness of Maharishi, movement officials, and the lack of uncensored outside news further strengthened my commitment.

At MIU and throughout the movement, guilt was used to manipulate students into never missing a flying session. When the Iranians seized the American Embassy, a MIU student friend who had missed a flying session was called into the Dean's office and blamed for the hostage-taking in Iran.

Leaving the MIU Environment

I graduated from MIU in 1980 with a BA in Interdisciplinary Studies and moved to Philadelphia to work with other TMers. Maharishi now stressed the importance of living and working with other flyers. Communities of TMers formed "Ideal Villages." By living together and flying together the world would be changed more rapidly for the better. An "Age of Enlightenment" would be realized. World peace would be achieved. I helped form a Philadelphia Ideal Village, a small community in South Philadelphia consisting of 16 row houses.

Living in a large city away from the Orwellian environment of MIU provided fertile ground for my first doubts. The promise of enlightenment had not dawned; the world did not seem changed; people suffered, be it their karma or not. Personal success, business success, the ideal life: Where was it, I thought?

I was depressed, chronically ill, and fatigued, which I later learned was a common side effect of meditation. One day my mother called and suggested that the meditation was causing my problems. Maybe I should join the real world, she said. The "affirmations" of the movement immediately entered my mind, overshadowing any doubts. "Rest is the basis of activity, deep rest for success. TM reduces illness, reduces stress, reduces depression. TM is the basis of all success, it is the solution to all problems," I repeated the well-learned doctrine, cliché after cliché.

I had so thoroughly absorbed the Maharishi doctrine that when my mother was taken to the hospital with a heart attack, I called her and said, "Mom, you have the solution to all problems at hand (she had learned TM) and you chose not to use it, thus you chose to suffer. When you don't want to suffer anymore, you will end it." I then hung up the telephone.

THE PROCESS OF LEAVING

In the fall of 1983 my sister Michele joined another controversial group – The Way International. My family began to plan an intervention, an exit counseling. The intervention involved assembling family members to give emotional support. I was asked to help by contacting the Cult Awareness Network (CAN) to gain information on The Way.

I initially contacted two CAN representatives. They were both friendly, yet our conversations left me unsettled. They asked questions about my family, my sister, and myself. I mentioned I was a member of TM. They suggested that TM may be controversial. I reflexively responded, "TM is not a cult, it is a scientifically validated program."

My sister's intervention was carefully planned and worked smoothly. I attended the sessions to give my sister support. I sat listening to the exit counselor elaborate the nature of group involvement, mind control, and disguised techniques of hypnosis. Red flags were raised in my mind. My years of movement training not to "entertain negativity" were shaken. Glimmers of independent thought began to surface in my mind. I was gaining a new view on hypnosis and the nature of trance states. TM teaches that hypnosis is dangerous. The more information I gained about hypnosis, the more I began to discover that in fact TM and hypnosis were one and the same.

This new information did not stop me from practicing the TM-Sidhi program, although it allowed me to begin to question the movement's "sacred science." Months passed before I allowed myself to entertain the idea of stopping meditation.

The Power of Information

My first step toward leaving the TM movement was to question everything I could about the movement. We had been taught that all critical nonmovement sources of information are invalid. I wondered whom I could trust. The beginnings of my journey of recovery had begun.

It took approximately one year to "physically" break my ties to the movement. During that year, I began to secretly contact former members, former MIU faculty, former aides of Maharishi. I was shocked by the specific information they provided about faked scientific research, transfers of money, studies of the negative effects of meditation, and details of Maharishi's personal life. I wanted more information. I became obsessed on finding everything I could. It was a time of both great exhilaration and hope, coupled with a sense of loss and mourning.

I knew I would lose all of my friends if they discovered I had stopped meditating. I began testing the waters. How would they respond to my questions? How would they respond when a standard cliché did not stop my questioning process? I knew how easy it was to dismiss and discard those who became negative, lost in the "mud."

I soon became persona non grata. My friends stopped inviting me to dinner. Then the phone calls stopped. My name was removed from the mailing list, and I was no longer allowed in the local TM Center. When fully involved in and believing in the movement, these actions would have been devastating; now, it was an opportunity for me to stand outside the movement's prison of specialness.

Breaking physically from the movement did not release me from the ingrained thought patterns that dominated me. How would I survive in the world without "nature's support"? How did people in the world function, without the grace of the gods? The power of Maharishi's meditation was essential to living my life. How would I find a parking space? How would I get a job? How would I succeed in this life and after without TM? How would I survive?

My transition out of the movement required a combination of factors: leaving the controlled environment of MIU, participating in my sister's exit counseling, and beginning to understand coercive influence. Then came the terrifying process of stopping meditation, which for so long I had been taught to be "the solution to all problems."

In 1986 I attended a session for former cult members at a national conference of the Cult Awareness Network. I listened to former members of "real cults" describing their experiences. They were talking about my experience! I had the same allegiance to and certainty about Maharishi that former Moonies had for the Reverend Moon. Both of these leaders were manipulating facts and lives in the name of spirituality.

RECOVERY

I discovered that making the break from the movement was only the beginning. I had difficulties with reading, memory, concentration, focusing, involuntary body shaking, and dissociation. I was afraid of temporal and spiritual reprisal. The movement's doctrines populated my thinking. At MIU I had learned that TM was connected to everything. I needed help in sorting out the spiritual baggage that was attached to every area of my life.

I broke the movement's code of silence for the first time by speaking to a reporter. As I told him the secret teachings, my body began to violently shake. There I was on my bed, body vibrating, head jerking back and forth; I was confused and frightened. At times I found myself defending the movement to him. I questioned my thought process. Was I a spiritual failure? Was I wrong to talk to him? Would I burn in hell?

At this point I knew I needed professional help to sort out my intellectual confusion, the movement doctrines that were controlling me, and the psychological difficulties that resulted from years of meditation. However, I still held the movement's prejudice that mental health professionals never solve problems, they only "stir the mud." I believed that psychological problems were only spiritual problems. How could a doctor stop my body from shaking, stop the Tourette's Syndrome-like utterances that I had been taught were the result of past-life misdeeds. I felt hopeless.

While at the CAN conference, I began asking professionals if they knew how to stop these problems. I was met with strange looks until I asked Dr. Margaret Singer, the noted cult expert, for help. To her, my problems were similar to those of other long-term group members. She armed me with an explanation of how these experiences come about, and she assured me that they do go away. For the first time I felt there was help for my difficulties. At Dr. Singer's recommendation, I began working with an experienced psychiatrist; I also continued a therapeutic relationship with Dr. Singer.

My recovery took on three major directions. The first was to work on my chronic states of dissociation and depersonalization. Second, to work on reality orientation: I used my therapist as a coach to help me work with my tendency to spiritualize everything. Third, I needed to develop social skills.

Dissociation and Depersonalization

In the TM world, it was okay to be a "Space Cadet." That was in fact what we called someone who was spaced out. Being "blissed out," mindlessly wandering, twitching, shaking, having unconscious vocalizations were all signs of spiritual growth. Forgetting one's name was funny. I would often begin tasks and in the process forget what I had started out to do—this was normal in the TM world.

Learning to live in the "relative" (the real world) required keeping these commonly experienced phenomena in check. Through therapy, I learned that these behaviors were positively reinforced, unconsciously learned habits that were difficult to break. By stopping the consciousness-altering practices of the TM movement, these behaviors occurred less frequently; but in periods of stress they tended to involuntarily recur.

It took many years for me to develop the skills to immediately label these states as they occurred. I had to learn coping strategies that returned me to a more balanced state of mental functioning. One of the most helpful strategies I found was to exercise. Exercise tended to reduce my episodes of dissociation by making me aware of my body. Every time I exercised, I became more aware of my body as being part of me. The more familiarity I developed with my physical body, the more aware I became of the subtle feelings that preceded my twitching, verbalizations, and so forth.

I began to identify things that caused sensory overload, that resulted in my spacing out, like shopping malls and video arcades. I learned to take them in small doses and gradually build up my endurance.

Upon completion of the TM-Sidhis course, I found myself having trouble reading. I would pick up a book, read the first few pages and then find myself lost, not knowing what I had read. I would reread the first page and again find myself lost. Then I would reread the first paragraph and find myself lost. I had no comprehension. After leaving TM I slowly developed reading stamina by setting a timer. I progressively increased my reading periods and attempted to read one complete news article daily.

Reality Checks

The basis of the TM program is that thoughts can magically materialize into matter. If you think a thought, it has an effect. If you want a Mexican dinner and you are pure enough via TM, it will spontaneously appear. Think negatively about someone and that person may get sick. Desire success in business and it will occur. In TM subjective experience determines reality. If it feels good, it must be right.

If objective sensory information is in conflict with group-generated subjective feelings, the objective intellectual perspective must be rejected and is considered a "mistake of the intellect." When the magical powers fail to produce results, it is thought to be the result of one's karma (i.e., past actions) from this and previous lives. The onus of all negative experiences in life falls back on the group member.

Thus, for my recovery I needed a therapist who had knowledge of group influences. Traditional therapy would diagnose me as delusional, possibly schizophrenic, and miss that my thinking process was systematically conditioned by TM ideology, which not only sanctioned but promoted magical thinking.

Through therapy with a person knowledgeable about cults, I learned that empty-mind meditation (such as we learned in our TM training) can cause cognitive inefficiencies: memory difficulties and problems with concentration and focusing. The prescribed Maharishi medicine was the cause, not the cure.

My learned reflexive tendency to spiritualize the mundane was the most difficult habit to break. TM doctrine connects all successes to meditation and all failures to personal or family karma.

I recall sessions with my therapist sorting out TM-generated feelings and comparing them to "accurate" information or perspectives. "Finding a parking space is not the result of meditation," Dr. Singer would say to me. Nonmeditators find them, too. "Successes in business are not the result of having taken an advanced TM training course. IBM is successful without meditation." Slowly I began to overcome the habit that I had been taught, which was to use my "feeling" states as my primary decision-making tool. I came to understand that the "mind" is not the enemy. In therapy I learned that I am a whole person and that I can make decisions as a whole person, with mind, body, and feelings.

Resocialization

I had lived outside of popular culture for 10 years. I lacked knowledge of popular music, film, literature, and world events. I now see how my isolation inhibited outside relationships. I had to learn how to carry on casual conversations without turning them into recruiting sessions. I had to get over the embarrassment of not knowing what someone was referring to when they talked about a movie or television program that everyone saw, or a song that everyone knew.

Resocialization sometimes requires disclosure skills and a sense of humor. Two years after completing litigation and putting my cult experience behind me I am still confronted at the most inopportune times with difficult questions. Recently at a meeting with a banking officer the question came up, "Where did you go to college?" "MIU," I responded. "What's MIU?" the bank officer asked. I paused. "Mid-Iowa

University. You've heard of it, haven't you? It's a small college south of Iowa City." "And what was your degree in?" he went on. "Business," I responded. That's the short answer, I thought to myself. What would he say if I fully disclosed . . . "research into consciousness as a field of all possibilities"? And then went on to explain that I had studied the mechanics of creation, that I learned to levitate two hours morning and evening . . . to save the world? The subject changed. It worked . . . and I felt relief.

Litigation

Shortly after leaving the movement I was feeling deeply deceived. I thought, Maharishi knew people could not levitate, fly, or become invisible. He had systematically covered up the adverse effects of his programs: suicides, mental breakdowns, memory difficulties, concentration problems, and more. He had created an organization that kept me engaged in his world plan by usurping my youthful idealism. I felt cheated.

A group of similarly minded former members contacted the administration at MIU; we requested a refund for the $1400 levitation course. Our request was met with "If you think you have a case, sue us." And that's what I did.

My lawsuit helped bring my group involvement to a conclusion. I chose to confront the TM movement's deception, negligence, and fraud in a court of law. The process of litigation required that I become very objective about my involvement. It required that I sort out in an objective way the movement, its claims and actions, and the effects they had upon me. The discovery process gave me access to carefully guarded movement secrets. This information confirmed my view of the movement as corrupt and harmful.

CONCLUSION

Leaving the group is like divorcing one's family. I had deep emotional bonds with the TM movement, Maharishi, and many of the caring members. The values that my family gave me were so subordinated to the group's ideology that I essentially lost contact with them while in the group. Recovery is a lifelong ordeal. Eighteen years have passed since my recruitment. I continue to uncover areas of my life that have been affected.

6

A PERSONAL ACCOUNT: BIBLE-BASED GROUP

Mark Trahan

In September 1986 I was indoctrinated into the New York City Church of Christ, the New York City branch of the Boston Church of Christ movement (known as the "Boston movement"). I remained a member for the next three and a half years.

THE INDOCTRINATION

In late July or early August of 1986 I received a call from an acquaintance I hadn't heard from in a long time. She called to invite me to a Bible talk that she was certain I would just love. My wife, Vicky, and I had met this young woman about eight months earlier when we were all exploring New Age techniques. We socialized for a while, but then had drifted apart. During that time because of an unsettling experience that both my wife and I had had with our occult involvement, we started reading the Bible and attending a local Baptist church.

Our friend from the past was now saying that she had found a great church, and she knew we would simply adore it ourselves because we were so "spiritual." Her first attempt was to get me to come to a Bible talk on Friday mornings at 10 a.m. I balked at giving her a definite commitment because my work schedule at the time required that I work late on Thursday evenings. I had no intention of being anywhere early on Fridays.

After a few weeks she changed tactics and turned her attentions to my wife, inviting Vicky to a Bible talk that was for women only. My wife and I had only been married about four months and soon after our marriage it seemed that all of our single friends abandoned us, which left Vicky quite sad. Eager to make new friends, Vicky quickly accepted the invitation.

I was rather surprised when I saw how much Vicky liked the Bible talk. In hindsight I realize she was mostly impressed by the people she met and then with the other aspects of the talk. Her enthusiasm motivated me to take the time to check out the men's Bible talk on Friday mornings. Our friend, of course, was ecstatic. She had introduced Vicky to a female leader of the group and that woman's husband just happened to be in the men's Friday morning group. Vicky's new friend said she would call her husband and have him meet me at the meeting so that I wouldn't feel too uncomfortable.

I geared myself up. Although I was curious, I felt sure that I was going to meet a bunch of "Hallelujah, Praise the Lord" types and would have to keep my sarcasm in check. Imagine my surprise when instead I found a gathering of people who not only had an interest in the Bible similar to mine, but who also amazingly came from similar backgrounds. I was impressed by the fact that people didn't rush out the door after the talk was over—they actually hung around and talked to one another. Even though I must have answered the same questions seven or eight times (What's your name? Where do you live? What do you do?), I was genuinely touched by their overt friendliness.

Soon after this Vicky and I were asked by the leadership couple, Sid and Nancy (pseudonyms), if we would like to do some one-on-one Bible studies with them. Since nobody else had ever made this offer before and we were anxious to learn more about the Bible, we readily said yes. Besides, here was another married couple who wanted to be our friends.

Something strange happened, though. It wasn't much, but it gave me pause. The one-on-one studies were never one-on-one. They were in fact two-on-one—two of them and one of us. And Vicky and I were never allowed to do the studies together. Nancy and the evangelist's wife studied with Vicky, and Sid and the evangelist studied with me. Also they swore Vicky to secrecy about what they studied with her as she was always one study ahead of me.

I silenced my doubts, however, and decided to continue the studies before making any hasty decisions. Vicky and I were both put through the same series of studies: The Crucifixion, The Word, The Kingdom, Discipleship, Light and Darkness, and Denominations. An additional study, The Holy Spirit, which dealt with charismatic "gifts" most commonly associated with the Pentecostal movement, was also given to me because I had a background in the occult. This particular study was done one-on-one, and in this case it was with neither Sid nor the evangelist. Instead, another "leader" who had a background in the charismatic movement did this study with me.

This was the next warning bell for me, and it was a big one. In reading the Bible myself I found that it was able to describe or explain a number of feelings that I had experienced in my practice of occultism. When I would talk of these things with other Christians who were not members of the NYC Church of Christ, they also had a basic understanding of the subject. When I talked about these things with people from the Church of Christ group, however, they seemed to have no understanding at all of what the Bible had to say on the subject. The Holy Spirit study, therefore, was a rather lame attempt on their part to answer any questions I had about it. I found it very unsettling that a "church" that claimed to know the Bible so well had no understanding at all of what the Bible had to say about these practices.

Again I swallowed my doubts about the group because everything else about it seemed so positive. The members were really committed and seemed to do what others only talked about. I was also impressed with the fact that during the studies they were able to answer many of the religious questions I had. Looking back now I see that many of these answers were wrong, but at that time I didn't know the Bible very well, and I was satisfied with almost any answer that seemed plausible.

Although I was unaware of it at the time, the studies that Vicky and I were being put through were the same for every person indoctrinated into the group. Each successive study was carefully designed to further narrow our options and lead us to the conclusion that this group was the only group on the face of the Earth which was *really* following the Bible and that we needed to become members *fast* or face the prospect of going to Hell.

The final stage of our indoctrination was a process known as Counting the Cost. This is usually the last study a person does before being allowed to become a member. It is far more involved than the previous studies. I consider it the final major breakdown of a person before entering the group.

During my time in the group I saw Counting the Cost go from taking about an hour and a half to sometimes as long as three hours a day for two or three days. Counting the Cost had to be done by someone in leadership, usually a Zone leader. In this process the person is asked about every sin he or she ever committed. When I eventually became a leader, I was taught not to ask *if* a person committed a particular sin, but *when* he or she last committed it. We were also taught that if we suspected someone of a specific sin, but we felt that the person wasn't telling us, we were to intimate that we had "struggled" with this sin ourselves . . . had he? or she? As I was to learn when I left the group, everybody "struggled" with the "sins" of rebellion and not trusting people (particularly group leaders).

In September 1986 Vicky and I were "baptized" into the group. We were now full-fledged members. It was only a matter of months, however, before I would have more misgivings about the group. For example, it was becoming increasingly obvious that Sid and Nancy, who had worked so hard to befriend us before we were members, no longer had time for us. We also noticed the formation of cliques within the group and the preferential treatment given to some over others. Certainly it was hard not to notice the unquestionable authority given to leaders of the group despite the fact that these leadership positions were not found in the Bible. Yet the leaders claimed the Bible to be the *only* foundation for the group's faith.

I saw so many things wrong that I banded together a small group of other recent converts and asked them if they saw the same things that Vicky and I did. To a person they described the same inconsistencies. We agreed to together confront the leadership of the group and either get some answers or consider the prospect of leaving. Alas, this mutiny never got off the ground. I "confessed" to my discipling partner, Sid, the problems I was having with the group, revealing that I had spoken to other members of the group about them. The leaders moved like greased lightning. The discipling partners of the other members we had spoken to were instructed to silence each of them. Vicky and I were ganged up on (separately) by the leadership and, using Scriptures out of context, were shown what audacity we had to question leaders that God himself had chosen!

For close to three more years Vicky and I remained in the group, but barely a day would pass when I wouldn't doubt the group for one reason or another. I remember one occasion when I was researching Bible translations and stumbled upon what I felt was strong evidence that the very opposite of something the group taught was really the truth. Greatly concerned, I called Sid and carefully explained the situation to him. It became quickly apparent that he had no concern for the facts. His main concern was that I was questioning a teaching of the group; he pulled out all the stops to silence me. Whether what I had to say was accurate or not was of no relevance.

THE EXIT

By February 1990 I was in such psychological and spiritual turmoil that it was no longer possible for me to remain in the group. After confronting leadership I made the difficult decision to leave. As a walkaway, however, I was beset with a number of problems. Although I didn't realize it at the time, I experienced most of the difficulties commonly encountered by those who leave high-demand groups.

Confusion

The first problem was confusion. The group had always made the claim that it was only going by the Bible. It had become increasingly evident, however, as the months wore on that not only was the group not going by the Bible, but also much of the doctrine and behaviors ran contrary to it.

When I left the group, my decision was based solely on that issue. As a result I was unsure if my decision to leave the group was correct. At that time I had no idea that the group was a cult. I strongly suspected that it was, but being unfamiliar with the specific criteria used to define a cult, I was constantly second-guessing myself. Had I done the right thing or was I just copping out because I was unable to make a commitment to God?

I was also confused about what to tell my friends in the group. I wanted them to know that I was leaving, and I wanted them to know my reason for making that decision. I knew the group wouldn't tell the members the truth about my departure so I wanted to speak with them myself. This created conflict because my desire to do what I felt was morally right was at odds with the group's teaching that to negatively influence others about the group was a grievous and unpardonable offense.

Especially painful was the fact that almost no one in the group knew the real details about my decision to leave. There was a lot of speculation, and already I was hearing slanderous accusations being made about me. Even close friends who had known me before my group involvement and who were also members ceased all communication. Because I had been so outspoken, members were being warned to avoid me. In fact, one woman who had been a close friend was so disturbed when she ran into me at a corner store that she was visibly shaking.

Loss of Support System

A second, serious post-cult problem I faced was the complete loss of my support system. I was married for my entire cult involvement, and my wife and I made the decision to leave the group together. Now, all we had left was each other. Neither my wife nor I had maintained any relationships outside the cult. During our membership all outside relationships had been initiated for the sole purpose of recruitment and indoctrination into the group. Almost all of our friends outside the group were gone, driven away by our ceaseless barrage of cult jargon.

Anger

Next, I experienced anger — at myself and the group. I wondered aloud, How could I have been so stupid? Why did I stick it out for so long? When did I stop thinking for myself? How could I have ever dreamed that these people really cared for me? Why do I still miss so many of them?

Guilt

Finally, I was overwhelmed with guilt. During the years of my involvement I had treated family and friends horribly, constantly judging them and trying to indoctrinate them. Also I felt guilty about bringing many innocent people into the group. What kind of strain had I unknowingly put their families through? Would I ever be able to get them out? I was ashamed of the kind of person I had become and of the things I had done.

Lack of Self-esteem

Because I had been a spiritual pariah in the group who was constantly reprimanded, I had little self-esteem. I had to regain confidence in myself and my abilities.

SOME SOLUTIONS

Despite the difficulties described above, I was able to find solutions and come to terms with my experience.

Self-education

Educating myself about cults in general and the one I had belonged to in particular helped tremendously in the process of recuperating and learning from the whole ordeal. It is probably the single most important step I took on the road to recovery. I read books, articles, and pamphlets; I watched videos; I spoke to numerous cult experts and ex-members. Their wisdom and advice shed new light on what I had lived through and how it happened. I learned about the specific criteria that so clearly define a cult and differentiate it from a legitimate church, religion, or other type of group.

Of utmost importance was learning about mind control: what it is and how it is used to indoctrinate people into cults and keep them under the group's influence once the indoctrination is complete. Understanding the power of mind control explained so many of the questions I had about my involvement with the group. Also it helped me to accept the difficulty I had in walking away from it.

Sharing

Talking to other ex-members was extremely beneficial. I truly believe that being a former member of a destructive cult is somewhat like being a war veteran. No matter how sympathetic a listener may be (although you will also find many who aren't), if the person hasn't been through the experience, then he or she cannot really comprehend what you're talking about.

Sharing the ordeal with others who had been through similar experiences was a great comfort. It also helped me prepare for the difficult task of reestablishing relationships with family members and old friends whom I had alienated.

Counseling

I sought counseling from mental health professionals who were specifically experienced in dealing with ex-cult members. They aided me in understanding not only what I had experienced in my cult but also what I could expect to experience after exiting the group. They helped me to see that my anger was natural and part of the recovery process.

Action

Finally, I took a position that I don't necessarily recommend to everyone but is one that has been invaluable to me. While I was educating myself on the modern cult phenomenon, I became aware of just how serious the problem really is. The group I was in was just one of literally thousands to be found both here and abroad! Because of this I made a decision to take an active role against cults and join the ranks of others who are concerned about this particular threat to our freedom.

I am currently working in cult education, speaking about cults to schools, churches, civic groups, and so forth. In addition, I work as an exit counselor, helping families who have lost a loved one to any one of these destructive groups. I've also counseled many people who walked away from cults and are seeking to understand their experience. I am the Associate Editor of *Thresholds*, a newsletter for ex-members of the Boston Movement.

Taking an active role against cults and helping to educate the public about such groups has greatly assisted in making something good come from a bad experience.

7

POST-CULT PROBLEMS:
AN EXIT COUNSELOR'S PERSPECTIVE

Carol Giambalvo

THIS CHAPTER IS WRITTEN FROM THE PERSPECTIVE of an exit counselor dealing with clients both during an intervention and during their recovery process, from my experience as the former National Coordinator of FOCUS (Former Cult Members Support network), and from my own recovery as an ex-member of a cult.

When *Combatting Cult Mind Control* (Hassan, 1988) was published, I began receiving many phone calls from ex-cult members who upon reading this book finally learned that they could get help for some of the residual effects of their cultic experience – or at least could begin to understand what had been happening to them. At one point those calls numbered over two hundred per month. Some former cult members had left their groups over five years prior to reading Hassan's book. From the book, they said, they finally understood some of the problems they had been experiencing and, in a way, it felt as though they had just recently left the group.

CLASSIFICATIONS OF
EX-MEMBERS

There are several classifications of ex-members, based on how they left the cult. Former members usually fit into one of the following:

148

1. Those who had interventions
2. Those who left on their own, or walkaways
3. Those who were expelled, or castaways

Walkaways and castaways need the most help in understanding their recovery process. Former members who were cast out of a cult are especially vulnerable; often they feel inadequate, guilty, and angry. Most cults respond to any criticism of the cult itself by turning the criticism around onto the individual member. Whenever something is wrong, it's not the leadership or the organization, it's the individual. Thus, when someone is told to leave a cult, that person carries a double load of guilt and shame. Sometimes walkaways also carry a sense of inadequacy. Often they can think through these feelings intellectually, but emotionally such feelings are difficult to handle.

A factor in any ex-cultist's recovery is whether or not the support of family and friends is available when he or she emerges from the cultic world. Former members who had family interventions and, in some cases, the opportunity to spend time at an appropriately oriented rehabilitation facility seem to make leaps in their recovery process (see Chapter 10 for a description of rehabilitation facilities). Because of the educational process inherent in exit counseling interventions and available at specialized rehab centers, these former members are equipped early on in their post-cult life with the tools necessary to begin to integrate their experiences and rebuild their lives.

ASPECTS TO CONSIDER IN POST-CULT RECOVERY

There are numerous aspects to consider when working with a person who has a left a cult. These factors will often influence the types of issues the ex-cultist will need to deal with. Some of the aspects affecting the recovery process that I've identified in my work with ex-members are:

1. How they left the group
2. Length of time in the group
3. Whether or not they were in a leadership position in the group
4. Availability of family and/or social network of support when they leave the group
5. Whether they have vocational skills or sufficient education to procure employment

6. The intensity of the residual emotional and psychological effects of their experiences
7. Financial resources available to them, or the ability to get help when they need it
8. Their age (for example, women leaving a cult after their child-bearing years, or young people who grew up in a cult)
9. Marital status and/or family they had in the group; whether it is still intact

Some former members have called me with an expressed desire and obvious need for exit counseling, but they cannot afford it. In fact, they can't even afford the cost of the long-distance phone call. There is a great need for financial assistance for former members who are crying out for help.

TOOLS FOR RECOVERY

In my experience the most helpful tool for recovering ex-cultists is learning what mind control is and how it was used in their specific cult. Understanding that there are residual effects from a mind-control environment – and that these effects are often transitory in nature – helps defuse the anxiety. Clients, especially walkaways and castaways, feel relieved when they learn that, given the situation, what they are experiencing is normal and the effects will not last forever.

Also integral to the recovery process is developing an attitude that there are some positives to be gained from the cultic experience. When former members learn about mind control, they can use that understanding to sort through their cultic experience, to see how they came to change their behavior and beliefs as a result of mind control. They can then assess what out of that experience is good and valid for them to hold onto.

When ex-cultists live in an area where there is an active FOCUS support group meeting, it is often helpful for them to participate. FOCUS is an international network of individuals who were once associated with high-demand groups. FOCUS offers support, referrals, and an opportunity to meet – both socially and at conferences – to dicuss common experiences and to assist one another in adjusting to life after a cultic or totalistic involvement. The meetings provide a safe place for ex-cult members to discuss their concerns with others who are dealing with similar issues. In this environment no one will look at them like they have two heads.

COMMON ISSUES IN
POST-CULT RECOVERY

Some of the recovery issues that keep recurring in my work with ex-cultists are:

1. Sense of purposelessness, of being disconnected. They left a group that had a powerful purpose and intense drive; they miss the peak experiences produced from the intensity and the group dynamics.
2. Depression.
3. Grieving for other group members, for a sense of loss in their life.
4. Guilt. Former members will feel guilt for having gotten involved in the first place, for the people they recruited into the group, and for the things they did while in the group.
5. Anger. This will be felt toward the group and/or the leaders. At times this anger is misdirected toward themselves.
6. Alienation. They will feel alienation from the group, often from old friends (that is, those who were friends prior to their cult involvement), and sometimes from family.
7. Isolation. To ex-cultists, no one "out there" seems to understand what they're going through, especially their families.
8. Distrust. This extends to group situations, and often to organized religion (if they were in a religious cult) or organizations in general (depending on the type of cult they were in). There is also a general distrust of their own ability to discern when or if they are being manipulated again. This dissipates after they learn more about mind control and begin to listen to their own inner voice again.
9. Fear of going crazy. This is especially common after "floating" experiences (see point 18 below for explanation of floating).
10. Fear that what the cult said would happen to them if they left actually might happen.
11. Tendency to think in terms of black and white, as conditioned by the cult. They need practice in looking for the gray areas.
12. Spiritualizing everything. This residual sometimes lasts for quite a while. Former members need to be encouraged to look for logical reasons why things happen and to deal with reality, to let go of their magical thinking.
13. Inability to make decisions. This characteristic reflects the dependency that was fostered by the cult.

14. Low self-esteem. This generally comes from those experiences, common to most cults, where time and again members are told that they are worthless.

15. Embarrassment. This is an expression of the inability to talk about their experience, to explain how or why they got involved or what they had done during that time. It is often manifested by an intense feeling of being ill-at-ease in both social and work situations. Also, often there is a feeling of being out of synch with everyone else, of going through culture shock, from having lived in a closed environment and having been deprived of participating in everyday culture.

16. Employment and/or career problems. Former members face the dilemma of what to put on a resume to cover the blank years of cult membership.

17. Dissociation. This also has been fostered by the cult. Either active or passive, it is a period of not being in touch with reality or those around them, an inability to communicate.

18. Floating. These are flashbacks into the cult mind-set. It can also take on the effect of an intense emotional reaction that is inappropriate to the particular stimuli.

19. Nightmares. Some people also experience hallucinations or hearing voices. A small percentage of former members needs hospitalization due to this type of residual.

20. Family issues.

21. Dependency issues.

22. Sexuality issues.

23. Spiritual (or philosophical) issues. Former members often face difficult questions: Where can I go to have my spiritual (or belief) needs met? What do I believe in now? What is there to believe in, trust in?

24. Inability to concentrate, short-term memory loss.

25. Reemergence of pre-cult emotional or psychological issues.

26. Impatience with the recovery process.

In my experience, there is no difference in the aftereffects experienced by those people who had family interventions or those who walked away or were expelled from a cult. Most ex-cultists—no matter the method of leaving the cult—experience some or all of these residuals. The difference is that the individuals who had interventions are more prepared to deal with them, especially those who went to a rehab facility.

It is important to note and to bring to the attention of the ex-cultist that each individual's recovery process is different and there is no manual to follow, step by step, telling you "How To Recover from a Cultic Experience." In fact, the desire for a quick and easy recovery may be in itself a residual effect of the cult.

PSYCHIATRIC ISSUES

Singer and Ofshe (1990) describe the types of psychological responses of people leaving thought-reform programs, or what is here referred to as "mind control groups." The majority reaction is "a varying degree of anomie — a sense of alienation and confusion resulting from the loss or weakening of previously valued norms, ideals, or goals" (p. 191). Most former cultists "need to put together the split or doubled self they maintained while they were in the group and come to terms with their pre-group sense of self" (p. 191). In addition to dissociative, depressive, and anxiety disorders, the most common psychiatric disorders seen in former members are:

1. Reactive schizoaffective-like psychoses occurring in individuals with no apparent personal or family history of mental disorder
2. Posttraumatic stress disorder
3. Atypical dissociative disorder
4. Relaxation-induced anxiety similar to that reported by Heide and Borkovec (1983, 1984) and Heide (1985) and resulting from meditation, chanting, or other trance-inducing exercises
5. Miscellaneous reactions, including concentration difficulties, memory impairments, phobias, self-mutilation, and so forth

CLOSING REMARKS

In closing, I would like to cite a letter — one of hundreds in my files — dated April 15, 1991. I believe this letter highlights the extent of the cult problem and the growing need for increased awareness on the part of families, helping professionals, and clergy — and an equally urgent need for expanded services for former cult members.

Dear Carol:

Presently I am in Saudi Arabia. My Army Reserve Unit was called up for active duty on _____. I have been in Saudi Arabia since _____ and have participated in "Operation Desert Shield/Storm."

In October '90, I left the _____ church after being involved for six years. Since I had some difficulties adjusting to life, my parents

persuaded me to seek counseling. I had just one session with a therapist before receiving my orders to deploy to Saudi Arabia. Redeploy-
ment back to the States is a slow process and my unit commander
does not know how long we will have to stay. I am willing to remain in
Saudi Arabia for however long it takes to complete the mission.

Even though I am assigned to the Chaplain's section and receive a
lot of spiritual enlightenment, I have found no one who can relate to
my experience in the cult. Writing to your organization is a shot in the
dark, but I felt it was worth a try. I need someone to relate to about
my experience in the cult. It would greatly help me to cope with my
present situation here. Can you help?

Sincerely,

(signed by a female officer)

REFERENCES

Hassan, S. (1988). *Combatting cult mind control.* Rochester, VT: Park Street
     Press.
Heide, F. J. (1985, April). Relaxation: The storm before the calm. *Psychology
     Today, 19,* pp. 18–19.
Heide, F. J., & Borkovec, T. D. (1983). Relaxation-induced anxiety: Paradoxi-
     cal anxiety enhancement due to relaxation training. *Journal of Consulting
     and Clinical Psychology, 51,* 171–182.
Heide, F. J., & Borkovec, T. D. (1984). Relaxation-induced anxiety: Mecha-
     nism and theoretical implications. *Behavior Research and Therapy, 22,* 1–
     12.
Singer, M. T., & Ofshe, R. (1990). Thought reform programs and the produc-
     tion of psychiatric casualties. *Psychiatric Annals, 20*(4), 188–193.

8

EXIT COUNSELING:

A PRACTICAL OVERVIEW

David Clark
Carol Giambalvo
Noel Giambalvo, M.S.
Kevin Garvey
Michael D. Langone, Ph.D.*

EXIT COUNSELING IS A VOLUNTARY, intensive, time-limited, contractual educational process that emphasizes the respectful sharing of information with members of exploitatively manipulative groups, commonly called cults. Exit counseling is distinguished from deprogramming, which received much media coverage in the late 1970s and 1980s, in that the former is a voluntary process, whereas the latter is currently associated with a temporary restraint of the cultist.

Many exit counselors, including those contributing to this chapter, when referring to their services, prefer terms such as "cult information consultant." At least for the time being, however, "exit counseling" is the term that most people use when referring to voluntary interventions designed to help cultists reevaluate their commitment to a group. Exit counselings are usually initiated by a cult member's parents or spouse.

What does an exit counseling entail? Briefly, a parent or spouse concerned about a loved one's cult involvement will arrange for a face-

*When exit counselors' experiences are described in this chapter in the first person plural, the "we" refers to the first four coauthors, who are exit counselors.

155

to-face or telephone consultation with an exit counselor or an exit counseling "team." If the exit counselor deems the case appropriate and the client agrees, they will proceed. First, the parents or spouse must learn about cultic manipulations (especially those employed by their loved one's group) and communication patterns that may interfere with their relationship with the cultist. If necessary, they may participate in family counseling with mental health professionals or, in some cases, in consultation with the exit counselor. Next, the exit counselor and client will decide on how most effectively to persuade the cultist to speak with the exit counselor.

When the family introduces the exit counselor to the cultist, the counselor will usually present the matter (of the cult involvement) as a family problem, which indeed it is. The exit counselor asks the cultist to participate in a review of information that may help him and his family better understand and cope with their problems. If the cultist agrees, which occurs in most cases, the exit counselor may spend one to several days discussing cults and psychological manipulation, reviewing written material, watching and discussing videos, and discussing the relevance of this information to the cultist and the family. The exit counselor, although not hiding his or her views about cults, takes care not to pressure or manipulate the cultist, who decides how to respond to this information. The exit counselor respects the cultist's final decision, whether that decision is to stay in the group or leave. If the cultist leaves the group, the exit counselor will provide information on how to continue the educational process begun in the exit counseling and where to get help coping with post-cult problems. (See Giambalvo [1992] for a detailed description of what happens in exit counselings and how family members can prepare.)

Although there are different approaches to exit counseling, they all respond to the family or loved one's needs, and seek to help cultists by providing them with information they are unaware of. The ultimate goal of the form of exit counseling described in this chapter is to restore cultists' individual judgment and enhance informed self-determination; the goal is *not* to pressure them to leave their group. This approach can be called information-focused exit counseling. It is related to but nevertheless distinct from process-focused exit counseling, or what Hassan (1991) calls "strategic intervention therapy," and from approaches that advance a particular theological agenda.

The approach described in this chapter presumes that families and loved ones who seek an exit counselor's assistance have six general needs bearing on their desire to help the cult-involved person. These are:

1. Identifying information relevant to assessment, decision making, and implementation of the family's action options
2. Effectively relating to the cultist
3. Assessing the nature, extent, and degree of destructiveness of the cultist's behavioral and personality changes
4. Exploring and evaluating options regarding intervention
5. Making a decision
6. Implementing the decision

RESPONDING TO FAMILY NEEDS

Before discussing the family's needs, it is important to clarify to whom the exit counselor is responsible and when. Until the exit counseling proper begins, the family (we include spouses in this category) is the client. A family seeks the exit counselor's assistance in order to determine how to most effectively help a loved one whose well-being is believed to be in jeopardy. If, after consulting with an exit counselor or other experts, the family decides that the most appropriate course of action is to try to persuade the loved one to talk to an exit counselor, the counselor should make it clear that when the exit counseling proper begins it is the cultist's welfare that is of paramount concern, rather than the family's. Although exit counseling is at heart a family intervention, exit counselors are not family advocates or agents who implement a family's wishes. They are consultants who provide information to help cultists make informed evaluations of their cult involvement.

Identifying Information

By virtue of their expertise regarding cultic manipulations and the practices and beliefs of specific groups, exit counselors are often able to provide families with substantial information pertinent to their deliberations. They also direct families to written information (books, articles, reports), audio- and videotapes, and people and organizations with relevant expertise. The basic goal of this information is to help clients evaluate the group in question and its impact on their loved one.

Sometimes exit counselors are called upon to help clients whose loved one is in an unknown or little-known group. In such cases, exit counselors will try to help their clients identify means of collecting information (see Chapter 9 for an illustration of this process). If exit counselors and their clients are not able to obtain sufficient information about the group, the exit counseling cannot proceed. This does not mean, obviously, that an exit counselor — someone in the helping profession who is knowledgeable about cultic processes — will not talk to a cultist in a little-known group. The interaction, however, will initially focus on collecting information from the cultist in order to assess the nature of his or her involvement. It is not, strictly speaking, exit counseling, which presumes that a particular group's harmful impact on a particular member has been established with reasonable confidence.

Relating to the Cultist

Families who consult exit counselors usually relate reasonably well to their loved one in the cult. This is because some screening, even if only informal, occurs. Screening may be performed by the exit counselor, by referral sources, including helping professionals (clergy, mental health workers), or by individuals who have had a cult-involvement or a family member in a cult. Referral sources realize that a successful exit counseling requires that the cultist's family members communicate with each other reasonably well, have the resources — including psychological — to effect an intervention, and be willing to explore honestly the pros and cons of an intervention. Referral sources who have some familiarity with the family's background will tend not to refer individuals for whom exit counseling is an inappropriate option.

We by no means want to imply that the families who proceed with an exit counseling are exceptional. They are, for the most part, average families who communicate with their loved one reasonably well. They can, nevertheless, often benefit from a professional family evaluation and from communication skills training (Langone, 1985; Ross & Langone, 1988). Indeed, we believe that the ideal model is that practiced by the cult clinics associated with the Jewish Board of Family and Children's Services in New York and Los Angeles (Addis, Schulman-Miller, & Lightman, 1984; Markowitz, 1989). In this model, families are interviewed by professionals, participate in support groups, and — when appropriate — are referred to exit counselors. The added family preparation clearly facilitates the exit counseling process. Although such professional preparation of families does not appear to be necessary for a successful exit counseling (most exit counselings do not involve such a level of preparation), the family's added psychological sophistication may contribute to the cultist's coping more effectively with post-cult problems. This hypothesis awaits testing by psychological researchers.

One should keep in mind that families' assessment of exit counselors may also function as a screening mechanism. In their research, families may request opinions from individuals who know exit counselors, or families may question exit counselors directly. If, for example, a family wants a helper who will be very controlling and focused on getting the cultist out of the group no matter what, the family is not likely to choose an exit counselor who subscribes to the educational, respectful approach described here. (Research comparing families who choose different types of actions – exit counseling, mental health consultation, waiting, deprogramming – might produce interesting and useful findings.) Some families, upon learning what an exit counseling requires, may decide that they lack the financial or personal resources necessary to carry out the exit counseling (for example, a husband and wife locked in disagreement about whether an intervention's probability of success makes it worth the effort of pursuing). Other families, even after being educated about cults and mind control, may be emotionally averse to sponsoring an exit counseling intervention because, for example, they fear the consequences of even asking their loved one to talk to the exit counselor. Thus, those families who engage the services of exit counselors may be a distinct subgroup of the general population of families seeking help for cult-related problems.

Because of such informal and formal screening, most families who hire exit counselors are able to participate in the process. They will tend to employ what Ross and Langone (1988) call the "learner-helper" style of family relating, rather than the "authoritarian" or the "laissez-faire" styles. According to Ross and Langone:

> Parents taking the learner-helper approach might say, "We think our daughter is in trouble. We want to help her, if that's what's best for her. But first we need information, we need to learn, and we are willing to change our own views and behavior, if necessary, so that we can help. Whatever actions we take, we want to respect our child's integrity, autonomy, privacy, and ideals. We want to be as flexible and unimposing as possible." In essence, these parents want to help their daughter help herself. (1988, p. 46)

Those families who want to pursue an exit counseling but are not prepared to follow the learner-helper model will usually require special preparatory assistance, which can be provided by exit counselors or other professionals knowledgeable about cult issues. However, even those whose communication skills are not clearly deficient can also benefit from training in this area.

Assessment

As noted earlier, exit counselors help families collect information pertinent to evaluating the group in question and its impact on the family's loved one. Exit counselors examine the following types of questions with the family. The family members answer these questions to the best of their ability.

- What is the name of the group?
- What information do you have about the group?
- What is the nature of your current relationship with your loved one?
- What specific behavioral, medical, or personality changes trouble you, for example, decreased frequency of contact, deterioration in school performance, decrease in sense of humor or warmth, changes in personal habits, marked changes in appearances?
- What actions have you taken thus far to try to help your loved one, for example, consulted with clergy or mental health professionals, attended family support group meetings, read relevant material?
- How do other members of the family feel about this problem?
- What can you tell me about significant aspects of your loved one's background, personality, and relationships with other family members, friends, authority figures, and so forth?
- What were the circumstances under which your loved one joined the group, including his or her psychological state?
- How deeply involved is the cultist?
- What is his or her status in the group?
- What is the nature and level of contact between family members and the cultist?
- What, if any, relationship have you had with members of the group, including the leader?
- What is the nature and level of the group's efforts to obstruct communication with the cultist?
- What aspects of the mainstream environment appeal to and repel the cultist?
- What aspects of the cult environment appeal to and repel the cultist?
- How do family members relate to the cultist?
- What role does the group play in producing the disturbing changes you have observed?

Some exit counselors (and mental health professionals who work with families) use questionnaires to collect specific information pertinent to the general questions listed above (Giambalvo, 1992; Hassan, 1988; Langone, 1983).

The most important question to discuss and answer is how the cultist has changed since joining the group, for concern about destructive changes is the family's ethical justification for considering an exit counseling (see Langone, 1985, and Langone & Martin, 1993, for a discussion of the ethics of a family intervention). Langone (1990) suggests using the following question to focus the assessment and distinguish valid from imagined or misunderstood concerns: "If your child (spouse) were not in a cult, what if anything would bother you about his or her changed behavior?" (p. 196).

After disturbing changes are identified, then the clients and the exit counselor can examine the group's role in producing these changes. The following is an example of the types of changes that trigger a family's alarm:

> The cultist is a 22-year-old male attending an Ivy League school. He needs two more semesters in order to complete a degree in architecture and art. Prior to his involvement with a cultic "Christian" group he had a good relationship with his family, including a very close relationship with his older brother, was very friendly and outgoing with many friends, and had a fine sense of humor (a family characteristic). He had dated regularly in high school and early college. He had been raised in the Presbyterian Church and was a leader in his church youth group. He was very talented in art and music, and he practiced his music daily. Drawing and playing his musical instrument were his favorite leisure activities.
>
> He had become involved with the group 14 months prior to the family's consulting the exit counselor. The family was struck by the following changes:
>
> - His decreased sense of humor
> - His judgmental attitude toward family members, especially his older brother
> - His self-imposed isolation when visiting the family
> - His lack of interest in music; he no longer played his musical instrument
> - His talk centered around the Bible; he seemed constantly to be trying to convert his family
> - He pressured the family to provide money for him to go on a "mission" on another continent
> - He planned to drop out of school before completing his degree

- He had dropped most of his current courses and was barely passing the two remaining courses on his schedule
- He broke contact with all of his former friends
- He had stopped creating his artwork completely
- He no longer showed an interest in going to museums and plays
- He no longer attended Christmas services with his family, which had always been a family tradition
- He had moved out of the dormitory into an apartment with "brothers," where he slept on the floor
- He had lost weight

The changes the family observed in this case would be disturbing even if the young man were not in a cult. The case becomes appropriate for exit counseling when there is reason to believe that the disturbing changes result to a large degree from the group's unethical influence on the family member. Sometimes psychological or psychiatric consultation with a cult-aware mental health professional may be called for if there is reason to suspect that a psychological disorder may contribute significantly to the troubling behavior.

It is interesting to note that in this particular case the background information revealed a significant fact to the exit counselor, who was familiar with this particular group: Because the cultist had to pay for his own mission trip, he was not in a leadership position. Such facts, which require an exit counselor's specialized knowledge to discern, can sometimes have important implications in planning the exit counseling.

Exploring Options

The assessment process is designed to help families make an informed evaluation of their options, which can be broken down into three categories:

1. The family may conclude that an exit counseling will not be appropriate, at least for the foreseeable future, for example, because the family has little hope of arranging a meeting between the cultist and the exit counselor, or because serious psychological issues must be addressed first. The family may, however, try to identify and pursue a strategy of gradually improving communication and rapport with the cultist. Or in some instances the family may have to accept and cope with a static,

though unacceptable, situation. Those families who are unable to pursue an exit counseling will often benefit from consultation with mental health professionals familiar with cult issues.

2. The family may conclude that an exit counseling will not be appropriate in the near future but may become appropriate sometime down the road. In such cases the exit counselor will help the family prepare over time for an unscheduled, though planned, exit counseling. The exit counselor and the family may work on improving communication and building rapport (or the exit counselor may refer the family to a mental health professional for communication training). They may continue to collect information in order to refine their assessment. And they may regularly discuss changes in the cultist's situation and factor these changes into their assessment and preliminary plan.

3. The family may decide to pursue an intervention. Sometimes interventions can be set up quickly; sometimes several months may have to elapse. Reasons for delays are diverse: The cultist may be in another state and will not be able to come home for several months. The exit counselor's schedule may require a long wait. A key family member may not agree with or may have strong doubts about the planned intervention. Or the family may require more time than usual to prepare for the intervention.

Making a Decision

The exit counselor stresses to families that no matter what choice they make, there are simply no guarantees with regard to the outcome. Many cultists ultimately leave their groups voluntarily, so even if the family does nothing, the cultist may at some point leave the group, although he or she may have many cult-related problems to contend with after departure. Sometimes exit counselings must be aborted for various reasons, for example, the cult suddenly forbids the cultist from visiting the family.

Although some relevant statistical estimates are available regarding the outcome of exit counselings, such statistics must be applied cautiously when estimating the probability of success for a particular exit counseling at a particular time. Generally speaking, most exit counselors believe that when the cultist gives exit counselors sufficient time to present their information — usually about three days — the person will decide to leave the cult about 90% of the time. If the cultist does not give the exit counselors sufficient time but does listen to their information to some extent, informal estimates indicate that about 60% will decide to eventually leave the group. However, there is no way of confidently predicting in advance whether or not a particular cultist (1) will give the exit counselor sufficient time, and (2) if so, whether or not he or she will be among the 90% who leave or the 10% who remain in the group.

Langone (1984) conducted a study of the outcomes of deprogrammings. In his sample of 62 deprogrammings, 63% of the cases resulted in the cultist leaving the group. Of the 37% who returned to the cult, 25% later left on their own. Although such formally collected data do not exist for exit counselings, the informal estimates noted above suggest that the overall probability of success is somewhat higher. It should be kept in mind, however, that the two populations may not be identical. Families who decide to pursue a deprogramming and the cult-involved loved one of such families may differ in important respects from those families and cultists who participate in an exit counseling. Further study is needed.

EFFECTING THE INTERVENTION

Giambalvo (1992) provides detailed, practical guidelines for families contemplating an exit counseling. She discusses the following preintervention issues:

- What not to say or do
- What to do
- Information gathering
- Readings
- Identifying the exit counseling team
- Timing and location
- Travel arrangements, accommodations, and meals
- Identifying the family team
- The preintervention family meeting
- Suggestions for presenting the plan to the cultist
- What to expect during the intervention
- Breaks/time schedule
- Possible exchanges that may occur
- Length of intervention
- Rehabilitation/reentry facilities
- Future plans

Giambalvo's philosophy of the family intervention holds for the point of view advanced in this chapter as well:

Family interventions are based on an educational model. The cultist has been a victim of a sophisticated set of manipulations. Once she or he becomes aware of these manipulations, basic integrity will usually not allow the cultist to remain a part of a system that victimizes others — no matter how lofty the goals.

The material is to be presented in a manner that shows respect for the cultist's dignity. In particular, it is important to be sensitive to the emotional trauma the cultist may undergo while confronting these issues. Material is to be put forth at a pace that allows the cultist to assimilate the information and, simultaneously, deal with its emotional impact.

The goal is for the client to reevaluate his or her commitment to the group. Although parents and exit counselors may hope that [the cultist] chooses to leave [the group], leaving is not the goal. *Informed* choice is the goal.

Once a person understands mind-control techniques, that person has the basic tools with which to sort out these issues and deal with them. But there is much less time involved and much less stress on the individual if she or he has had the opportunity for exit counseling and rehabilitation. It is imperative that family [members] understand this whole process so they can be supportive to the cultist. (1992, pp. 29–30)

Phases of the Intervention

The phases discussed below are not sequential, clear-cut steps or stages. They are aspects of a long and involved give-and-take in which movement is largely a function of the cultist's comfort level. Exit counselors share information (such as personal knowledge, published information, internal documents from the group, video- and audio-tapes, personal reports of ex-members of the group), and cultists process this information as they are able and willing. Although the specific content of the information exit counselors share will vary from case to case and from exit counselor to exit counselor, it usually involves the following:

- The family concerns that led to the exit counseling
- The nature of mind control, for understanding mind control is relevant to understanding the factors that gave rise to the loved one's behaviors that concern the family
- Doctrinal, ideological, and organizational issues that relate to mind control, including information not generally available to the cultist, such as an analysis of internal documents of the group
- Common post-cult difficulties and helping resources

Presentation of this information is not mechanical or didactic. Exit counselors understand how cultic manipulations can distort the interpretive functions of cultists and, therefore, know how to present the information with sensitivity and tact.

The Exit Counselor's Introduction   At the beginning of the intervention proper the family introduces the exit counselor(s) to the cultist. Exit counselors will try to put the cultist at ease by explaining their purposes. Exit counselors stress that they are there to respond to a familywide concern resulting from the person's cult involvement. Exit counselors' specialized knowledge enables them to communicate and explain this concern. They do not deny that there may be many genuinely good points about the cultist's group involvement. In order to establish rapport, which is vital, exit counselors must communicate that they are honest and willing to listen. From the exit counselor's perspective, however, a cultist does not have enough information to make an informed evaluation of the group. Moreover, prolonged contact with the group may have diminished the cultist's capacity to think critically and make genuinely autonomous decisions. The exit counselor's main objective is to review pertinent information *with* the cultist and the family, not to argue or "persuade." The information will speak for itself. The cultist will decide what impact this information will have on his or her life.

Although some exit counselors are more willing than others to engage in debate or rational argument, they (if they are behaving ethically) do not harangue or denigrate the cultist. In other words, ethical exit counselors do not engage in the kinds of assaultive "confrontation" sometimes associated with certain intense forms of drug "counseling" and some cultic groups. Some confrontation may be used, however, in response to the cultist's attacking the family or the exit counselors with confrontational techniques learned in the cult.

Hostility, Denial, and Dissociation   Although a cultist may exhibit hostility, denial, and dissociation at any point during the exit counseling, these reactions are most commonly observed during the early stage of the intervention. Despite exit counselors' sincerest attempts to be respectful and open-minded, a cultist will typically display at least a muted hostility. Cultists may, for example, demand more information about the backgrounds of the exit counselors, which they will provide.

During these give-and-take discussions, a cultist will often deny or dissociate certain facts or memories (saying, for example, "I keep in touch with my family just as often as I always did"). In denial, the fact or memory is suppressed or reinterpreted in a way that makes for a tacit suppression. A dim awareness remains. Later, when the cultist no longer feels a need to deny, he or she can "take back" what was said earlier. Dubrow-Eichel (1989), for example, notes in his discussion of a

Hare Krishna deprogramming that the cultist initially denied lying to get money from people but later openly acknowledged it. Similarly, in the film *Moonchild*, the cultist initially responds to a claim that he lied to people by saying, "You cannot tell the truth to people who are not prepared to hear it." Later he acknowledged that what he did was indeed lying.

At the time of denial, cultists are not *consciously* lying, even though what they say is a lie. Denial, as we use the term, is an unconscious deception; lying is a conscious deception.

The fundamental denial which must be dealt with in an exit counseling is the tendency for a cultist to deny, through repression or extreme reinterpretations of experience, that lies occur at all. Cultists are so indoctrinated with the belief that the end justifies the means that they will tend not to see lies as lies but will rationalize them as "heavenly deception," "transcendental trickery," or whatever. Helping the cultist acknowledge one lie, however small, can set the stage for questioning the fundamental assumption that neither the group nor the individual member lies. Once the cultist begins to question this assumption, the person is much more capable of recognizing the countless deceptions upon which cultic groups depend.

In dissociation cultists don't suppress facts or memories; they simply do not have access to them — even if only temporarily — because these facts or memories are "split off" from consciousness. Although dissociation has causes, these causes are not typically motivational in character, as is the case in denial and lying. During rituals that utilize hypnotic practices, for example, cultists may not register — may not "encode" — certain experiences or aspects of the experience, for example, that a leader's intoning "You and I are one" during a training session may subtly cause the cultist to unknowingly take on the leader's identity. The cultist's saying, during an exit counseling, that the leader was not being manipulative during a particular event under discussion may indeed be absolutely honest from the cultist's perspective. There is no denial of an unpleasant truth. There simply was never any awareness of manipulation inherent in the event.

Cultists can often, in retrospect, begin to "put things together" and see how the cult's trance-inducing practices and denigration of reflective, critical thinking reduced their awareness. This leads to many former cultists' not being able to describe precisely when and how they came to accept certain aspects of the group's doctrines or ideology. These processes are dissociated, are split off from their consciousness.

Although distinguishing denial from dissociation is sometimes difficult, it is important to keep the distinction in mind because each requires a different approach if the person's critical thinking skills are to be awakened. Patience is probably the most effective way to deal with denial. Exit counselors tend to tolerate the cultist's denial and simply continue to share information. At some point when the cultist begins to make connections, the exit counselor can return to the initially denied item and review it again. As the cultist's understanding grows, his or her need to deny diminishes. With regard to dissociation, the process is similar in that patient presentation of information is required. In dissociation, however, a special type of information—that is, mind-control tactics related to hypnotic practices—must often be discussed before the cultist can begin to understand why his or her awareness was diminished. The point under discussion when the dissociation initially took place is reviewed in order to analyze and possibly reinterpret the remembered experience, not to confront it more honestly.

Resistance   The cultist's demonstrating resistance to the exit counselor's information is a positive sign for it is weaker than denial in that the person simply tries to avoid the subject, rather than deny it. Signs of resistance typically include changing the subject or nitpicking.

Exit counselors respect the emotional message of resistance: "This information makes me uncomfortable." They don't push the client because (1) their approach is premised upon respect for the client, and (2) pushing is likely to raise the client's fear level and increase the likelihood that the client will resort to denial as a means of dealing with emotional discomfort. Instead, the exit counselor will simply make a mental note of the resistance and proceed with the discussion of the information. When a return to the subject is appropriate, it can be discussed again. When the cultist is no longer threatened by the information, the resistance will evaporate.

Interest   When the cultist begins to ask questions about the information and request additional information, that person is exhibiting interest, which is definitely a sign of further progress. Other signs of interest include a change in the quality of the relationship—for example, muted hostility changing to warmth, appreciation, friendliness; examining literature without being asked; staying awake to read materials after the exit counselors have retired.

Participation   Participation is, in a sense, interest compounded. In addition to requesting information, the cultist who is "participating" *gives* information, for example, discussing concern for a friend in the group or revealing things about the group that heretofore had been denied. Although the cultist may still disagree with the exit counselor (who seeks an open, questioning mind, and does not require agreement), the disagreement tends not to be hostile. At this point the cultist is participating in the *search* for truth, not simply responding positively or negatively to the exit counselor's information.

When truly participating in the exit counseling, cultists begin to stop seeing the world in black and white. They show a capacity to look at events from multiple points of view. They begin to see the internal logic to be found in alternate points of view, including those with which they disagree. This is a critical change, for the cult typically presents its view as the only one with merit. When cultists realize that the cult view is merely one point of view, they are able to begin seeing the pros *and* cons of that point of view. The exit counselor's goal during this phase is not to push a particular point of view on the cultist. Rather, it is to help the person see the positives and negatives of different points of view in order to lay the groundwork for a coherent, self-chosen, and informed perspective.

Making Connections   When the cultist spontaneously begins to make connections between bits of information, participation has reached a very positive level. The person not only begins to see the pros and cons of different perspectives but also begins to evaluate and compare them and at least begins to create the coherent, self-chosen, and informed point of view that is the sign of an exit counseling's success. The cultist begins to *think* independently.

Ironically, longer-term members often tend to respond more quickly to the exit counselor's information because they have had some opportunity to see the cult's "dark side." Recent joiners who are still in the "honeymoon phase" will often have more difficulty attributing credibility to the exit counselor's information because it seems so incompatible with their own experience.

Signs that clients are making connections include the following:

- They begin to see the outside world in a way that reveals an appreciation, as well as a recognition, of different perspectives. For example, rather than seeing the family's setting up the exit counseling as an evil desire to control (the "black" view of the cult), they will recognize it as a multifaceted act of love and will begin to feel some appreciation, some gratitude even, for the family's actions.

- They begin to truly recognize that they were victimized and, as a consequence, come to understand how they had been manipulated into misinterpreting their family's past actions.
- They spontaneously relate new information to the subtle influence techniques associated with mind control, saying, for example, "That's an example of a message within a metaphor."
- They spontaneously volunteer examples of how their group used mind-control techniques.
- They begin to recognize and acknowledge instances of denial, resistance, and dissociation.
- They begin to see alternatives to the group, not only as intellectual alternatives, but as *real choices* that they have the capacity to make.

When a client begins to exhibit these behaviors and insights, departure from the group becomes very likely. If the exit counseling was based on a correct assumption – that is, that the cultist was adversely affected by a highly manipulative group – rarely will the cultist freely decide to return to the group. Usually those who do go back to the cult do so because of very strong interpersonal bonds with other members, a belief that they will be able to use their knowledge of mind control to maintain a reasonable level of autonomy even in a powerful group, or a profound discouragement about their capacity to build a new life outside the group.

Although they obviously have a preference, exit counselors respect whatever choices clients make. If a person chooses to remain in the group, the exit counselor will remind him or her – and the family – that the cultist now has knowledge that can be used to strengthen his or her autonomy and improve family relationships. If the client chooses to leave the group, which occurs in the great majority of cases that reach the "making connections" phase, the exit counselor will provide information about what lies ahead and which resources can help. (See other chapters in this book for specific information on the recovery process and ways in which it can be facilitated.)

A Note on Fees

Exit counselors typically charge between $500 and $1000 a day, plus expenses – a fee schedule similar to that of many other consultants. Individuals unfamiliar with consulting fees are sometimes taken aback by these figures. Several points, however, should be kept in mind in evaluating these fees. First, exit counselors – even more than most consultants – must put in long hours keeping abreast of developments pertaining to cults. They are not paid for this time. Second, many exit counselors do not charge for preliminary phone time. Third, many offer free consultations or workshops for former cultists. Fourth, their typical paid workday is 12 to 16 hours in length, and they are often "on call." Fifth, most exit counselors annually devote hundreds of hours to public and professional educational activities. Sixth, exit counselors are frequently targets of verbal abuse, harassment, and, at minimum, the threat of spurious lawsuits. Lastly, exit counselors have special-ized knowledge and skills that require years of study and preparation, including, in most cases, a personal cult experience. One does not be-come a competent exit counselor merely by "taking courses."

EXIT COUNSELING
AND DEPROGRAMMING

The only necessary distinction between exit counseling and depro-gramming is that the latter physically confines the cultist, at least initially, in the home, a hotel room, a cabin, or some other convenient and private location. This distinction, however, tends to cause three further differences between exit counseling and deprogramming.

First, exit counselors *must* be capable of quickly establishing a rap-port with the cultist; otherwise the person would simply leave. Even though some deprogrammers are as respectful and polite as exit coun-selors, the deprogramming situation does not *require* that they behave this way. Therefore, some deprogrammers may be unnecessarily con-frontational.

Second, because of the physical confinement, cultists involved in a deprogramming are much more likely to become enraged than they would during an exit counseling. They may curse and insult the depro-grammers and their parents. They may threaten revenge. They may become physically violent. They may even attempt suicide or physi-cally harm themselves in order to get to a hospital, from where they can call their cult leaders. Such behavior can test the patience of even the most mild-mannered deprogrammer, and in cases with a confronta-tional deprogrammer may lead to a destructive escalation of harsh words and behavior. Indeed, even though most deprogrammings may be successful in that the cultist leaves the group (Langone, 1984), psychotherapists who work with ex-cultists have noted many in-stances in which a "successful" deprogramming had harmful afteref-fects.

Third, some, but not all, deprogrammers act as though cultists are so deeply under the influence of cults that physical confinement is necessary in order to persuade them to listen to information not available in the cult. Although this point of view may sometimes be true, the success of exit counseling suggests that often this is not the case. One may conclude, therefore, that the deprogramming situation tends to exaggerate the power and malevolence of cults. This, especially in combination with the emotions engendered by a deprogramming, results in a tendency for deprogrammers to focus on attacking the group and the group leader much more than exit counselors do. It also results in a tendency for deprogrammers to require, for all intents and purposes, that the cultist come to accept the deprogrammer's assumption of powerful mind control; otherwise the cultist's physical confinement would not have been justified. Although this process may resemble in some ways the mind control it seeks to undo, it differs in two very important respects: Deprogrammers do not seek to persuade cultists to adopt the deprogrammer's personal belief systems, nor do they seek to control the cultist's behavior after the deprogramming is over. As one deprogrammer put it, "I don't believe in vegetarianism, but I'm not out to make [the cultist] eat meat" (Dubrow-Eichel, 1989, p. 25).

Although most exit counselors reject deprogramming because of ethical and practical concerns, many recognize that in certain special cases deprogramming may be an ethical last resort for parents. Sometimes families may not believe that an exit counseling will work and feel that deprogramming is their only viable option for helping a loved one whom they believe to be in imminent physical danger. Sometimes groups may send members to foreign countries or refuse to tell families where they are, in which case families may opt for a deprogramming when they do finally locate their loved one. Sometimes cultists may exhibit psychotic behavior or become medically ill as a result of their group involvement, in which case deprogramming may be ethically and legally defensible.

If parents believe that deprogramming is their only viable option, they should realize that should legal entanglements arise (for example, the deprogramming fails and the child or the cult sues and/or files criminal charges), the burden of justification will fall upon the parents and the deprogrammers. Often parents and deprogrammers who are sued or arrested will rely on variations of the necessity defense, which maintains that the harm resulting from the cult involvement justifies the extreme action of deprogramming. Sometimes this or other defenses are accepted by the legal system, but sometimes they are rejected. Parents should also keep in mind that even successful legal defenses can cost tens of thousands of dollars.

Langone and Martin (1993), who discuss ethical and legal implications of deprogramming and exit counseling, suggest that the greater the danger to the cultist and the lower the probability of success of less-restrictive alternatives, the greater will be the ethical defensibility of a deprogramming. Ethical defensibility, however, does not guarantee legal leniency.

Part of the controversial nature of deprogramming stems from actual abuses of the process. Although cult propaganda about deprogramming is often ridiculously hysterical (e.g., comparing deprogramming to the tortures of the inquisition!), instances of sexual or physical abuse are not unknown.

VARIED APPROACHES WITHIN
THE EXIT COUNSELING FIELD

All exit counseling approaches depend upon building rapport with cultists in order to help them make a more informed evaluation about their cult involvement, which exit counselors view as an exploitatively manipulative situation (otherwise they wouldn't conduct the exit counseling). Hassan (1988) contends that cultists are in a trap that (1) they did not choose (we would qualify this statement by saying that their choice was not informed and was manipulated), (2) is similar to traps experienced by cultists in other groups, and (3) is possible to get out of. For Hassan the exit counselor's job is to bring about behavior change in cultists in order to lead them out of their traps. In a paper distributed at the Cult Awareness Network's 1991 National Conference, Hassan (1991) said that exit counselors, in contrast to deprogrammers, "effect change with finesse not force."

This statement includes the three key variables that not only distinguish deprogramming from exit counseling but also distinguish varieties of exit counseling. As noted above exit counseling is distinguished from deprogramming by the lack of force and all that it entails. Exit counseling approaches differ among themselves according to the degree to which they seek to *effect* change, versus *invite* change, and the degree to which they rely on the deliberate use of *technique,* that is, "finesse," vs. the degree to which they rely on *information.* Our approach differs from others in that we believe that the exit counselor's approach ought to be to invite change by sharing information, rather than to effect change through the skillful use of technique.

The word *ought* in the preceding sentence was chosen deliberately. Our concerns result from ethical judgments, not judgments about the efficacy of approaches that stress effecting change. We do not claim that our approach is more effective. No scientific data exist to support the efficacy of one form of exit counseling compared to another.

Nor do we suggest that other approaches are unethical. In some respects, however, approaches emphasizing the effecting of change do trouble us.

Our disagreement with change-oriented approaches parallels disagreements among Christians who have examined the ethics of evangelization. In a special issue of the *Cultic Studies Journal* devoted to this subject ("Cults, Evangelicals," 1985), all contributors agreed that ethical considerations should restrain social influence, regardless of its efficacy—that is, the end does not justify the means. They disagreed, however, on where the ethical boundary should be drawn. Mark McCloskey of Campus Crusade emphasized persuasion: "The Christian communicator, then, is an unashamed and conscientious persuader—unashamed because of the good news of our message and conscientious because of the urgency of our message" (1985, p. 308).

Father James LeBar (1985), on the other hand, emphasized "invitation," rather than "persuasion," as did Rev. A. Duane Litfin of Dallas Seminary: "As the appointed messenger he [the preacher] is responsible for seeing that all hear and that, to the best of his ability, all understand. But the response of the hearers is not the messenger's affair. He is not called upon to persuade the hearers to respond" (1985, p. 272).

Because cultists have been victimized by groups that rely on high-pressure persuasion, we feel that, although exit counselors cannot absolutely avoid persuasive communications, they should not center the exit counseling on persuasion. The exit counselors should not feel obligated to "effect change." Nor, as a consequence, should they feel obligated to master the skills of persuasive communication in order to achieve the requisite "finesse" to effect change. Exit counselors should focus on presenting pertinent information in a way that makes it comprehensible to the cultist. Being honest human beings they should not, and cannot, hide their preference—that the cultist decide to leave the group. However, their preference should be communicated as an open invitation, rather than function as a hidden agenda.

Hassan is the most prominent exit counselor with whose approach we disagree in some ways. Calling his approach "strategic intervention therapy," Hassan (1988) stresses that, although he too tries to communicate a body of information to cultists and to help them think independently, he also does formal counseling: "For me, encouraging the person to think for himself was paramount and that I was careful not to impose my own belief system on a client. My role was to present information, to do individual and family counseling as needed, and to facilitate family communication" (p. 115). He further states that his approach focuses "on the process of change" (p. 123), is family-centered, and rests on four core beliefs about people: (1) "people need and want to grow," (2) "people focus on the here and now," (3) "people will always choose what they think is best for them at any given time," and (4) "everyone is unique and every situation is different" (pp. 121–122).

These four core beliefs are vague and rather standard fare for counseling approaches within the field of humanistic psychology. As with many humanistic counseling approaches, Hassan's runs the risk of imposing clarity, however subtly, on the framework's foundational ambiguity and thereby manipulating the client. Hassan says: "My approach depends on having faith that deep, deep down even the most committed member of a mind control group wants out" (1988, p. 122). This assumption may be true. But it also implies that the counselor knows better than the cultist what the latter *really* wants—which also may be true. If not extremely careful, however, the counselor may in fact manipulate the cultist from point A ("I'll talk to you because my family requested it") to point B ("I want to leave the cult") while mistakenly believing that he or she is helping the cultist "grow" by effecting the changes that the cultist really wants deep, deep down. The ethical propriety of such manipulation is made even more dubious by the fact that the cultist has not *sought out* the exit counselor's assistance.

In information-focused exit counseling, we tell cultists that our goal is to share information and that our methods will include discussion, videos, and the examination of written documents. We intentionally avoid the use of counseling techniques designed to change the person's behavior because doing so entails pursuing an unstated goal to which the client has not given his or her approval. Whatever techniques we use are educational, designed to enhance the communication of information, not to change behavior.

Some might argue that our ethical restraints decrease the probability of getting the cultist out. This may be true, although our experience indicates otherwise and no scientific evidence exists that would argue one way or the other. But even if there were such evidence, we could not in good conscience *invite* cultists to return to a free society while violating one of its central tenets: that the end does not justify the means.

Hassan (personal communication with M. Langone, December 17, 1992) says that our critique exaggerates the manipulativeness of his approach. He is aware of the danger of manipulation in strategic intervention therapy, or in any therapeutic approach for that matter, and tries to minimize this danger by taking a step-by-step approach to helping the cultist "grow." Instead of trying to move the cultist from point A to point B (a goal established by the counselor), Hassan tries first to identify the implicit goal the cultist has at point A (let us call this goal, "A.1"), then tries to help the person achieve this goal. He next identifies the next implicit goal (let us call this goal, "A.2"), counsels the cultist to achieve that goal. And so on. The cultist may or may not arrive at point B ("I want to leave the cult"). By staying focused only on the immediate present, Hassan can take a change-oriented approach to exit counseling without necessarily becoming blatantly manipulative. Furthermore, to the extent possible, he tries to structure the exit counseling as a family counseling situation so that the cultist's goals and needs are inextricably connected to the goals and needs of other family members. This will necessarily illuminate conflict areas, for example, the cultist's desire for his or her family's love and approval vs. the family's need for greater contact with the cultist. Working out these conflicts one at a time can lead the cultist farther and farther from the cult.

Despite these clarifications of Hassan's approach, we still have several concerns. First of all, Hassan's sensitivity to the potential for manipulation in his approach is not clearly communicated in his writings. We trust that this will be corrected in future writings. Second, exit counselors, would-be exit counselors, and mental health professionals who rely on Hassan's writings may not be sufficiently sensitive to the potential for manipulation. They may as a result depend more on effecting change than inviting change. Third, even when practiced in its most pure form, strategic intervention therapy is still overly intrusive. As Ofshe and Singer point out (1986), cults manipulate central elements of cultists' selves. Respecting the magnitude and pain of this "mind rape" requires, in our view, that exit counselors lean very heavily on the side of inviting, rather than effecting, change. Fourth, subordinating the exit counseling to a family counseling structure is usually not necessary for a successful exit counseling.

It is quite possible, however, that due to a self-selection process families who think they need a family counseling approach may be inclined to engage Hassan's services, while families who are not as interested in a family counseling approach may seek out information-focused exit counselors. To the extent families are making informed decisions—and it is the responsibility of all exit counselors to help families make informed decisions—the existence of different approaches to exit counseling is a plus for "consumers" because they have more choices.

We have been able to critique Hassan in such detail because he has written so clearly about his approach, for which we commend him. There is another change-focused approach to exit counseling that also troubles us in certain respects, but about which very little has been written. This approach seeks not only to *effect* changes that bring cultists out of their cults but that also lead them toward a particular theological perspective or faith. Again, the distinction between "invitation" and "persuasion" is central, and again we come down on the side of "invitation."

Most of the information on which our concerns are based is anecdotal and unconfirmed. Therefore, we do not want to criticize anyone in particular. We would rather that our critique be used as a framework with which to evaluate certain approaches to exit counseling. We also want to make clear that these change-focused theological approaches can be Christian, Jewish, or even non-Western (several cultic groups, for example, have had programs aimed at helping people in cults, such as the Rajneesh group). We also want to stress that we are *not* criticizing evangelical ministries that focus on cultists (Enroth & Melton, 1985). Preaching the Gospel to cultists may sometimes result in their leaving their cults. Our concern is with persons who preach the Gospel (or push other theological agendas) in a manipulative way within the context of an exit counseling. We do not define exit counseling so broadly as to include any communications that may contribute to a person's deciding to leave a cult.

Admittedly, we are in a gray area. An evangelist may capture the interest of a cultist while talking on the street and may, as a hypothetical example, engage in a lengthy, intensive dialogue that might resemble the information-focused exit counseling described in this paper. In a similar way, a good Samaritan of any faith may begin talking to a suicidal person on a street and wind up doing something resembling what mental health professionals would call a "crisis intervention." However, neither the evangelist nor the good Samaritan has a professional relationship with the person on the street. Exit counselors do have professional relationships with their clients. This is a vital distinction because professional relationships have ethically grounded boundaries.

We believe that change-focused exit counselings with theological agendas are inappropriate because they contradict the assumption on which all exit counseling rests, that is, informed consent. A cultist who has followed a group for several years, for example, is asked to give the exit counselor several days to examine information that may affect his or her evaluation of the group in question. The family's appeal is that the cultist make an *informed* evaluation. How can an exit counselor advocate the vital importance of informed decisions and simultaneously suggest that the cultist move from one religious perspective (however cultic) to another (however traditional) on the basis of what may be no more than a few hours or at most a few days of discussion? This rhetorical question becomes even more pointed when one considers that most cultists remain psychologically vulnerable and suggestible for some time after leaving their groups. Cultists are accustomed to letting authority figures make major life decisions for them. Exit counselors, if they are to remain ethical, must not exploit this vulnerability by implicitly taking the place of cult authority figures and manipulating the cultist – however subtly – to follow such and such a faith.

Some have criticized information-focused exit counselors because the information they share may contribute to a person's renouncing a cult, without embracing another religious belief system. This is a valid criticism, but it overlooks the vital fact that exit counseling, as a professional relationship, has boundaries. Exit counseling focuses on helping cultists make informed decisions regarding their relationship to a cult. It may also address their relationship to God when the cult has exploited, obscured, or distorted this relationship. This is not to say that cultists' relationship to God is unimportant. On the contrary, resolving spiritual issues is the most difficult and important task for many, if not most, former cultists. The depth and importance of this spiritual need, however, demands extensive study, dialogue, contemplation, and deliberation. It would be arrogantly simplistic for exit counselors to claim that in a few days they can help a cultist make an informed evaluation of a cult involvement *and* make an informed decision about post-cult religious commitments. Resolving these spiritual issues is part of the *recovery* process, not exit counseling. Clergy – especially pastoral counselors – could be the primary helpers for former cultists grappling with spiritual issues.

Similarly, substantial psychological change also takes time and effort. An exit counseling does not cause substantial psychological change. It merely provides information that is a catalyst for change, that *awakens* cultists, who are then able to make genuine choices originating from within rather than without. A reliance upon psychological "techniques" in exit counseling may ultimately make it more difficult for cultists to determine whether or not the choices they made in the exit counseling were indeed theirs, rather than the exit counselor's.

CLOSING COMMENT

Information, especially that related to mind control, is the key that unlocks cultists' minds. Exit counseling as we conceive it is merely the means by which that information is made available. Exit counselors are not psychological alchemists. Nor are they spiritual wonderworkers. They are simply human beings sharing what they know with other human beings.

REFERENCES

Addis, M., Schulman-Miller, J., & Lightman, M. (1984, November). The cult clinic helps families in crisis. *Social Casework: The Journal of Contemporary Social Work,* 515–522.

Cults, evangelicals, and the ethics of social influence. (1985). [Special issue]. *Cultic Studies Journal, 2*(2).

Dubrow-Eichel, S. (1989). Deprogramming: A case study. *Cultic Studies Journal, 5,* 177–192.

Enroth, R., & Melton, J. G. (1985). *Why cults succeed where the church fails.* Elgin, IL: Brethren Press.

Giambalvo, C. (1992). *Exit counseling: A family intervention.* Bonita Springs, FL: American Family Foundation.

Hassan, S. (1988). *Combatting cult mind control.* Rochester, VT: Park Street Press.

Hassan, S. (1991). Strategic intervention therapy: A new form of exit-counseling which is better than deprogramming. Unpublished paper.

Langone, M. D. (1983). *Family cult questionnaire: Guidelines for professionals.* Weston, MA: American Family Foundation.

Langone, M. D. (1984). Deprogramming: An analysis of parental questionnaires. *Cultic Studies Journal, 1,* 63–78.

Langone, M. D. (1985). Cult involvement: Suggestions for concerned parents and professionals. *Cultic Studies Journal, 2,* 148–169.

Langone, M. D. (1990). Working with cult-affected families. *Psychiatric Annals, 20,* 194–198.

Langone, M. D., & Martin, P. (Winter, 1993). Deprogramming, exit counseling, and ethics: Clarifying the confusion. *Christian Research Journal,* 46–47.

LeBar, J. (1985). Evangelization and freedom in the Catholic Church. *Cultic Studies Journal, 2*(2), 340–347.

Litfin, A. D. (1985). The perils of persuasive preaching. *Cultic Studies Journal, 2*(2), 267–273.

Markowitz, A. (1989). A cult hotline and clinic. *Journal of Jewish Communal Service, 66*(1), 56–61.

McCloskey, M. (1985). What is evangelism. *Cultic Studies Journal,* 2(2), 308.
Ofshe, R., & Singer, M. T. (1986). Attacks on peripheral versus central ele-
    ments of self and the impact of thought reforming techniques. *Cultic Stud-
    ies Journal, 3,* 3-24.
Ross, J. C., & Langone, M. D. (1988). *Cults: What parents should know.* New
    York: Lyle Stuart.
Singer, M. T., Temerlin, M. K., & Langone, M. D. (1990). Psychotherapy cults.
    Cultic Studies Journal, 7, 101-125.

9

THE IMPORTANCE OF INFORMATION IN PREPARING FOR EXIT COUNSELING: A CASE STUDY

Kevin Garvey

THE SUCCESS OF AN EXIT COUNSELING is directly related to the quality of available information and the effectiveness with which that information is applied to the case in question. Equally relevant to the eventual recovery process is for the cultist to understand the environment in which he or she existed. In the early years of exit counseling, most interventions involved a small number of well-known groups. There was a surplus of reliable, well-documented information about those groups, and there were ex-members able and willing to lend their expertise. For the most active groups today, this situation still holds. In recent years, however, hitherto unknown cults, sects, and training systems have proliferated to such an extent that even the most experienced exit counselors are challenged and sometimes stymied. Too often distraught relatives with little understanding of how vital information is to the exit counseling process ask exit counselors to deal with a cultic system about which little or even nothing is known. This chapter outlines an esoteric, idiosyncratic, little-known group. As more and more such groups are appearing today, there is a greater need for exit counselors to gather information in order to learn about them.

Although an initial lack of information makes the exit counselor's task more difficult, it is not necessarily an unresolvable problem. This optimistic assertion is mainly due to the fact that the proliferation of groups is not a random process. In many cases cultic groups will have intellectual and sometimes even personnel connections with other groups. This occurs because, for example, an "entrepreneurial" follower of one group sets out to create his or her own group. Cults with similar dynamics and characteristics also tend to fall into certain categories. For example, destructive fringe Christian groups are very similar, even though the specifics of their "theologies" may differ. Ostensible reliance on the Bible at least gives these groups a common language, however much they may interpolate their own neologisms and distort the Bible text. The cultic fringe of the New Age movement (which includes most psychotherapy cults) on the surface is much more heterogeneous and fluid. Because there is no single "book" upon which all New Agers rely, their "theologies" or philosophical bases are as unbounded as the human imagination. In exit counseling situations with New Age groups, therefore, acquiring information is often much more important and difficult than is the case with Bible groups. Nevertheless, connections between groups and common themes among New Age groups reduce the exit counseling burden.

An important dynamic common to New Age groups is the exploitation of personal anxieties that have been made more painful and persistent by a strained social environment. The connection between a fragile social environment, personal anxieties, and the growing New Age movement is perhaps most clearly reflected in the well-publicized attitudes and beliefs about the approaching millennium. Several years ago a surprising number of journalists trumpeted the Harmonic Convergence, a New Age event which focused on the rare circumstance of three planets situated in the same sign of the Zodiac. This incident of contrived mysticism composed of abandoned traditions, pseudoscience, and manufactured scholarship was ballyhooed as the advent of profound cosmic changes, expected to culminate in the year 2001, 2010, or whatever year is designated by a person's philosophical calendar of choice. The attention that supporters of this bizarre event procured and the alacrity with which literally millions grasped at these straws-in-the-wind underline the degree of vulnerability in our culture. In our society's eagerness to disconnect from the past, we have lost touch with traditions that have mercifully relieved millions of individuals of the spiritual, moral, and physical suffering that too often accompanies and punctuates life. We are also too willing to discard the accumulated practical wisdom earned by our ancestors.

There is a disturbing, emotionally charged component to the vulnerability of such people. Their spiritual anxiety, exacerbated by the pace and complexity of modern life, leads to an immediate pursuit of "meaning," rather than a prolonged effort at moral evaluation. The resulting internal paralysis produces a fear of further searching. Having lost the motivation for intellectual effort, these anxious and weary seekers cross an internal threshold, where the New Age version of the supernatural beckons. The essence of the New Age vision that captivates these seekers is that meaning is not cognitive; it is primarily an emotional experience; it is not necessary to be logical, rational, or even reasonable. The ultimately dominant criterion of what is good is a totally subjective feeling state. The goal of life becomes a good feeling, a never-ending "high."

What is not made clear to New Age recruits, however, is the degree to which spiritual and psychological hucksters can manipulate the feelings of their vulnerable targets. The New Age movement, with its wide array of programs for rationalizing personal and social problems, is a spawning ground for such hucksters. They appear armed with a dazzling melange of psychological techniques refined over decades of experimentation, contrived myths, and seductive appeals to a person's most sublime yearnings. The silliness of much of what is offered does not offset the dangerous behaviors that lead too many New Agers into tragedy. These tragedies, whether immediate, such as suicide, or prolonged, such as madness, are disturbingly intrinsic to the New Age's bizarre fringe. Because new groups with shifting emphases are constantly emerging within this fringe, the roots of this phenomenon are obscured and the tragedies produced by the techniques and pursuits of this fringe are increasingly difficult to prevent and treat.

My colleagues and I have recently conducted 15 exit counselings with clients who adhered to one or another of the various manifestations of this New Age eruption of bizarre groups. We have encountered groups that preach that their members are transplanted space spirits; others that follow channeled entities from Atlantis, Lemuria, and other "manifested space/time equivalencies," several of which believe that their sacred copulations are producing a new Angelic Species; and, frighteningly, three recently emergent groups plainly engaged in criminal activities. These latter were mainly drug-related, although two of these groups also had ties to call-girl operations and one was suspected of selling youths into slavery. Exit counselings involving such groups obviously entail the risk of legal entanglements, physical danger, and unfortunately a greater potential for failure. These risks produce a demand for greater-than-average discretion and diligence in the information-collection phase that precedes the exit counseling proper. The following illustrative case study describes this vital process of information collection. The case is inspired by the 15 cases alluded to earlier and is a composite derived from four of those cases.

Each facet of the composite case is derived from events and themes of real cases.

Using a composite protects the confidentiality of those with whom we have worked, allows for a discussion of a greater variety of issues, and permits a truly inclusive discussion of the tools exit counselors regularly employ. Because the composite case depicts the extremes with which exit counselors might have to contend, it will, I hope, give the reader an acute appreciation of the importance of information in cult cases, even certain information that may at first inspection seem mundane. Developing such an appreciation is important for anyone helping ex-cultists deal with recovery issues, for ex-cultists can be relieved of a great deal of unnecessary and unwarranted self-blame by coming to understand how the cult manipulated and exploited them.

Although this case may at first glance appear incredible, I wish to stress that nothing is exaggerated. Unfortunately, extremes are not rare within the world of cults. And in our work we must remember that what is bizarre to one person may be a cherished belief to another. It is, however, the ethics of persuasion used in the inculcation of those beliefs that is addressed here and throughout this book.

THE INITIAL CALL
FROM THE FAMILY

The initial call from the family was deceptively typical; hence, it proved to be typically misleading. As is often the case, we heard a simple tale with simple details; as with many cases, the initial story is direct, and details often sound alike. We have learned over the years not to take the family's recounting at face value.

We were told that the family's 23-year-old daughter had disappeared from graduate school without warning, without leaving traces of her whereabouts. One year later she called her parents (collect) to demand her inheritance. Her perfunctory style of speech contradicted her claims that she was happy and increasingly spiritual and that her parents should be proud. She had, she now ebulliently informed them, "demonstrated her worthiness" by giving birth to a "Boy Child." She needed her inheritance because she was now going to Hawaii to be prepared for her next sacred copulation. This, she breathlessly confided, would produce the Girl Child. She went on to state that these children, conceived by disincarnate beings from the region of the Southern Cross constellation, were the first Earth Plane Manifestations of a new evolutionary species. They were, she further blurted out, the psychic Adam and Eve, "sort of a reincarnation of the ancient pharoanic pairings," which "we know protected the earlier descent of the spiritualized DNA." The same phenomenon, she insisted, "produced the Hawaiian royalty conceived by Polynesian nobility via marriages of brothers and sisters." This was, she added, "how the earlier and enlightened societies joined in the creative work of the Bisexual Deities."

As the parents tried to assimilate all this, they heard a muffled voice tell their daughter to "quiet down" and "get the money." At this command their daughter's breathless enthusiasm disappeared, her voice suddenly grew cold, barely recognizable; her last statement was a direct command to her parents to send her money to a specific post office box number.

The family found that the box number was merely an overseas mail drop for a numbered bank account. The number from which the collect call originated led to a pay phone in a parking lot in the Midwest. The mention of Hawaii led nowhere. The family retained investigators who learned that Hawaii is a focal point of bizarre cults; yet, they found no record of the young woman having been there, nor could they identify any group pursuing the imaginative practices she described.

For a year the family restricted their efforts to this type of general investigation. Their reasons were based on a combination of fear for their daughter, a reluctance to face having this problem bantered about by friends and acquaintances, and an understandable ignorance of where to turn for experienced assistance. A business acquaintance of the father's confided to him that he had recently had a son "exit counseled" out of a well-known, commercial training system. The description appeared to echo the father's situation, which inspired him to open up to his acquaintance. Because of this conversation, the family contacted me.

After listening to the family's initial description of what had transpired, my first request was for a personal meeting. It was carefully explained that this meeting would focus on introducing ourselves to one another, the family members and me and my team of exit counselors. The complexity of the situation was apparent to all; it was readily agreed that the issues of comfort with each other, combined with the family's need for confidence in our reasonableness, knowledge, sensitivity, experience, and discretion could only be explored in such a face-to-face setting. We wanted to find out if there were undercurrents within the family structure that needed open discussion.

A good portion of this initial meeting was spent giving the family a presentation on cults, on our approach to exit counseling, and on the New Age itself. This included an educationally oriented discussion of a variety of hypnotic-induction techniques often found in cults and the related emotional and intellectual dissociation often produced by cult practices. These educational methods reveal our counseling style and are helpful in identifying and explaining the impact produced by a cult's techniques.

We pointed out that the ideas the daughter espoused, combined with the practices mentioned, placed this group into a specific category. With more information we hoped to discover the connection between the contents the group taught and the psychological control techniques they used to produce compliance with whatever actions members were led to carry out.

We ended on the theme that the family should take time to privately assess us before formally engaging our services, and that we would assess whether we felt we could be of further service to the family.

PHASE ONE:
PERSONAL SOURCES
OF INFORMATION

After a few days we reached a formal arrangement with the family and began an intensive study of the situation. First, we wanted to expand the information we received at the initial meeting and prepared a questionnaire that each family member completed. Such a questionnaire is important, especially when the person to be counseled is in a new or unusual cult. The family's answers invariably reveal aspects of the cultist's background that subsequently prove to be crucial leads into the group's appeal and tactics. Later discussions stimulate memories the family had not thought pertinent, instill an expanded understanding of the cult's processes, reveal who in the family is emotionally close to the prospective counselee and who understands the person, and help to identify the next level of contacts and leads.

We often ask to talk with persons outside the immediate family to learn possible details the family may not know. This involves consent and introductions by the family to doctors, clergy, teachers, friends, and acquaintances of the cultist. It is important to work with the family and rely upon their instincts about who should be approached. From a small pool of helpful people we learned details the family had not known, some of which were decidedly unpleasant.

The daughter's college years were punctuated by a painful romance, a prolonged bout of promiscuous sexuality, and a drug dalliance. She had an abortion during her junior year, which precipitated an extreme moral crisis.

The family told us that they had been concerned about their daughter's tendency toward religious zealotry and that they had, when the daughter was 17, taken steps to curtail her religious interests, an action that probably deterred the young woman from finding comfort and guidance in her religious traditions.

College friends reported that during the summer prior to her senior year she became acquainted with a young, wealthy, and exotic set of New Age practitioners who used peyote and (the laboratory-designed drug) Ecstasy. Her friends reported that after this brief drug use she sought help from a local drug clinic that was well-thought-of by the college's counseling center.

This summary does not convey the many hours it took to collect background information. The family encouraged us to pursue our instincts and supported each request for additional time and effort.

PHASE TWO:
FURTHER INFORMATION
COLLECTION

The identification of the drug clinic opened many avenues. A young relative was a recovered addict who knew the addictive-services world and maintained a healthy concern about the way this field was being influenced by disastrous programs run by cults. He knew of people lost to cults because they thought a cult recruitment program really was what it claimed to be—that is, an addiction service.

With his help we learned about the clinic's counseling approach, which was decidedly "spiritual" and emphasized a set of techniques we recognized as potent guided-imagery exercises. These intrinsically hypnotic inductions were used for two purposes. They ostensibly guided the person back through a sequence of painful memories. They would also, it was claimed, facilitate the person's contact with his or her "spiritual center." By practicing these techniques, the addict was told that he or she would be armed against the emotional and psychological storms that kept the person from spirituality and love. It was, the clinic claimed, these storms that blocked the person's center and caused the pain the addict fled from by using the drugs.

The clinic's literature advertised that each administrator and counselor was a trained practitioner of Neuro-Linguistic Programming, which meant that each was trained in certain techniques of hypnotic induction. Neuro-Linguistic Programming (NLP) was cited by the National Research Council's study (Druckman & Swets, 1988) as a "system for modeling a person's behavior and thought processes in relation to a specific topic or behavior" (p. 140). This is why NLP has been adopted by even benevolently inclined clinics. It's a tool for generating change for change's sake. We knew that NLP is also used by some very aggressive cults because the NLP method can be used by such groups to instill a reliance upon the cult, and provides a conditioning method to further induce compliance.

The clinic's literature included copious instructions for implementing the guided-imagery exercises. While in a trance state, the person is encouraged to "Float above your time line and drift comfortably into your past. Choose an incident and get the emotions that are there. Float back to the time line and go 10 minutes in front of the incident. Now glance forward to NOW. Do the feelings disappear? Did the choice you made disappear? Is the incident's memory now flat?" (Note: These and other quotes describing the guided-imagery technique paraphrase instructional literature from an actual clinic involved in one of our cases.) The significance of this exercise was pointed out at the bottom of the clinic's instruction sheet, which said that if the emotions stemming from the original incident do not disappear, then simply "reframe" the memory. This means telling yourself that it is "okay to let the emotions go and to let the memory disappear." This reliance on "disappearance" is a form of manufactured amnesia found in several of the most well-known New Age systems.

The recovering addict is told to "Program your future by *creating memories* for your future Time Line." You are, in other words, going to get healthy by cooperating in your personal flight from reality! This is another technique often found in major destructive cults. This information also revealed a major overlap between the clinic's methods and participants' subsequent susceptibility to a more direct cult involvement.

We had to acknowledge that this literature did not provide total insight into our case's evolution, but it gave us important guidelines. Our analysis satisfied us that the clinic's administrators had been exposed to well-known cult practices via this New Age thinking and methodology. The cited material, for example, is an almost word-for-word quotation of training criteria devised by a large international group and sold in their bookstores. In addition to the already-cited methods, the material also parallels elements of the original est training. In each case where these methods and beliefs are used, a discernible pattern exists; these and other themes and beliefs pervade the New Age world, which was the dominant ambiance of the clinic.

The guided-imagery, or trance, exercise allegedly moves the person into a state where reflective reasoning decreases, sensory responses fade, and the person becomes more suggestible and acquiescent. Thus, the person develops a marked tendency to accept what he or she is being told as the product of his or her own mental process. Such a state renders the person highly vulnerable to manipulation. If the suggestions include the admonition to "live by" the implanted ideas, the person will have the urge to do so. This urge to assent to the implanted ideas is normally accompanied by instructions implying a great sense of unease should the ideas be resisted.

The technique of guided imagery is a potent tool. It can turn a person's response to stress and anxiety into a control device. The leaders of the program and the subject together identify what prove to be stress-laden thoughts and activities for that person and counter the stress by focusing on soothing images. Through repeated practice, conditioning comes into play in that the stressful sensation or idea prompts a desire to return to the solace of the trance state brought on by the guided imagery. The individual is now locked into a prescribed, noncognitive, noncritical response pattern, not only *not* of the person's choosing but also beyond his or her immediate understanding.

First learning about the clinic's use of guided imagery from the literature and later learning about the group's use of these techniques from ex-members answered many of our questions about the young woman's vulnerability. These methods do not merely serve as a one-time treatment. They are intended to be used repeatedly whenever the person encounters anxiety-producing situations. In other words, the methods are to be practiced; when practiced, they become conditioning procedures. Each time one is used, the person sacrifices another piece of emotional resilience, avoiding another opportunity to examine a perhaps painful but important incident. As the influence accumulates, the person becomes less and less willing to examine the roots of anxiety — and more and more dependent on the cultivated ability to return to a learned "dissociative" state, a term often used by mental health professionals to describe the effects of such practices. This sequence of acts leads a person to accept the product of imagination as equal to the product of judgment.

Our experiences with and observations of hundreds of other New Age participants verify that in order to accept the new cosmic, philosophical, and psychological concepts demanded by a cult, such mind-altering techniques are required. If an individual's previous support systems have been entwined with painful incidents and thus proved deficient in that person's eyes (as was the case with this young woman), he or she can be led to increasingly accept these New Age concepts. Often the result is someone who is eager for almost any transcendent, or "transformational," ideology.

We were informed that the clinic itself espoused several New Age ideologies, some derived from existing cults. Staff members' personality characteristics, background experiences, behavior in the parent cult, and adherence to specific ideologies contributed to our picture of how the young woman had crossed the threshold into the cult.

PHASE THREE:
FORMER CULT MEMBERS
AS INFORMATION SOURCES

A major door opened when the parents received a call from a young man previously involved with the cult. When we met him, he was stable, free of the cult's dominance, and concerned about those still involved. From him we learned more about the group's sophistication, energy, criminality, and violence-oriented ideology. This former member was privy to most of the leader's business plans but was not a great source of information about the group's indoctrination techniques. His lengthy absences from the group when sent out to conduct business for the leader prevented him from giving us a good picture of day-to-day activities, and his exposure to our client's daughter was limited.

He explained why the woman's phone call apparently emanated from a Midwest parking lot when she was actually somewhere in Latin America. The group used modified cellular phones and switching mechanisms to re-route incoming and outgoing phone calls, making it impossible to trace a call to its actual point of origin. This is an increasingly common cult practice.

The ex-member gave us a sketchy description of the group's mythological belief structure. It was a hybrid system concocted out of the top members' former cult experiences, the leader's experience and study, the leader's psychopathologies, and a large dose of sheer criminal ambition. Its main points reflected an artful reworking of ancient Aztec, generic New Age, and ancient Hawaiian concepts and rituals. The participants saw themselves as an elite corps chosen by "highly evolved spirits" to be the agents for the creation of a superspecies. This honor could, of course, be withdrawn by the leader. A member's worthiness was based on his or her adherence to criteria set by the leader. Fear of "withdrawal" was the base of his power. In sum, he availed himself of the services of a totally dedicated crew of personal pawns: members fulfilled his fantasies and functioned as operatives in his international "business."

Even though our informant knew much about the group's antecedents, history, and intentions, there was also much he could not tell us. He knew only that the leader's villa headquarters was in a Latin country. But he had never been to the villa.

The ex-member's outline of the group's ideology did not allow us insight into the relationship between the indoctrination, the theoretical content of the system, and the applied results. Without this vital area of insight we could not formulate an exit counseling strategy. We needed better knowledge, better understanding of the effect the system had on our client's daughter.

We knew little about the cult's public demeanor and its internal style. The scope of its "business" also remained a mystery. Eventually through friends in the overseas country we learned that local citizens feared the inhabitants of the villa. There were rumors that the villa was a drug center, that its owner (the leader) was a black magician, that many federal "political types" were observed around the villa at strange hours. These informants said it was known locally that the American women from the villa artfully worked the area as call girls. Our prospective counselee was, in fact, among the most artful at choosing well-heeled vacationers. Her routine was to spend time with them, invite them to the villa, and there, often with their wives, they would be compromised.

The ex-member's story had convinced us that this group was far too sophisticated to be a simple, deranged cult. It was too complicated, actively involved in many business arrangements in dangerous fields, and brazen about its activities. The group went about its activities as though it were protected.

The family retained a corporate security firm to unravel the business trails. Within a few weeks we received information about the leader's financial history, the group's banking transactions, transactions with verified criminal organizations, and transactions that appeared to be with companies that were fronts for other interests.

Other ex-members were found who reported that the group's top six leaders were formerly involved in groups that various of our team members had also once embraced—est, Transcendental Meditation, Scientology, Ramtha, and Neuro-Linguistic Programming. The two female cult leaders were into an Earth Goddess worship that did not appear too exotic; in fact, it explained elements of the fertility rituals that the young woman referred to when she called her family. The leader was the fulcrum as well as the lever of this cult's existence. He was the Savior, but he was also the Satan who could whimsically deal out pain.

The security firm's expertise and contacts further uncovered a trail of convoluted business deals, murky bank transfers, a list of creditors and tales of drug-related violence. The leader was also the subject of rumors about his penchant for ritualized sexual tableaux, a man with a long history of cult affiliations, a mercurial and violent temperament, and a host of former acquaintances from whom he had stolen money, respect, and reputation. He had more enemies than friends.

He was in his late thirties, normally used a European passport, held a degree in finance from one university, had studied comparative religion at another university, and had an extensive New Age résumé. He had been in a theosophical school, was well acquainted with Maori myths and practices, had studied hypnotherapy and Silva Mind Control, and had spent time with an overseas Gurdjieff community. He purports to have taken est training, to have become an NLP practitioner, and to have immersed himself in Aztec lore.

Further, ex-members warned us that the leader "was very charismatic, very powerful!" A reflection of this power was the way he took control of the original group. Although he had not founded the group, its progenitors – two married couples – instantaneously fell under his spell. They readily adopted his system, eagerly adapted themselves to his polymorphous tastes, and never questioned his methods for raising money. Drug trade, prostitution, and blackmail became mere "manifestations of highly evolved entities," as these former members described it. (Note: This reference is from the personal notes of a member of one of the fully evolved cults used for this composite.) Just as the group expanded, these so-called manifestations also evolved!

We learned that our prospective counselee had traveled widely in Latin America. Each trip was paid for by a separate corporate entity, some tied to the leader, some obviously his customers. The pattern suggested the young woman's role as a possible financial courier, a liaison agent, a sexual favor, or all of the above.

At this point we were still unaware of the techniques used to ensure the leader's control while his agents were away from the headquarters. Finally, the internal control devices were made known to us through personal notes provided by another ex-member, who stated that the leader chose his pawns well. Once his drug interests led him to the crew running the drug clinic, he instinctively recognized that the clinic's guided-imagery exercises were a godsend! The leader appeared to recognize the origins of these methods, and knew how to use their spiritual implications to alter a person's ethical base.

The clinic placed a large emphasis on personal "affirmations," which are positive slogans a person is trained to say after entering a relaxed state. "I am the source of my love," "I am the positive force," "Only I control my inner space" are examples of the clinic's format. (Note: Again these references are from the personal notes of a former member of one of the cults used for this composite.) When repeatedly practiced by a person plagued with self-recrimination, such phrases possess a conditioning effect — as do the guided-imagery exercises with which they were paired — and contribute to the decline of critical judgment. Persons appear to adopt the positive message and lose the capacity to reflect upon its implications. Affirmations were to be repeated when a cult member felt even mildly anxious.

The ex-member's notes described the control system the leader used on her. During private sessions he simultaneously praised her spiritual progress, sexually trained her, and castigated her for her retention of ethical doubts. To overcome such doubts he told her that her new life was one of sweet bliss ("cosmic innocence") and that any judgments she had about her actions were merely the last gasp of her former egotism. To overcome this trap she should perfect her "inner voice" via affirmations. Among those on her list were: "My body is a joyful lie." "All people are innocent." "Even the drug lords are innocently engaged." "My sex is a game of the spirit." "The General is an innocent." and "Death is the final innocence." (Note: This information was verbally provided by several ex-members of one of the fully evolved cults used for this composite.)

Our constantly expanding body of information forced another meeting with the family. Our information was drawing a portrait of a criminal group with far-reaching connections. The security investigators reported that there was a pattern of drug trading and money laundering, and possible arms sales to terrorist groups.

The cult's companies, named after mythical warrior gods, showed up on lists of companies suspected of dealing arms to Middle Eastern nations. What was also certain was that this type of operation was progressive: You kept growing or got out, and few got out on their terms. Those who worked for such people were expendable. If the situation heated up, our young would-be counselee might be beyond our reach: She might be dead.

This presented a terrible impasse for the family. If an attempt to reach her was made and failed, the young woman might be killed. If no attempt was made, the chances of serious harm striking her would

grow. A botched attempt would also endanger the family, the ex-
members, and the counseling team. The father asked for a few days to
sift through his dilemma. He preferred a unanimous choice among all
his family's members, which could not be properly pursued through
hasty phone calls. We readily agreed and waited out the family's decision.

A few days later the father called, presenting us with the family's
reasons for going ahead. He instructed us to proceed into our final
preparatory stage.

We were confident that we possessed an accurate account of the
young woman's odyssey from disaffected student to international call
girl, from a professed Christian to an amalgamated New Ager. We
also had an adequate picture of the group's outside operations and
were able to constantly update this information through contacts with
ex-members. The woman could not travel far without us knowing of
her plans. This was the tactical advantage that permitted the eventual
counseling.

PHASE FOUR:
DISSECTING THE CULT'S IDEOLOGY

Once the counseling started, its success would rest upon our grasp of
the leader's ideological system, its delivery, and its use as a control
device. We found an enormous amount of useful material; the following summarizes a section of what we eventually used.

The members of the original group, including the man who became
the ultimate leader, shared a common set of prior experiences: est,
Transcendental Meditation, Scientology, and Neuro-Linguistic Programming. Each teaches that the perceived world is an illusion, that
to think otherwise is a reflection of one's ego having succumbed to the
deceptions perpetuated by the world, and that their path is the right
way to a spiritual development that leads a person to freedom from
the material prison mistakenly regarded as your body.

Each of these groups says that your mind is an enemy and each
teaches techniques for escaping from the mind's grasp. With the exception of NLP, each espouses a mythology in which the group's leader is
elevated to cosmic importance, while the individual member is told
that the fulfillment of spirit is dependent upon sacrificing individual
personality and assuming the leader's essence. The founders of the
group we were investigating carried such conditioning with them when
they set up their original group. The leader merely fulfilled needs cre-

ated by prior experiences, but he still needed to make this group his own. He did so in an ingenious way.

He built upon the existing tendencies by first elevating one of the married women into an Earth Goddess figure. The "Mother" blessed any yearning, any personal inclination, as a benevolent expression of the universal, creative spirit. She also became the portal through which males were welcomed into the group, through an act of "Celestial Unseparation." This act, witnessed by the group, served several purposes. It removed sexual inhibitions, gave license for the absence of future restraint, and bonded the person to the group. It allowed the leader control without having to be heavy-handed. The person never thought he or she was being coerced. Once this threshold was crossed, additional controls were easier to impose.

The Mother's female acolytes, for example, quickly learned that serving as a "portal" was a great honor. This was an especially honorable act when the male happened to be tied to the "degenerative" realms of government, business, the underworld, the Church, and education. In this way prostitutes served the temple—never contemplating why the worshipping males they welcomed were always selected by the leader!

The leader established a liturgy that celebrated this and other activities. There was group praise for the acolytes, with a persistent demand for open discussion of any qualms. Those who did share doubts were physically chastised, immediately forgiven, and enveloped in acts of "sweet strokes." This pleasure-pain-pleasure sequence was effective in eradicating individual resistances. For those needing additional persuasion, the leader held private "spanky toon" sessions, a preadolescent title that belies the nature of these intense sadomasochistic rituals. The leader possessed an artful combination of charm and rage and an uncanny sense of how to arouse sensation and emotions in a staccato and confusing pattern, which he called the *wave of ego*. He identified this pain sensation as the world's unrelenting grip. In time, and with whatever number of sessions were required, a young woman learned to equate pain with pleasure, except for those states the leader permitted as pleasure. Women also learned to redirect spontaneous responses with a privately written set of affirmations. The practice of affirmations, which the leader adopted from the drug clinic, was the ultimate control device. (Note: The ex-members emphasized that this was the most confusing technique. Unraveling the apparently individualistic content from the technique's impact took many months of patient self-examination and diligent therapy.)

When a young woman was chosen for a specific role, the leader drew her into private sessions, which permitted him to identify her deepest traits, vulnerabilities, and needs. He would write her affirmations accordingly. In this way the woman believed she was special and actually the architect of her actions; in essence she remained an effective tool for her leader.

This leader individually imposed a group doctrine in a manner that closed the person off from the world. He also made it an internally consistent system, with a logic that could not be upset by anyone locked into it. The fulfillment of his systematic ambitions, however, required a final step. To generate the verification of his cosmic importance, which was restricted solely by the scope of his pathologies, he needed unlimited moral authority. His experience taught him that mere conditioning produced a person who was too capricious. The mind, he knew, had too much resilience; too many thoughts remained untouched by pure technique. He liked to refer to Hitler's propaganda chief, Joseph Goebbels. "Goebbels," the leader would frequently declare, "realized that Descartes was wrong. Descartes's maxim, *Cogito, ergo sum*, never engages the will. *Credo, ergo sum* is what people need: I believe, therefore I am!" As did Goebbels, this leader conjured up an ingenious belief.

When he took over the group, he carefully built upon the beliefs already held by the group's following. He wove the old beliefs into a contrived myth, which conveniently placed him at the center of each follower's conscious and unconscious thoughts. The original group's system started with the concept that all material things were the result of one malevolent act committed by two evil spirits who decided that male and female actually were two distinct essences. To enforce their view they tricked other spirits into thinking that matter – hence distinct objects and people – was real. This spawned such delusions as sexual appetite; concepts about love, hope, and compassion; and, of course, confusions about body-mind distinction.

The higher truth held that what was truly real – pure spiritual essence – was all one thing, was male *and* female, and incorporated within itself all things – objects, ideas, spirits. This truth could only be "known" by "passing the portal" from separateness to oneness. Whatever they willed, whatever whim they felt, whatever they did, was really the One's intention acted out through them. They were extensions of the One's pure essence! (Translation: Separateness [individuality] is illusion. Devotees function as an expanded unity of One [the leader]. Hence, amorality is justified.) Their task was to change the world from its delusion of separateness to an embrace of the One.

They could not be judged by the world's deficient standards. The original group saw itself as transcending any materially based and reasonably derived law. But they also lacked direction, lacked a leader. One day on a beach, he appeared.

The ex-members' accounts closely matched our collected documents. Their experiences also fell within the range of criteria we knew applied to cult indoctrination phenomena. The female ex-member's handwritten affirmations, although not a uniform code intended for all the group's women, did verify the mode the leader used with each woman. We now were confident that we had a solid picture of how this leader "transformed" his followers. The last step in our preparations involved taking what we knew and what we surmised and turning it into a foundation for a counseling strategy. This entailed moving from the general realm of the group to the specific person, our prospective counselee.

We needed to know, for example, what she believed she believed. This is not a mere play on words. The leader's system depended on his ability to get a person to accept certain ideas and attitudes. These, in turn, had the same effect as the clinic's affirmations. They prompted her assent to actions or they prevented actions. Once these "beliefs" were known, we would be able to identify the emotional and psychological stimuli that activated their power over her behavior and choices.

Our final hurdle proved to be former members' amazing memory blocks. Although individuals mentioned a pattern of capricious violence, no one could actually describe these patterns. Group discussions with ex-members apparently gave individual ex-members sufficient permission to slowly recall and reveal minute details of their experiences. By comparing what the others said with their own experiences, several of the women slowly began to grasp the significance of little actions and subtle comments made during private sessions with the leader. In an agonizingly deliberate process, in which each person voluntarily engaged, these ex-members groped their way toward increased understanding and, more importantly, toward increased memories. This discussion stimulated the healthier aspects of each person's intellectual and emotional resilience. From these ex-members' memories emerged facts, insights, and conceptual patterns, providing the counseling team with the tools it needed.

The ex-members' recollections filled the gaps in our knowledge of how the leader manipulated the preexisting reliance upon the affirmation technique. By adding content that aggravated a person's inner crises, the leader forced each person's inner "voice" to constantly refer to him. He became the subject of the inner voice's dialogue between the person's self and its own higher self. The next step was to use private sessions as the vehicle for inserting his persona as the One, the Higher Self, the sole authority. This was aided by his use of "spanky toons," which opened up an appetite for pain. Pain became a personal "portal" into deeper aspects of self.

By observing the dilemmas each ex-member experienced during these revelatory group sessions, we became aware of what our prospective counselee would face during a counseling. This prepared us for our job of assisting her through these crises. The ex-members were able to describe the focal point of what these crises would conjure up: Tlaceapele!

This mythical creation was the name of the leader's persona, a spirit who absorbed the leader and infused him with cosmic wisdom, the One's desires, and gave him his awesome powers. The power was invoked during the "spanky toon" sessions when the leader entered a state of barely restrained rage. What transpired was held in secrecy, with affirmations producing the necessary acquiescence. The participant was locked into a conditioned pattern that blocked any urge to question or reveal what took place. In other words, the young woman we hoped to meet with and counsel would no doubt have problems recalling these sessions, as was displayed by the group of ex-members. When challenged, she would retreat into a dissociative and amnestic state. The ability to thus retreat was the group's badge of loyalty and acceptance. She was totally accepted.

Our group sessions drew out detailed information sufficient to identify the myth's origin and intent. When the leader exerted his power over the initial group, he did so by convincing them that he was the reincarnation of an Aztec warrior-priest, Tlacaleal. This historic figure was the instigator of the vast human sacrifices that dominated the last period of Aztec power: Under Tlacaleal "the new cosmogony incorporated the belief that the very existence of the universe and mankind was dependent on the continuous provision of victims taken in war for sacrifice on the altars of the sun god" (Keen, 1971, p. 12). Tlacaleal, the leader claimed, was him, sent by the space spirits of the Southern Cross constellation. He was the One's sole representative on earth. When the Aztecs failed him by succumbing to the dark forces of Spanish Christianity, he was forced to preserve the secret of his being. He also had to release the spirits of his entourage so they could assist his work. To release the spirits he slit the throats of seven priests and four temple concubines. After exiting the bodies through the opened throats (so they would not be defiled by any dying utterance should they exit through the mouth), he and the spirits went to the pristine setting of Hawaii.

Hawaiian priests and deities were now the vehicle; Hawaiian rituals the norm. It was during this sojourn in Paradise that the goddess Pele was married to Tlacaleal. Once she had "passed the portal," she no longer had a separate essence. She was now returned to the One. In this way the group's prime myth created the androgynous god, Tlaceapele. This myth also conveniently provided the model for each female's "passing of the portal" during the tortured sexual rituals.

The myth carries the obligation for cosmic successes into the present. The leader firmly implants the idea of slit throats during his private sessions. A hint of this rite punctuates the group liturgies. These suggestions jointly enforce the hypnotic-like commands for unyielding obedience and personal dedication. Our prospective counselee would carry all this into a counseling session and would be prone to even violent action to preserve her part of the secret.

This myth explained the moves the group made between Latin America and Hawaii. (It also provided a magnificent cover story should any of the leader's minions get caught by authorities. The story is so bizarre that any who revealed it would be grist for psychiatric diagnosis.) When combined with the other facts obtained through our research, the young woman's story was illuminated.

Her "passing the portal" exercises elevated her to the status of suitable concubine for Sacred Copulations. We now saw the pattern. Her first child represented the Aztec side of the myth. The next child was meant to represent the Hawaiian. The subsequent marriage of these siblings would consummate the celestial union of Tlacaleal and Pele. The myth would be reenacted in reality. In this way "the ancient of most ancient religions" would be restored, and the seed of her sacred copulations would repopulate the heavens.

The information we gathered enhanced our understanding of the generic New Age control systems that the leader employed. It gave us accurate criteria for what proved to be her trigger points. The information gathered from many sources gave us the means to isolate her from the leader, approach her, and elicit an agreement to discuss her situation. It was a successful counseling.

This chapter cannot fully explain all the issues confronted by the family and the team. Nor is this chapter an appropriate place to expand on all the concerns related to the exit counseling process. It is hoped, however, that this account demonstrates the value of extensive probing into a cult's ideas as well as its practices. For only when the ideas are known can the scope of the influence truly be known.

It has been four years since the counselings used in this composite took place. The counselees whose experiences are reflected are totally free of the groups. Each is living a life based upon a realistic acceptance of limits and obligations as well as possibilities. The young woman is in graduate school. Her son is with his grandparents and looks forward to the day when he and his mother are living together. A recent letter from her wryly noted the accelerating attention being paid the approaching millennium. She observed that society has become more and more susceptible to force-fed myth as the increasingly complex information needed for daily existence comes more and more from impersonal and inanimate sources. It was ironic, she wrote, that as the New Age mania spreads, along with a resurgent appeal for spiritualized feminist religion, the most renowned female icon is . . . Madonna. Our former counselee's experiences — which make Madonna's persona appear quite nonthreatening — have forced her to conclude that for a society whose beliefs are severed from the logic that spawns those beliefs, the appropriate icon is not a pseudochristian mockery of Aphrodite. It is the one image that the blandly ebullient New Agers never want displayed . . . the Mater Dolorosa.

REFERENCES

Druckman, D., & Swets, J. A. (1988). *Enhancing human performance.* Washington, DC: National Academy Press.
Keen, B. (1971). *The Aztec image in western thought.* New Brunswick, NJ: Rutgers University Press.

Section III

FACILITATING RECOVERY

10

POST-CULT RECOVERY: ASSESSMENT AND REHABILITATION

Paul R. Martin, Ph.D.

IN THIS CHAPTER I DESCRIBE MY clinical observations concerning the problems former cultists encounter during the recovery process, discuss the assessment procedures I use at Wellspring Retreat and Resource Center, a residential rehabilitation center for former cultists, and briefly describe Wellspring's treatment program. Our experience has been mainly with members of fringe Christian groups, so my observations and recommendations may apply more to this group than to others.

MYTHS

First, however, I would like to discuss common myths surrounding the cultic experience (Martin, 1989). Some of these myths can be found among persons of all faiths; others are most commonly held by Christians. The myths are expressed in questions or statements such as the following:

- "Why didn't you leave that group?"
- "I certainly could think of some other people who would join a cult, but frankly you were the *last* person I would have expected would join a cultic group!"
- "Why see a psychologist? You know you were deceived in your

spiritual walk with God. You need to repent of your sins so that
the deceiver cannot tempt you anymore."

- "I don't know why you are complaining so, your group wasn't a
  cult. Why, they preach the gospel. Perhaps you're just bitter and
  need to get your heart right with God."
- "Perhaps your leader was right – you are not committed enough
  and your leaving was just an excuse for not totally surrendering
  your heart to God. You're using your rebellion to authority in
  general as an excuse to criticize this group. Take the beam out of
  your own eye first."
- "It's been my experience that people who join these groups are
  troubled or have come from dysfunctional homes. I didn't know
  you had problems before but I guess I was wrong."
- "I don't know why you're not reading your Bible – after all, the
  Word is truth and that is what will help heal you. You need to
  get back into fellowship; the people at church are going to start
  to wonder about you."
- "You know, you started slacking off on your Bible study and
  prayer during college. I'm sure if you would have kept up with
  those two essentials the group involvement wouldn't have deceived you so much and you wouldn't be in the shape you're in
  now."

When ex-cultists hear any of the above statements, they hear messages that say: "Something is wrong with you," "You must have some
psychological problems," "Perhaps your spiritual life isn't what you
thought," "Maybe you are not submissive and indeed are rebellious."
For the ex-cultist who hears and believes these distorted messages,
recovery is impossible until the erroneous messages are dealt with.
(Most of these people have already spent endless agonizing hours re-
penting and confessing their sins to no avail. This is not the time to
prescribe more of the same.)

Anyone can get involved in cults regardless of spiritual or psychological condition. Cults exploit the weak, the strong, the idealistic, and
the person looking for a cause. Cults exploit and worsen preexisting
problems. To blame a person for being in a cult is like blaming a
toddler for falling down, blaming a victim of rape, or blaming one who
suffers from a terrible disease.

THE STAGES OF RECOVERY

The first thing parents or friends should do if a loved one comes home
from a cult is to take care of any medical or nutritional needs to make

sure the ex-cultist is physically healthy. They should also assess which stage of recovery the person is in because former cultists' needs can vary markedly as they progress through the recovery stages. At Wellspring we have observed that people usually go through three stages of recovery after leaving a cult: (1) developing a conceptual framework; (2) grieving, reconciliation, and reaching out; and (3) reintegration into society.

Stage One:
Developing a Conceptual Framework

The focus of Stage One is education and self-acceptance. A thorough look at the group in question and the techniques of psychological manipulation used by cults is in order. Along with this, it is important to remember the loss of closeness and companionship that the ex-cultist experiences upon leaving the group.

The Possible Need for Exit Counseling   If ex-cultists still exhibit considerable confusion about their cult experience, if they tend to blame themselves, if they do not recognize the manipulative techniques to which they were subjected, and if they do not recognize or they deny having been victimized, then they can probably benefit from exit counseling, even if they have been out of the cult for a long time. Indeed, some people who left cults more than 10 years ago have sought out exit counseling.

The exit counseling may be performed at the person's home by an exit counselor (see Chapter 8). It may occur at a residential rehabilitation facility, such as described later in this chapter, or it may occur in an unsystematic manner, for example, by reading about cults, talking to former cultists, attending seminars, and so forth; this latter method is why we occasionally hear statements such as, "He exit counseled himself."

Obviously, when possible, a formal, systematic exit counseling is preferable. Exit counseling gives former cultists a framework with which to understand post-cult problems and, thereby, facilitates the recovery process.

Recognizing the Importance of Relationships   Cults lure people primarily because of the relationships the cult experience offers. Cultic involvement is an intensely personal experience. Correspondingly, recovery must be intense and personal. The therapist, counselor, pastor, and parent must be able to relate to the ex-member's emotional needs for acceptance, belonging, friendship and love. Cultic involvement can produce serious psychological problems, though the problems of ex-cultists may not all be cult-related. Pastors are well advised to seek mental health consultation if they desire to treat these people.

Harold Bussell notes that he seldom saw an Evangelical who entered a cultic group for doctrinal reasons. Among the factors he describes that make a group attractive is the cult's emphasis on "group sharing . . . community and caring" (1985, pp. 111–113).

Evaluating the Group   The first step in working with an ex-member is to do a sound intellectual and theological (or philosophical) evaluation of the group's teachings.

Second, the group's ethics – for example, its use of money, its methods of thought reform, and its practice of deception – all need to be thoroughly examined. Parents (or friends) can be of great service to exit counselors or mental health clinicians by providing information they have acquired about the cult in question. Likewise, the counselor may well have information about the group that parents are not aware of.

Third, the ethics and theology of the group need to be examined within the context of the person's psychological needs. This third step in evaluating the group is similar to Carl Rogers's concepts of congruity or genuineness, that is, that a person "is freely and deeply himself" or that there is no "discrepancy between the actual experience of the organism and the self picture of the individual insofar as it represents that experience" (Rogers, 1992, p. 828). In the specific cult treatment situation the therapy must focus on the particular needs and vulnerabilities of the former cult member and demonstrate to that person how these needs were exploited by the cult. For example, many cults prey upon the concepts of perfection or of being the best. Many clients enter a cultic group with perhaps high values around perfectionism and being the best among the best. It is important then for the therapist to see how the cult exploited those values, so that the experience becomes integrated into who the person was prior to the cult involvement and how the cult exploited or changed those core values. In this third step it is essential to tell the client that *all* cult members have particular values and needs that the cult took advantage of. Clients need to understand that cult recruitment is not something that happened because they were uniquely vulnerable, but rather each person has a set of factors that a cult can exploit.

Recovery of Fellowship and Recognition of Group Processes   In recovering from a cult experience, typically the issue that takes longest to resolve is the aching search for the love, fellowship, and caring experienced while in the group. It is extremely important to establish a trusting relationship. The helper must work hard. Sullivan (1984) found that only one-half of ex-cult members who sought help were able to engage in a successful working relationship with a counselor. Counselors or pastors (especially if other church members are assisting) must provide warmth and care, but they should take care not to become a substitute or imitation of the intense social "high" the former member experienced in the group. The tremendous fellowship and warmth that the ex-member longs for is often an artificial high. Yes, the group experience felt great, but was it true and was it always produced by genuine love and acceptance, or was it really more like the feeling of euphoria produced by some drugs?

There are many group processes that can make people feel wonderful, even euphoric. And it is to be noted that these processes or euphoric feelings are not unique to cults or fringe churches. What becomes troublesome for the recovering ex-member is coming to understand that such processes are not unique to their group. Moonies have told me of the tremendous feelings of rapture, love, and warmth they have experienced at some of their services. Members from The Way International have told me how they sensed the presence of God at some of their conferences. Ex-members of Great Commission International long for the "fellowship" and feelings they experienced while in the group. Former members of fringe churches tell of how good they felt after attending one of their services; some later named the experience "The Carl Stevens Show" after their leader, or called it a "buzz." A woman I counseled continued to go to a charismatic sect even after it had nearly destroyed her family. She admitted the people there skillfully used many techniques to induce guilt, even causing her to become estranged from her family; yet she had to go the service because she "felt so good" when she was there.

Consistently, former drug addicts who later joined cultic groups referred to the experience as a "high" or as "getting high." In a different but similar example, a Christian friend of mine returned from a Buddhist meeting and related how she too was moved by the testimonies and the group's singing. She became quite caught up in the entire experience and felt particularly enraptured.

The longing to duplicate such experiences can be one of the most difficult problems for ex-cultists to overcome. They have learned to love a feeling, and they begin a search to find that feeling again outside the cult. It then resembles an addiction. Just like the drug addict they maintain that there is no greater feeling in the world. But look at the result of drug addiction — a most pitiable condition that wrecks lives, health, careers and often kills. A similar process that leads to destruction can be found by the cultist who will sacrifice everything simply because he can't seem to find that "feeling" anywhere else.

While the group member was on a "high," he may have unknowingly repressed or dissociated emotional pain, doubts, and the telltale signs that his health was being neglected. Such highs (which are certainly not unique to religion) can be psychologically and spiritually unhealthy (Ash, 1984; Martin, 1989). For the most part this experience in the cult produces a strong sense of dependence on the group and its leaders. Consequently, helpers must be very careful not to foster dependency toward them or toward other group processes. Dependency conflicts are typically a major concern for the ex-member. Good rehabilitation and therapy will seek to achieve a movement away from dependency toward group support and healthy relationships.

The Recognition of "Floating"   "Floating" in the cult field refers to altered states of consciousness, that is, states between waking and sleeping, "states that differ from those usually experienced in the world of everyday reality. Included are states such as those induced by creative work, meditation, drugs, sleep, alcohol, and hypnosis" (Pollio, 1982, p. 240). When an ex-cultist gets back into the high after leaving a cult it is called "floating." If he snaps back into the shame-based motivations experienced in the cult and again believes the cult was right, that too is called floating. Floating episodes are handled by discovering what triggers the episodes and by grounding the client in some reality-oriented rational exercises. Madeleine Tobias in Chapter 16 provides advice on dealing with triggers.

Understanding Trauma   In attempting to understand what has happened to the ex-cultist, it is often helpful to employ the victim, or trauma, model. According to this model, victimization and the resultant distress are due to the shattering of three basic assumptions the victim held about the world and self. These assumptions are: "the belief in personal invulnerability, the perception of the world as meaningful, and the perception of oneself as positive" (Janoff-Bulman, 1985, p. 15). The ex-cultist has been traumatized, deceived, conned, used, and often emotionally, physically, sexually, and mentally abused while serving the group and/or the leader. Like other trauma victims (for example, of criminal acts, war atrocities, rape, and serious illness), former cultists often reexperience the painful memories of their group involvement. They also lose interest in the outside world, feel detached from society, and may show limited emotions (Janoff-Bulman, 1985, pp. 16, 17).

Thought Reform   Ex-cultists still in Stage One of their recovery process must thoroughly understand how they were under the influence of a thought-reform system. Lifton's work (1961, 1987) has been especially useful to former cultists. Geri- Ann Galanti (Chapter 3) discusses Lifton's identifying criteria of a thought-reform program.

I would like to expand on Galanti's formulation by discussing Lifton's eight themes according to the degree to which they contribute to a constriction of members' relationship with the world, their selves, and the cult.

Cults alter the boundary between members and the world by essentially erecting a psychological wall. Obviously Lifton's milieu control is the primary factor in constricting members' relationship with the outside world, but mystical manipulation and sacred science also contribute significantly. The euphoria that mystical manipulation produces—for example, through chanting, speaking in tongues, and so forth—creates a sense that the group is radically different from the outside world. This difference is, of course, interpreted positively, for example, as "the presence of God," "the moving of the Holy Spirit," "the sign of God's presence," "bliss consciousness," or "inner enlightenment." They doubt if this feeling can be found outside the group. Similarly, the sacred science underlines the special quality of the group. Cults have answers for virtually everything. And there is no truth outside their "science," or there is at least no fulfilling truth outside the group. The net result is that cultists begin to doubt if truth is outside the group, so in effect they set up their own internal censoring of outside information.

Cults alter members' relationship with their selves through doctrine over person, according to which the group's doctrine takes precedence over the members' personality, interests, and health—over virtually everything. Thus, cults broadly define sin and narrowly define human nature. This tends to alienate members from themselves. For example, some cults teach that being an artist or musician is settling for God's "second best." Those who are artistically inclined are thereby made to feel unspiritual, immature, sinful, or rebellious. Yeakley's (1988) research on the pressure to conform to a certain personality profile (see Chapter 1) is consistent with the view that cults cause an alienation within oneself.

The loaded language is the flip side of doctrine over person. In other words, doctrine over person "pushes" or "squeezes" the person's personality. Normally human nature fights such strictures and tries to stretch back into place. Here the loaded language "blocks" the normal pushing back by inserting into the cultists' minds such thought-stopping phrases as "Your question is of the Devil" or "Your desire for art is middle-class decadence." So the practice of doctrine over person and loaded language combine to alter the boundaries between the pre-cult and in-cult personality.

Cults control and change members' relationship to the cult through the demand for purity, the cult of confession, and the dispensing of existence. After the recruitment "honeymoon" is finally over, these factors work together to markedly increase cultists' dependency with regard to the group. The cult of confession enables the group to learn about the person's weak spots and provides ammunition for future encounters. The demand for purity means that members will feel per-manently inadequate. It keeps them in a perpetual cycle of "trying harder" and yet never reaching the required goal. The net result of the practice of confession and purity is to severely limit the vast array of behaviors that people are normally allowed to express. Hence there is a behavioral restriction, or boundary, on the cultists as well.

The combined effect of milieu control, doctrine over person, and the cult of confession places the concept of dispensing of existence in vivid and horrifying terms. Cultists who have lost faith in the outside world, and have lost faith or confidence in themselves, and who come to understand that they must be remolded by the processes and teach-ings of the cult are faced with a horrifying perspective when encounter-ing dispensing of existence. Hence, if one has already lost the outside world believing it is evil and lost one's self believing it too is evil or "bourgeois," then the prospect of losing one's affiliation with the cult presents the cultist with the phenomenon of the total annihilation of the self.

The dispensing of existence accentuates members' anxiety because their often-hidden feelings of inadequacy render them vulnerable to being judged unworthy. Having been indoctrinated to believe that rejection from the cult is tantamount to personal annihilation, mem-bers will obviously do all that they can to remain in good standing.

The thought-reform program changes the relationships cultists have with themselves, the cult, and the world. These relationships become constricted because of the new boundaries thought reform places on each of these areas.

If former cultists do not understand the thought-reform program, they will not be able to resolve their tangle of emotions — guilt, fear, shame, sadness, and anxiety. They will not appreciate the extent to which these emotions result from a constricting of their relationship with self, world, and cult.

Even if cultists do understand thought reform, two powerful and fundamental emotions will emerge: joy at being free and rage at having been violated. The former emotion affirms their identity as a free and independent person; the latter emotion affirms their sense of right and wrong. It is vital that ex-members' moral outrage not be treated as pathological. They have been wronged. They have been made to feel helpless. Their former sense of right and wrong—one of the most central elements of the human identity—has been turned upside down. Rage fortifies the weakened remnant of their moral self against the lingering power of the cultic evil.

The joy at being free and the rage that comes with understanding what happened serve to clean the human spirit. These feelings must run their course. At this point, recovery to post-cult life begins. The person is at Stage Two.

Stage Two:
Grieving, Reconciliation, and Reaching Out

In Stage Two the former cultist will be dealing with some or all of the following thoughts and questions:

"I feel sad that my friends are still in the group."

"I can't believe this happened to me."

"I've lost so much time."

"Can I find any legitimate spirituality?"

"What can I believe about God?"

"How could I have been so stupid?"

Stage Two is the beginning of the grieving process as well. People who grieve must be understood. They must be allowed to talk and to feel.

Regaining Purpose   At this stage recovery must focus on helping these people regain less unsettling beliefs about the world and themselves. Most of the stress symptoms can be attributed to victims' lack of belief in a meaningful world in which they saw themselves as positive and somewhat invulnerable. The cultic experience is often a crisis of faith. Many ex-cultists' say to themselves, "How could God allow this to happen to me?" or "I feel like a fool." Their belief in a just world is shattered. They can no longer say, "It won't happen to me."

A quest for meaning among ex-cultists is paramount. Victims must be helped to regain a belief in themselves and in a world that allows room for bad things happening to good people. Also, they may need to

talk out and relive the trauma again and again, as do the victims of
other types of crises (Horowitz, 1990). Sadly, the process of talking
about the trauma is sometimes short-circuited by well-intended helpers who view such rumination as unedifying or focusing too much on
the past.

Effective therapy must be very supportive and reaffirming, as self-
esteem needs to be rebuilt. Victims need to be freed of the view that
they were somehow solely responsible for their plight. They must be
able to forgive themselves. This task is especially problematic for
those who had strongly believed in a version of the "Prosperity Gospel." (The prosperity gospel holds the conviction that if a believing
person has enough faith, is completely repentant of all sin, and gives
at least 10% of his or her income to the church or to some Christian
ministry, then he or she will have good health, obtain financial wealth,
and experience general prosperity in all areas of life.) Meaning and
regained trust must be achieved. For those coming out of religious
cults, theological reconstruction is often most helpful if they can see
the event in view of a benevolent God who truly loves them (see also
Chapter 16).

The Need for Reconciliation   At times the ex-cultist may realize
his words or actions while in the cult offended others. It is very healing
to go to these others and ask for reconciliation. Although the offender
fully recognizes his intentions were not always meant to harm, he now
realizes his words or acts may have been hurtful to others. (One word
of caution to the ex-cultist: Don't commit the mistake of taking what
you have learned after leaving the cult and applying it back in time—
that is a sure formula for undeserving guilt! Once a person learns of
cult dynamics and recruitment techniques, it is counterproductive to
take that knowledge and apply it retrospectively—for example, to
think to oneself, "I should have known this" or "I should have seen it
coming.")

The Request for Information   Almost invariably most former
members going through Stage Two recovery have a lot of questions to
ask about the specifics of their group, the Bible (if it was a Bible-based
cult), religion, or other philosophical beliefs. These questions need to
be thoughtfully answered and thoroughly discussed. Helpers should
beware of the pitfalls of working with a former cult member.

Pastors who work with ex-cultists should know that the chances for
and speed of the ex-member's recovery may depend in part on how

similar the church's and pastor's style are to that of the extremist group. If there is a marked similarity between the former group and the present church, then there will be a greater probability the church setting will trigger traumatic memories. Consequently, the ex-member should seriously consider buying a different Bible translation, finding a pastor unlike his past leader in personality or teaching style, and a church or fellowship providing a welcome contrast to the cultic milieu. Far too often ex-cult members drop out of noncultic churches because they remind them too much of their former group. What is tragic is that these people are sometimes viewed more as "backsliders" than as victims.

The Need for Support   Support groups or professional counseling can contribute significantly to post-cult recovery by teaching ex-members strategies and skills that will enable them to avoid being victimized in the future. They will, as a consequence, regain some sense of personal strength and self-esteem.

As with other victims, finding and talking with other former members (preferably from the same cultic group) is an essential step to recovery. Often through this process former members become close friends. Their experience is similar to that of "war buddies" or to that of members of support groups for victims of drug or alcohol abuse, divorce, cancer, or the like.

Rediscovery of the Gospel   For those coming from aberrational Christian groups, it is essential for them to rediscover the New Testament gospel. All aberrational Christian cults distort certain aspects of the gospel. These groups, especially those that proclaim loudly that they are the "true" Christians, tend to define "Christian" much too tightly. What makes one a Christian? By definition, groups that are Christian recognize, articulate, and display the gospel of Jesus Christ. They are groups that have adhered to the major creeds of the Church and believe in the authority of the Bible. But in cultic groups something is missing in regard to the recognition, articulation, and demonstration of the gospel, such as its clear teachings on sexual behavior.

Recently at Wellspring there were two young women from two different sects. The leader of one group justified having sex with some of the women in the church as permissible because "God's grace is so great that he can forgive anything." Under this banner he had oral sex, group masturbation, group sex, and individual sessions of intercourse with the women because "God's grace was so great." This pastor also talked to the women and girls about how special they were. Using the banner of Christianity and the gospel, this pastor engaged in the wildest forms of sexual excess.

The other sect taught a version of the gospel that emphasized "mortification of the flesh." For them the gospel was to see how Jesus "mortified his flesh" and each Christian then was to do the same in order to be saved. Salvation for them was in the imitation of Christ as the perfect person. Christ was to be the example. In addition, the young woman who had been in this sect had believed that all other denominations were "without any scriptural base." By implication there was no salvation outside the little group. This second sect took the opposite extreme in regard to sin. Anything besides prayer, Bible study, evangelism, and attending church meetings would be very carefully examined before it could be permitted.

One thing that causes confusion here is that with many of these cultic groups the public facade and the public statements of faith seem quite sound. But much of the distortion often happens with the communication that goes on in the inner circle. Here the leader reveals his own insights and practices that he may well justify because (he says) the world can't yet grasp them, but because of his own spiritual advancement (he says again) he can understand and practice these hidden or secret truths. In this way the cult leader "hooks" those in the group by arguing that they can become a part of this inner circle of more enlightened and more spiritual persons.

Yet in both of the above examples, mainstream Christianity would recognize the extremes of both groups as well beyond the bounds of reasonable interpretation of the Bible and traditions of the church.

Less extreme examples could also be given, such as the Shepherding movement. Typically, one would be hard pressed to find fault with much of the doctrinal beliefs of this movement. The error there is with the authority structure, which stresses unquestioning submission to leadership in every area of life, and goes beyond the boundaries of accepted biblical authority.

What is disturbing is that many of these cultic groups could, with a clear conscience, subscribe to a most orthodox, fundamental, and evangelical statement of faith. But phenomenologically and practically they are living a subtle but deadly religion of "performance," of trying to live up to essentially nonbiblical standards imposed by the leader. Often these standards change from month to month or week to week, creating a destabilized environment that makes the members even more dependent on the leader. Through the biblical gospel, however, meaning to life is restored and self-esteem is regained. Bussell (n.d.) maintains that, with regard to aberrant Christian groups, a clear understanding of the gospel is the single most important issue in a cultist's recovery and future immunity to further cultic involvement (see also W. Martin, 1980, pp. 71–81).

Rescuing Others   During Stage Two ex-members will often direct some energy into trying to get their friends out of the sect. Without careful planning such efforts may prove fruitless. Moreover, the care and energy devoted to helping a friend may work to the detriment of the ex-member's own recovery. Therefore, it is always best for ex-members to first grow strong and then develop a plan that may best help their friends. One form this may take is having parents contact the friend's parents to share the information about the group. Once this information is shared, it is the friend's parents' decision to develop a strategy for helping their loved one.

An ill-planned phone call, letter, or article hurriedly sent to a friend will usually result in the friend innocently sharing the information with the leader. Invariably the leader will quickly refute the material and the hapless sect member will believe that the ex-member is the misguided one.

Contact by the Cult   Some former members don't know what to do if they should be contacted by people still in the cult; thus, preparation is needed. Most cults will still try to control the departed member. The cults' purpose is first to try to persuade the member to come back. If they don't succeed with that, then they will go for damage control; that is, they will try to discredit the former member and limit any contact he or she may have with those in the cult.

Generally it is fruitless for ex-members to argue with cult members who contact them. Their tack is to say things like, "We miss you," "We love you," "We have been so worried about you," "We have been praying for you," "We would like to be with you." It is best for the former member to express appreciation for the concern and tell the others that perhaps in the future a meeting may be arranged. The ex-member should not make any promises; instead, he should let the cultists play their hand. If there is some indication that the group members who make contact have genuinely sincere questions about their own involvement in the group, then the ex-member may safely but cautiously share some information. If a meeting is called for, ex-members should not go alone, should clearly set the terms of the meeting, and should limit their remarks in order to stick to those terms.

Retributions of the Cult   A more serious concern is actual fear generated by the cult's threats. If the group is known to be violent toward ex-members, then the former member must protect himself. Madeleine Tobias in Chapter 16 provides practical advice on how ex-cultists can protect themselves against their former group.

Reemergence of the Past   Invariably as Stage Two issues are resolving, the past will replay itself: "There are issues I never dealt with before joining this cult." Some of the issues that may surface are:

- Unresolved grief over divorce of parents
- Death of parents
- Drug/alcohol or other addictions in the family
- Personal problems
- Loneliness
- Unsatisfactory relationships with the opposite sex

At times a crisis—such as seeing a family member join a cult and then return home after much family anguish—may trigger a completely new awareness of unresolved issues.

Recently I dealt with a young man, Charles, raised in a very dysfunctional home. His father left for several years when Charles was a child. During this time, the mother leaned on Charles for emotional support. As a result Charles felt smothered and helpless and could not really live as a child; he had to be "strong and responsible." Bitterness and resentment ensued.

Miraculously, the cult crisis caused all family members—Dad, Mom, Charles, and the other son, Jerry—to see the problem. At the same time, they discovered some books about codependency and discovered that the family had some serious problems. Although there was much grief and tears, the denial and resistance were gone. The steps for recovery proceeded rapidly with good progress.

The actual crisis can be an excellent opportunity to improve family relations, heal wounds from the past, and develop patterns of healthy relations that will benefit the next generation.

In summary, Stage Two recovery involves the successful resolution of regaining meaningful beliefs about themselves and the world. Self-esteem must be reestablished and former members must be freed from the idea that somehow they were responsible for the abuse suffered from their cult experience. During this stage the gathering of information about the group and the general religious or philosophical traditions upon which the group allegedly based their beliefs is essential. Support from friends, ex-members, and loved ones is the indispensable matrix in which Stage Two proceeds. For those emerging from Christian-based groups the rediscovery of the Gospel, that is, the nonmeritorious forgiveness and acceptance through Jesus Christ, is essential.

Invariably during this stage recovering ex-members want to get their friends out of the group, or the ex-members may be contacted by the cult. Caution is advised here; a very careful plan and thorough preparation are essential before any communication with the cult member ensues.

Successful progression through Stage Two will also result in the reemergence of pre-cult issues. The crisis of the cult experience itself often paves the way to realistically deal with such issues. Finally, the ex-member must contextualize the entire cult experience by recognizing the positives of the experience. Not only must self-esteem be recovered but also, through the support and affirmation of caring loved ones, the whole self or those parts of one's personality that were repressed and not nurtured during the cultic experience will reemerge.

Stage Three: Reintegration into Society

When the former cult member begins talking less and less about the cult and spending more time in career, relationship, and personal issues, then he or she is in the third stage of recovery. In many cases, the cult experience was a temporary diversion on the road to adulthood, with the cult often thwarting or confusing the cultist about career and school aspirations. Many case examples show that once a person joined a cult, the leaders often counseled people to switch majors, drop out of school, and so on. Leadership's decision to demand a different career direction is couched in phrases like, "This will be more productive for the kingdom of God," "God would be more pleased if you chose to do . . . ," "The world will be enlightened more quickly if you did. . . . "

Positives of the Cult Experience   As strange as it may sound, there is often some positive benefit to the cultic experience. Perhaps unhealthy shyness has been overcome because the person has been challenged to accept leadership opportunities that were never available prior to the cult experience. Discovering an innate talent to organize and administrate may have surprised the cultist. Anyone in a cult learns about discipline, hard work, long hours, specific job skills, and teamwork. These skills, when applied in the environment of true freedom, can serve a person very well.

Recovery of the Whole Self   What is important, though, is to extract the positive from the cult experience and tie it into pre-cult aspirations. I have found some very insightful clues into a person's personality and interests by exploring with my clients their childhood activities, dreams, wishes, and talents. As an example, I look at my own childhood: I was filled with love for the out-of-doors, nature, fishing, hunting, travel, adventure, and a strong penchant for the informal. I hated protocol, such as wearing my Sunday suit, doing my homework, and taking piano lessons!

Now, what clues from my own childhood could be helpful in understanding myself as an adult who had been in a cult? My childhood did not give many clues as to career or vocation. But my childhood experience did provide very valuable insights concerning my future temperament, interests, and life-style. To this day I am still an avid outdoorsman. I love nature – the hills, lakes, sky, clouds, sun, animals, and flowers. My love for nature made me feel uncomfortable with eight years of city living while in the cult. I now live in the country and feel much more at home. I still am uncomfortable in formality. I only wear a suit if I must. I am much more comfortable with jeans and a flannel shirt.

However, my years in a cult put my real self into question. My love for nature and the rural settings didn't seem to fit our group's call to engage in aggressive evangelism. I began to think more and more that I was somehow less spiritual than others. My love for the arts and for the creative spirit in others didn't seem to fit anymore. Life was primarily to be a passion for duty to reach the world for Christ. Life went from color to black and white. Roses no longer smelled sweet. In fact we were too busy to ever see the new black-and-white, odorless roses. Parts of me were dead during those seven and a half years in the cult and I know that others were likewise living an existence that did not fully validate the richness of their talents and temperaments.

Recovery processes in Stage Three help bring the ex-cultist back to being a whole person in a whole world, devoid of black-and-white thinking and undue influence. In other words, in Stage Three recovery the reemerging former member begins to make a series of successful readjustments to society.

The Self and Religious Commitment   Cults often teach the black-and-white order by pointing to Christ's commands to "deny self" and "forsake all." For many recovering cultists, the understanding of Christ's words is a pressing issue. Former members who wish to embrace Christianity may want to ask, Does God really require a truncated version of ourselves? Why would He have created us in our richness of talents, interests, and temperaments to only tell us it is all evil? Isn't Christ's message one of giving the entire self with its richness and with its needs unto God to be used for His glory and His kingdom? Do the words of Christ pierce to the spirit of the law itself and reveal in our hearts and our will that we cannot possibly be accepted by God on the basis of good works? Hence, don't Christ's commands to forsake all, to deny self, to take up our cross, and to have a righteousness greater than the scribes and Pharisees point out the utter impossibility of anyone ever achieving such a state of goodness by following strict demands? A recovering cult member may want to ask, as Peter did to Jesus when the rich young ruler went away, "Who then can be saved?" Wasn't Jesus so instructive in his reply, "With man it is impossible, but with God all things are possible"?

A healthy spiritual life, therefore, is distorted if two things aren't kept in mind. First, the impossibility of being reconciled to God apart from God's initiative, unconditional love, and empowerment. Second, the affirming acceptance of ourselves. Do we have to lose our talents and personalities to be accepted by God? Doesn't it seem that only a "sick," nonexistent god would make such demands? Former Bible-based cultists who have experienced the act of being reconciled to and having accepted God have been provided with a way to see growth and healing in their lives that was hitherto unavailable to them. The act of grace provides two miracles: love for God and love for self. Clarifying what the self is and that God indeed accepts and affirms people helps to put into focus career, school, and self-identity issues.

Recovery of the Practical   Practical issues such as management of time, money, goal setting, and a general regaining of a normal life-style must also be addressed. The Wellspring program offers career and vocational tests to help clients explore fruitful avenues regarding future career and schooling plans.

In working with the recovery of practical skills it is sometimes necessary to help the former member get a grasp of which skills are necessary to successfully negotiate pursuing job, school, or relationship goals. For example, sometimes a series of career and vocational tests are given. The results are discussed in light of the person's pre-cult personality, identity issues as defined by the cult, and current aspirations. Practical skills may also need to be taught: the effort needed to look for a job, preparation for job interviews, how to handle the cult experience on a résumé, proper dress and manner for interviews, typical employer expectations regarding work habits, interpersonal skills, and so forth.

Recognition of Sexuality and Intimate Relations   Sexuality and dating can be troubling issues for recovering cultists. Many cults distort intimate relationships. Some cults arrange marriages, for example, the Unification Church and the University Bible Fellowship. Many cults do not permit dating at all. Celibacy is also typically seen among Hare Krishnas, upper-level leaders in Transcendental Meditation, and members of Ananda Marga Yoga. Still other groups permit dating within the group, but only if chaperoned or approved by the leadership. In the Boston Church of Christ dating has been almost exclusively in the form of double dating; apparently, however, according to some former members, recently there has been some relaxation about this rule. Former members of Great Commission International (GCI) have told me that dating was discouraged or even forbidden except with the approval of the elders. The founder and former leader of GCI, Jim McCotter (1984, p. 40), wrote that dating was a type of faction not unlike other factions which can divide a church. (McCotter's exact quote is: "What we call 'dating,' the Bible may call 'partiality' [James 2:9]. What we call 'boyfriend/girlfriend,' the Bible may call a 'clique' or 'faction' [Galatians 5:20].) Reports from Maranatha Ministries reveal that dating rules were so strict that members had to get permission from the leaders and could only date people within the movement. Dating as a single couple was permitted only if the partners were engaged.

Some cults suggest that any sexual feelings are sinful and lustful. One of the prime examples of this type of cult would be the Unification Church (Moonies). The Hare Krishnas also take the extreme view that sex is for procreation only (not for pleasure between marriage partners) and may be engaged in only once per month.

By stark contrast, nudity and premarital sex is permitted, encouraged, or even required in other cultic groups and churches. One female client at Wellspring reported that members of her former church were told to remove their clothes in mixed company to prove they were "open" to one another. In another group, in Racine, Wisconsin, the leader, Larry Yarber, reportedly told one woman, "Unzip your pants. You shouldn't be inhibited. God wants your needs to be fulfilled. You don't have a husband right now; you'll have one someday" (Burger, 1989, p. 5). Other female members reported that he had told them the same thing. The women interviewed said that Yarber used sex under the pretext of helping them with their "sexual problems" (Romenesko, 1990, p. 95). In addition, ex-members reported that Yarber advocated wife swapping (p. 96).

John Gottuso, pastor of Park View Christian Fellowship in California, reportedly convinced a number of women to become sexually involved with him as an aid to their spiritual life (Milligan, 1989, p. A-8). Another member of Gottuso's church said, "The theme was masturbating your deepest darkest secrets . . . a lot of times he'd challenge men or women to take off their clothes or pants—to demonstrate their genital area or breasts" (Nelson, 1988, p. 6). Examples from many other groups could be cited. But these illustrations are given as examples of the types of sexuality exhibited in cults, some of which (including Gottuso's) boast evangelical statements of faith.

The broad range of sexual attitudes and practices seen in cults underscores the confusion that arises for many ex-members as they readjust to sexual behavior and values outside the cult. At this point it is helpful to allow the former cultist to see how the group's standards deviated from the accepted norms of dating in our society, from his or her own conscience, and from the heritages of mainstream religions.

It is not uncommon for former cultists to go to extremes upon leaving a group. The sexually "pure" may become promiscuous and the sexually active may become unbearable prudes. Helpers can't offer quick fixes to these wild extremes. Such behavior only exposes the damage and abuse of the cult. Helpers observing such behavior can usually conclude that the former cultist is dealing with tremendous rage and can probably benefit from professional help.

Longing for Friends in the Cult   Even during Stage Three the ex-member will continue to miss friends left in the cult and may desire to try to get them out. Reasonable approaches to helping a friend are encouraged once the cult victim has recovered sufficiently. If the ex-member continues to obsess about getting people out, that is, if he is constantly thinking and talking about his friends remaining in the cult and his desire to assist them, then it is wise to talk seriously with him about it. Explore possible reasons for such strong concerns, such as codependent relationships with those in the cult, excessive guilt over recruiting some of these people, an inordinate desire to rescue friends, or simply the desire to help. After these issues are discussed, the former member will be in a better position to know if there are any issues that may require further attention.

It's always a good sign if the ex-cultist desires a better relationship with his or her parents. Encourage this. Perhaps that long family vacation that never materialized could finally be realized. A few family counseling sessions would not hurt. At the least it is now the time to regularly set aside on a weekly basis some space for family activities. Parents should plan something the entire family has to participate in, such as a game, a work project, or just eating out.

POST-CULT ASSESSMENT

Thus far I have discussed issues that are critical to the recovery of former cult members. These issues are relevant to a general assessment of how to help ex-cultists. Now, for the benefit of psychologists and other mental health professionals, I want to describe the formal assessment procedures we use at the Wellspring Retreat and Resource Center.

Many believe that once an individual is out of a cult, that is, successfully exit counseled and rehabilitated, the problems are over. Many do not understand that exit counseling per se, as valuable as it may be, does not relieve the overall distress of the ex-cultist. The ex-cultist's decision to leave may be firm, but there remains a plethora of unresolved issues that invariably cause high levels of stress. My own research on clinical profiles of those who have left cults (Martin, Langone, Dole, & Wiltrout, 1992) shows that walkaways (those who leave cults without counseling) do not differ statistically in their Millon test profiles from those who have received exit counseling. This difference cannot be explained by other moderator variables.

Why, then, are the distress levels between walkaways and those exit counseled so similar whether or not they participate in a rehab program? Probably because they both must still contend with a multitude of issues that exit counseling cannot fully address, including:

- Unresolved grief issues over loss of friends in the group
- Unsettled issues about what was right and wrong in the group
- Insecurity about who they are
- Unrecognized dependency issues
- Uncertainty about career and vocational plans
- Unresolved issues about God, sacred writings, religious authority, spiritual calling (for those exiting religious cults)
- Unclear thoughts about therapy, validity, personal "growth," their own identity, and the struggle to change in a positive direction (for those exiting psychotherapy or human potential cults)
- Untangled conflict about whether they were "victims" or "agents"

- Incapacitating fear about moving forward with new friends or new career, overfocusing on the past
- Unmet communication needs with parents and their expectations

What then is the best way to assess the factors contributing to post-cult distress? At Wellspring we have gathered and developed a battery of standardized instruments which are used to assess clients in all of the major domains so affected.

Currently, at Wellspring, we use the following test battery for our post-cult evaluations:

1. *Intake Interview.* Gathers general biographical information, background information of family and social framework, health and mental status, special characteristics of cultic group. Time: 1 hour or more depending on interview style.
2. *Life Orientation Inventory (LOI)* (Kowalchuck & King, 1988). Consists of a preliminary screening questionnaire of 30 questions to determine the client's potential suicide risk. If screening device is near 70 or above, a long-form test (113 questions) can be administered to determine area of greatest conflict (work, relationships, family, and so forth). Test time: 10 minutes; long-form time: 45 minutes.
3. *Millon Clinical Multiaxial Inventory (MCMI)* (Millon, 1987). Standard clinical device for measuring personality characteristics and affective states. Similar to Minnesota Multiphasic Personality Inventory (MMPI) in setup; assesses test taker on scales of: dependency, obsessive-compulsiveness, passive-aggressiveness, narcissism, and psychotic tendencies, to name a few. Profile determined and represented through graph. Time: 45–90 minutes.
4. *Beck Depression Inventory (BDI)* (Beck, Ward, Mendelsohn, Mock, & Erbaugh, 1961). Informal questionnaire of 21 questions assessing current level of depression. Designed by well-known cognitive therapist Aaron Beck. Approximate time: 5 minutes.
5. *Interpersonal Behavior Survey (IBS)* (Mauger, Adkinson, Zoss, Firestone, & Hook, 1980). Survey designed to distinguish assertive behaviors from aggressive behaviors such as "expression of anger" or "refusing demands" and conflict avoidance and "dependency." Time: 30–40 minutes.

6. *Hopkins Symptom Checklist (HSCL)* (Derogatis, 1977). A quick and accurate measure of affective status in psychological distress. A shortened version of the SCL-90. Time: 10–15 minutes.

7. *Post-Cult Needs Assessment.* An information checklist developed at Wellspring that ascertains clients' personal desires for rehabilitation focus, such as emotional concerns, social concerns, family issues, spiritual concerns, cult education needs, vocational needs. Time: 30 minutes.

8. *Self-Directed Search* (Holland, 1990). A self-administered vocational interest survey to determine client's choice of preferred career paths. Time: 1½ hours.

9. *Adult Child Distortion Scale (ACDS)* (Crites & Russell, 1988). Assesses dysfunctional codependency areas of family of origin and current family structure, as well as personal communication style. Test time: 30 minutes.

10. *Dissociative Experiences Scale (DES)* (Bernstein & Putnam, 1986) and *Splitting Scale (SS)* (Gerson, 1984). Combined scales have 60 items or less and measure levels of susceptibility to dissociation and the amount of cult-induced dissociation. Time: 15 minutes.

11. *Religious-Metaphysical Index.* Index of person's religious belief system prior to group involvement, during involvement, and desire for future belief boundaries. (Under development at Wellspring.)

The battery used by Wellspring is by no means complete. A critical weakness is the lack of an instrument that can objectively evaluate the degree to which groups are cultic. Drs. Michael Langone and Robert Chambers are currently developing such an instrument.

The very nature of post-cult assessment requires the skills of trained psychologists, psychiatrists, clinical social workers, and mental health counselors. Consequently, post-cult assessment should be organized and supervised by such qualified personnel.

In addition, post-cult assessment requires, at the least, several days. In my opinion any less time would be incomplete or viewed as too intense, if thorough. I doubt that many people fresh out of a cult are ready to handle the necessary test taking and interviewing in a one-day period. Spreading the testing out over two or three days, however, allows ample time for relaxation, recreation, and reflection.

Reflection is important because the thoughts, emotions, and behaviors of those recently out of a cult change from day to day. When therapists can see an ex-cultist for several days, the practitioners get a better overall impression of the client's status. Assessments must be dynamic because the client's needs and perceptions will change significantly as time progresses.

THE WELLSPRING TREATMENT PROGRAM

Post-cult assessment and rehabilitation issues blend together. The first few days of rehab (at least at Wellspring) are periods for such assessment. Debriefing is essential during this time. Current research shows that trauma becomes crystallized a few days after a traumatic event (see, for example, Scurfield, 1985, pp. 240, 241, 242). The quicker the debriefing (for example, crisis intervention and education on what happened, how it happened, and feelings to expect), the less likely that post-traumatic stress disorder (PTSD) will develop. Problems and needs are identified and many are worked on during their usual two-week stay at the facility.

General Description

The goal of Wellspring's program is to assist ex-cult members return to normal life again, free of the deleterious effects of their cultic experience, which include false guilt, depression, anxiety, fear, confusion, and anger. Thus, we help our clients return to *emotional* stability. We also assist them in returning to *social* stability by helping them reintegrate themselves with family, friends, and career—relationships and life goals that are often interrupted by the cult. In addition, we help those who so desire (and most do) to establish or reestablish a wholesome and biblical relationship with God and church or synagogue—in other words, a return to *spiritual* stability.

Clients are referred to Wellspring by a variety of means. Many are referred by personal counselors who work with parents, siblings, and/ or children of cult members in extricating their loved one(s) from the cult through voluntary dialogue and counseling regarding the errors and dangers of the cult. Some individuals are referred by exit counselors and others associated with various anti-cult organizations. Others are referred by pastors and campus ministers familiar with Wellspring; still others are referred by friends and former cult members who have been helped at Wellspring. Individuals who choose to come to Wellspring have *already* decided to leave their particular group *before* they come: no "deprogramming" takes place at Wellspring.

Clients are generally accompanied to Wellspring by one or both parents, by one or more siblings, by a husband or wife, by a child or children (adult), and/or by their exit counselor (if one was employed in helping them leave the cult). Upon arrival the client and those with him or her are welcomed to the guest house, where the client is shown to his or her room and introduced to the staff and other clients who may be there. The client and family member(s) or loved one(s) are invited to one of the staff homes where they are helped to relax and feel at ease while they and the staff get to know one another in an informal atmosphere, often over a meal.

Family members and exit counselors usually remain only until the following day, just long enough to transition the client into the Wellspring program, and to assure the family that they are committing their loved one into capable, compassionate care.

The core of Wellspring's program consists of psychological counseling and instructional sessions on cultic dynamics and religious and spiritual issues. Due to the nature of the problem, each client is treated as an individual with a unique combination of needs and personality traits, including strengths and weaknesses. Therefore, the specific counseling and instruction offered is tailored to the individual. In general terms, however, the counseling sessions are designed to enable the client to focus on his or her cult-induced emotional problems and develop effective solutions to them. Theological instruction (offered only to those who desire it) centers on specific theological and interpretive errors taught in the Bible-based cult and demonstrates how such errors deviate from traditional Judeo-Christian thought. For those interested in personal Bible study we teach standard methods of biblical exegesis and hermeneutics. Finally, various findings on the dynamics of psychological coercion and indoctrination are presented to help clients see that the process whereby they were drawn into the cult was a subtle but powerful force over which they had little or no control and therefore they need not feel either guilt or shame because of their experience.

In the formal counseling and instructional sessions much use is made of Wellspring's extensive library of books, articles, and audio- and videotapes covering a wide variety of topics, from specific cultic organizations and cult-related issues, to counseling issues such as depression and addiction, to more general psychological and theological books and tapes.

In addition to formal sessions there is plenty of provision for rest and recreation in order to afford the client a chance to recuperate from the usual exhausting rigors of cult life and to provide a preliminary model for a workable life-style, which contains a healthy balance of work, play, and relaxation. The close proximity of Wellspring to numerous state and local parks and lakes and to the Ohio University campus makes possible many different types of recreation for our clients.

Intake and Program Content

Before any formal counseling take places, the client is interviewed by a staff member and a series of standard tests and questionnaires is administered to determine areas of greatest need for psychological, social, and spiritual counseling. Additional input is obtained, if possible, through consultation with the parent(s), other family members, and/or exit counselor who may have accompanied the client to Wellspring. (Often extensive consultation has already taken place by telephone prior to the client's arrival at the center.) Using the information thus obtained a specific program of counseling and instruction is tailored to meet the client's needs and desires.

Although each client's experience and needs are unique, there still exist many areas of commonality among former cult members. Hence a wide variety of issues and topics have been developed for presentation and discussion as required. These include the following:

- Characteristics of cultic leadership, authority, and influence
- Mind control and group manipulation
- Addiction and dependency
- Independent critical thinking
- Assertiveness training
- Dealing with negative emotions (e.g., anger, anxiety, depression, guilt)
- Family relationships
- Sexuality
- Resocialization
- Decision making
- Spiritual and religious disillusionment
- Comparative religions
- Interpretation of the Bible
- Various specific theological doctrines and issues as requested (e.g., the nature and character of God, the grace of God, the gospel, Christian liberty vs. legalism, biblical discipleship, finding the will of God, the unpardonable sin)

- Philosophical concepts and ideas (e.g., theories of knowledge, ulti-mate reality, the meaning of life, man's place in the universe)
- Career goals
- Selecting healthy religious affiliation

No client is compelled or required to discuss religious or spiritual issues if he or she prefers not to. Wellspring does not seek to convert clients to any church or denomination. The vast majority of our clients from Bible-based cults have been eager to study the Scriptures to understand what they really teach and weed out the distorted and false teachings of their former group. Wellspring offers this assistance to such individuals.

As much as possible clients are encouraged to set the pace and intensity of their own schedule while at Wellspring. Nondirected time can be spent hiking, fishing, exercising, or pursuing other personal or group leisure activities. Trips into town can be arranged for shopping, entertainment, using the athletic facilities at Ohio University, or other reasons. The mix of activities at Wellspring is meant to provide a preliminary model for a workable life-style in contrast to the former demands of cult life.

Rarely do we find an ex-cultist who wrestles exclusively with cult-related issues. Clients' needs must be prioritized: The most urgent and most closely cult-related are dealt with during rehab. Remaining issues—those that are not as urgent and could be dealt with by other qualified professionals—are identified, briefly addressed, and referred to outside resources. Consequently, when a person leaves rehab, there is, it is hoped, a sense of structure, direction, and support for that individual.

Program Termination and Follow-up

Termination of the client's resident program occurs when staff, client, and family are confident that the client has made sufficient progress in overcoming the particular negative effects of the cultic experience to be able to return to a normal life-style outside the cult. Often the client's parents or other family members return to the center to trans-port the client home. Before leaving, though, the family members join the client in joint counseling sessions designed to aid in the reintegra-tion of the family, as well as reconciliation of the client to the family when that is needed.

An attempt is made by the Wellspring staff to maintain contact with former clients through periodic letters and telephone calls. Occasionally former clients who are doing especially well following their rehabilitation may be encouraged to participate in conferences, seminars, or media forums on cults sponsored by other organizations or churches. Sometimes former clients make themselves available as reference or resource persons to provide information on their former cult and/or to help in intervention and counseling with other members of their former group (or other groups).

Before leaving Wellspring, each client who so desires is given guidelines on how to select a warm, caring place to worship that will continue to assist in wholesome growth to spiritual maturity.

Approximately six months after leaving Wellspring the former client is asked to retake one of the standard psychological tests given upon entering the program (the MCMI). This retest serves as an objective evaluation of progress during the intervening months, and is a good indicator of the effectiveness of the Wellspring program, helping to show where adjustments may need to be made. A thorough review of these follow-up scores conducted in the summer of 1989 revealed that virtually every client seen at Wellspring had recovered from his or her cult experience and was living a healthy, productive life. In particular, their scores on the depression, dependency, and anxiety scales evidenced statistically significant improvement.

All of these things help to confirm and solidify the former client in his or her decision to leave the cult, and strengthen his or her resolve to press on in a responsible and productive way.

CONCLUSION

In summary, post-cult assessment and rehabilitation are invaluable tools for those who have walked away, for those who have been exit counseled, and for those who have gone through the trauma of involuntary deprogramming. Post-cult assessment can help identify issues. It can also help relieve people's fears of excessive damage done by the cult. Some parents, for example, might tend to catastrophize: "Oh, my son will be incoherent for the rest of his life." Post-cult assessment is a way to alleviate that type of fear.

The following is a list of the objectives to be accomplished by former cult members via assessment and rehabilitation:

1. Understand how thought reform has affected them
2. Be able to recognize their own level of distress, and know which stage of recovery they're currently working through

3. Understand the nature of rehabilitation and how it can assist their needs
4. Be familiar with support resources (such as the American Family Foundation and the Cult Awareness Network) and related victim assistance programs
5. Become acquainted with the option of short-term professional counseling with a qualified counselor
6. Be able to address the pros and cons of returning to school, moving, finding employment, finding appropriate support and counseling (e.g., ex-members group, pastoral, individual therapy)
7. Become more aware of the family dynamics that may have existed prior to the cult involvement that now need to be addressed
8. Recognize career avenues

In conclusion, I would add that post-cult assessment and rehabilitation are effective and invaluable tools that can bring new insights to relationships, as well as bring an awareness of possible resources for becoming whole again.

REFERENCES

Ash, S. M. (1984). A response to Robbin's critique of my extremist cult definition and view of cult-induced impairment. *Cultic Studies Journal 1*(1), 27–35.

Beck, A. T., Ward, C. H., Mendelsohn, M., Mock, J., & Erbaugh, J. (1961). An inventory measuring depression. *Archives of General Psychiatry, 4,* 561–571.

Bernstein, E. M., & Putnam, F. W. (1986). The dissociative experiences scale. *Journal of Nervous and Mental Disease, 174*(12), 727–735.

Burger, S. (1989, November 5). Summary of meeting. Unpublished letter.

Bussell, H. (n.d.). A study of justification, Christian fullness, and super believers. Unpublished manuscript.

Bussell, H. (1985, March). Why Evangelicals are attracted to cults. *Moody Monthly,* pp. 111–113.

Crites, F., & Russell, J. R. (1988). *Adult child distortion scale.* Fort Worth, TX: Association for Pragmatic Therapy.

Derogatis, L. R. (1977). *SSCL-90: Administration, scoring and procedures manual for the revised version and other instruments of the psychotherapy rating scale series.* Baltimore, MD: Johns Hopkins University School of Medicine, Clinical Psychometrics Unit.

Gerson, M. J. (1984). Splitting: The development of a measure. *Journal of Clinical Psychology, 40,* 157–162.

Holland, J. L. (1990). *The self-directed search.* Odessa, FL: Psychological Assessment Resources.

Horowitz, M. J. (1990). Psychological response in serious life events. In V. Hamilton & D. Warburton (Eds.), *Human stress and cognition.* New York: Wiley.

Janoff-Bulman, R. (1985). The aftermath of victimization: Rebuilding shattered assumptions. In C. R. Figley (Ed.), *Trauma and its wake: The study and treatment of post-traumatic stress disorder.* New York: Brunner/Mazel.

Kowalchuck, B., & King, J. D. (1988). *Life orientation survey: A method for assessing suicide risk.* Austin, TX: PRO-ED Inc.

Lifton, R. J. (1961). *Thought reform and the psychology of totalism.* New York: W. W. Norton.

Lifton, R. J. (1987). *The future of immortality and other essays for a nuclear age.* New York: Basic Books.

McCotter, J. (1984). *Chapter seven.* Silver Spring, MD: Great Commission International.

Martin, P. (1989). Dispelling the myths: The psychological consequences of cultic involvement. *The Christian Research Journal,* Winter/Spring, 9–14.

Martin, P., Langone, M. D., Dole, A., & Wiltrout, J. (1992). Post-cult symptoms as measured by the MCMI Before and After Residential Treatment. *Cultic Studies Journal, 9*(2), 219–250.

Martin, W. (1980). *Essential Christianity.* Ventura, CA: Regal Books.

Mauger, P. A., Adkinson, D. R., Zoss, S. K., Firestone, G., & Hook, D. (1980). *Interpersonal behavior survey.* Los Angeles: Western Psychological Services.

Milligan, M. (1989, April 30). Arcadia counselor stripped of licenses. *Star-News,* p. A-8.

Millon, T. (1987). *Millon Clinical Multiaxial Inventory-II.* Minneapolis, MN: National Computer Systems.

Nelson, L. (1988, August 3). Church practices revealed, counseling said to include sexual contact. *Arcadia Highlander,* p. 6.

Pollio, H. R. (1982). *Behavior and human existence.* Monterey, CA: Brooks/Cole.

Rogers, C. (1992). The necessary and sufficient conditions of therapeutic personality change. *Journal of Consulting and Clinical Psychology, 60,* 828.

Romenesko, J. (1990, March). The false prophet. *Milwaukee Magazine,* p. 95.

Scurfield, R. M. (1985). Post-trauma stress assessment and treatment: Overview and formulations. In C. R. Figley (Ed.), *Trauma and its wake: The study and treatment of post-traumatic stress disorder.* New York: Brunner/Mazel.

Sullivan, L. B. (1984). Counseling and involvements in new religious groups. *Cultic Studies Journal, 1*(2), 178–195.

Yeakley, F. (Ed.). (1988). *The discipling dilemma.* Nashville, TN: Gospel Advocate.

11

GUIDELINES FOR THERAPISTS

Lorna Goldberg, M.S.W., A.C.S.W.

RECENTLY A 25-YEAR-OLD WOMAN came to my office. At age 17, while in high school, she joined a Bible-based cult; she left the group seven years later. Her consultation with me occurred one year after her cult departure. She described how her high school boyfriend's family were, and continue to be, members of what appeared to be a fundamentalist Christian church. They were the ones who had encouraged her to become involved. At the time the young woman's parents were not unduly concerned about her involvement in the group, believing it was simply a church.

Over a period of time the church leader, a married man with four children, exerted more and more control over this young woman. Eventually he seduced her into a secretive sexual relationship, redefining the relationship as being "God's will." The woman was 18 years old; the preacher was 60. After six years in the cult, her closest friend told her that the same minister had been secretly having a sexual relationship with her. Breaking the secrecy surrounding this leader's sexual improprieties (and the eventual discovery that he had been having sex with at least 12 other members) propelled this young woman and her friend to leave the cult.

Upon leaving, the young woman was filled with self-loathing and shame. She sought out therapy with a woman who claimed to be an expert in the area of sexual abuse. After learning about her client's situation, the therapist told the young woman that it was clear that she was reenacting a sexually abusive situation from childhood. The therapist told her client that her father had, most likely, abused her. When the former cultist was unable to recall such an incident, the therapist reassured her that she would remember it in time. She was placed in a group for incest survivors; during a group guided-imagery process, she remembered that she felt uncomfortable whenever her uncle hugged her. However, she remained unable to remember any sexual contact with her father. Although she could empathize with the feelings of the women who had experienced childhood sexual abuse, she continued to have difficulty remembering abuse from her own childhood.

After several months of therapy she joined other members from her cult for an exit counseling session. During the exit counseling she learned how cult leaders manipulate recruits to do many things contrary to the recruits' own beliefs. The exit counselors told her that it was possible to be sexually abused by a cult leader without having been sexually abused in childhood.

As we can see from this example, cult life can have a traumatic impact on cult members. In working with a former cultist, a therapist who minimizes the cult experiences and sees all cult actions exclusively as indicative of experiences in early life and not, to a greater degree, due to the manipulations of the cult leader is further victimizing the former cultist. Of course some individuals have had traumatic experiences in their childhood, which are remembered or repressed prior to their cult involvement, while others who join cults are not traumatized by such an experience. However, therapists need to recognize the impact that cult life can have on former cultists and not make a priori judgments about cult involvement.

TYPICAL PRESENTING PROBLEMS

Former cultists who enter therapy show a wide variety of presenting problems. These problems have changed in some respects over the years. The former cultists that I began seeing as clients 16 years ago typically had been in the larger cults that were prevalent in the early 1970s. These ex-members had spent up to five years in these groups, had entered the cultic environment during late adolescence, and generally had left because of a deprogramming, usually arranged by family members.

In a study coauthored with William Goldberg (Goldberg & Goldberg, 1982), we described former cultists seen for counseling or therapy within two to three months of having left their cult as continuing to show the character traits and hold some of the attitudes of their cultic group. For example, those who were in Eastern religious cults that focused on subservience to a spiritual leader kept their heads bowed, spoke with a sing-song cadence, and continued to struggle with their desire to be good and holy, while those who were in cults that emphasized sexuality as a lure for recruitment continued to relate to others in a seductive manner. Most of the former cultists seen at that time also showed what appeared to be diminished abilities in the areas of perception, decision making, discrimination, judgment, and memory. It took time for them to collect their thoughts; speech was often colorless and halting. Former cultists who sought counseling within two months of leaving their cult were described as being in the first stage of a process that typically lasted about two years. Usually by the two-year marker the individual had integrated the cult experience and moved into the wider world, no longer primarily defining himself or herself as a former cultist.

Although these individuals no longer wished to remain in the deceptive and controlling environment of the cult, they initially experienced a sense of confusion, manifest in their continued automatic expression of the cult's attitudes and beliefs. They had difficulty integrating the bizarre cultic world from which they had exited with the outside world – the world in which they had spent their youth and adolescence. They were strangers to their own families and to their former selves; they showed symptoms that revealed their sense of disorientation, alienation, and identity confusion. Singer and Ofshe (1990) note that these individuals feel like immigrants entering a new culture. However, they are actually reentering their own culture, bringing with them beliefs from their cult life that conflict with the norms of the larger society. Their pre-cult personality (or real self) struggles with the personality that was imposed by the cult. West (1992) labeled this the *pseudopersonality*.

Case Example

Several years ago I interviewed a woman who had left an Eastern meditation group one month prior to entering therapy. She had returned home suddenly after a heated dispute with one of the leaders. Her parents arranged for her to see me after she had gone through a voluntary exit counseling. (For a description and discussion of exit counseling, see Section Two.) After five years of "doing service," she became disillusioned with some of the deceptive practices of the leadership. In her first therapy session, however, she expressed a concern about whether I would be "spiritual" enough to work with her, a question that indicated she was continuing to hold onto her group's doctrine. I responded that I wasn't sure if I was spiritual enough because I wasn't sure what she meant by the term. Thus began the long process of attempting to define, and thereby demystify, the former cultist's cult jargon and ideology.

The young woman often used amorphous language, speaking in such an abstract manner that it was difficult to follow her. At the same time, the difficulty I experienced in concentrating on what she was saying helped me understand the diffuse and trance-inducing environment that she had been in. Telling her of my confusion in sessions helped her objectify her experience. To serve as someone who aids the client in relearning how to speak more concretely and clearly is a crucial therapeutic function. The goal here was to "ground" this young woman, who seemed to float on air with language and a demeanor that might lead me, her therapist, to float along with her.

Upon leaving her Eastern meditation group, she continued to dress in a "hippie" style, to practice yoga, and to maintain a vegetarian diet. These decisions were not challenged. In our sessions, however, we explored how yoga affected her, whether it was a regressive experience, returning her to cultic thinking, or a progressive experience, providing her with more structure and a sense of well-being in her current life. Her cult had encouraged long periods of meditation. After her departure, she often found herself dissociating, automatically drifting into a trance state. Once she began to link dissociation to yoga, she gave up the practice of yoga on her own.

Although she had attended college, she at first believed she was too much of an outsider and too "slow thinking" to succeed in a conventional job. She was an excellent typist but could only get temporary employment. She sensed that her behavior and dress were too offbeat for her to gain rapport with other workers. Sometimes she had trouble following complex directions and she had difficulty concentrating. Although she was a voracious reader prior to cult involvement, she found it difficult to read after leaving her group. She feared that she had lost some of her intelligence. In time, however, to her relief and mine, her cognitive and social abilities returned.

CHANGES IN RECENT YEARS

In contrast to those ex-members seen years ago, the majority of ex-cultists seen in recent years do not initially present themselves as dramatically different from the outside world. Their appearance is not as otherworldly as those who left cults in the 1970s. This difference results from several factors.

First, the majority of cults today are not as isolated from the outside world as were cults in the 1970s. Although the individual still enters into a new belief system when joining a cult, now a connection is often kept with the outside world. Typically believers continue working at their pre-cult jobs and more often tend to remain in contact with family and friends, even though this contact becomes more strained as the cult member's behavior, attitudes, and language begin to change.

Second, while in the late 1960s and 1970s there were more cults with an Eastern religious doctrine, today there are more Bible-based, new age, or psychotherapy cults. Therefore, on the surface at least cult members do not appear to be as otherworldly as their earlier counterparts.

Third, those who seek help today are more likely to have left a cult on their own (as opposed to leaving as a result of a deprogramming, which was more prevalent in the 1970s) and may not be seen for several months or even years after their departure. Therefore, the residual identifications with the cult and the cult leader have loosened.

However, some cultic identifications and attitudes do remain. For example, some former cult members describe having more critical attitudes toward themselves and others after leaving their cult. It seems that they have incorporated the harsh attitudes of their cult leaders. Some continue to believe that they have no personal worth now that they are separated from the group that claimed all responsibility for their accomplishments. One woman, for example, formerly an editor of her cult's newspaper, was doing simple clerical work several months after her cult departure. She was certain that all her editing skills were attached to the cult; she was terrified that she would fail at a more demanding job.

Without an understanding of their cultic experience, those who leave cults on their own tend to be plagued by aftereffects longer than those who gain such an understanding, for example, because they have been exit counseled. This is particularly true for individuals who have spent most of their young adulthood in a cult. We are now seeing an increasing number of former cultists who have spent 10, 15, or even 20 years in a cult.

Case Example

One 36-year-old man did not enter therapy with me until five years after he had left the psychotherapy cult he had been in for 10 years. In the years following his departure from the group he had no idea that he had been in a cultic group nor that his experience had harmed him until he came across Hassan's (1988) book, *Combatting Cult Mind Control.* An intelligent man, he also appeared to be somewhat intense and moralistic. He was having difficulty settling on a career (he was working well below his potential) and was having problems developing intimate relationships. Three years after having left his cult, he was disturbed enough by these problems to have sought out therapy, which focused mainly on his current life and its relationship to early childhood experiences. He felt uncomfortable with his therapist, had concerns about being "controlled," and terminated the therapy after a brief period. Thus, his first therapy experience touched on but did not explore his cultic involvement.

He consciously understood that it was in his best interest to have left his cult; yet he still believed that he had failed, thereby minimizing his cult experience. In our therapy sessions he realized that his sense of shame and feeling that he was a bad flawed person made him suppress his painful feelings about the group. He had held onto the belief that the group's doctrine was perfect, although he regarded the middle-management types who administered the "program" as manipulative and, therefore, flawed. Yet he continued to hold the cult leader – a more distant figure – in high esteem.

Due to his sense of being a failure for having left the group, he unconsciously undermined his ability to succeed in new projects. Because of his unconscious sense of feeling trapped in the cult, he feared new commitments. After some time in therapy he was able to begin to speak of the antisocial, even criminal, activities that he had engaged in while in the cult. He was extremely ashamed of this behavior, and it helped him to be reminded that these actions were put forth by his cult leader as having been in the service of the "greater good." His distaste for these irregular activities and the group's attitude toward them in fact had eventually played into his decision to leave. At times during therapy, his highly moralistic demeanor led to feelings that the therapist was not "up to par"; this demeanor in fact was a reflection of his own feeling of worthlessness and served as a "cover" for, or characterological defense against, his feelings of shame.

RECOGNIZING
CULT-INDUCED EMOTIONS

In the cult, emotions are manipulated by others. When cultists leave the group, they continue to feel unable to control their affects. While some former cultists will appear lacking in affect, others will appear to be overwhelmed by their emotions. For example, a man who left a mass therapy group not long before coming in for therapy felt anxious all the time. He appeared to be jumping out of his skin, expecting to be "nailed" by those he came in contact with. In his group, members were videotaped, then picked apart by the leader and other members. In addition to anxiety, he suffered from periodic depression. The intensity of these feelings was not noticed prior to his cult involvement. This creative man was dissuaded from continuing his artistic profession and for some time found it hard to return to his career because of the cult-induced feeling that to pursue his art was "selfish," and because he feared criticism from others. Ironically it was the promise of enhanced creative ability that lured him into participating in this cult's workshops in the first place. It was only after examining how the cult had manipulated him that this young man was able to begin to succeed in the art world.

Many former cultists, particularly those from new age, mass therapy, or other cults that violate their members' natural boundaries and defense mechanisms, describe feeling flooded with emotion all the time. Halperin (1992) notes that some former members initially appear to be in a manic state. Others, particularly those from religious groups, appear to suffer from symptoms related to depression. They describe feeling racked with guilt or shame; they believe that they no longer are "good" people and are now on the path to Hell. Ex-members of cults that required long periods of chanting, meditation, visualization, or other hypnotic techniques often appear detached from their emotions. They suffer from anxiety about entering into trance states involuntarily; as a result they have difficulty with concentration and other cognitive abilities. Those who experienced repeated verbal, physical, or sexual abuse often develop several of a cluster of symptoms (classified as post-traumatic stress syndrome), including flashbacks, nightmares, amnesia, phobias, anxiety, depression, emotional numbing, shame, guilt, self-loathing, and social withdrawal.

Most former cultists suffer from a strong sense of loneliness. They were constantly surrounded by others in the cult and induced to identify with the leader. Cultic friendships usually are conditional, based on the individual's loyalty to the cult. For some afterward in therapy there is a discovery that part of the cult's appeal was to escape from a sense of loneliness that developed in early childhood and adolescence. In any case, a group of former cultists is a helpful adjunct to individual therapy for those who are feeling lonely or isolated from others who had similar experiences.

Coupled with loneliness are feelings of sadness and grief — sensing a loss of a life that promised total fulfillment. Former cultists are mourning the loss of a period in their lives that appeared to fulfill their idealism. Sadness is a healthy reaction to loss. Former cultists need to come to terms with how their normal idealism and perhaps youthful grandiosity were exploited and destroyed by the cult. For some the sadness focuses on the years of missed possibilities while in the cult, for example, not having had the opportunity to enter into a satisfying relationship, to have children, or to acquire career skills.

After a time there is often an expression of intense anger at the cult leader and/or a desire to act against the cult. Social or legal action is usually seen as a progressive step. Rather than directing anger primarily at the self, the former cultist is now taking constructive actions against the manipulators or, through education, is preventing others from getting ensnared.

Anxiety is commonly experienced by former cultists. One woman told me, "The hardest thing for me to face is the feeling that I am no longer protected from the forces of the outside world." It is difficult to face a world without the magical powers of the cult leader and the protective mechanisms of decreeing, chanting, meditation, and so forth. Once away from the cult, however, the former cultist no longer needs to feel the conditioned anxiety that all can be taken away from the individual at any time based on the predilections of the cult leader. Ex-members sometimes fear their fragility upon leaving the group. This is not only because of the symptoms they are experiencing but also because family members or friends treat them as if they were made of porcelain and will easily break. It is important for ex-members to see that if they have survived their cult experience, they have survived the most difficult part. Now they can begin to recover.

INITIAL ASSESSMENT: UNDERSTANDING THE CONTEXT

All those recruited by cultic groups are not necessarily living under mind-control influences. Conversely some individuals are involved in very controlling relationships that might not appear to be cults. It has become clear to me that what is important in terms of therapeutic intervention is not whether a person has left a group that fits within the definitional boundaries of a cult, but whether that individual reacted to involvement in that group in a particular way, as described in this chapter. That is, the issue is not the group itself but a particular reaction of the individual to the group's pressures while in the group and to the experience of leaving that group. Sirkin and Wynne (1990) describe the cultic relationship as similar to a folie à deux.

Upon ascertaining if a particular client indeed was in a high-demand situation and in fact had been controlled within that situation, it is important that the therapist "normalize" post-cult symptoms and emotions. Ex-cultists need to know that their reactions usually are related to cultic suggestions, practices, and manipulations, and to their actual separation from the cult.

After helping former cultists understand that separation from their cult may normally induce a variety of symptoms and emotions, the clinician should begin to focus on how these symptoms might be related to several factors. Factors to be considered include the individual's experience in the cult, the nature of the cult, the duration and intensity of involvement, the type of departure from the cult, and the degree of emotional support and understanding received after departure. For example, somatic complaints might be related to the cult's suggestion that a person's body will rot or the person will contract a severe illness upon leaving the group. Fear of accidents, death, or negative life circumstances might have to do with cultic suggestions and a general fearfulness of disaster now that the cult's supposed protection no longer exists in the former member's life. And as mentioned previously, for some, it is quite painful to consider getting through life without protection. A homosexual man, for example, was lured into a cult by the leader's promise that by following her practices he would be safe from AIDS.

Many former cultists suffer from sexual difficulties after having been forced to practice celibacy for many years or after having been sexually manipulated or abused within the cult. This makes it difficult to trust new relationships. Ex-cultists usually feel awkward in social situations; to their alarm they often find themselves behaving in the manner deemed "proper" by their cult. This behavior, however, usually contrasts sharply with their pre-cult behavior and post-cult values.

THE PSYCHOEDUCATIONAL
PROCESS

From the beginning the therapist joins the former cultist in a psychoeducational process. According to Singer (1991), "Therapy cannot begin until education ends." The therapist and the ex-cultist first must have knowledge about cult recruitment and control processes, particularly the specific methods used by the former cultist's group. In order to further analyze this process, the therapist needs to help the former cultist explore his or her vulnerability to recruitment – a vulnerability that we all have under certain circumstances, unless we are informed about mind-control techniques and can identify those techniques as they are being used by the recruiting group.

Exploring Vulnerabilities to the Recruitment Process

Vulnerability to cult recruitment is particularly high during transitional periods. Those who entered cultic groups in late adolescence should be helped to see the degree to which their involvement parallels the developmental process. In adolescence there is a push for separation. Healthy late adolescents value a sense of their own autonomy and attempt to develop a vision of the world that is different from their parents' view. Offer and Offer state that "The establishment of a self separate from the parents is one of the major tasks of young adulthood. The young adult must disengage himself from parental domination" (1975, p. 167). Erikson (1950) defines the consolidation of identity as the life crisis of adolescence. Even though adolescents have made numerous identifications with their parents throughout their early life, they are pressured by cultic groups to give up these identifications and to replace them with the group's values. The clinician should help the former cultist see how he or she was pressured to make these new identifications, which met the group's needs rather than his or her own.

An ex-member told me, for example, that when she informed her group that she was planning to attend graduate school in clinical psychology she was told that she was "copping out on her responsibility to God" by thinking only of her own needs. The leaders encouraged her to be a counselor to the youth group; as a result, she placed her career on hold during her four years of cult membership. Therapy involves reworking pre-cult, cult, and post-cult values to help the individual gain a better integrated and more autonomous sense of self. Now that this woman has left the cult, she plans to fulfill her career goal.

Working with Adolescents

During late adolescence vulnerability to cult recruitment can be intensified because of the individual's physical distance from the family, perhaps on a college campus or while traveling during a vacation period. Many cults recruit on or near college campuses or at youth hostels or transportation centers. Separation from home might increase an adolescent's feelings of anxiety and sense of loss. Living in a college dorm can increase an individual's concern about his or her sexuality and anxiety about how to deal with increased personal and sexual freedom. Additionally there are specific personality dynamics of adolescents that make them vulnerable to cults. Anna Freud (1966) describes how the defenses of intellectualization and asceticism are often utilized in adolescence. Blos (1962) notes a tendency toward inner experience and self-discovery—the religious experience.

Adolescents tend to be idealistic, and cults hold out the promise of the fulfillment of idealistic dreams. William Goldberg and I (1988) noted that adolescents who seem particularly vulnerable to cults are those who have high expectations for themselves and are ready to see the best in others. This characteristic might play into their faith in the cult's idealistic words and a tendency to ignore the disparity between the group's words and actions. The demand for perfection might be related to growing up in families where high standards of performance were set by one or both parents. Vulnerable individuals may feel that they could not measure up to these expectations on their own. The cult promised a way to achieve a high standard or a means to escape from some minor or major disappointments in themselves or others.

By looking at the vulnerability of all adolescents, the former cultist is helped to feel less embarrassed and weak-minded. What happened to him or her could have happened to anybody who was in the wrong place at the wrong time. Ex-members tend to believe that this bad event (that is, joining the cult) happened because of something they lacked. They often feel ashamed of, and responsible for, the events in their lives—a vestige of the childhood magical thinking that is also part of the belief system of many cults. Former cultists need to understand that even if they were initially attracted to the structured and communal environment, if they had known that they were being deceived and manipulated by a variety of highly sophisticated techniques orchestrated by a sociopathic leader, they would not have joined.

Working with Adults

There are other vulnerability factors not related to late adolescence. Those who joined cults may have had a desire for a sense of community, acceptance, or increased skills at a time in their lives when they were experiencing loneliness or anxiety about the future. They may have been vulnerable because of a loss or fear of loss. This may be related to internal factors such as a disappointment in themselves causing a loss of self-esteem, or external factors such as divorce, physical illness, death, change in physical location of their residence, or a change in employment that caused a disruption in their life. They may have been vulnerable because of pressure to take a training workshop run by a cult in connection with their job. Some individuals joined cults as a restitutive attempt to deal with chronic depression or various character disorders. Others joined as a way of fending off ensuing psychotic behavior, which rarely works because nonproductive members are usually thrown out since cults demand a high level of functioning and effectiveness at fund-raising, recruitment, and other cult-directed work. Those with antisocial tendencies often use what they have learned in one cult to form a new group in which they can control others. (Although over the years former cultists have given me numerous anecdotal accounts of sociopathic cult leaders or members, I have not seen antisocial ex-members in my practice.)

EXAMINING
THE CULT EXPERIENCE

Cults often deceive new recruits about requirements, the doctrine, and the sponsorship of the group itself. Rarely does the initiate understand that he or she will be induced to become involved in a regressive, totalistic environment. Doctrine is given in a piecemeal fashion so that initially members see only the most universally acceptable ideas and practices. Thus the initiate is not making an informed choice when he or she joins a cult.

Certainly understanding the powerful effect of group processes is not new. In 1895 LeBon (1972) emphasized the power of suggestion and contagion in groups. Freud elaborated on this theme by noting that an individual "liability to affect becomes extraordinarily intensified, while his intellectual ability is markedly reduced" (1921, p. 20) when he participates in a group. Freud also referred to the tendency of groups to temporarily or permanently suspend feelings of hostility toward members and to use the mechanisms of identification and reaction formation to further defend against hostile feelings. He also noted that group leaders are seen by members as a new ego ideal and this further encourages the identification process with the leader.

Modern-day cultic groups have incorporated sophisticated manipulative techniques that capitalize on the normal group tendencies previously described. Ofshe and Singer (1986) have noted that destructive cults have further refined programs of coercive influence that have been employed by the communists in the former Soviet Union and China. Cult techniques have now gone beyond political "thought reform" to focus on central (intrapsychic) rather than peripheral (political) aspects of an individual's self. The cults of today use techniques to break through and change an individual's coping strategies and defense mechanisms.

According to former members, in order for cults to gain new adherents, they use sensory bombardment through such tactics as prolonged lectures, sleep deprivation, environmental control, and love bombing. They encourage the breaking of ties with the recruit's usual sources of information and support, such as family and friends. Recruitment is most effective when the group is able to completely monopolize the member's time. Cults induce recruits to be caught up in hypnotic emotionality rather than the intellect through stirring songs, chants, and confessional guilt-inducing sessions. All of this can serve to bring on a dissociative state, that is, an altered state of increased suggestibility. To protect oneself in the midst of confusion, loss of former ties, induced guilt, and dissociation, the recruit tends to reorganize reality through a new defensive system in which identification with the aggressor (the cult leader) predominates.

Although the recruit experiences the positive effect of belonging to a community in which there is unanimity of thinking, the pressure for such unanimity precludes any type of critical assessment of this coercive experience and precludes the retention of a sense of the pre-cult self. The recruit is unable to differentiate his or her thoughts and feelings from those of the group, as boundaries between the individual and others in the cult have merged. Ex-cultists report that at this point they experienced a sense of peace, a euphoric feeling. The cults attribute this to a mystical or religious experience. Many cult members, in fact, describe the fantasy of merging with their leader — a fantasy often suggested by the leader. This fantasy further induces the recruit to serve the wishes of the leader, who is presumed to know the recruit's every thought. The leader is now imagined to be carried inside the recruit's own body — as a new foreign superego. Some groups induce depersonalization in their pressure on members to have out-of-body experiences. One woman, for example, was encouraged to transport herself to other planets. After leaving the cult, she continued to be plagued by out-of-body experiences until she was able to identify how depersonalization was induced in her cult and the triggers that re-induced these experiences after she left the group.

Although cults hold out the promise of solving pre-cult difficulties for some, after an initial period of excitement and relief, most former cult members describe in retrospect feeling that the promise was only the "hook" and that their need for personal growth was in fact suppressed or overridden by the needs of the group. Members are often encouraged to work for the group full-time. Cults encourage passivity by teaching members to follow their leader without question. Those who attempt to act independently are humiliated by the leader and treated as object lessons for the others.

Assessing the Influence of
Mind-control Techniques

In the initial stages of therapy it is particularly important to assess the influence that mind-control techniques continue to have on the individual's behavior and thoughts. The cult's persuasive techniques, for example, continue to have an impact to the extent that there is a belief that every thought and action has cosmic significance, that individuals create their own reality, that there is overwhelming guilt or fear when entertaining thoughts considered negative by the group, and that there is a need to employ what Lifton (1961, p. 29) refers to as the "thought-terminating cliché" when confronted with information that does not fit into a simplistic black-and-white view of reality. This all indicates that the individual views the locus of control as stemming from the cult rather than from the self.

TAKING AN ACTIVE AND
RESPONSIVE STANCE

Former cultists need to be told when their emotional state is a natural reaction to separation from a cult. Since they were coerced to restructure their personalities in order to conform to cultic attitudes and behavior, they tend to feel completely depleted upon leaving that environment. Their task is to begin to deal with not being tightly orchestrated by others. This orchestration, plus the pressure to conform to the cult's view and ignore their emotions, leads cult members to a passive and robotic existence. When they don't know what they feel, they find themselves going through the motions at the request of others.

In one cult, for example, a woman was told that whatever she felt, the opposite was the truth, which was her cult leader's way of controlling individuals and putting them into a disoriented state. The woman was hospitalized after she was mauled by a dangerous bull, which she ignored, believing that what she was seeing was a friendly cow. The help that she received during her hospitalization led to her cult departure.

Why Not Silence?

Although silence with other types of clients can promote the development of the client's fantasies about the therapist and allows the transference to evolve, silence can be particularly anxiety provoking for a former cultist. He or she might be at a loss about how to fill such a vacuum after years of automatically responding to a structured life. A silent therapist can unduly burden some former cultists or can become a blank screen for the projection of paranoid ideation that was induced by the cult. Such projection can lead to premature termination of therapy. Solomon (1988) points out that silence also is contraindicated for those prone to dissociation. Lack of structure can induce trance.

Common Reactions to the Therapist

Many former cultists initially fear being manipulated and controlled by the therapist in the same manner that they were manipulated by the cult leader. Therapists should not jump to the conclusion that they are seeing a paranoid character trait or that this paranoia is the result of the individual's experience of early childhood relationships. In former cultists such behavior more often is a displacement of feelings that were induced by the cult experience. Having a concern about being manipulated following cult involvement in fact can be a healthy sign of increased skepticism. (Most cultists tended to be too trusting prior to their cult experience.) Furthermore, former cultists are struggling with their cult-induced passivity and they initially might not be in touch with what they actually think. Therefore, they correctly sense that they can be easily influenced by others.

Some former cultists tend to idealize their therapists, especially in the early stages of therapy. Again this can be a way of filling the vacuum created by cult departure. It is vital that the therapist not play into this idealization by assuming the role of rescuer and violating therapeutic boundaries. Therapists should be seen as co-workers in the self-discovery process, not as gurus. The former cultist should be a participating member in a team of equals. The therapeutic rules and process need to be clearly explained to show that nothing magical occurs, that the therapist has no special powers but does have human limits. It is helpful to remind former cultists to put their thoughts into words, because the therapist is unable to read minds. Equally important is to help former cultists see that the therapist has human flaws and makes mistakes. In fact, when it seems appropriate, I often laugh at my mistakes. This seems to help former cultists deal more effectively with their unusually harsh attitudes toward themselves, those self-critical attitudes that may have been exacerbated or even instilled by their cult.

In contrast to former cultists who idealize or want to please the therapist, some relate in an angry, devaluing manner. They will zero in on every character flaw and mistake made by the therapist. It is important to face this anger with equanimity. However, the therapist should not allow herself to be abused, thereby repeating her client's cult experience. Several authors, including Deutsch and Miller (1983) and Halperin (1990), have focused on how some cultists have had a preexisting difficulty with tolerating anger or with assertion. Former cultists need to know that they will not be punished for displaying anger. Anger may also serve to protect former cultists from their fear of being unduly influenced by the therapist. Additionally perhaps, for some, there may be a need to displace anger from the cult leader onto the therapist, who is seen as a less powerful and vengeful figure.

Many former cultists may decide to see the therapist only for short-term goal-oriented therapy. For obvious reasons, these individuals are sensitive to and resentful of pressure to remain in treatment. Therapists should consider working with these clients on a goal-oriented periodic basis if that seems desirable and potentially more productive. Former cultists need to know that they can leave therapy with positive feelings on both sides and be welcomed back at a later date.

On the other hand, Dubrow-Eichel and Dubrow-Eichel (1988) describe the tendency of some former cultists to expect therapy to be the "quick fix" that was promised by the cult. Although it is useful to focus on specific goals, the therapist must clearly state that there will be no quick, dramatic transformation. The therapist cannot make promises of cure: only cult leaders do that. Therapy requires hard work on the part of the client and the therapist; if all goes well, in time, the former cultist will have a clearer understanding of his or her experience.

Focusing on the Positive

Former cultists have survived a major crisis in their lives and have learned a great deal from this experience. Not all cult-induced behaviors are negative. Some former cultists express that they can be proud of having pushed themselves to the limit for their goals. Others state that they became more outgoing and self-confident as a result of the proselytizing demanded by the group. Many learned valuable skills, which can be used in post-cult life; this is generally true for those who worked in cult-owned businesses. Generally cultists are induced to credit the cult with the responsibility for all their achievements. It is therefore helpful to remind former members that they, not the "magic" of the cult, were responsible for their successes.

THERAPEUTIC GOALS

The primary therapeutic goals are to help former cultists gain an understanding of their cult experiences and of themselves. By inducing regression, suppression, identification with the aggressor, and numerous other defensive strategies in their members, cults often intensify the dependency feelings and uncertainty of childhood. Because a cult member is trained to no longer trust his or her inner emotions, which have been reinterpreted by the cult as indicators of the individual's "selfishness," the cultist finds it necessary to constantly check with the leader for a sense of what behavior and which attitudes are correct. In the cult, correct behavior is rewarded and incorrect behavior is punished.

Initially, the therapist is providing information to help the former cultist gain a better comprehension of how mind-control processes at work in the cult tended to obliterate the members' sense of self. Along with this, the therapist is providing a safe environment for the former cultist to tap into what he or she truly feels, particularly in remembering the cult experience. The toleration of a wider range of shared memories, emotions, and spontaneous responses in proportion to the situation at hand is the therapeutic goal. For example, individuals need not be "up" all the time, as was necessary in the cult. Yet it is important to combat the ex-member's cult-induced passivity by encouraging the expression of spontaneous reactions and autonomous behavior so that former cultists can begin to make independent life decisions and manage more successfully the tasks of work, school, and relationships.

CONCLUSION

A therapist who sees only family life experiences as the genesis of the difficulties experienced by ex-cultists is not dealing with the precipitating, more recent traumatic event in the individual's life that has led to the presenting difficulties. Although cults of the late 1980s and early 1990s appear different from cults of the 1960s and 1970s, the differences are merely superficial. For the most part, former cultists today are struggling with the same post-cult reactions as did ex-members of earlier years. Cults use a variety of manipulative techniques that superimpose new identifications and values on individuals. These cult-induced identifications and values clash with pre-cult and post-cult beliefs.

Although they have left their cults, ex-member clients initially enter therapy with many cult-induced behaviors, emotions, and beliefs, which the therapist and client must begin to identify. Therefore, the therapist needs to utilize a psychoeducational approach, initially giving information about the cult's manipulative techniques to explain how this has influenced post-cult behaviors, emotional reactions, and beliefs, while at the same time creating a safe environment for the expression of memories and spontaneous reactions. Although the therapist needs to take an active role in the therapeutic process, it is necessary that the former cultist be a participating member in a team of equals. This contrasts sharply with the cultic relationship in which the leader is seen as godlike and the cultist is denigrated and seen as having little of value to contribute.

REFERENCES

Blos, P. (1962). *On adolescence.* New York: Free Press.

Deutsch, A., & Miller, M. J. (1983). A clinical study of four Unification Church members. *American Journal of Psychiatry, 140,* 767–770.

Dubrow-Eichel, S. K., & Dubrow-Eichel, L. (1988). Trouble in paradise: Some observations on psychotherapy with new agers. *Cultic Studies Journal, 5*(2), 177–192.

Erikson, E. H. (1950). *Childhood and society.* New York: W. W. Norton.

Freud, A. (1966). *The ego and the mechanisms of defense.* New York: International Universities Press.

Freud, S. (1921). *Group psychology and the analysis of the ego.* London: Hogarth Press.

Goldberg, L., & Goldberg, W. (1982). Group work with former cultists. *Social Work, 27,* 165–170.

Goldberg, L., & Goldberg, W. (1988). Psychotherapy with ex-cultists: Four case studies and commentary. *Cultic Studies Journal, 5*(2), 193–210.

Halperin, D. (1990). Psychiatric perspectives on cult affiliation. *Psychiatric Annals, 20*(4), 204–213.

Halperin, D. (1992, April). Presentation at the NY/NJ regional conference of the Cult Awareness Network, Wayne, NJ.

Hassan, S. (1988). *Combatting cult mind control.* Rochester, VT: Park Street Press.

LeBon, G. (1972). *The crowd.* New York: Viking Press.

Lifton, R. J. (1961). *Thought reform and the psychology of totalism.* New York: W. W. Norton.

Offer, D., & Offer, J. B. (1975). *From teenage to young manhood: A psychological study.* New York: Basic Books.

Ofshe, R., & Singer, M. T. (1986). Attacks on peripheral versus central elements of self and the impact of thought reforming techniques. *Cultic Studies Journal, 3*(1), 3–24.

Singer, M. T. (1991, November). Presentation at the annual conference of the Cult Awareness Network, Oklahoma City, OK.

Singer, M. T., & Ofshe, R. (1990). Thought reform programs and the production of psychiatric casualties. *Psychiatric Annals, 20*(4), 188–193.

Sirkin, M. I., & Wynne, L. C. (1990). Cult involvement as relational disorder. *Psychiatric Annals, 20*(4), 199–203.

Solomon, A. O. (1988). Psychotherapy of a casualty from a mass therapy encounter group: A case study. *Cultic Studies Journal, 5*(2), 211–227.

West, L. J. (1992, May). Presentation at American Family Foundation conference, Arlington, VA.

12

GUIDELINES FOR CLERGY

Richard L. Dowhower, D.D.

MY EXPERIENCES WITH EXITING MEMBERS of manipulative and abusive religious and psychotherapy cults have repeatedly impressed upon me the universal need of these former cultists for a certain type of counseling. In most cases, they need a significant encounter, connection, and relationship with a pastoral counselor who is spiritually developed, theologically trained, and knowledgeable about cults. Someone who was in a religious cult needs a counselor who will affirm the legitimacy of that person's spiritual quest, no matter how misdirected it may have become. In this chapter I will discuss issues that I believe clergy should consider when working with former cultists.

Ex-members and helping professionals who are strictly "secularist" may not want to concern themselves with the spiritual issues discussed here, although it is my belief that certain general principles and guidelines for understanding and counseling former cult members can be gleaned from what is expressed in this chapter.

THE VOICES OF RECOVERY

"Spiritual rape was more painful in my cult than sexual and physical abuse."

"When I was joining my group, I thought it was God calling to me, and now I just don't know where that call came from."

"Did I betray God by joining a cult? Will He forgive me?"

"Is it okay not to believe anything right now after the experience I just had with that New Age group?"

"My problem isn't with people, but with God. I was sincerely wanting to do the right thing . . . now I can't pray anymore. If this [cult experience] was your will for me, God, then f--- you! I don't believe it was God's will, but it hurts."

"Although my group wasn't religious, it still spoke to the same needs that a religious group speaks to. My leader offered me spiritual answers. I don't think I betrayed God, but I betrayed my friends and family."

"I went to my family's clergy but he was no help at all. I feel that the Bible's not interested in organized religion."

"The adults in my childhood ritual-abuse experience were the elite of our town – doctors, lawyers, even a Protestant minister!"

"After getting out of my group, I wanted to be spiritual. To me, love is love. I have a problem with needing to believe in a being who is bigger than us. I like the idea of 'Trust yourself.'"

These are just a sampling of some former cult members' candid reflections on the religious and spiritual issues that remained unresolved after their exit from a destructive group. Some of these were voluntary reports given at a recovery weekend sponsored by the American Family Foundation. Some came from private interviews over the past 17 years.

Revelatory disclosures such as these are typically heard by many sensitive and available clergy in congregational settings, military chaplaincies, campus ministry outposts, college and seminary classrooms and faculty offices, as well as the offices of specialized pastoral counselors and psychotherapists. They may even be heard by executive clergy in denominational offices and councils of churches.

A THEOLOGICAL ORIENTATION

My own theological tradition gives highest priority to the need of the human spirit and being for the experiential knowledge of the person's own unconditional acceptance by the Holy Other, Almighty God, The Creator of the Universe, The Ground of Being, The Ultimate Reality. To know Yahweh's *chesed*, the steadfast love that lasts forever, or the "grace" of the Lord Jesus is to be "known through and through and loved still and all." It is love with no strings attached.

Therefore, my goal as a pastor who does counseling with ex-cult members is to reflect that *chesed*/grace in our meetings. I want, within my conditioned limits, to accept that person as unconditionally as possible. I want to accept that person where he is, and seek by the *chesed*/grace inherent in such an encounter, to help him define his own theology and set and pursue life goals based upon it.

That means that as a Christian clergy of the Lutheran tradition, I am not in that particular relationship trying to move the person toward a predetermined conversion decision. Not only does "missionary" counseling of ex-members violate my theology of *chesed*/grace, but also it represents a direct threat of another religious attack upon the person, not unlike the cult's manipulation and abuse. My education in a church-related college included a required course in Judeo-Christian ethics; a major thesis of the Judeo-Christian tradition is that we consider people as ends in themselves and not as means to another's end.

I believe we develop our human capacities to receive and understand *chesed*/grace from brief experiences of unconditional acceptance in interpersonal relationships, beginning with one's family of origin. Thus, I aim to make the pastoral counseling session with an ex-cult member one in which he or she experiences *chesed*/grace. Then, the person can determine within a noncoercive setting what theologizing and life-style decisions may come next. My theology tells me that the work of conversion is God's; my job is to faithfully serve the mutually identifiable needs of the cult victim.

HELPING A PERSON
"DO THEOLOGY"

The purpose of the spiritually developed, theologically trained pastoral counselor is to assist in the person's effort to "do theology," that is, to engage in a thinking, feeling process by which the person reflects upon the ultimate meaning of his or her own life experience, and articulates that meaning in a rational and coherent manner. In most cultic environments the group and its leader(s) make grandiose claims to having the truth. All of this, meanwhile, is fraught with massive contradictions, especially in the cult's actual practice and in the leader's lifestyle. This hypocrisy and the intellectually untenable theology leave the ex-cult member with great confusion over what is valid theologically, and what is not.

In the voices of the ex-cultists quoted above, one hears the hunger to affirm spiritual needs and to sort out healthy religion from a theology that is unhealthy, immature, and makes one vulnerable to abuse

by others. This process of reflection and deliberation seeks to identify
the divine presence and activity in, with, and under the ordinary experiences of a person's life. It seeks to explore and identify the major
theological motifs in the cultic theology and to bring to the surface
the needs of the individual that were drawn to such an appeal in the
first place.

The immediate objective is to raise, develop, and heighten the spiritual gift of discernment. Persons whose spirituality matures and develops in a consistent manner are able to discern the difference between
the spirits: those legitimately attributable to God and those that are
not. Many former cult members evidence a lack of wise discernment in
their decisions to join and commit themselves to groups that turn out
to have destructive effects on their lives.

I proceed from the assumption that there are claims to truth that
are theologically respectable on the basis of internal coherence, valida-
tion in the history of religious thought, and the capacity to give meaning to life experience. Most groups known to be intentionally destructive have truth claims, or theologies, that are wanting.

THE THEOLOGICAL ORIENTATION
OF CULTS

Religious and psychotherapy movements that violate human rights
have some common theological traits. They are usually contemporary
versions of the ancient Christian heresy known as Gnosticism, the
teaching that one can only be saved by special enlightenment, the
privilege of the spiritually elite.

Most religious cults deny the claims of Judaism to be the fullness
of God's revelation. Many of them claim that Jesus of Nazareth did
not provide all that needed to be done for salvation, nor did he provide
the full revelation of God. Each of these cults has a leader who claims
to complete the job of saving humanity and to provide the fullness of
revealed truth. Therefore, from their point of view, the Holy Bible is
inadequate, just as mainstream synagogues and churches are inadequate as fellowships to nurture souls to salvation.

My colleague Richard Jensen (1990), a Lutheran radio evangelist,
pointed out that the revelation of the Biblical accounts was made
publicly; that is, God disclosed the divine identity to groups of people
who were eyewitnesses to these historical events. By contrast, cult
leaders receive private divine self-disclosures not subject to review by
believers or critics. Some New Age cults offer the believer the hope of
becoming God, a possibility enacted by many cult leaders.

COMPARING AND CONTRASTING

My first ex-member counselee taught me a lot. He was a six-foot-six, almost-bald, Dutch ex-Hare Krishna. A deprogrammer (as we called them in that era, the late 1970s) brought him to see me so that I could assist with the reentry process. The deprogrammer needed someone to help the young man distinguish between healthy and sick religions.

The following list of contrasts and comparisons reflects the contrasts that began to emerge for me from those conversations.

Religions respect the individual's autonomy.

Cults enforce compliance.

Religions try to help individuals meet their spiritual needs.

Cults exploit spiritual needs.

Religions tolerate and even encourage questions and independent critical thinking.

Cults discourage questions and independent critical thinking.

Religions encourage psychospiritual integration.

Cults "split" members into the "good cult self" and the "bad old self."

Conversion to religions involves an unfolding of internal processes central to a person's identity.

Cultic conversion involves an unaware surrender to external forces that care little for the person's identity.

Religions view money as a means, subject to ethical restraints, toward achieving noble ends.

Cults view money as an end, as a means toward achieving power or the selfish goals of the leaders.

Religions view sex between clergy and the faithful as unethical.

Cults frequently subject members to the sexual appetites of the leaders.

Religions respond to critics respectfully.

Cults frequently intimidate critics with physical or legal threats.

Religions cherish the family.

Cults view the family as an enemy.

Religions encourage a person to think carefully before making a commitment to join.

Cults encourage quick decisions with little information.

REGARDING AMBIGUITY:
A PHILOSOPHICAL FOOTNOTE

A universal theme that runs through my experience with recovering ex-cultists is the manner in which they deal with ambiguity, that is, the presence of complexity and uncertainty in the face of religious believers' need for absolute assurance.

Cultism, even more than religious fundamentalism, plays to this hungering to overcome complexity, uncertainty, and the issues of debatable interpretation in order to grant what an old-time hymn called "blessed assurance." Evangelical Harold H. Bussell (1983) has good reason, therefore, to express concern as to why fundamentalist Christians seem to be so vulnerable to cults. Cults, especially Bible-based cults, go the extra mile, so to speak, and may thereby provide some fundamentalists with an even greater sense of certainty.

I believe that the intolerance of ambiguity is an invitation to the unambiguous worldview characteristic of cults. This rigid and simplistic style of processing ideas typical of the recovering ex-cultist presents a challenge to the pastoral counselor, especially one who does not share this propensity.

I find it necessary to give the ex-cultist permission to explore other ways of thinking, providing the encouragement to do so and teaching skills that broaden and offer alternatives to the ex-cultist's habitual ways of processing faith issues.

In the conflict between the uncertainties that intellectual honesty must confront and the emotional need for assurance of salvation, cult leaders and, to a lesser extent, fundamentalists usually throw the issues of ambiguity overboard for the sake of the secure feeling of certainty. This can turn out to be a very expensive choice.

UNDERSTANDING
THE CONDITION OF
RECOVERING EX-CULT MEMBERS

The effectiveness of the pastoral care of former cult members depends in large measure upon the clergy person's understanding of and empathy toward the ex-cultists' experiences and the abuse they suffered.

Some members were physically or sexually abused while in their cults. And all ex-cult members have psychological abuse from which they are still healing.

Longtime cult watcher Ronald Enroth studied abusive evangelical Christian congregations, referred to in the anti-cult movement as "shepherding/discipling" churches. Enroth (1992) describes the condition of these victims:

Unlike physical abuse that often results in bruised bodies, spiritual and pastoral abuse leaves scars on the psyche and soul. It is inflicted by persons who are accorded respect and honor in our society by virtue of their role as religious leaders and models of spiritual authority. . . . But when they violate that trust, when they abuse their authority, and when they misuse ecclesiastical power to control and manipulate the flock, the results can be catastrophic. The perversion of power that we see in abusive churches disrupts and divides families, fosters an unhealthy dependence of members on the leadership, and creates, ultimately, spiritual confusion in the lives of victims. (p. 29)

Dealing constructively with this spiritual confusion is the goal of the pastoral care of recovering cultists. The good news is that clergy often are best prepared to do so; the bad news is that not only are clergy suspect as potentially just another abuser like the last one, but also some clergy have difficulty understanding and accepting the experience of abuse that is being described.

Perhaps clergy can better appreciate victims' experiences by keeping in mind Enroth's 10 identifying traits of abusive churches:

1. Control-oriented leadership
2. Spiritual elitism
3. Manipulation of members
4. A perception of being under persecution
5. A demanding, rigid life-style
6. Emphasis on experience rather than rationality
7. Suppression of dissent
8. Harsh discipline of members
9. Denunciation of other churches
10. A painful exit process

To these I would add other traits common to the wider range of abusive religious and therapeutic groups:

- Extreme manipulation by guilt and fear
- Sexual abuse of women and children
- Economic exploitation

COMPLICATING FACTORS

A survey of the work I have done with ex-cult members in recovery in the past four years reveals a number of complicating factors. These factors influence the pastoral care and theologizing issues but are not totally caused by the cult, nor are they always theological in nature. But they do influence the theologizing process. These are often issues emanating from the ex-cultist's background, including dysfunctional families and a history of drug or alcohol abuse.

One young man at a recovery group session announced that he had been raised in a dysfunctional family and then went off and joined a dysfunctional religious group. This example illustrates the findings of family systems pioneer and therapist, Rabbi Edwin Friedman (1985). In Friedman's postgraduate clergy seminar on Family Emotional Process he speaks of the need for individuals to differentiate and the tendency of some family systems to promote fusion instead. "Families that produce cult members are invariably fused and not differentiated," states Friedman. "Cults don't destroy families; families breed people for cults." Although most clinicians who have worked with cultists (Clark, 1979; Singer, 1979) would vigorously disagree with Rabbi Friedman and call his statement hyperbole, I don't believe that they would disagree that a sizable minority of cultists do come from such families. When these persons leave cults, their family conflicts re-emerge and sometimes obscure or complicate spiritual needs.

Other ex-members with whom I have worked have demonstrated thwarted or blocked development in such maturation tasks such as socialization and sexuality and its management. In the case of two single heterosexual males in their mid-20s, the inability to enter into meaningful intimate relationships with women and accept their own sexual drives produced massive attacks of guilt. These feelings not only drove one young man into a totally controlling celibate religious group but also fueled a tremendous drive for a religious or spiritual release from the burden of guilt. According to a psychologist who had worked with one of the young men (and I agreed), the issue was not the extremism of the young men's religious pursuits, but the fuel that propelled it, namely their unmet social, intimacy, and sexual needs. I talked with each of them in the arena of their prime interest – namely, Biblical theology – until the cows came home and it had not the slightest impact as long as the fuel kept pouring through the pipeline. We did not make any headway until we focused on the struggles of men in the Bible to manage their sexuality responsibly before God.

SPIRITUAL VOIDS

There are a number of spiritual deserts that show up on the landscapes of recovering ex-cult members. Sometimes there is a childhood in which the family and personal experience is totally devoid of any meaningful education in a religious tradition, spiritual experience, or religious formation or organized activity. In some cases, nominally religious families tend toward a process of secularization of their life-style. For example, as I drove an ex-Moonie from dinner to a television interview show where we were to appear with his bishop and his parents, he confided to me that although his parents had sent him to religious schools for 16 years, they had not allowed much of that tradition to affect how they lived, worked, or played. For others there may be no viable religious tradition to return to.

Enroth (1992) observes, "They will share the pain of leaving an abusive church and the struggle to adjust to life on the outside. For many of them, life in an all-encompassing Christian environment has been so devastating that they find it difficult sometimes to read their Bible, attend church, or even believe in God" (p. 30).

The recovering cultist may well be in a time of spiritual nothing-ness, having given up an all-consuming system that sought to give meaning and direction to life. The cult may have provided a spiritual mentor from whom the ex-member is now separated. Although the ex-cultist may have left the group by making a rational and liberating choice generated by an increasing and healthy awareness of the de-structiveness, hypocrisy, and manipulation of the group, that person still feels a great loss that the sensitive pastoral counselor needs to be aware of. Thus, a crucial element in pastoral care is to support the ex-member's grief over the loss, a grief that is still complicated by mixed feelings over that which was left behind.

A CHECKLIST OF SPIRITUAL AND THEOLOGICAL ISSUES

There is a menu of spiritual issues that is useful in the clarifying, contrasting, and informing work of the clergy counselor. The categories outlined below need to be addressed and the cult's theology articulated and tested. In addition, the counselor needs to offer a tempered encouragement to the recovering ex-member to move toward one of the more creditable approaches to religion or philosophical systems.

The following are significant issues to cover:

1. *Personal unworthiness and guilt.* As I described earlier, the need for forgiveness and the building of self-esteem based upon a sense of divine affirmation is crucial.

2. *Apocalyptic dread.* Every cult I have known has a tremendous sense of urgency that drives the potential recruit to immediate decision, total commitment, and radical action. Most of these cults are all fueled by a belief that we are living in the time when God will end this era of human history by some dramatic and destructive event from which only the specially enlightened/saved will be part of the delivered remnant of God's own people. I believe this picks up on a theme present in the spirit of our times; it needs to be explored and addressed.

3. *Demonic realities.* While the secularization of Western culture has been taking place, the three-story universe complete with angels and demons has fallen into disrepute with much of sophisticated society. However, the visceral sense of the demonic in some cultic thinking and practice and the pervasiveness of sin and evil has led many sophisticated persons to reexamine the old worldview. Karl Menninger's *Whatever Happened to Sin?* (1973) and M. Scott Peck's *The People of the Lie* (1978) have done much to sound an alarm warning us to be open to the existence of spiritual forces.

4. *The debate over exorcisms and deliverance ministries.* While affirming an awareness of spiritual powers in the tradition of St. Paul in Ephesians 6, I also admit that in over three decades of pastoral ministry, half of that as part of the anti-cult network, I have never encountered human dysfunction based upon alien spiritual beings who have taken up residence in a person's body, in the manner of the little girl in William Blatty's *The Exorcist,* a novel and movie allegedly based upon the pastoral care experience of a priest in Mt. Ranier, Maryland, near my current home.

On one hand, I am suspicious that the diagnosis of demon possession may be an illegitimate avoidance of responsibility in the hard work of psychotherapy. On the other hand, my pastoral experience has been punctuated with enough extramedical healings rooted in healing ministries to keep me open to what many would call "miracles of divine intervention" and what others would explain in other terms.

When respected colleague Fr. James LeBar (1991) reports authenticated cases of "diabolic presence" and appears on ABC's "20/20" to narrate an exorcism, I must remain open to possibilities beyond the range of my experiences to date. I invite other clergy to do likewise.

We need to keep a balanced perspective. A recovering multiple personality disorder victim introduced me to the work of Dr. James Friesen (1991). He reports on his therapeutic team's learning from childhood trauma victims who developed alter personalities in order to escape the pain of their immediate experience. An articulate evangelical Christian, Friesen argues persuasively that deliverance ministries do not heal multiple personality disorders, but retard real therapeutic practice; at the same time, he affirms demon possession as a reality with which to be dealt.

5. *Fear of eternal damnation.* Cults cut people off from everything, including the possibility of eternal life outside the group. Powerful fears are intentionally planted and stimulated within the cult: "If you ever leave us, God's only true people, you will be cut off and cut down by God. Terrible things will happen to you and everyone you care about. You will burn eternally in hell." Assisting a person to overcome this legacy of influence, which is similar to posthypnotic suggestion, is a major pastoral counseling task in cult recovery situations. We must help ex-members realize that the group was wrong, they have been liberated, and God is favorably disposed toward them.

CONCLUSION

Spiritually developed, theologically trained pastoral counselors with a working knowledge of destructive cults can be helpful to recovering ex-members if they consider the following:

1. In addition to a general knowledge of cults, one needs to know the specifics of the particular group's teachings and practices. Both the American Family Foundation and the national office of the Cult Awareness Network have packets of materials on many specific groups. The peculiar theology and emphases of a group are crucial materials for the pastoral counseling process. I have also found that other ex-members of the group in question can be extremely helpful in coaching the pastoral counselor as well as serving as co-counselors.

2. As one creates a trusting and trustworthy relationship with the recovering person, it is helpful to explore the person's childhood religious experience and tradition. This helps assess how much substance there may be to build upon, or how little foundation material there may be. Why did the person abandon the faith traditions of childhood? Is a return to that faith tradition a healthy and sound new direction?

3. It is very important to help identify and articulate the spiritual needs that may have contributed to that person's entry into the cult. Was it the need for unconditional acceptance, or to be at the messianic

cutting edge of God's transforming activity, or to be included in the divine elite corps, or the need to expose the older generation's hypocrisy? All personal needs are important. Many deserve our affirmation.

4. After identifying the illegitimate ways in which the cult sought to meet these spiritual needs, one needs to open new possibilities and options by which the particular needs may be met. This may involve referral to religious organizations whose doctrinal priorities, worship forms, and life-style teachings provide better ways to meet the person's needs, even if the pastoral counselor might not choose the same for himself or herself.

5. Instead of the obvious interpretation that the recovering person has suffered a totally destructive episode during cult membership, a pastoral counselor might be well-advised to explore the more beneficial aspects of the cult experience. If God uses all things to work for good, where is the good to be found in this person's cult era?

6. What actions of restitution need to be made by a person to reestablish himself or herself, in his or her own eyes and also in the eyes of friends, family, and others who may have been abused or offended by the person during the cult experience? There are often very specific steps in that reconciliation process.

REFERENCES

Bussell, H. (1983). *Unholy devotion: Why cults lure Christians.* Grand Rapids, MI: Zondervan.

Clark, J. G. (1979). Cults. *Journal of the American Medical Association, 242,* 279–281.

Enroth, R. (1992). *Churches that abuse.* Grand Rapids, MI: Zondervan.

Friedman, E. H. (1985). *Generation to generation: Family process in church and synagogue.* New York: Guilford Press.

Friesen, J. G. (1991). *Uncovering the mystery of MPD.* San Bernardino, CA: Here's Life.

Jensen, R. (1990). Cult Awareness Network national conference, Chicago, IL.

LeBar, J. (1991). American Family Foundation annual meeting, Philadelphia, PA.

Menninger, K. (1973). *Whatever happened to sin?* New York: Hawthorn.

Peck, M. S. (1978). *The people of the lie.* New York: Simon & Schuster.

Singer, M. T. (1979, January). Coming out of the cults. *Psychology Today, 12,* pp. 72–82.

13

GUIDELINES FOR PSYCHIATRIC HOSPITALIZATION OF EX-CULTISTS

David Halperin, M.D.

A VARIETY OF SOURCES MAY REFER FORMER cult members, and occasionally current members of cultic groups, to psychiatric hospitals. Sometimes cultists are self-referred. Most often, however, they will be referred by families, helping professionals, social service agencies, or the police. The latter two are most likely to refer cultists whose groups have "dumped" them on the street because, for example, their mental illness makes them unable to continue to raise money for the group or function adequately to serve the group's purposes.

If psychiatric intake workers are not sensitive to cult issues and do not bother to inquire about their patients' possible cultic involvements, they will not realize the extent to which a patient's presenting symptomatology may be related to powerful group pressures and their aftereffects. As a consequence, they will tend to overestimate and misunderstand psychopathology and inappropriately treat the cult-involved individual.

Sometimes such misdiagnosing can result in unnecessarily prolonged inpatient treatment. Cults tend to indoctrinate members with the belief that the group is always right and, when dissenting, members are always wrong. By overfocusing on searches for "unconscious motivations," mental health professionals may unwittingly reinforce cultists' tendency to blame themselves and thus may waste much therapeutic time.

This chapter seeks to shed light on these issues by describing cases that illustrate the types of problems encountered by psychiatric hospitals treating cultists. Three broad categories of patients deserve examination: individuals who prior to cult affiliation appeared to be without significant mental illness; individuals who prior to cult affiliation evidenced significant psychopathology; and individuals who ascribe to Satanism. Cult affiliation may significantly exacerbate the individual's difficulties in adaptation, whatever overt symptoms of preexisting psychopathology are present. Thus, in considering guidelines for the inpatient treatment of cult members, the relationship of the cult member to his or her family, ego strength prior to affiliation, and community resources available to the individual upon discharge need to be considered for meaningful aftercare planning. Guidelines can be best formulated and issues considered in the context provided by the examination of specific cases within the three categories outlined above.

THE HOSPITALIZATION OF INDIVIDUALS WITHOUT APPARENT SIGNIFICANT ILLNESS PRIOR TO CULT AFFILIATION

Many of the important issues and parameters for the formulation of guidelines are presented in the case of Benjamin C.

Benjamin C. was referred for psychiatric evaluation because his family noted that he was becoming increasingly anxious and hostile. A recent graduate of a prestigious law school, Benjamin had found it surprisingly difficult to obtain a position with a law firm despite his remarkable law school record. His family had noted that his difficulties had intensified after he had begun to focus more and more of his attentions on Patricia, a trainer for a mass therapy group. At Patricia's insistence, Benjamin participated in a weeklong intensive leadership seminar sponsored by Patricia's group. Benjamin's family felt that this experience seriously exacerbated his condition.

When seen in initial psychiatric consultation, Benjamin was a fearful, exceedingly anxious, suspicious male who was extremely confused and unable to provide a recent history. He discussed the "seminar" and his relationship with Patricia in a circumstantial and disjointed manner. Clearly judgment was impaired. He had little insight into his situation. After consultation, discussion with his family, and considerable persuasion, Benjamin grudgingly accepted hospitalization.

During hospitalization Benjamin required treatment in a closed setting. His manner was aggressive and threatening. He required significant levels of neuroleptics. However, within six weeks he was discharged. After discharge Benjamin was followed in psychoanalytically oriented psychotherapy. Neuroleptics were soon discontinued. During the course of treatment he was strongly encouraged to discontinue contact with the mass therapy group and to reexamine his relationship with Patricia. Ultimately Benjamin was able to meet and marry a less controlling woman. He returned to the practice of law.

The case of Benjamin illustrates the profoundly disruptive impact that a cult (in this instance, a mass therapy group) may have on a previously high-functioning, apparently intact individual. His degree of decompensation was extraordinary considering his prior history of academic achievement, social adaptability, and vocational functioning. He responded to structured inpatient treatment combined with psychotherapy and pharmacotherapy. Because of his preaffiliation strengths and the presence of a concerned and supportive family, Benjamin's social and vocational rehabilitation was accomplished with relative ease. His willingness to reexamine his preaffiliation personality in psychotherapy contributed significantly to his positive posthospital experience.

Despite the absence of preaffiliation symptomatology, a less sanguine outcome occurred in the case of Sharon B., where there was a greater resistance to ongoing posthospitalization psychotherapy.

Sharon B. was the Chair of the Department of Mathematics at a prestigious preparatory school. Despite her professional success, Sharon had difficulty forming and sustaining relationships with men. The product of a conforming and religiously focused background, she had found it difficult to reconcile her sense of probity with a more permissive social environment. Finally, a former boyfriend encouraged her to attend the recruiting meeting of a mass therapy group. She attended the meeting and an initial "seminar" without apparent ill effects. She was so enthused about her experience that she encouraged her friends to attend and contracted for an "advanced weeklong training seminar."

Unlike the previous meetings, this training seminar was conducted in a rigidly structured, coercive manner. One exercise required her to parade about scantily clad, discussing her masturbatory fantasies. During the course of this "seminar," she was frequently referred to by a sexually demeaning nickname. Twenty-four hours into the program she became increasingly anxious. She obsessed about the "parade." She became so visibly disturbed that the trainers separated her from the other group members. Despite her obvious decompensation, no attempt was made for her to receive emergency psychiatric care. Eventually Sharon was unceremoniously dropped off at her parents' home. Her parents hospitalized her immediately.

Sharon's initial hospitalization was brief. In the absence of apparent sequelae no effort was made to arrange for psychiatric follow-up. However, three weeks later she experienced severe anxiety and phobic symptomatology. Sharon was rehospitalized. This second hospitalization was lengthier; she required lithium and neuroleptics prior to discharge. This time psychiatric follow-up was arranged. Despite this provision Sharon has not been able to return to her former position. Her life-style has changed radically. She currently functions at a diminished position and has plans for graduate study.

Similar issues were presented in the case of Cathy I.

Cathy I. was a successful articulate junior executive in an investment bank. At her boyfriend's insistence, she attended an employment seminar sponsored by a mass therapy group. During the course of an exercise she began to dissociate and experienced depersonalization. In a panic she sought emergency psychiatric consultation. She described her sense of depersonalization in graphic and vivid terms. She was placed on and rapidly responded to high doses of anxiolytic agents. Intensive outpatient treatment was required.

These cases illustrate the potential for rapid decompensation in individuals after exposure to certain types of cultic experiences; in these examples they were all mass therapy sessions. These persons were apparently functional and without significant history of illness. No prodromal signs of decompensation were noted, reflecting the difficulties in attempting to assess the premorbid vulnerability even of high-functioning individuals to the aggressive, coercive, and demeaning procedures routinely employed in mass therapy groups (and other cults). Finally, these cases illustrate the importance of making provision for structured aftercare in aiding the individual to reconstitute after these harrowing experiences.

Similar issues arose in the case of Yves T., illustrating the potential for a more chronic illness with a more problematic outcome.

> Yves T. became depressed while at graduate school. He dealt with his depression by attending a seminar sponsored by a mass therapy group. After attending the seminar he became so distraught and disorganized that he was asked to take a leave of absence from the graduate program. Hospitalization was not required, for the most part because of the support provided by his exceedingly nurturing family.
>
> After leaving graduate school he found work in his field but on a master's level. Three years later his depression returned. Despite his previous experience he returned to the mass therapy group for support. After attending the initial seminar he became agitated. When seen in psychiatric consultation, he was grossly confused, disorganized, suspicious, and threatening to his family and himself. Yves was hospitalized immediately.
>
> During hospitalization he reintegrated rapidly. Initially he required neuroleptics, but within a week only anxiolytic agents were required. In total his hospitalization lasted 10 days. After one outpatient visit Yves discontinued treatment. He has not been able to return to work. He and his family are essentially supported by his parents.

These cases illustrate the spectrum of hospitalizations that result from contact with a cultic group in the apparent absence of severe preexisting psychiatric illness. In all cases, the patients decompensated rapidly under the intense group pressure generated within the mass therapy context. The experience within the group precipitated a brief psychotic episode. However, despite an initial clinical picture marked by affective volatility, suspicion, agitation, and confusion, these individuals have reconstituted rapidly and remained outpatients without the prolonged use of mood-stabilizing agents and/or neuroleptics. Nonetheless, their paranoid and quasimanic agitation is evidence that even intelligent individuals with a high level of functioning, living in a context of social support, can decompensate and — as demonstrated by Sharon B.'s radically changed life-style — can experience significant sequelae even with outpatient psychotherapy.

Outpatient psychotherapy is a necessity if these cult victims are to return to their former level of functioning. A significant characteristic of these patients, however, is their absence of interest in and/or lack of insight into the need for outpatient psychotherapy. It is not surprising that previously high-functioning individuals will readily lay the primary burden for their episode at the feet of the cult experience. Nonetheless, it is extremely important to encourage them to consider the possibility that in addition to the destructive impact of the cult experience there may have been some preexisting vulnerability and that full recovery often requires further psychiatric consultation.

Individuals who seek help from mass therapy groups are often skeptical about mainstream mental health approaches. If psychotherapy is approached in a task-oriented fashion, however, without cant and with a view toward helping the individual work with specific stressors, it may be accepted. Consistent work with significant family members is particularly important in this process. Even if the relationship of the ex-cultists and significant parental and/or family figures was marked by ambivalence, work with family members is often extremely useful in allowing an otherwise skeptical patient to accept hospitalization and/or outpatient care. Moreover, family members themselves may have many doubts, for example, about their parenting, and will deserve the support the psychiatric contact can provide.

The four patients described above were high-functioning individuals with little overt psychopathology prior to their cult affiliation. Involvement with a cultic group resulted in brief, time-limited psychotic episodes with relatively benign sequelae. When hospitalization is required of an individual with chronic illness secondary to cult affiliation, we see clinical issues that are different from those in the previous situations.

THE HOSPITALIZATION OF
INDIVIDUALS WITH CHRONIC ILLNESS
PRIOR TO CULT AFFILIATION

The case of Henry S. illustrates the issues that arise when hospitalization occurs in the context of overt psychiatric illness and subsequent cult affiliation.

Henry S. attended a prestigious college. In the latter half of his junior year, his academic performance declined. He involved himself in hostile, argumentative interchanges with teachers (with whom he had previously had amicable relations). His performance on the varsity lacrosse team declined. Following his girlfriend's return to her parents in Europe, Henry became extremely despondent. He began to isolate himself. He related to friends with an ill-concealed grandiosity and hostile detachment. His parents noted a growing religious preoccupation. During this period of increasing agitation he contacted and joined a cultic group. In a panic his parents sought psychiatric consultation. They were able to obtain a court order directing Henry to undergo a psychiatric evaluation.

On psychiatric evaluation Henry was an anxious, distraught, fearful young man in poor contact with his environment. He grudgingly accepted hospitalization. During the course of his brief hospitalization his condition improved rapidly. He responded well to anxiolytic agents. Contact with the cult was discouraged. Also during the course of his hospitalization he was exposed to exit counselors on a voluntary basis. He formed a good relationship with them and foreswore his membership in the cult group. Upon discharge he attended a halfway house for ex-cultists. Apparently reintegrated, he returned to college in the fall.

Within two to three weeks of his return to college, however, he began to act in a bizarre manner. He became extremely agitated and confided to his roommate that God was speaking to him by telephone. In this state of agitation he contacted the cult and on the cult's advice he left college. With the cult's encouragement he refused psychiatric care. He currently functions as a member of the cult's fund-raising team.

Henry's history raises significant issues. His cult affiliation occurred during a severe depressive episode. His isolation, alienation, hostility, and grandiosity evidenced severe psychiatric illness. Because of his history of social and intellectual strengths, however, his family focused on his symptomatology as primarily the product of his cult affiliation. Thus, he was encouraged to return to college, but without adequate provision for psychiatric follow-up. This, in effect, denied that his cult affiliation was in and of itself symptomatic of an underlying process of real severity. The very flamboyance of the symptom of cult affiliation obscured the actual depth of his illness.

Other aspects of the interface of chronic psychiatric illness and cult affiliation are illustrated in the case of Sheldon Z.

Sheldon Z. had attended law school. In his third year, preoccupied with a sense of anxiety about his future direction, Sheldon attended meetings sponsored by a variety of New Age groups. He left law school to pursue his new enthusiasms. Ultimately he was forced to return to his parents' home because he had depleted a large trust fund.

On his return home he acted in an increasingly bizarre manner. He would talk at great length about plots directed against him by malevolent entities; he frantically telephoned his "masters" for support in this battle of "cosmic" importance. Eventually his behavior became so disorganized that he required hospitalization.

During the course of his hospitalization he responded to neuroleptics and lithium. However, the core of his delusional system remained untouched. He continued to obsess about the "cosmic" battle and repeatedly verbalized intense suicidal ideation. Even though the "master" encouraged Sheldon to participate in psychotherapy and to continue with his medication, this "master" also reinforced Sheldon's bizarre belief system. Sheldon was quite willing to continue his outpatient treatment with the proviso that his belief system and/or contact with his guru not be touched.

Sheldon Z.'s outpatient treatment illustrates the challenge that the psychiatrist faces in working with an individual who is chronically ill and at the same time continues to be invested in a bizarre belief system. While most cultic groups discourage contact with mainstream mental health professionals, it is my experience that not all cult leaders will discourage contact with usual professional channels, particularly when they feel overwhelmed with the demands made by a devotee. Indeed, in this context, the psychiatrist may have to establish a relationship with the cult leader to obtain his or her support for a patient to pursue appropriate psychiatric care. While it is exceedingly difficult to maintain a nonjudgmental approach toward a belief system that includes irrational references—such as multiple higher planes of existence and possession by dark forces, as in Sheldon's case—these bizarre ideas could be approached existentially as metaphors for the patient's sense of isolation and depression. Thus, Sheldon's belief system, which defied credibility and rationality with its multiple entities without limits was not challenged. Instead, the focus of his treatment remained the establishment of a therapeutic alliance that would enable Sheldon to pursue his worldly activities while he explored noncult-related social options (and enable him to resist impulsively acting out his suicidal ideation).

Sheldon's particular obsessions had a gnostic quality. Other patients may be members of groups that espouse racist or anti-Semitic doctrines. In all of these cases, if the psychiatrist is to work with these individuals in a productive manner, he or she must be alert to the intense countertransference that almost certainly will be evoked. In Sheldon's case, mainstream psychiatric activity on the "material" plane was constantly denigrated; in other cases, the psychiatrist may be constantly challenged because of his or her background. However, if it is recognized that these productions are part of the patient's attempt to maintain some self-esteem and/or independence from a psychiatrist on whom the patient feels more and more dependent, these ideological productions need not interfere with the progress of treatment.

WORKING WITH INDIVIDUALS
WHO PROFESS BELIEF
IN SATANISM

The issues that arise in working with individuals (primarily adolescents) who profess satanic beliefs differ significantly from the issues previously discussed. The case of Edward Y. is suggestive:

Edward Y. was brought in for psychiatric consultation because he had recently begun to frequent a crowd of grossly disaffected youths at his high school. His mother noted bizarre inscriptions on his bedroom wall – inscriptions with a morbid cast, such as disfigured animals, tortured women, and so forth. She had also noted his increasing interest in heavy metal music and a reliance upon black and otherwise provocative clothing. There had been a recent epidemic of suicides at Edward's high school. His mother was concerned that Edward might be vulnerable to this group contagion.

On psychiatric examination Edward was a severely dysphoric youth in good contact with his environment. He readily admitted to suicidal ideation, described recent cross-dressing activity and significant substance abuse. In addition, he admitted to an increasing interest in Satanism and occult activities. Past history was significant in that Edward was the product of a broken home and his two subsequent stepfathers were heavily alcoholic. His relationship with his mother was extremely ambivalent – at times excessively close and at other times distant and detached.

Because of the multiple difficulties that Edward was experiencing, a voluntary hospitalization was arranged. Over the course of some months Edward was able to separate himself from his delinquent associates, establish a more appropriate relationship with his mother, and stop substance abuse. He has continued in outpatient psychotherapy.

Edward's case is representative of adolescents who profess an interest in Satanism. Unlike cult members, adolescents who dabble in Satanism are usually the products of much more significantly pathological backgrounds. Their pathology and current situation is often exacerbated by significant drug abuse, and antisocial trends and associations are present. Adolescent dabblers are much more significantly at risk for suicide. Indeed, they may engage in self-destructive activity because of the fantasy that they will emerge from the afterlife as much more powerful entities (à la Freddy in the *Friday the 13th* movies).

During the course of hospitalization satanic dabblers may assume a bullying role within the ward culture and/or tap into antisocial potentialities within the hospital environment, that is, get involved in delinquent activity and substance abuse. It is vitally important that contact with other members of satanic groups be proscribed. In addition, extensive education of staff members is important when working with satanists because of the intense countertransference issues that may arise in working with individuals who have been active participants in destructive, sadistic, and other antisocial behavior. Finally, since satanists are often the products of significantly pathological backgrounds, a careful evaluation for child physical or sexual abuse is required.

DISCUSSION

After careful consideration of these cases, certain guidelines reflect the realities of working with individuals who have joined cultic groups and who require hospitalization. These are:

1. Careful assessment of the individual's preaffiliation status. Cult affiliation may precipitate a brief psychotic reaction. It may also be symptomatic of severe underlying pathology and chronic illness. Even in an otherwise intact individual, the brief psychotic reaction may be surprisingly severe with the patient manifesting agitated, suspicious, confused, and quasimanic behavior. However, hospitalization, which places the individual in a structured and protected setting without further contact with members of the cultic group, is usually successful in terminating the brief psychotic reaction.

2. Treatment of an individual with a problematical preaffiliation history is often protracted and complex. Mood stabilizers, anxiolytic agents, and neuroleptics may be required. While contact with members of the cultic group should be discouraged, the mental health professional should be prepared for the possibility that even though the patient reconstitutes from this episode, he or she may still consider himself or herself to be an active cult member and espouse the cult's ideology. Since many cultic groups disparage or actively discourage psychotherapy, exit counseling should be considered an essential element of long-term hospitalization or in working with long-term cult members who are chronically ill. In selected cases an effort to enlist the cultic group in supporting mainstream psychotherapy should be made and may be useful.

3. Follow-up care in halfway houses and other supportive settings, in particular rehabilitation centers for former cultists, may be extremely helpful. In most cases follow-up care should include exit counseling, psychotherapy, family therapy, and pharmacotherapy. Other chapters in this book provide information on all but the last of these types of follow-up care.

Regarding pharmacotherapy, let me cite the recommendations made by Dr. John Clark:

> In deciding whether or not to prescribe medication for former cult members, the physician should keep in mind that it is difficult to determine the extent to which the ex-cultist's symptomatology is a function of the cult experience or a function of a true psychiatric illness. Therefore, the physician should (a) be more cautious than usual in making the decision to prescribe, and (b) follow the patient's progress very closely when medications are given.
>
> This latter point is especially important, for the clinical evidence suggests that ex-members respond to medications more rapidly (and sometimes more adversely) than one would normally expect. This appears to be the case whether or not the symptomatology is psychotic or nonpsychotic or whether or not a history of psychiatric disorder exists. Consequently, when prescribing medications for ex-cultists, the physician should be prepared to decrease dosages or discontinue the medication sooner than customary practice would suggest. (Clark, Langone, Schecter, & Daly, 1981, p. 79)

Let me also add a note about exit counseling. Exit counseling is an educational intervention that provides former cultists with a conceptual framework for understanding how they were seduced and exploited by high-intensity groups. Sometimes it is appropriate to begin an exit counseling on the inpatient unit. Often it can occur as part of the follow-up. Exit counselors, however, can also play a useful role in educating hospital staff about the realities and impact of cult affiliation, even if the exit counselors do not work directly with the patient during his or her hospital stay. This is especially true when the exit counselors have special knowledge about the group to which the patient belonged.

Cult members who require hospitalization face a double burden of dealing with a severe mental illness precipitated or exacerbated by an exploitatively manipulative cult environment. Mental health workers who encounter such patients must be alert to the possible role of destructive groups. Otherwise they may augment, rather than relieve, their patient's burden.

REFERENCE

Clark, J., Langone, M. D., Schecter, R. E., & Daly, R. C. B. (1981). *Destructive cult conversion: Theory, research, and treatment.* Weston, MA: American Family Foundation.

14

GUIDELINES FOR SUPPORT GROUPS

William Goldberg, M.S.W., A.C.S.W.

AN INDIVIDUAL'S GROUP AFFILIATION is an important and necessary factor of human existence. All of us need to feel accepted by others, and the power of groups can be used to help or to harm. Every former cultist recognizes the power of groups because all cults use group dynamics to manipulate and control their members. (One-on-one cultic situations are unusual, but they do describe a group. In this case, the group is a dyad.)

In this chapter I shall examine the malignant use of group dynamics by cults and cult leaders and suggest ways that positive group dynamics can be used to help former cultists in the recovery process. Finally, I shall offer suggestions about rules and policies that can be adopted by recovery groups for former cultists.

THE POWER OF GROUPS

Human beings are social animals. In fact, the first sign of humanness is the infant's social smile. We define ourselves by identification with reference groups, including our country, religion, race, class, political party, and occupation. As Bion has pointed out (Rioch, 1972, p. 20), even a hermit in a desert cannot be understood unless we know which group he has been separated from.

With respect to behavior, the whole of a group is greater than the

275

sum of the individual group members. People in a group tend to act differently than they would as isolated individuals. LeBon (1960) points out that, "In a crowd, every sentiment and act is contagious to such a degree that an individual readily sacrifices his personal interest to the collective interest" (p. 30). Dictators and cult leaders, as well as more benign leaders, can induce people to do things that they would not normally do by relying on the contagion that occurs in the group.

Vulnerability

In times of personal transition, group affiliation and identification are particularly significant. Adolescents, for example, are no longer comfortable with answering the question, Who are you? by defining themselves as their parents' child, a definition that satisfied them when they were younger. Since most adolescents in our society have not yet determined exactly who they are, they tend to answer the question by reference to groups they identify with. Adolescents tend to adopt a style of dress and a view of the world that reflect this group identification.

Young adults who are away from home and, therefore, away from the groups they previously identified with, seem to be particularly vulnerable. Halperin (1983) describes the initial contact with a cult under these circumstances as one that "promises a context in which to relate. It provides a time and place for the individual who is literally at loose ends . . . to establish some human context in which to function" (p. 225). Halperin reminds us that this need for boundaries and a human context in which to meet, eat, and relate is hardly pathological (p. 225). Adolescence is the most common period of transition and, therefore, the most common time for familiar affiliations and identifications to be disturbed. However, other periods of transition can also affect vulnerability. These periods can include divorce, loss of a spouse, loss of a job, a major disappointment, or a debilitating illness.

Malignant Use of Group Dynamics by Cults

In cults, a person's natural and healthy desires to identify with a peer group are regulated to change their views of themselves, their families, and the outside world. It is necessary to note that in the initial stages of affiliation, individuals who join cults rarely know that is what they are doing. They usually believe that they are joining a Bible study group, learning a meditation technique, becoming part of a commune, and so forth. Once the new recruit enters the cult's confines, manipulative techniques are used to produce conformity. These include love bombing, the withholding of approval for healthy self-assertion, and the positive reinforcement of childlike, accepting behavior.

As with all groups, cults require new members to go through an initiation period, during which the recruit is expected to be childlike and accepting of the cult's doctrine. This initiation period facilitates a resocialization into a new way of viewing the world. New cult members are often required to perform demeaning tasks as a means of reinforcing their novitiate state. They are usually discouraged from and often forbidden to contact family and friends—a different peer group with which they could identify.

Within the cult, orchestrated group dynamics are used to enhance the sense of being part of an elite vanguard as old methods of thinking and behaving are ridiculed and new ones are presented. The cult member receives positive reinforcement for adopting the group's jargon and conforming to its standards. Many cults even confer a new "rebirth day."

Support Groups in the Recovery Process

Because manipulative and exploitative group dynamics have been used to infantalize, enslave, and harm cult members, former cultists are often reluctant to enter into new relationships (Goldberg & Goldberg, 1988). Former cultists may fear intimacy on a one-on-one basis and may even fear entry into a growth-enhancing, nurturing group. Because group dynamics have been used to harm them, however, it is particularly efficacious for a group to be one of the tools used to help them to recover.

Two of the major tasks that former cultists must accomplish are regaining a sense of mastery over their environment and a sense of trust in their own instincts. Group dynamics were used within the cult to disempower them and to encourage them to suppress and defend against their feelings. A nurturing group can help former cultists feel more comfortable in assuming a mature, independent, self-directing stance. It can also help them to feel that they can trust others again.

Groups are a particularly salutary means of helping former cultists. First, the group helps to break down feelings of isolation and loneliness. Few friends and family members can understand and empathize with former cultists' experiences. Others may be quick to explain, interpret, or simplify former cultists' own experiences to them. The recovery group gives former cultists the opportunity to describe their experiences to a sympathetic audience of people who have been through a similar experience. It is particularly helpful for individuals who have recently left a cult to see others who already left such groups and who have become involved again in the world outside the cult. The group helps members understand that the manipulative techniques used by their cult were also used in other cults. This recognition further serves to objectify and thus dispel the magical significance of cult rituals and techniques.

Another helpful factor of recovery groups for former cultists is that other group members can offer practical advice for handling difficult situations. For example, groups can discuss what to write on a job resume; how to respond when contacted by members of the cult; how to deal with positive and negative feelings about the cult, the cult leader, and cult members; how to overcome feelings of loss and sadness; and how to relate to family members and friends regarding the cult experience.

A RECOVERY GROUP MODEL

Having suggested the positive effects that groups can have on the recovery process for former cultists, I would like to describe one successful recovery group. I will also discuss some of the issues that must be considered when planning such a group.

For the past 16 years, Lorna Goldberg and I have co-led a support group for former cultists. The group meets monthly in our home and the formal part of the group lasts for two and one half hours. The group may be attended only by individuals who have been prescreened and invited to the group by one of the co-leaders (see below). The group has ranged in size from 6 to over 30 members.

Meetings begin with a statement of the group's contract (that is, the purpose of the group): This is a group for former cultists and everyone in the room, with the exception of the group leaders, has been in a cult. Everyone has been screened by one of the group leaders. The purpose of the group is to discuss the experience of being a former cultist and to explore the issues and feelings that former cultists must contend with. Everything that is discussed in the group is confidential.

The next stage of the group is devoted to introductions. All the participants introduce themselves and tell something about themselves and their reasons for attending the meeting. Usually, they say which cult they were in, how long they were in, and how long they have been out; then they may bring up issues which are particularly troubling to them at that moment. In this manner, the ice is broken and group members find it easier to speak up. This method also permits group members to have a sense of the others and the commonalties that may exist between them.

After the introductions, the meeting is thrown open for spontaneous comments. Usually something that has been said in the introductions will evoke a reaction from another group member. For example, one member might comment on how she handled a particular obstacle or emotion. Sometimes one of the group members will ask for clarification of an issue that was mentioned in the beginning of the group. If no one comments, one of the group leaders will point out the themes running through participants' initial comments that night. This statement will usually be sufficient to provoke interchange among the group members.

The Group Leader's Role

Throughout the meeting, the leaders act as catalysts for interchanges between the members. We do not attempt to be experts, nor do we pronounce judgments on different ways of dealing with issues that come up. It is the healing atmosphere of the group and the support of the other group members that provides the impetus for the meeting. If the group leaders assume too active a role, or if they intervene too quickly with possible solutions, they would be circumventing the healing and empowering process of the group.

During discussion we do point out certain consequences of their adopting a particular stance. For example, if a group member were to say that his way of dealing with the hurt and betrayal engendered by the cult is to resolve never to love or trust another, we may point out the high emotional price that is being paid for that solution. We would then ask for comments from other group members or ask whether other group members have found different solutions to this problem.

There are times when it is important for the leaders to intervene and to use the authority inherent in the leadership role to guide the group to a more therapeutically productive path. We constantly reinforce the concept that there are different, equally valid solutions to problems; we try to intervene in situations when the group sees one and only one solution as acceptable. For example, if the entire group were to agree that it is best never to attend church again or if we sense that one member is being pushed to do something that he or she is not ready to do, we will point out alternative methods of handling the situation. We stress that these alternative methods can also be valid or that alternatives might change for the same individual throughout the recovery process. Our goal is to avoid simplistic answers to complex issues and the notion that there is a right answer if only the individual can discern it. In so doing, we are drawing a distinction between cultic and noncultic behavior.

Group leaders may also intervene to refocus the group. For example, group members may display resistance to dealing with feelings by discussing related but tangential topics (such as legislative attempts to deal with the cult phenomenon). As interesting and valuable as these discussions can be in another context, the purpose of this group is to talk about feelings and issues related to being a former cultist. If the discussion gets off on such a tangent, the leaders will refocus the group.

At other times, group leaders intervene to clarify issues, to point out parallels and differences between points of view, and to illuminate issues that may have been overlooked or taken for granted. We may encourage the group to listen to members whose voices are not being heard, or we may tone down the message of members who are overwhelming or monopolizing the group. For example, when someone is monopolizing the group, we may cut in by asking if other members have had similar feelings. This intervention gives another group member the opportunity to speak without unduly embarrassing anyone.

Again, it is important to remember that the major tasks of the group leaders are to facilitate, support, and encourage productive problem solving by the group. The group process itself should be the vehicle for helping the individual group member.

The Meeting's Conclusion

Near the end of the meeting time, one of the leaders will summarize that evening's discussion and try to determine if there are unresolved feelings on the part of any of the group members. If there is a sense that some individuals have not had the opportunity to speak about a topic of concern to them, the leaders will ask if there are any other topics that should be addressed by the group. Sometimes this question will help a quieter member contribute.

At the end of the session, time is left for announcements of upcoming events and the schedule for the next meetings. We save these announcements for the end of the group rather than the beginning so that these more impersonal issues will not set the tone for the entire meeting.

The meetings end with informal socialization and often with exchanges of telephone numbers among the participants. It is important to note that although the formal part of the meeting is the most structured, the informal socialization part of the meeting, which occurs before and after, can be equally valuable and should be built into the time sequence.

As has been described elsewhere (Goldberg & Goldberg, 1982), the typical pattern is for group members to attend two or three meetings immediately after their decision to leave the cult and to attend subsequent meetings occasionally. Members are free to attend as many or as few meetings as they desire.

ISSUES FOR RECOVERY GROUPS

Having presented a model that has been found to be helpful, I would like to highlight some of the issues that are important to consider.

Frequency of Meetings

The advantage of more frequent meetings (weekly rather than monthly) is that the group provides a structure that can compensate for the loss of the cultic structure (Spero, 1982). Also, there is less group turnover, which leads to greater continuity in group process. Group roles emerge and become more clearly defined, thus lending themselves to scrutiny and analysis. More frequent group meetings more closely approximate the traditional group therapy model.

There are also advantages to less frequent meetings (monthly). Former cultists tend to be wary of making a commitment to a group that meets frequently because of their previous negative experience of group pressure while they were in the cult. A less frequent group meeting may provide sufficient distance for ex-cultists to be willing to attend the group without feeling that they are surrendering their autonomy. The higher rate of group turnover may not be a major impediment to the group's helpfulness. As Bailis, Lambert, and Bernstein (1978) point out, there is a continuity that evolves in an open group despite turnover. There is a transmission of norms from one group meeting to another as long as one or two experienced members attend each new group. Further, the higher turnover rate encourages former cultists who took a hiatus from the group to come back and attend a meeting when they feel the need to do so. They would be less likely to do so if there were a more steady membership with the concomitant sense of obligation to be there every time.

Finally, the less frequent group meeting more closely approximates the psychoeducational model, which is more helpful when dealing with people who have been involved in cults. The most effective method for helping cultists examine their cult membership (that is, exit counseling, see Chapter 8) employs an educational approach.

Recommendation   The frequency of the group meeting should reflect the group's purpose. If the group has been formed to help people who have recently left their cults, or to offer an explanation of cultism and mind control (as may be done, for example, when a cult disintegrates), a more frequent meeting schedule should be adopted. On the other hand, if the purpose of the group is to provide more general support for former cultists, less frequent meetings can be held.

Group Leadership

The issue here is whether it is more advantageous to have support groups for former cultists led by professionally trained individuals or whether these groups should be leaderless or led by peers. There are several advantages to having a professional lead the recovery group. First, a professional, because of his or her training and objectivity, is more likely to keep the focus of the group on meeting the members' needs. The professional is more likely to feel comfortable about intervening to mitigate the negative effects of comments or behaviors that are exploitative, insensitive, or destructive to others.

The group's norms, as previously mentioned, should support independence and self-autonomy in contrast to the cult's demand for obedience and conformity. An objective professional can ensure the fact that divers points of view are acknowledged and respected rather than allow one or another course of action to be seen as "proper." Thus, the professional's role and status will permit him or her to abort destructive or unhealthy avenues of discussion. Also, the professional can act as an interviewer in the screening process (see below).

There are also several advantages to leaderless or peer-led groups. In the first place, professionals are not always willing, able, or available to lead the groups. Professionals usually wish to be paid for their time and former cultists may not have the resources or be willing to pay a professional fee. Professionals who have not been in a cult themselves, or who have not had experience in working with former cultists, may misinterpret cult phenomena and mislead the group (see, for example, the story of the former cultist who joined an incest survivor's group in Chapter 11 by Lorna Goldberg). Furthermore, having a leaderless or peer-led group initially might be more comforting for those who are feeling distrustful of authority after having been abused by a cult leader. A leaderless group can also be seen as empowering for the members.

Recommendation   It is advisable that each group have a leader, regardless of whether that individual is a professional or a more experienced former cult member. It is the leader's responsibility to keep the conversation moving and focused on the needs of all the participants. It is also the leader's responsibility to make sure the group is not dominated by one individual or by one point of view. Group leadership can be assumed by a more experienced group member or it can rotate from meeting to meeting among those who are willing to assume this role.

Screening Group Members

A mechanism for screening potential group members should be established. The purposes of this screening are to ensure the fact that no active cult members attend the group and to explain the purpose for the group and its rules to the prospective member.

Clearly the presence of an active cult member would be discomforting and inhibiting to former cultists when they attempt to discuss their own recovery. Active cultists may not consider the rules of confidentiality to be more compelling than their loyalty to their cult. Also, active cult members may make provocative statements that could shift the focus of the meetings from that of helping the group members deal with being former cultists to helping the cult member see his or her group in a different light.

The initial screening interview is also useful for explaining the group and its purpose to prospective members. They can be told what happens at the meetings, who may attend, and what they will be called upon to do. It also may allay their fears of attending a group of strangers to know that there will be at least one person whom they have met beforehand. (For a more in-depth discussion of the screening process, see Goldberg & Goldberg, 1982.)

CONCLUSION

In this chapter I have discussed the power of groups, the malignant use of group dynamics by cults, and the way positive group dynamics can be helpful in the recovery process. I have presented a recovery group model, which has been used successfully by one recovery group, while also suggesting that other models can be employed to help former cultists recover from the experience. Similar groups can be helpful for families of active cultists. Everyone whose life has been touched by a cult knows how necessary support and encouragement can be. Groups can be an important vehicle to help people receive that support and encouragement.

REFERENCES

Bailis, S., Lambert, S., & Bernstein, S. (1978). The legacy of the group: A study of group therapy with a transient membership. *Social Work in Health Care, 3*(4), 405–418.

Goldberg, L., & Goldberg, W. (1982). Group work with former cultists. *Social Work, 27*(2), 165–170.

Goldberg, L., & Goldberg, W. (1988). Psychotherapy with ex-cultists: Four case studies and commentary. *Cultic Studies Journal, 5*(2), 193–210.

Halperin, D. A. (1983). Group processes in cult affiliation and recruitment. In D. A. Halperin (Ed.), *Psychodynamic perspectives on religion, sect and cult.* Boston: John Wright PSG.

LeBon, G. (1960). *The crowd.* New York: Viking Press.

Rioch, M. J. (1972). The work of Wilfred Bion on groups. In C. J. Sager & H. S. Kaplan (Eds.), *Progress in group and family therapy.* New York: Brunner/Mazel.

Spero, M. H. (1982, July). Letter to the editor. *Social Work, 27*(4), p. 384.

15

GUIDELINES FOR FAMILIES

Arnold Markowitz, M.S.W., C.S.W.

PARENTS WITH AN ADULT SON OR DAUGHTER in a cult often need to encourage and, in some cases, sponsor their child's departure from the cultic group. For most parents this is an uncharacteristic involvement in the personal life of their child; however, the parents' intervention may be justifiable if the cult has adversely affected their child. The decision to encourage a son or daughter to reconsider membership in a cultic group is not an easy one and often creates a dilemma for parents. First, there is the question of how much a parent should intervene in the life of an adult offspring. On the other hand, by not intervening or expressing concern, parents run the risk of appearing to accept, even support, the cult affiliation. Making complaints about the group is often viewed as a control issue and may be taken by the child as a personal criticism.

To offer an effective argument against the cult, parents often need to rely on the services of former cult members and professional exit counselors, who can be very effective in their discussions with the cult-involved son or daughter. Voluntary exit counseling has proven to be effective precisely because it is a respectful process based on the love and support of concerned family members and friends, those who have enough status to ask the cult member to participate in an exit counseling intervention.

Carol Giambalvo (1992; Chapters 7 and 8), a highly respected exit

285

counselor, offers helpful suggestions for understanding the exit counselor's role in initiating the post-cult recovery process. Exit counseling is often the first educational step in this process. If the former cult member is planning to stay at a residential rehabilitation center (preferably one that specializes in cult-recovery issues), the exit counselor should make the trip with the ex-cultist to ease the transition from the cult and the exit counseling sessions to the rehab center. Issues of concern can be brought to the attention of the center's staff at this time. Certain issues may have emerged during the exit counseling sessions that pertain to family conflict and areas of family dysfunction. The exit counselor's job is to focus on cult-related matters, such as mind control, and to steer around family matters that have the potential to jeopardize or derail the intervention and a successful outcome. Hence, exit counselors generally do not, and probably should not, get involved in family therapy.

Exit counseling is an intense and powerful experience, one that can foster dependence on the counselor through the transference phenomenon that often occurs in therapeutic treatments. Once the cultist has made the decision to leave the cult, whether or not he or she goes to a rehab center, it is desirable now for the former member to reconnect with family members and to establish a therapeutic alliance with other professional helpers who may enter the picture at this time. Cult members often have a propensity toward idealization; therefore, care should be taken that the exit counselor not be viewed as the next guru.

In the case of those who leave their cults without formal intervention, their post-cult symptoms are similar. It is necessary, however, for these ex-members (often called walkaways or castaways) to come to understand how the cult manipulated and exploited them before they can fully recover.

POST-CULT SYMPTOMS

An early observer of cultists and ex-cultists, psychologist Margaret Thaler Singer (1979) was the first to identify the type and severity of psychological symptoms manifested in these individuals. Since then many other clinicians, including myself, have confirmed Singer's findings and added additional observations (Clark, 1979; Hassan, 1988; Spero, 1983; West & Singer, 1980). Many former cult members, particularly those with experience with lengthy or intense periods of meditation, repetitious prayer, or chanting, present with some or all of the following symptoms:

- Dissociation ("floating"): involuntary drifting off into altered states of consciousness
- Difficulty concentrating: loss of critical thinking; poor judgment
- Dependency, submissiveness, suggestibility
- Memory loss
- Anxiety
- Guilt: for leaving friends in the group, for having caused trouble for their families
- Fear: of retribution from God, from the group itself, and from the threats invariably made by the leader toward members who leave

Anger is another commonly felt emotion. Former cult members who receive psychotherapy eventually express anger over having allowed themselves to be controlled and used by the cult group or the leader. It is interesting to note, however, that many former members remain protective of the leader, tending instead to focus their anger at others in the group. It is typical, at least initially, for ex-members to say the leader is well-meaning while it was other members who ruined the group's ideals.

Psychotherapy helps the individual integrate his or her pre-cult personality with his or her post-cult personality as a way to make the former member whole again. The task is to achieve a stable sense of self and deal with the issues of adult life.

FAMILY ISSUES

Family dynamics, including past and present interaction, conflicts, and patterns, are evident when the crisis of a child's cult involvement reaches the family's awareness. The stress parents feel and their reactions to it are a particular concern for therapist and parents alike. Reduction of stress and the development of a good support network is most helpful for parents. Prior to the consideration of an exit counseling intervention, parents should learn about the psychological functioning of the family in order to anticipate and defuse any conflicts that may undermine the exit counseling process.

Issues and dynamics common to families of cult members include:

- Parents blame each other for their son or daughter's cult involvement.
- The cult problem exacerbates parental conflicts or reawakens dormant marital problems.

- One parent is emotionally overinvolved with the cult member, and may be emotionally distant from the spouse.
- Parents are often afraid to evoke their child's anger; they tend to defer. For example, they probably did not express their concerns about the group in the early stages of their child's involvement.
- There is a sense of despair and hopelessness; parents feel hurt by their child's rejection of family values and the family's religious views.
- Parents are angry that their offspring allows his or her life to be controlled by the group or the leader.
- Parents feel anger at the cult, the leader, and other members for having recruited their child.
- Parents sense a loss of such pleasures as seeing their child develop a career, have a family and children (for them, grandchildren); parents often feel upset that their son or daughter has not made a good enough adjustment to adult life.
- Parents feel shame, guilt, and a sense of failure.
- The child uses the cult to separate from parents, to create emotional distance.
- Cult affiliation, with its alternative life-style and beliefs, enables young adults to define themselves as totally different from their parents.
- Love bombing and approbation by the cult gives the participant an initial feeling of competence and acknowledgment outside of the family.
- Despite the cult's authoritarian and rigid structure children often feel they have become independent by joining the group.
- Adolescent depression over the need to separate from parents may be temporarily assuaged by joining a cult that relieves one of autonomous responsibilities.

Based on my work with families of cultists, I postulated (Markowitz, 1983) that the family often has unrealistic or unobtainable expectations of achievement and success for the child who is in the cult. The child's acceptance, or internalization, of these expectations leaves him or her vulnerable if the parents' expectations aren't met. This child is unable to separate personal aspirations from the family's expectations. While all parents and family members have expectations of one another, and parents are certainly gratified by their children's successes, it is important for the parents to accommodate to the abilities and desires of each child.

Families that are able to discuss their mutual expectations, and allow for negotiation of differences where everyone has the ability to influence family decisions, will fare better in discussing cultic involvement. In her work at the Cult Clinic operated by the Jewish Family Service of Los Angeles, Cathy Gordon (personal communication, 1991) found that in "open, honest, and well-prepared families the result is a healthier dynamic among everyone." Gordon further noted that family therapy that explores family dynamics and relationships leads to a "realistic and positive recovery process."

RECOVERY ISSUES

Once the cult member decides to leave the cult, attention turns to the individual's recovery from the experience. A particular individual's recovery will depend on a variety of factors, including the type of cult, intensity of the group's practices, the extent of control and submission, pain and suffering experienced in the group, personality factors, and available social supports.

Both resiliency and protective factors are affected by cult involvement, making it pertinent to look at how cult members fare in terms of these factors.

Resiliency Factors

Researchers have been interested in the development of children who grow up in the midst of severe emotional and social deprivation yet seem to develop healthy and gratifying adult lives. In studying these survivors, Benard and others (Benard, 1987) attempt to delineate the protective factors that create such resilient children.

Resiliency is viewed as the ability to bounce back or make a positive adaptation in the face of adversity. *Protective factors*, which may sometimes overlap resiliency factors, are the mechanisms by which a person avoids the social and emotional hazards in his or her environment. Examples would be children of alcoholics, children with mentally ill parents, and children surrounded by family criminality or such destructive neighborhood elements as poverty, drugs, alcohol, and crime. Assessing these adaptive factors can be useful in determining how resilient a former cult member is after departure from the group and also may be helpful in observing the ex-cultist's recovery over time. Development of these attributes can be used as positive markers of recovery, as goals to be achieved. While the literature is quite extensive, here we highlight only a few of the resiliency factors that are significant in gauging the post-cult recovery process.

Autonomy   A strong sense of independence, a sense of personal power, a sense of having a compelling future, achievement orientation, self-directed (Anthony, 1987, cited in Benard, 1991; Garmexy, Werner, & Smith, 1974, 1991, 1992, cited in Benard, 1991).

Purpose   Related to fostering autonomy, includes having a vision for the future, goal directedness, success orientation, education or career aspirations, persistence, hopefulness, and a belief in a bright future. According to Benard, "this factor appears to be the most powerful predictor of positive outcome" (1991, p. 5).

Self-Esteem/Sense of Self   An internal focus of control, feelings of personal worthiness, the belief that one can control events rather than be a passive victim (Benard, 1987).

Coherence   A sense of confidence that the external world and one's internal environment are predictable and hopeful (Benard, 1987).

Social Competence   Feeling at ease with social demands at work and with peers, includes the ability to form romantic relationships and friendships; use of humor, flexibility, and adaptability are significant assets.

The five factors just described can be used to gauge resiliency and can serve as a guide for the recovering ex-cultist, family members, exit counselors, and psychotherapists. The extent to which these factors are present or absent helps to determine the progress as well as the prognosis for a faster or slower recovery.

Protective Factors

Protective factors that may be useful for recovery are:

Attachment to an Adult   Having access to at least one warm, supportive relationship where there is a low level of criticism can have a healing effect. Many tend to join a cult following a disappointment in life or the rupture of a significant relationship. It will be restorative for the ex-cultist to establish a good post-cult attachment.

Problem-Solving Skills   Learning to make decisions and tolerating ambivalence are helpful to the former cult member in overcoming his or her dependency on others, submissiveness, and suggestibility. The ex-cultist needs to learn to live without the simplistic answers the cult offered.

Sense of Purpose   Feeling that life has meaning and that goals can be developed is another sign of health. Almost all ex-members will say they were attracted to the greater sense of purpose that the cult seemed to offer. Having a sense of direction and goals will help protect against returning to a cultic relationship.

Control over One's Fate   Having a sense of control over one's life is an indication of self-assertion and self-esteem. Cult members often enter cults at a time of confusion, when they feel hopeless about their lives and lack a sense of control over their future.

Participation in a Positive Structure   Finding some structured activity that organizes the former cultist's life is helpful to the recovery process. Cult members are often recruited during periods of transition, such as during a vacation, after graduation, when starting a new school or job, at those times when the sense of structure is lacking.

Stress Management   Having the ability to manage stress and disappointments is an important attribute for recovery. Self-reflection, the use of humor, accepting one's mistakes and limitations are aspects of adult development that former cult members can use in place of rigid perfectionist expectations.

AFTER THE CULT: FAMILY ISSUES

Post-cult family issues need to be examined to minimize conflicts and to enable the former cult member to recover without the emotional baggage we often see in treating the former cultist and family. Minuchin's (Minuchin, Rosman, & Barber, 1978) description of issues that arise in the treatment of enmeshed families can be useful, with particular attention focused on matters of individuation, competence, and intrusiveness (Markowitz, 1983).

Individuation

Families with rigid and unflexible expectations run the risk of undermining autonomy by holding to rigid expectations. In addition, if the expectations are unachievable, unrealistic, or of no interest to the son or daughter, they need to be changed. Family members, parents in particular, need to adjust their hopes to the reality of a child's abilities and interests. Often young adults, even older adults, do not want to disappoint their parents out of a desire to avoid parental disapproval. It is more constructive, however, when parents can own up to their unrealistic hopes, for example, what one father called his "middle-class expectations."

Former cult members need to develop autonomy by learning to tolerate the frustrations of adult life with its ambiguities, mixed messages, and trials of self-reliance. After the exit counseling is concluded or after a stay at a rehabilitation center, participation in family therapy sessions is most helpful in assisting individuation and autonomy. In family therapy each family member is encouraged to talk about personal feelings and how he or she experienced the period of the loved one's cult involvement; at the same time, the family is encouraged not to dwell on the experience in the cult.

In the case of parents of young adults, the parents will need to make the transition from parenting a younger child, where the parents made decisions, took care of environmental supports, and provided food, shelter, money, a car, and other amenities, to forming an adult relationship with their child. There should be a decline in the parents' responsibility for providing basic financial support except for special reasons such as illness, unemployment, and the immediate post-cult period. Emotional support and encouragement should be the mainstay of a parent's relationship with a young adult son or daughter.

Competence

Parents tend to view their child's cult involvement as an indication of poor judgment, immaturity, and incompetence. Yet cult life demands discipline and forbearance, along with additional challenges for cultists who are required to master strenuous yoga exercise, fasting, sleep deprivation, and long hours of work. The former member's accomplishments in the group need to be acknowledged by the parents even though these activities were conducted under the influence of mind control. The reality is that while in the cult the individual usually acquires new skills and knowledge, which afterward can be added to the personal inventory of competence. Parents need to accept those experiences the ex-cultist feels were positive developments while in the cult. Some experiences were positive, others will take time to sort out before the former member can truly judge their impact. Parents must give the loved one time, must trust their child's innate sense of competence and mastery.

Having the opportunity to make a meaningful contribution to family life or the community at large is most helpful in giving the former cult member a sense of competence. Hence, shopping or other chores should be encouraged, as should the resumption of school or work when the member is ready.

Parents are understandably afraid when their child has contact with members still in the cult. Even though these concerns may be realistic, parents must be careful not to undermine the ex-member's autonomy or erode any remaining sense of competence. It is helpful to have an open discussion of these concerns, for example, to openly say it makes the parents uncomfortable, while at the same time knowing that their daughter feels she can manage the contact. Consultation with a therapist or exit counselor who is familiar with the situation can help to relieve the tension over this issue.

Intrusiveness

The former member may have a strong emotional response to leaving the cult. Feelings of loss and anger, along with some of the symptoms noted earlier, can be frightening to observe. Family members, parents in particular, in an attempt to be supportive, can be overly intrusive with questions about what's wrong, what happened. A delicate balance is needed here between parents' saying they are available to listen and not becoming overly intrusive in pursuing issues that the child may not want to share with a parent.

The message should be that the individual has a right to privacy, a right that was not respected in the cult. The human organism is a self-correcting system that, given time and a variety of paths, will follow a process that leads to the individual's most competent adjustment, once that individual is free to explore new opportunities.

Other Suggestions

Some additional ways that family members can help the recovery process are:

- Be a good listener; if the ex-member is talking, don't interrupt; let him continue. Prompt with an open-ended question if you want to stimulate conversation.
- Provide help when asked for suggestions or ask if you can make a suggestion. Be careful not to try to provide too much information, advice, and help unless it is sought out by the former member.
- Avoid being overprotective; allow the person to make mistakes.
- Provide access to a full medical check-up.
- If you observe the floating phenomenon, speak clearly and directly; touching a hand or shoulder may help bring her back from drifting off into an altered state of consciousness. Looking a per-

son in the eyes will help catch her focused attention, but blink naturally and periodically avert your gaze. Blinking and looking away help reduce the ex-member's propensity to develop the wide-eyed, staring-into-nothingness look, a prehypnotic state.

- Be an educated cult observer by reading such books as *Cults: What Parents Should Know* (Ross & Langone, 1989), *Exit Counseling: A Family Intervention* (Giambalvo, 1992), and *Combatting Cult Mind Control* (Hassan, 1988), as well as other books and articles recommended by the cult education groups.
- Review the policy you had with family and friends regarding social contact with the former cult member. Although the parents may want to handle whatever socializing occurs with extended family members or friends, they should discuss this point with the ex-cultist.
- If the cult involvement was kept secret from some or all of the family, ask your child what feels comfortable. It should be left up to the former cult member to decide whom to tell about the cult affiliation. If the parents kept it a secret, the former member should not be burdened with having to keep this secret unless it in some way serves a need. Generally one can assume that the people around you know these "secrets" and in fact most would be supportive. The goal is to allow the former member the latitude to discuss his cult experiences with anyone of his choosing.
- If it appears that the former member is not progressing rapidly, learn to tolerate the slowness of recovery. The development of new interests, goals, and a life purpose takes time. Ex-members can also be impatient. They and their families are encouraged to compare their current situation to their recent past and not to compare it with peers. It is more useful to say "six months ago I was in a destructive cult and now I'm free" than to compare oneself to former classmates or colleagues with degrees or careers. Progress can be looked at in terms of the changes made in three-month increments of the ex-member's life. (Anderson, Reiss, & Hogarty, 1986).
- Respect the ex-cultist's privacy and need to be alone at times. Expect and encourage rest, time out, and recuperative social withdrawal, particularly in the early stages of recovery. Offer opportunities to join in on activities but accept it if the ex-member declines the invitation.
- Create an environment that is low in tension, conflict, and over-stimulation. Intense affect and tension in the family can precipitate internal stress for the former cult member. Conflict, intense

group discussions, verbal interruptions, and arguments can be difficult to manage. Decrease stress by reducing the emotionality and intensity of family life.

For example, following a break-up with his first girlfriend since leaving the group, a 20-year-old former member of the Unification Church spent the weekend at his parents' home. His parents were so worried about his distress — an appropriate reaction to disappointment in romance — that he had to be hospitalized briefly as a way to alleviate the parents' tension and severe anxiety.

Decreasing stress includes avoiding the following unhelpful behaviors:

- Criticisms of family members
- Criticisms of the recovering ex-cultist
- Extreme involvement with the ex-cultist
- Expressions of intense anger
- Nagging
- Rejection
- Threatening to withdraw support and help
- Patronizing extremes of encouragement and enthusiasm that are not genuine, such as enthusiastic compliments to the ex-cultist for doing her own laundry or some other basic chore

While some of these suggestions may seem contrived, it is helpful to try to contain the family atmosphere in a fashion conducive to recovery and rapprochement with the ex-cult member. Respecting good interpersonal boundaries and family boundaries is the goal of the above suggestions. Good boundaries will lead to autonomy and healthy separation as the young woman or man becomes an independent adult.

STAGES OF
POST-CULT ADJUSTMENT

There are three basic stages in the post-cult recovery process: reentry, reemergence, and integration. Generally the ex-cultist completes these stages over a three-year period following departure from the cult. Bear in mind that each individual, and therefore each recovery, is different. Parents should not expect their son or daughter to run like clockwork.

Lorna Goldberg and William Goldberg (1988) have provided excellent insights into the different stages former cult members pass through on the road to recovery. Using the Goldberg's observations, I have outlined some suggestions for parents, which can help ease their children's distress.

1 to 3 Months: Reentry

The first three months after departure from the cult are usually the most intensely difficult for everyone. The cult experience is regressive and may elicit childlike behaviors and appearances. During this first stage of recovery the ex-member begins to lose the cultlike characteristics and demeanor. The dependency, suggestibility, and grandiose thinking fostered by the cult slowly give way to more realistic thinking.

Dependency   Often a renewed parent-child relationship develops during this early period. Eventually this relationship should become more of an adult-adult relationship; but for now the former cult member will be somewhat more dependent on parents than one would expect of an adult child. Parents and other family members need to be prepared to spend time with the former member – time exercising when he or she feels up to it or joining in new interests, such as a cooking or painting class. Short visits by friends and extended family should be controlled and remain within the comfort zone of the former cultist. Parents and other family and friends need to strike a balance between their own participation and respect for the ex-member's boundaries.

This period of dependence can be a difficult dilemma for both parents and children alike. Rabbi Yehuda Fine (1988) found in his counseling that at this point the parents' role is sometimes confusing: There is an ongoing risk of parents either overwhelming the ex-cultist with too much closeness or leaving too much distance between themselves and their child. Emotional closeness vs. distance is a typical dilemma for everyone involved – both the parents and the former cult member.

Two brief examples of recently exited members may be helpful. In the first case, a 21-year-old college graduate reluctantly returned to her parents' home in a small western town after a brief affiliation with the Unification Church. Spending this period of time together allowed the family to reconnect, to attend family therapy sessions, and to help the young woman figure out a direction for her life. In the second case, a 45-year-old woman found it supportive to spend some time with her parents at their vacation home to recapture some of the time lost during her 20-year cult involvement.

The period of initial dependency can be used to help sponsor a reattachment to the parents that will be healthy, open, and supportive. There is no place here for parental criticism or negative assessments, such as "I told you that group was no good." By being there and being supportive, the parents replace the cult leader who formerly served as an idealized parent surrogate.

Other Characteristic Symptoms   Floating, guilt feelings, and loneliness are also common during the reentry period (Goldberg & Goldberg, 1988). Suggestions on dealing with floating (dissociation) were noted above.

Many former members feel guilty for leaving the cult, for leaving the people they care about, and for their own dishonest or poor behavior while in the group, as well as for the expense, trouble, and heartache they have caused their parents. Persistent feelings of guilt can be symptomatic of depression and should be evaluated by a mental health professional. Parents and others may help to assuage the guilt feelings by accepting them and offering an opinion that perhaps the ex-cultist need not feel guilty. Self-reproach, shame, and guilt are not helpful to the recovery process. Despite parents' encouragement, the former cult member will need time, patience, and repetitious discussion to relieve the sense of guilt.

The intensity of the cult experience with its focus on group experiences may leave the former member bereft of the stimulation and company of peers. A good deal of rest is initially needed, but also the good company of people who are interested and able to listen to the cult experiences can be helpful.

6 to 18 Months: Reemergence

In this second stage, former cultists should be able to return to school or work. Age-appropriate developmental tasks should resume with the exception of dating and socializing on a broader scale. This is a time when much emotional sorting out is needed for the former member to consolidate identity issues, including sexuality and romantic relationships, which may be delayed in this population. Some former cult members embark on a mission to warn others about destructive cultism or work with exit counseling teams as a way to express their anger at having been manipulated by the cult or its leader. During this period parents need to pull back and not be overprotective.

The parents' fear that their child may return to the cult is a realistic one, especially as parents observe life's frustrations and displeasures emerge during their child's struggles to establish life away from the group. Parents, understandably vigilant, who try to prevent setbacks may actually prolong their child's dependence and undermine autonomous growth. Emotional support is needed and should be liberally applied, while lavish financial support can backfire. In some instances grateful parents pay expensive rents and support their unemployed adult child with little expectation that he pursue a job or care for his own needs in a significant way.

In one case, for example, a 25-year-old man with an Ivy League education worked as a carpenter while in a cult. Upon his departure from the group, his parents continually provided him with paid projects rather than allow him to compete in the marketplace as a skilled craftsman. They were concerned that if he did not do well enough on his own he would return to the "protection" of the cult. Those parents needed to have confidence in their son's ability to tolerate the frustrations of daily life. Their well-intentioned efforts only served to deny their son the opportunity to use his inner strengths to develop his competence as an adult.

Also at this stage, the issue of telling others about the cult experience can become significant. The former cult member will also need to decide what to tell prospective employers and how to make adjustments on a résumé for the time spent in the cult.

18 to 36 Months: Integration

During this stage of recovery there is an integration of the pre-cult, cult, and post-cult personality. The time needed for a thorough integration and moving on varies widely, but ideally this should occur within three years. Life no longer revolves around cult-related issues; other tasks such as career goals, friendships, and romantic relationships should predominate. Generally the person now exhibits a more assertive stance toward life and begins to move forward. It is clear to many of us that post-cult psychotherapy facilitates the recovery process.

CONCLUSION

Dealing with a child's cult involvement can be a terrible ordeal for parents. Parents observing frightening changes in a loved one will struggle with the question of whether or not to intervene. If they decide to intervene, they must then contend with the sometimes frightening demands of a successful exit counseling. If the intervention succeeds, or if the adult child leaves the group on his or her own, the parents must then try to be supportive of their child, now a former cult member. Parents must strike a balance between overprotectiveness and distance.

People do recover from cults. And their families, despite the difficulties, can be instrumental in that recovery.

REFERENCES

Anderson, C. M., Reiss, D., & Hogarty, G. E. (1986). *Schizophrenia and the family.* New York: Guilford Press.

Benard, B. (1987, March). Protective factor research: What we can learn from resilient children? *Illinois Prevention Forum, 7*(3), 3–9.

Benard, B. (1991, August). *Fostering resiliency in kids: Protective factors in the family, school, and community.* Western Regional Center for Drug-Free Schools and Communities, Far West Laboratory. Portland, OR: Northwest Regional Educational Laboratory.

Clark, J. (1979). Cults. *Journal of the American Medical Association, 242*(3), 279–281.

Fine, Y. (1988). Toward family reunification: Counseling the cult recruit. In G. Eisenberg (Ed.), *Smashing the idols: A Jewish inquiry into the cult phenomenon.* Northvale, NJ: Jason Aronson.

Gimabalvo, C. (1992). *Exit counseling: A family intervention.* Bonita Springs, FL: American Family Foundation.

Goldberg, L., & Goldberg, W. (1988). Group work with former cultists. In G. Eisenberg (Ed.), *Smashing the idols: A Jewish inquiry into the cult phenomenon.* Northvale, NJ: Jason Aronson.

Hassan, S. (1988). *Combatting cult mind control.* Rochester, VT: Park Street Press.

Markowitz, A. (1983). The role of family therapy in the treatment of symptoms associated with the cult. In D. Halperin (Ed.), *Psychodynamic perspectives on religion, sect and cult.* Boston: John Wright PSG.

Minuchin, S, Rosman, B. L., & Barber, L. (1978). *Psychosomatic families.* Cambridge, MA: Harvard University Press.

Ross, J. C., & Langone, M. D. (1989). *Cults: What parents should know.* New York: Lyle Stuart.

Singer, M. T. (1979, January). Coming out of the cults. *Psychology today, 2*(1), pp. 72–82.

Spero, M. (1983). Individual psychodynamic intervention with the cult devotee: Diagnostic and treatment procedures with a dysautonomous religious personality. In D. Halperin (Ed.), *Psychodynamic perspectives on religion, sect and cult.* Boston: John Wright PSG.

West, J., & Singer, M. T. (1980). Cults, quacks, and nonprofessional psychotherapies. In H. Kaplan, A. Freedman, & B. Sadock (Eds.), *Comprehensive textbook of psychiatry* (Vol. III, 3rd ed.) (pp. 3245–3257). Baltimore, MD: Williams & Wilkins.

16

GUIDELINES FOR EX-MEMBERS

Madeleine Landau Tobias, M.S., R.N., C.S.*

THE FOLLOWING GUIDELINES ARE BASED on my experiences as an ex-member of a destructive group and on the work I've done in counseling and consultation with over two hundred ex-members in the last three years. The suggestions for managing cult-related difficulties are aimed specifically at former cult members; however, I believe others involved in or close to the post-cult recovery process will benefit as well.

NATURE OF POST-CULT PROBLEMS

The degree and type of damage suffered as a result of cult membership vary greatly. Some individuals are able to leave their groups with a minimum of distress, readjusting rapidly to life out of the cult. Others may exhibit serious difficulties in coping with even simple activities of daily living. Factors explaining pre-cult vulnerability and the variables within a cult that influence and account for these differences in the recovery process are discussed in other chapters. Outlined here are the major areas of post-cult vulnerability and the associated problems typically encountered by ex-members.

*I would like to thank Paul Ford and Hana Eltringham Whitfield for their contributions to the body of this paper, and Michael Langone for his patience and editorial assistance.

PROBLEM AREAS
FOR EX-MEMBERS

Difficulties for ex-members tend to fall within life's general aspects of survival and growth, as listed below. Specific needs within each of these problem areas are then more fully developed.

Psychological:
Separating the Wheat from the Chaff

- Sorting through beliefs and values, before, during, and after the cult
- Identifying and disarming cult mind-control techniques
- Unloading the language, or disavowing and discontinuing use of the cult's internal terminology
- Floating, or dissociation, altered states
- Indecisiveness, black-and-white thinking, and obsessional thoughts

Emotional: Dealing with Feelings

- Grief work
- Depression and feelings of failure
- Shame and guilt
- Fear, including nightmares and panic attacks
- Anger and rage

Physical: Helping the Neglected Body

- Health issues and medical care
- Exercise and diet

Vocational: Focusing on the Future

- What to do with your life now
- How to explain the years of life in the cult
- Reevaluation of career goals and skills
- Going back to school

Relationships: Dealing with Trust Issues

- Trusting self and others
- Loneliness, including "cult hopping"
- Reconciling with family and former friends, making new friends

- Need to separate from family and friends still involved in the cult
- Dating and sex

Spiritual/Philosophical:
Reassessing What to Believe In

- Where's God after the guru?
- Reclaiming spirituality or other beliefs and philosophies

UNDERSTANDING IS
HALF THE BATTLE

Before you can recover from anything, first you must know and understand what you are healing from. Although ex-members who left their groups at least in part because of outside assistance (such as an exit counseling intervention, see Chapter 8) may have some understanding of what was done to them; those who were ejected from cults ("castaways") or left on their own ("walkaways") often have little such understanding. Indeed the latter frequently have a strong need to deny they were manipulated and exploited.

On an unconscious level, some ex-members may have difficulty moving beyond a position of shame and guilt, finding it preferable to acknowledging that they were helpless and victimized. The fear—and sometimes rage—experienced when they fully confront helplessness and victimization—that is, having no control over their lives—can at times be overwhelming and more distressing than denial, shame, or guilt. Thus, even many years after leaving their groups, ex-members often withdraw from families and friends, hide or deny their problems, and defer seeking help for cult-related issues. Frequently, when castaways or walkaways do enter therapy, it is to deal with relationships or other issues that are a direct or indirect result of their cult involvement, a connection that often is not initially apparent to them.

Obviously denial of the cultic relationship—either in a small or large group or in a one-on-one relationship—needs to be dealt with first. The recovering ex-member needs to understand mind control, cult recruitment techniques, and his or her particular vulnerabilities. Ex-members need to read and hear everything they can about destructive groups and mind control, which helps to validate their experiences and end their feelings of isolation.

The checklist below may help ex-members sort through what they do and do not understand about their cultic experience and mind control, and begin the recovery process.

MAKING SENSE OF
YOUR EXPERIENCE

The following sets of questions are aimed at exposing the real nature of the cultic group, the leader, and the techniques used. Dealing with the issues raised by these questions begins the process of education and critical examination, a process that is crucial to post-cult recovery.

Recruitment

1. What was going on in your life before joining or meeting the group or leader?
2. How were you approached?
3. What were your initial reactions to and feelings about the group, other members, the leader?
4. What first interested you in the group?
5. How were you misled during recruitment?
6. What did the group or leader promise you? Did you ever get it?
7. What didn't they tell you that might have influenced you not to join had you known?
8. Why did they want you?

Mind Control

1. What mind-control techniques were used by your group? Chanting, meditation, sleep deprivation, isolation, drugs, hypnosis, criticism, fear?
2. What was the most effective technique? the least effective?
3. What are you still using now, such as chanting, that you have a hard time giving up or not doing?
4. What are the group's beliefs and values?

It is useful here to have knowledge of Lifton's (1961) eight criteria for mind control to use as a measuring stick against your cult experience (see explanations of Lifton's criteria in Chapters 3 and 10).

Doubts

1. What are your doubts about the group now?
2. Do you still believe the group or leader has all or some of the answers?
3. Are you still afraid to encounter members or your leader on the street?

4. Do you ever think of going back? What's going on in your mind when that happens?
5. Do you believe your group or leader has any supernatural or spiritual power to harm you in any way, physically or spiritually, now that you have left?
6. Do you believe you are cursed by God for leaving?

This last group of questions serves to indicate what degree of cultic influence is still operating.

UNLOADING THE LANGUAGE

Once out of the group, ex-members may discover they are using group jargon without being aware of it. Group slogans and terminology become a shortcut for communication within the group; they also stop creative, inquisitive thinking and mark you as a member of that group. After you leave the group, this language interferes with and creates barriers to communication with others; when the language is heard, seen, or felt unexpectedly by the ex-member, it may even produce altered states, confusion, anxiety, terror, guilt, and shame.

Some ex-members find that they need to make a special effort to relearn their native language. Cults change the meanings of so many common, everyday words and expressions; thus, for former members, communication outside the group becomes painful and confusing. Ex-members no longer have a meaningful vocabulary to understand their own inner world. This is truly thought stopping and isolating.

To rebuild a normal vocabulary and confidence with words, a former member of an extremist political group recommended doing crosswords and other word puzzles, available in most supermarkets, bookstores, and daily newspapers. Start with the easy ones and build up.

To unload the cultic language, some have found it helpful to list all words used in the group that mean different things outside. Then look up their "real" meanings in a dictionary. Television, newspapers, and books can also be helpful in determining how the rest of the world views certain words and their meanings.

DEALING WITH ALTERED STATES

A common post-cult problem is dealing with "floating," also called trancing out, spacing out, and dissociation. When floating, an ex-member feels disconnected from his or her environment. Concentration becomes difficult, attention spans shorten, and simple activities become major tasks. The need to make minor decisions may produce confusion and panic.

The best way to deal with floating is to discover the trigger that provides the stimulus to float. Obvious triggers include music that was sung or heard in the cult, prayers or chants, or a certain tone of voice. Triggers are particular to each group. Some are simply incidental to the environment of the group and are reminders of experiences in the cult; other triggers are specifically installed during altered states to bring about programmed responses in members.

Triggers may be:

- *Sights:* special colors, flags, pictures of the leader, hand signals, facial expressions, symbols of the group, items used in group activities or rituals
- *Sounds:* songs, jargon, slogans, clicks in the throat, special laughter, mantras, decreeing, praying, speaking in tongues, curses, cue words and phrases
- *Touches:* certain gestures or types of touching, handshakes, a kiss
- *Smells:* incense, perfume or cologne of leader, foods, room odors, body odors
- *Tastes:* certain foods, blood

Merely becoming aware of your triggers is the first step in becoming immune to them. If you have any souvenirs or reminders of your cult's rituals and observances, consider getting rid of them. It's not necessary to keep testing yourself and feeling the pain.

One of my clients became enraged with me whenever I used what she considered to be cult jargon. As these were words that are part of normal everyday usage, and there were so many of them, it quickly became apparent I couldn't eliminate them from my vocabulary. It was imperative to reframe the meaning of the words for her. Reframing (or reprogramming) eliminated the emotional hold of the words and thus the group. She was able to regain more personal power and choice and was also less isolated from others whom she previously viewed as insensitive and cruel.

Figure 1 is a Reprogramming (reframing) Worksheet for triggers developed by Caryn StarDancer (1990).

Use the worksheet with each remaining troublesome trigger. First name the specific *Trigger.* Identify your *Immediate Response* to it, both intellectually and emotionally. Ask yourself, what does it mean to me now? The following case example illustrates the usefulness of the worksheet.

TRIGGER:
IMMEDIATE RESPONSE:
    Emotions:
    Message:
SHORT-TERM CONSEQUENCES:
    Emotion:
    Message:
CHALLENGE:
    Old Message:
    Is this message based on fact?
    What facts refute this message?
    What facts, if any, support it?
RESULTS:
    What is the worst that could happen?
    What favorable things, if any, might happen?
NEW PROGRAM:
    What alternative thought could I try to replace the old message?
    How might I defuse my negative emotions?
    What things can I do to replace them with positive emotions?

Figure 1. Reprogramming Worksheet*

* Reprinted with permission, Survivorship, 3181 Mission St., #139,
San Francisco, CA 94110.

Barbara was a member of an Eastern religious cult who had difficulty concentrating and solving problems; she suffered from anxiety and depression following her cult departure. She kept as a "souvenir" several scrolls that contained prayers chanted in the group. Chanting was believed to bring earthly and spiritual happiness, and those who left the group were to be cursed with a variety of unexpected calamities.

Seeing the scrolls was a *Trigger* for Barbara. Her *Immediate Response* was a vague feeling of dread, a slight dizziness, and a reminder of the group's threats. The *Short-Term Consequences* for her were continual doubting of her decision to leave the group, and a sense of failure and low self-esteem. The message was that she was in danger spiritually, physically, and emotionally for having left the group: she would be punished.

In the *Challenge* section you may need to do some research. What are the facts? Does the rest of society believe this to be true? In examining her beliefs, Barbara was able to intellectually understand that the scrolls and chants did not have any power and that many others had left the group without experiencing harm and were indeed doing well. In fact, Barbara left the cult because her marriage and family life had been deteriorating since joining; now the quality of her life and her family's had already improved in the few months since leaving! Reviewing this made Barbara realize that there were no objective facts to support the group's threatening claims.

Use your imagination in the *Results* section, see if you can picture and change the things that may happen. Remember times in the past when your cult or leader was wrong about something. In the cult you were expected to believe and did believe that your leader was infallible. Remember your doubts! After reviewing the course of her time in the group, Barbara was able to discard the scrolls.

Use the *New Program* section to try out new messages to replace the old and examine your feelings about these changes. Be patient with yourself. The magical beliefs of some groups take root in our imaginations and some creativity may be needed to yank them out! With use of these guidelines, Barbara was able to look at the scrolls with objectivity; she was able to let go of them once they were divested of their power.

When you take the effort to reprogram your triggers, you can make huge strides in regaining your freedom from cult mind control. The worksheet can also be modified and used to examine the cult's beliefs. The *Challenge* portion is useful for this. In the group you were taught not to trust your own thoughts and inner feelings. Now there may be times when you become confused about which thoughts are your own and which are the cult's. As you go through the worksheet and examine different ideas, you can decide what to believe and how you wish to interpret *your* reality. This is also the beginning of trusting yourself again.

DEALING WITH FEELINGS

Some feelings were encouraged and exaggerated in the group: Guilt, fear, and shame, for example, were all used to foster compliance and control. Other feelings were harshly punished, suppressed, or forbidden, such as anger at the leader or group. It's likely that angry feelings were channeled by the group onto outsiders, family, or the government, and were used to rationalize antisocial behavior and isolationism.

Having feelings is good news and bad news for ex-members. While in the cult, members learn to survive, in part, by denying and suppressing their feelings. Once they are out, they are often flooded with feelings that are difficult to identify and deal with.

Grief and Mourning

Almost all ex-members experience grief and mourning. Leaving the group means experiencing many losses:

- Loss of the group
- Loss of time while in the group
- Loss of innocence, naiveté, idealism
- Loss of spirituality or other beliefs
- Loss of family
- Loss of meaning in life

Grief and mourning, especially when combined with anxiety, anger, and shame, can produce an incapacitating depression. It is not uncommon for ex-members to be dealing with such emotions months after leaving. The key to dealing with these and other intense feelings is to express them somehow, sometime, to someone. Expression can be through keeping a journal of thoughts and feelings. Writing an account of your cult experience is an excellent way to make sense of it by getting the feelings out of your head and body and onto paper. Write poetry, draw, paint, knit, and crochet it. Use your imagination!

In Connecticut several women's groups got together to draw attention to and share their rage and grief over sexual trauma in their lives. Each woman made a piece of quilt expressing her thoughts and feelings about sexual abuse. The pieces sewn together made five 12 ft × 12 ft quilts, creating a moving and inspiring story of strength and survival.

Finding someone to listen to your story, your experiences, and your feelings is vital to recovery. Choose someone who will be able to listen to you nonjudgmentally and sympathetically, someone who is interested in learning about cults and mind control, someone who is objective and supportive of your efforts to heal.

Feelings of Failure, Guilt, and Shame

Ex-members who were not exit counseled frequently feel that somehow they are failures or inadequate for not having been able to stay in the group. They may feel that there is something lacking in themselves, or they were not good enough for the group or leader. If their leader left, was jailed, or died, they may think it was their fault for not being good or spiritual enough. Cults typically blame the members for everything bad. Ex-members have a tendency to continue this practice of self-blame after they leave.

Guilt is experienced when thoughts and behaviors run counter to beliefs about what is right and wrong. In a cult these beliefs may be discarded, distorted, or reversed through thought-reforming processes in order to control members. Ex-members may feel guilt for a variety of reasons:

- Hurting and disappointing family, causing them worry, pain, and anger
- Recruiting friends, relatives, and other new members
- Participating in cult-directed activities that go against previous ethical values, such as drug-related activities, begging, lying, spying on friends and other cult members, cult-enforced prostitution and pornography, violence, murder, and other criminal activities
- Attaining a position of power and authority in the group and using it to support the leader and control others
- Participating in the "victim chain" by abusing their subordinates even as they themselves were abused by their superiors

Shame is felt when you see yourself as bad through the eyes of others; guilt is felt when you do something you believe to be bad. For example, a cult member may be given a daily quota for fund-raising. Unable to meet it, he returns to the group and must report his low earnings. Feeling guilty that he didn't earn enough even though he may have worked until exhaustion, he is now made to feel that he is morally inferior, if not evil, for his deficiencies. Shame is now heaped onto the guilt. The cultic system thus produces a continual cycle of guilt and shame.

Since so much of cult behavior is aimed at controlling members through guilt and shame, the challenge is to identify those actions ex-members would normally regret, given their pre-cult ethical systems, and at the same time identify the factors within the group that diminished members' capacity to make voluntary, informed choices. They must sort out which actions they should take responsibility for from those that are the responsibility of the group and leader.

Forgiveness as a Means to Recovery

Forgiving yourself is essential to eliminating shame and reducing guilt. Shame is toxic: It cripples self-esteem and retards emotional healing. Although guilt may help us avoid making the same mistakes again, excessive amounts of it prevent us from growing and learning from those mistakes.

Working through guilt and shame is crucial to the recovery process. The following technique, adapted from 12-step programs, is a useful mechanism to gain control over self-deprecating emotions.

1. First, make a list of all that you have done in the group that produces shame and guilt related to the group experience.
2. Share this with someone you trust who will not judge you. Talking it over with a therapist, exit counselor, clergyperson, or an-

other ex-member is very helpful. You need someone else's perspective and objectivity. You need to get it out of you!

3. Realistically look at this list and see if you can make amends to any of the people involved. This should not be done if it causes further pain to another or puts you at risk of reinvolvement with the group.

4. If you can, and if you find it helpful, ask for forgiveness from God, your higher power, or whatever your spiritual source is.

5. Don't forget to forgive yourself. This is both the hardest and the most important part of all. As long as you are operating on guilt, you are emotionally handicapped.

6. Ex-members *do not* have to forgive their leaders to heal. They can if they want and are able. They should, however, avoid continuing to set impossible standards for themselves, as is the norm in cultic groups.

We can seek forgiveness from those we hurt, from God, and from ourselves, but forgiving those who hurt us is a different issue. This is a highly personal matter. As one ex-member said, "For those in the group who hurt me, as a fellow member, I can forgive them. They were as much under the influence of our leader as I was. As for the leader, since he shows absolutely no indication of sorrow for what he has done to me and what he continues to do to others, and for what he would still do to me if he could, I do not forgive him."

Fear

Fear is the backbone of mind control. Cults control by fear: fear of those outside the group; fear of failure, ridicule, and violence within the group; fear of spiritual failure. Comparing notes with other ex-members is the best antidote to fear. One source of ex-member mutual support is FOCUS, a support network for former cult members affiliated with the Cult Awareness Network. There are numerous FOCUS groups throughout the United States. (For information contact Cult Awareness Network National Office, 2421 W. Pratt Blvd., Suite 1173, Chicago, IL 60645.)

Recognizing that your fear results from outside manipulations becomes easier when you talk to others who have similar doubts and fears. Common expressions of fear are:

• Fear we made a mistake in leaving the group: What if we were wrong and our leader really is the messiah?

- Fear of physical, emotional, financial, and/or spiritual disasters: What if, as the cult leader predicted, these harmful events actually do befall defectors?
- Fear of violence and retribution from the group: What if the group follows through on its threats?

Be aware of the possibility of posthypnotic suggestion as a possible explanation for some post-cult symptoms or problems. Remember the power of triggers; review or redo the reprogramming worksheet as often as necessary.

If you've been taught for years about the dangers to you and your family upon leaving the group, then you may blame yourself for everything bad that happens. Do some reality checking. If you believe the cult is responsible for anything bad that has happened to you since leaving, then who do you think is responsible for the good? Be realistic about the powers of your former leader and the potentiality of the cult's follow-through on threats. If real harm from the cult is a possibility, then take the necessary precautions, some of which are outlined below.

Protecting Yourself

If your group is known to be violent toward ex-members, in that case you must protect yourself. The issue of protecting ex-cultists is a complex one. The following suggestions come from Kevin Garvey (personal communication, 1991), an experienced exit counselor.

Stage One: Reality Testing

1. Has your group ever hurt, sued, libeled, slandered, or actually killed or kidnapped someone?
2. Have you ever met anyone who was so harmed?
3. Has anyone in your group admitted to hurting or harassing others?
4. How important were you to the group? Do they have any reason to fear you now that you are out?
5. How emotionally stable are the leader and the group's members?

Garvey notes that 80% of his cases do not generate safety concerns. The remaining 20% involve aggressive efforts to contact the person, harassment, and legal threats. He calls this the "hollow threat" category, as it is rarely followed through on. "It usually reflects a leader's need to impress the followers," states Garvey.

Stage Two: Putting the Cult on Notice

1. Write your cult leader and state emphatically that you are leaving the group and do not wish to be contacted. Send it by registered mail and keep the receipt.
2. Hang up on all cult calls. Get an unlisted number if you get crank calls.
3. Go to the police and make a complaint. You may be able to get a restraining order if you are being seriously hassled.
4. Get professional legal help for yourself if you are subject to legal harassment from the cult.

Stage Three: Protecting Yourself   If there are direct threats of physical violence:

- Assess the extent of the threat
- Notify law enforcement and arrange for their help
- Take protective countermeasures
- Be aware of surveillance
- Never travel alone
- Monitor your telephone calls
- Keep family cars protected
- Carefully monitor family and small children
- Alter familiar daily patterns
- Keep exterior house lights on at night
- Install a home security system
- Buy, borrow, or adopt a big or loud dog
- Move to another locale

Anger

Emerging anger is one of the first signs of recovery from the cult experience. Anger is a normal and healthy reaction to the numerous harms and assaults perpetrated upon us. Anger is the most appropriate response to the abuse and manipulations of the cult and is also the hardest for some ex-members to get in touch with and deal with. *Anger means you are now ready to acknowledge that you were victimized.* That is incredibly painful. What was done was heinous, evil. Ex-members are entitled to their rage.

Anger may be hard for family, friends, and sometimes even therapists to accept. You may be urged to "forgive and forget." Ex-members who have been brought up to hide or deny "negative" feelings may not have the tools or experience to know how to express this potentially healing emotion.

Ex-members of cults and adult survivors of childhood physical and sexual abuse share many things in common in their recovery. Both have been victimized by those they trusted and depended upon. Many cult members have been sexually and/or physically victimized and abused; all have been emotionally and spiritually vandalized.

Just as fear is the backbone of mind control, anger is the powerhouse of recovery. Anger is an extremely valuable tool in healing: Anger fortifies your sense of what is right by condemning the wrong that was done to you. It provides the energy and will to proceed through the difficult task of getting your life back together. It is through anger that ex-members tap into a source of motivation and energy which enables constructive and reconstructive action. Suppression of such anger in the cult contributed to depression and a sense of helplessness.

Anger can also be a two-edged sword. Anger can motivate to heal or be turned inside, against the self. Blaming yourself may be easier than using anger to make the necessary changes in your life. Anger can be suppressed, resulting in addictions, physical illness, or emotional disorders, including depression and suicidal thoughts and behaviors; or anger can be directed at innocent others. Anger can further isolation from others when it is expressed inappropriately, or when you are unaware of it. Anger, to be used effectively, must be focused on its source – the cult's leadership.

Anger can be expressed and transformed creatively and powerfully through the use of such techniques as the following:

1. Keep a diary and write about your anger and other strong feelings.
2. Write a letter to your cult leader. Tell him or her off. It is not necessary to send it, especially if doing so would put you in danger! You don't have to mail it to feel the positive effects of having written the letter.
3. Talk to someone about your feelings.
4. Turn on the shower, get in, and scream.
5. Turn the car radio on loud and scream in the car, but not while driving.
6. Do something physical: pound pillows with a whiffle bat or tennis racket. Go into the woods and pound boulders with a sledge hammer (wear protective goggles). Direct your anger into the activity.
7. Fantasize taking revenge – it's okay to imagine it. We all go through periods of creating scenarios whereby our injured pride is restored. It is not okay, however, to do anything illegal or dangerous to another.

8. Speak out publicly about your cult experience. Get involved in an anti-cult group. This is not something that everyone must do to recover, but it is a therapeutic activity for many ex-members.
9. Get the law on your side. If your group has been involved in criminal activity, seek a lawyer before going to the police. You need to protect yourself first.
10. Consider a civil suit against the cult for damages. Again seek legal advice about this.
11. Take an assertiveness training course at your local "Y" or community college.

It has been said that success is the best revenge. Becoming happy outside of the cult, rather than getting sick and dying as the cult wishes, is the best evidence of your success and the best exposure of the cult's lies about life outside of the group.

TAKING CARE OF YOUR BODY

For many ex-members the last thing they were allowed to care for in their group was their health. If you were in a group that didn't allow for proper nutrition, medical care when you were ill or pregnant, dental hygiene and care, or proper dress and exercise, you may have special health needs.

Most ex-members come out of their cults with no medical insurance or savings. If you are in that category, you may have to register as an outpatient in a large community health center to find good care. If you have a job with medical coverage, take advantage of it. In this case, you can usually choose your own doctor.

A medical checkup is essential if:

1. You are presently suffering from any medical condition – chronic (long-term) or acute (recent and severe) – since you entered or now that you are out of the group.
2. You were pregnant while in the group.
3. You were physically or sexually abused in the group.
4. You were exposed to serious infectious diseases, such as AIDS, TB, venereal and tropical diseases.
5. You have a prior history of a chronic illness, such as diabetes, epilepsy, or high blood pressure.

All children who were in cults need a complete physical examination and need to be updated on vaccinations against serious childhood illness, such as polio, measles, whooping cough.

Using the System: Public Assistance

Some ex-members come out of their groups seriously ill and disabled. As distasteful as it may seem, temporary reliance on the state or federal government's public assistance programs can be an excellent means for helping you get back on your feet. State agencies can be helpful in assisting you to find housing, health care, and employment.

If you were employed before joining the group, you paid taxes to the state and federal government. You can look at that as money you deposited for your future; now your present situation requires use of that resource. If you had earnings withheld for social security, you are entitled to use that money now if you are disabled. This is not charity – this is survival!

As soon as you are on your feet and working, you will automatically be paying taxes again. You will be contributing to the well-being of the economy, aiding the same programs that assisted you, and therefore helping others. You will also be independent again.

VOCATIONAL NEEDS

For some ex-members, their first employment opportunity was while in the cult. All ex-members – unless they were in the group only a short time – must consider their experiences in the cult in their search for employment. At first, this may seem impossible but force yourself to sit down and list what you learned in your cult. Many ex-members resist looking at the positive side; nevertheless, some good must have occurred, even if it is only to acknowledge to yourself that you could survive incredible hardship.

Cult members learn sales and recruitment skills, office skills, farming, communication skills, publishing skills, and administrative and leadership abilities, to name just a few. Write it down and put it in your résumé. It is often helpful to consult with other ex-members, family, and friends to strategize about proper wording in your résumé and before job interviews.

While you are reviewing the benefits of your cult experience, try to look for the hidden, less tangible benefits. One ex-member's family, for example, often teased her about being lazy because of her avid interest in reading as a child. In her Eastern meditation cult, she worked full time while going to school at night, frequently taking four courses a semester so she could complete her degree quickly enough to satisfy her leader. In addition, she had housekeeping and child-care duties. When she finally left her group, she was able to retire the label of "lazy" forever!

Also, don't forget that it's never too late to go back to school. Frequently ex-members return to college with new goals and careers in mind.

RELATIONSHIPS

In rebuilding your life, you will undoubtedly face the rather unsettling dilemma of reestablishing former relationships and figuring out how to have new ones. Trust, loneliness, and dating are areas of great concern.

Trust

Many leave their groups with deep suspicions of others' motivations and feelings. The betrayal of trust by the group, with its residue of hurt, rage, and fear, presents problems for the ex-member. Knowing whom to trust and to what extent takes time.

Trust should never be absolute. In the cult you had no choice but to rely on and trust the group completely. Absolute trust was demanded by the leadership: anything less was a sign of Satan, gross imperfection, disobedience, or worse, and was a punishable offense.

Learning to trust in stages is important. Experience has taught you that those who present themselves as friendly, interested, and helpful may have darker motives. The key to trusting is to proceed slowly. Trusting is a process, not a final act. It must be earned by those who desire to get close to you.

Learning to trust again also involves learning to tolerate the foibles, sensitivities, and eccentricities of others. This in turn helps you to tolerate and trust yourself, your imperfections and idiosyncrasies.

Loneliness

Perhaps the single largest difficulty for those who walk away from their cults is isolation and loneliness. Without a network of family, friends, and other survivors, recovery is much more difficult. Some ex-members return to their cults or inadvertently join other destructive groups (known as cult hopping) in order to fill the void created by leaving the intense group experience provided by the cult.

In some cults, members live at home and continue working. For them, feelings of isolation and loneliness may not be as intense. The emotional and spiritual needs met by the group may in time be replaced with safer and rewarding outlets, which already exist in their family and community.

For those who relied on the group to meet all their essential needs, such as safety, food, and shelter, as well as spiritual and relational needs, they experience a vast void upon leaving. In *Trauma and Recovery*, Judith Herman (1992) states that a key factor in recovering from traumatic events is being able to talk about it in groups with others who have had similar experiences. By sharing stories and feelings, participating in group problem solving, and meeting and making new friends, isolation is diminished and the cultic experience detoxified. Ex-members who have FOCUS groups in their area have an opportunity to meet with others with similar experiences. For some former members, 12-step meetings provide a safe environment to talk about addictive problems the person may be dealing with.

Building new networks of friends and regaining a sense of community can sometimes be done by returning to the religious faith you were brought up in, if that seems to be an appropriate route for you at this time. For many ex-members, however, organized religion may not be an option they wish to consider for some time. Indeed, after their experience, many former cultists remain wary of any kind of organized group for quite some time.

As trust in self is regained, trust in others can begin. As your sense of vulnerability lessens, you will slowly open yourself to others. Perhaps first allowing yourself to find people with similar hobbies, interests, skills, and occupations may provide "safe" topics to relate to. One ex-member found friends through a computer bulletin board. Only after considerable correspondence and trust building was she able to meet with a new friend. By that time she had gotten to know him rather well.

Dating and Sex

Many former cult members have difficulty resuming normal relationships. This happens for a variety of reasons:

- They had little or no dating experience before joining the cult.
- They were born into the cult or were young when their families joined.
- They were subject to enforced strict celibacy in the group.
- They were in a cult that practiced sexual abuse and/or enforced promiscuity or prostitution.
- They were in a cult where marriage and childbearing were determined by the group leader(s).

Certainly for the above reasons, but also simply because of having lived in a closed, controlled environment, adjustment to dating and socializing may seem quite strange and even frightening. Compounding the confusion, popular television, movies, and books present a distorted picture of the norm.

The following guidelines have proven useful in helping former cult members resume life's challenge of involvement in intimate relationships:

1. First, you may want to examine your beliefs about relationships before and during your cult experience. What did the group believe, or profess to believe, about relationships? Do you continue to hold those values?

2. Use the Challenge section of the reprogramming worksheet if these beliefs are difficult to sort through.

3. If you had little or no dating experience before the cult, give yourself permission to be a novice in relationships.

4. Remember, relationships begin with friendships. Liking precedes loving. Give yourself permission to take your time.

5. If celibacy was practiced in your group and you wish to reexamine these values, discuss your sexual options with knowledgeable counselors. Pastoral counselors and mental health and medical professionals can provide sex education and contraceptive advice as well as help you clarify your values.

6. If sexual trauma, such as rape, prostitution, and pornography, was practiced in your group, then psychotherapy is urged to help you resolve any post-traumatic symptoms that may interfere with having healthy intimate relationships. (See also the section below on selecting professional help.)

7. If you were married in the group and your spouse remains in it, decisions about marriage and children (if any) need to be resolved. This may require help from clergy and legal and mental health professionals.

8. If both you and your spouse left the group, issues surrounding the cult and its effect on your roles, values, and life-style need to be resolved.

9. If your spouse was chosen for you by the group, very basic decisions about your marriage need to be explored and your commitment to each other reevaluated. For some, this may mean recognition of irreconcilable differences and a basic mismatch and perhaps a decision to divorce. For others, a reevaluation of the relationship may mean a new and deeper level of commitment and appreciation.

SPIRITUAL AND
PHILOSOPHICAL ISSUES

Perhaps the most emotionally upsetting and talked about phenomenon at ex-member meetings is the difficulty in coming to terms with spirituality. Although the focus in this section is on religious beliefs, the disruption of fundamental personal beliefs extends to all areas since there are all kinds of cults—political, therapy, new age, health, and so forth. Thus, the suggestions here need to be extended to other philosophical or political beliefs for ex-members from another type of cult for whom religion per se may not be the main issue of concern. The reevaluation of personal beliefs and the resumption of activities in support of those beliefs remain to be resolved for ex-members of all cults—religious and otherwise.

Ex-members often describe their cult experience as a spiritual rape. It can be likened to having fallen totally in love, changing and conforming yourself so as to merge with your loved one, giving up everything to love and serve, only to be betrayed. The wound is very deep and will take time to heal.

Most ex-members shy away from organized religion (or even any kind of organized group) for a while after their cult departure. For those who were comfortable with their previous religious affiliation, a return to their church or synagogue is welcome. That, however, seems to be the exception rather than the rule.

Ex-members are advised to take their time in choosing another religious affiliation. If you have any doubts at all whether you have chosen another cultlike group, contact the Cult Awareness Network (CAN) to see if there are any complaints against the group in question. Most of all, if you are in any doubt, trust yourself, check it out with others who are not in the new group.

For further discussion on spiritual issues related to cult recovery, see Chapter 12 by the Reverend Richard Dowhower.

TAKING INVENTORY:
GETTING THE HELP YOU NEED

Questions commonly asked by ex-members are:

1. Why is this such a big deal? Why do I have to work on these things at all?
2. When can I finally stop working on these issues?
3. How do I know if I need professional help?

Briefly, the answers to the first two of these questions can be found by examining your psychological health, that is, your capacity to work, love, play, and – if you have religious faith – pray. The post-cult period often requires close examination because of the damage to ex-members' psychological health. When their health is recovered, they can stop working on issues particular to the post-cult experience and begin to focus on other life issues.

Self-help

Many ex-members recover from their cult experiences on their own. Some of the activities they have described as useful in this self-help process are:

- Reading all they can on cults and mind control. There is a growing body of literature on these subjects. Several good books are available about specific groups and types of cults. Organizations like the Cult Awareness Network (CAN) and the American Family Foundation (AFF) have extensive bibliographies and also sell relevant books and literature.
- Joining FOCUS or other ex-member support groups. FOCUS is an organization of former cult members, with regular meetings in states throughout the country. These groups meet monthly or more frequently.
- Talking to friends, family, and clergy about their experiences. The process of understanding and working through the cult experience begins by sharing thoughts and feelings with those who care. Talking about it, rather than silently rehashing it within, helps to put it in perspective and give vent to feelings.
- Writing about their experiences.

Professional Help

A recent survey of ex-cult members (Langone, Chambers, Dole, & Grice, in press) found that 70% sought professional help after leaving their groups. Regarding professional help, you can benefit from it if:

- You are having difficulty functioning fully or enjoying life.
- You had emotional difficulties prior to joining the cult, which are now resurfacing.
- You feel overwhelmed by such emotions as depression, anxiety, guilt, shame, and rage; or you are unable to deal with floating,

have nightmares, insomnia, intrusive thoughts about the trauma experienced in the group, panic attacks, numbing of emotions, a feeling of deadness inside, or detachment from others. These latter are symptoms of what is called post-traumatic stress disorder; they are commonly found in survivors of destructive cults, incest, rape, and war, as well as in victims of natural disasters, such as floods, tornadoes, and earthquakes. (APA, 1987)

If you have not been through a formal exit counseling, you are strongly urged to find someone who has expertise in post-cult work, or at least is willing to learn about the special problems of former members. Referrals can often be obtained from the previously mentioned cult educational organizations.

There are four types of professional assistance ex-members may seek. They are:

Exit Counseling   Consider meeting with an exit counselor. Just because you left the group voluntarily, or were kicked out, doesn't mean you cannot utilize, or benefit from, a professional exit counselor. An intensive day or two with an exit counselor with expertise in your particular group may be all you need to sort through the various cult mind-control issues. You are able then to follow up your recovery in an informed manner.

Rehabilitation Center   Rehabilitation centers for ex-cult members are live-in facilities where clients can continue their education about cults, examine their psychological needs, prepare for returning to their families, explore vocational interests, and rest and relax. A brief stay with intensive support, education, and counseling can be very helpful in coming to terms with the cult experience, dealing with its aftermath, and preparing for a productive return to the "real world."

Pastoral Counseling   If religion is an issue for you, it is important to locate a clergyperson who has familiarity with cults and mind control. Churches and religious organizations are increasingly confronting the issues of cult conversion, as they, like the family, are being hard hit by losing their members to cults.

Psychotherapists   Therapists can be mental health practitioners with master's or doctoral degrees in a variety of disciplines, for example, nursing, social work, psychology, marriage and family counseling, pastoral counseling, and psychiatry.

How to choose a therapist. It is important that your therapist view your cult experience as a major contributing factor to your current problems, a factor that should be addressed very early in therapy. Your therapist then can assist you as a coach, an ally, in a psychoeducational process.

The following are questions to consider asking during the first session with a therapist. Remember, you don't have to select the first therapist you talk to. Don't be afraid to "interview" the therapist to make sure that he or she will be able to meet your needs. (The questions in this section were adapted for ex-cult members from Judith Bentley's *How to Choose a Therapist,* copyright 1985 by VOICES in Action, Inc., P.O. Box 148309, Chicago, IL 60614.)

1. What is your educational background? Are you licensed or accredited?
2. What is your counseling experience and training in cults and mind control?
3. Are you an ex-member of a destructive cult? What kind of postcult counseling did you have?
4. What kind of therapy do you do (e.g., cognitive, Freudian) and what will it involve?
5. Do you believe in "therapeutic" touching of clients? What is permissible touching?
6. Do you believe that it is ever appropriate to have sex with clients or former clients? (Run, don't walk, out of the office if the answer is anything other than never!)
7. Are you reachable in an emergency?
8. What is your fee?
9. How do you feel about the New Age? Do you incorporate any new age techniques in your therapy (e.g., crystals, past life regressions)?
10. Would you tell me a little about your philosophy of life?

Suggested questions to ask yourself after the initial interview:

1. Did you feel accepted, respected, and comfortable with the therapist? Do you like yourself a little more now?
2. Did the therapist make you feel comfortable or did you notice things that made you feel uneasy? You are not strange for noticing the furniture, paintings, or books in the office.
3. Was the therapist direct and open in answering all your questions or did he or she dodge any of them?

4. Did you get the impression that this person feels she or he has all the answers to every problem (if so, run like mad!), or did you get the feeling she or he was interested in exploring with you, with no preconceived expectations, where you'd be going in your therapy?
5. Did you get the feeling that this person is a sensitive, wise, mature person with whom you feel safe?
6. Did the therapist overreassure you that you now had the right counselor to take care of you? In other words, were you being set up to idealize him or her as the perfect therapist for you, the only one who could heal you?

Some general matters to keep in mind when selecting a therapist:

1. Trust your own judgment! You have the right not to trust immediately. Trust needs to be earned; there are no shortcuts.
2. Interview several therapists. You wouldn't buy the first car you see.
3. Get referrals from agencies and people you trust, if you are able.
4. Remember, you can stop therapy any time you want. Therapy is for you, not the therapist.
5. Discuss touching early on. Touch is a highly personal issue. Some therapists will hug a client, but this activity should be initiated by the client, not the therapist. Say something if there is touching involved and you feel uncomfortable about it.
6. Remember, it is *never* okay to be touched on the chest, genitals, or any place else that makes you feel uncomfortable.
7. Work with a therapist who will interact with you during the session. Ex-members need a therapist who is actively involved in the recovery process.

GETTING ON WITH YOUR LIFE

I am often asked, "When am I done working on this stuff?" "When is being in a cult going to stop being a big thing in my life?" The answer is not simple. Gradually, preoccupation with feelings, thoughts, and behaviors associated with the cult will lessen. As ex-members resume taking responsibility for their lives, personal empowerment increases. As soon as ex-members start to look forward to their careers, relationships, and even simple pleasures, life in the cult recedes into the past, rather than lingering in the present and future.

For some of us, the experiences of our cult past get transformed into a viable present by influencing our life work. Many ex-members become therapists or lawyers who may work with former cult members. Some will continue friendships and relationships with other ex-members. For most, recovery means getting on with life and coming to terms with the past through self-acceptance and self-forgiveness.

Recovery means accepting a new view of the world and life. This view perhaps does not see the world as safe, as fair, or as rosy as before, rather it sees human nature with less naiveté, and sees oneself as less vulnerable, yet with a new compassion for self and humanity. By avoiding the challenge of recovery, an ex-cult member runs the risk of using cynicism, pessimism, and hatred as defenses against vulnerability, and of using isolation and denial as weapons against future hurt and pain.

Recovery means full acceptance of our humanity – the good as well as the bad. Recovery means recognizing that we must struggle for betterment while we accept our own and others' imperfections.

REFERENCES

American Psychiatric Association. (1987). *Diagnostic and statistical manual of mental disorders* (3rd ed.-rev.). Washington, DC: Author.

Andres, R., & Lane, J. R. (Eds.). (1988). *Cults and consequences: The definitive handbook.* Los Angeles: Commission on Cults and Missionaries of the Jewish Federation Council of Greater Los Angeles.

Bentley, J. (1985). *How to choose a therapist.* Chicago, IL: Voices in Action, Inc.

Crowley, K., & Paulina, D. (1990, November). Exit counseling workshop. Preconference, National Conference of the Cult Awareness Network, Chicago, IL.

Hassan, S. (1988). *Combatting cult mind control.* Rochester, VT: Park Street Press.

Herman, J. (1992). *Trauma and recovery.* New York: Basic Books.

Langone, M. D., Chambers, R., Dole, A., & Grice, J. (in press). Results of a survey of ex-cult members. *Cultic Studies Journal.*

Lifton, R. J. (1961). *Thought reform and the psychology of totalism.* New York: W. W. Norton.

Ross, J. C., & Langone, M. D. (1989). *Cults: What parents should know.* New York: Lyle Stuart.

Singer, M. T. (1979, January). Coming out of the cults. *Psychology Today,* pp. 72–82.

StarDancer, C. (1990). Reprogramming worksheet. *SurvivorShip.*

Section IV

SPECIAL ISSUES

17

CHILDREN AND CULTS

Michael D. Langone, Ph.D.
Gary Eisenberg, M.A.

THIS CHAPTER WILL EXAMINE THE CAPACITY of certain cultic and related authoritarian groups to harm children, physically and psychologically. The particular groups with which we are most concerned are exploitatively manipulative and threaten children because they (1) live by an absolutist ideology that dictates harsh physical discipline and/ or the rejection of medical intervention; (2) function as closed, often physically isolated, societies that resist any investigation of possible child abuse; and (3) use religious beliefs to justify their ideology and reclusive nature. Their absolutist ideology provides a rationalization for child abuse. Their limited interaction with members of mainstream society (for example, members don't visit doctors, children attend group-run schools) tends to close off the normal means by which authorities learn about child abuse and neglect. Their religious nature magnifies their capacity to avoid scrutiny because they can invoke the First Amendment in order to curtail investigative efforts. For these reasons, raising the question of child abuse and cults is not analogous, as some have suggested, to asking about child abuse and Episcopalians, or Catholics, or Baptists. The social structures and psychological dynamics of mainstream religions simply do not incline them toward child abuse and neglect as do the structures and dynamics of cultic groups.

Not surprisingly, child protection authorities cannot easily measure the scope of the problems these groups pose. Scientific literature on child abuse in cultic groups is almost nonexistent. Official investigations cover only a handful of extreme cases in which the death of a child served as the stimulus to governmental action. Nearly all of the other available information comes from individual court cases, about which newspaper reports are the only readily available sources of information. An early survey of such reports can be found in Landa (1984). Consequently, it is impossible to estimate the extent of the problem with any confidence. Moreover, the connection between a group's practices and child abuse and neglect is not always clear. Nevertheless, on the whole the evidence is sufficiently compelling to warrant examination. Much more research must be conducted, however, before we can draw confident conclusions about the relationship between cultic groups and child abuse and neglect.

This chapter will try to make the best of this unfortunate situation. We will first examine the psychological dynamics that make cultic groups especially prone toward child abuse and neglect. We will then describe the types of harm that have been observed in cultic and related groups. Lastly, we will offer some thoughts on treatment issues pertaining to children coming out of cultic groups.

PSYCHOLOGICAL DYNAMICS

Markowitz and Halperin (1984) provide the most complete and compelling explanation of why child abuse and neglect is likely to be associated with cultic groups. First of all, because these groups are centered on the personality of a charismatic leader, the leader's idiosyncratic beliefs, no matter how mundane, may influence the group's childrearing practices. A leader's fear of dentists, for example, may result in a requirement that children avoid dentists. The totalistic structure of these groups—that is, their controlling sometimes even the most minor aspects of members' lives, such as what clothing to wear—potentiates the destructive power of the leader's idiosyncracies.

Because these groups' ideologies tend to be nonfalsifiable, subjectivist systems that are threatened by the outside world, ideology must be treated as sacred and unchallengeable. This feature becomes especially destructive with regard to children, in that, as Markowitz and Halperin note, "there is a primacy of ideology over biology . . . childcare may be seen as a disposable superfluity" (1984, p. 145).

The cult's hierarchical structure and its setting itself up as "family" turn parents into "middle management" with regard to their own children. How they discipline their children, what activities they encourage in their children, what they teach their children: such decisions are dictated by the group's leader. The parents' role as middle managers can become especially dangerous for children when the leader measures the parents' dedication to him by their willingness to abuse their children at his request (Landa, 1990/1991). In addition, the parents' dependence on the leader, the either-or mentality of the group, and the frequency with which members are subjected to oscillating rewards and punishments can, in conjunction with group strictures against dissent, result in a great deal of suppressed anger. Parents may then vent their frustrations on their children. Such projection of anger becomes even more destructive when the group's doctrine emphasizes harsh physical discipline.

Environmental control is of paramount concern to a cult's leader(s). Self-expression and/or rebelliousness is natural for children, especially during certain developmental stages, such as "the terrible twos." Consequently, cults tend to impose severe controls to curtail the expression of natural impulses, thereby stifling creativity, individuality, and sexuality (an exception being groups that advocate unrestrained sexuality, although even in these groups the leadership may exercise considerable control over the choice of partners and the manner of sexual expression).

Many observers believe that cult leaders tend to be psychopaths. Therefore, they will tend not to show empathy for children who are being beaten or neglected. Because of the control these leaders exert over their followers, as well as the fear they engender, followers will often tend to identify with the leader. Such identification can further inhibit or distort the expression of natural impulses because most followers, who are not psychopathic, will be inclined to feel empathy with victims. Moreover, followers who participate in events in which they inhibit natural impulses of compassion and empathy will experience cognitive dissonance and will tend to alter their beliefs to make them consistent with their behavior. The leader's control and the consequent vulnerability of children are thereby strengthened.

TYPES OF HARM

The child abuse and neglect to be described here offers only conspicuous, documented examples, and is broken down into two categories: medical neglect and physical abuse and neglect. We do not separately discuss psychological abuse because, as the previous section implied, it is an inherent feature of the cultic structure. Nor do we discuss indirect cult influences on children, such as cult-sponsored programs being taught in the public schools, or deleterious influences on cult children that are not necessarily physically or medically harmful, such as custody disputes or developmentally inappropriate educational programs. The information base for these two areas is limited and the problems they pose are not as directly linked to the psychological and social dynamics of cults as are abuse and neglect.

We have located only one study that systematically examined the question of children in cults. Gaines, Wilson, Redican, and Baffi surveyed 70 ex-cult members in order to "determine the effects of cult membership on the health status of current and past members, including children" (1984, p. 13). Among their findings relevant to the treatment of children were the following:

- 27% of the respondents said children in their groups were not immunized against common childhood diseases
- 23% said children did not get at least eight hours of sleep a night
- 60% said their groups permitted physical punishment of children
- 13% said that children were sometimes physically disabled or hurt to teach them a lesson
- 13% said that the punishment of children was sometimes life-threatening or required a physician's care
- 61% said families were encouraged to live together and share responsibilities
- 37% said that children were seen by a doctor when ill

Medical Neglect

Swan (1990) examined more than one hundred legal cases in which religious beliefs against medical care impacted on children. In dozens of these cases, children died. Although not all of these cases involved groups commonly considered to be cults (most were associated with the Christian Science Church), cults can, and do, take advantage of religious immunity laws pertaining to health care, against which Swan and the American Academy of Pediatrics have protested ("Pediatricians urge," 1988). Even though religions do not have absolute immunity, they are in large measure shielded from official scrutiny.

The Fort Wayne (Indiana) *News-Sentinel* published a series of investigative articles on the Faith Assembly, an ultrafundamentalist sect that shuns medical care and was then led by the now-deceased Hobart Freeman. This group had a maternal death rate nearly 100 times that of the state average and a perinatal death rate nearly 3 times the state average ("Pre-natal," 1984). As early as 1984 the *News-Sentinel* had documented the deaths of "84 people who died after they or their parents followed the sect's teachings" (Zlatos, 1984a). Despite a series of legal investigations, this figure climbed to more than 103 deaths ("Faith Assembly pleas," 1991). Among the deaths reported in this story were a five-month-old boy (son of a man who had dropped out of a medical residency to join the group) who died of bacterial meningitis, normally a treatable disease ("Faith Assembly pleas," 1991) and the 103rd identified death, an infant boy who died of untreated pneumonia ("Faith healing in court," 1990). These fairly recent deaths occurred despite a string of similar deaths in the same group. For example, in 1984 a nine-month-old girl died from untreated bacterial meningitis (Zlatos, 1984b) and a 26-day-old infant died of untreated pneumonia ("Faith-healing believers," 1984).

A two-year-old boy whose parents belonged to the Faith Tabernacle, died of a Wilms' tumor because his parents relied on prayer rather than medicine. Experts at the parents' trial testified that medical intervention is successful against Wilms' tumors more than 90% of the time ("Couple asks," 1988).

In 1991 another child of a Faith Tabernacle family died of dehydration and malnutrition, because he couldn't keep nourishment down, after contracting ear and sinus infections. In 1981 parents in the same group were convicted of manslaughter for letting their son die of highly treatable cancer. A judge refused to order medical examinations for the couple's nine surviving children because of the state's religious exemptions to the juvenile code ("Tabernacle couple," 1991).

In 1990 six Philadelphia children, whose parents were associated with the Faith Tabernacle, or First Century Gospel Church, died of complications from measles. With one exception, the children could have been saved with medical care, according to a local health official. Of 900 measles cases during a six-month period in 1990, 492 took place among members of two sects that ran schools with hundreds of unvaccinated students ("The measles," 1991).

In 1986 Jon Lybarger was convicted of felony child abuse for denying medical care to his seriously ill five-week-old daughter. Lybarger and his wife founded a group called Jesus through Jon and Judy, which held that Jesus should be their only doctor ("Convicted," 1986). His conviction was overturned (People vs. Lybarger).

Not all cases that come to the attention of authorities involve deaths. The following report from the *Cult Observer* ("End Time couple," 1991, p. 6) is a telling example of how limited are the actions of courts when seemingly well-intentioned parents allow their children to suffer or die because of their religious beliefs:

Charles and Marilee Myers, members of the End Time Ministries in Lake City, FL, were charged with child abuse in December for their failure to seek treatment for their 16-year-old son, who almost died before heart surgery to remove a tumor. End Timers believe exclusively in faith healing. Although other members in several states have died in such circumstances, this is the first time a member has been charged with a crime.

Before his operation, young William Myers, unable to eat, had lost 30% of his weight and was suffering from liver and kidney failure. In October, a physician from the Child Protection Team said William, whom he described as if he had been living in a concentration camp, was "at great risk of death, not only from his cardiac lesion but also from the complications of long-term malnutrition."

The Myers, who say they feel they made a grave mistake in not seeking medical treatment, add that they did not realize the severity of their son's condition. In April, the Myers' newborn grandson died from massive hemorrhaging when their daughter and her husband failed to get medical treatment for the infant. The inquest judge ruled that the "religious shield" protected the couple from criminal prosecution. From "End Time couple is first ever charged," by Cindy Swirko, *Gainesville (FL) Sun*, 12/25/90, 2B.

On Dec. 20 Eighth Judicial Circuit Judge Nath Doughtie ruled that William should be sent home to his parents. . . . AP in the *Miami Herald*, 12/20/90.

In March 1992 the Florida Supreme Court threw out the murder convictions of two End Time parents, whose comatose seven-year-old daughter had died after they treated her with "spiritual healing." It was the first time a state's high court has overturned the criminal convictions of parents who cited religious beliefs in denying a child medical care. The court said Florida law did not give the couple "fair warning" that they could be prosecuted if they relied solely on prayer. Also reversed was a probation stipulation that the parents seek conventional medical care for their other children. Only three days after this decision, two other End Time parents were found guilty by a Live Oak jury of felony child abuse, nearly two years after their severely handicapped daughter died of pneumonia without medical care ("End Time reversals," 1992).

Physical Abuse

Child advocate and journalist Kenneth Wooden investigated child abuse in Jim Jones's People's Temple. In his book, *The Children of Jonestown*, Wooden states:

Physical abuse of the young was part of the routine at People's Temple. As Jones began to exercise total control, children were beaten if they failed to call him Father or were otherwise disrespectful, or if they talked with peers who were not members of People's Temple. Belts were used at first, then were replaced by elm switches, which in turn were replaced by the "board of education," a long, hard piece of wood, swung by 250-pound Ruby Carroll. (1981, p. 11)

A People's Temple member described the escalation of punishments that the children faced:

Mild discipline gave way to making young girls strip almost nude in front of the full membership and then forcing them to take cold showers or jump into the cold swimming pool at the Redwood Valley Church. Unequal boxing matches gave way to beatings with paddles, then electric shock, and finally something [Jones] called a "blue-eyed monster," which hurt and terrorized the younger ones in a darkened room. (Wooden, 1981, p. 11)

These abuses occurred while the People's Temple was in California and regularly winning praise from newspapers and politicians.

Allegations of child abuse in the House of Judah, an ultrafundamentalist Michigan sect, resulted in the removal of 62 children from a camp run by the sect ("Sixty-two youths," 1983). This action was prompted by the death of a 12-year-old boy who was beaten to death for refusing to do his chores. A report by Ray E. Helfer, M.D., of the Department of Pediatrics/Human Development of Michigan State University stated:

These nutritionally healthy bodies have been moderately to severely injured by repetitive beatings and other physical insults. Of the first 50–55 children examined by a physician after John's death a full 20% had signs of severe physical abuse. For the children greater than 5 years of age this percentage increases to approximately 40% and for boys in this age range, the figure is 70–75%. Thus, the likelihood of a male child reaching adolescence without showing physical signs of severe physical abuse to his body is less than 25%. (1983, p. 253)

House of Judah leader William A. Lewis was convicted along with seven other members of the group for enslaving children and holding 12-year-old John Yarbough in involuntary servitude until he was beaten to death in 1983 ("House of Judah," 1987). Lewis is now out of jail and has created a new community of 70 people in rural Alabama ("Michigan cult," 1991).

The Northeast Kingdom Community Church, which has branches in Island Pond, Vermont, and Clark's Harbor, Nova Scotia, was the subject of much controversy during the mid 1980s (Grizzuti-Harrison, 1984). On June 22, 1984, Vermont state authorities raided the sect's houses and took 112 children into custody, intending to examine them for signs of abuse. But a district judge found the action "grossly illegal" and ordered the children returned to their homes. Fortunately, the group apparently instituted changes in its practices, including registering births and seeking outside medical help, which greatly lessened the reports of child abuse and ultimately led to a relative acceptance by the local community ("Island Pond," 1989).

The leader of a controversial group in Quebec, Roch "Moise" Theriault, received a two-year prison sentence for beating a child to death and burning and burying the body ("Gaspe cult leader," 1982). Having served his sentence, the leader then set up another base in Ontario, from which 14 children were removed due to further charges of child abuse (Bellefeuille, 1986).

The Stars and Stripes, a military newspaper in Europe, described a taped sermon by a fundamentalist preacher: "The tape tells parents when disciplining children to 'break their will,' to 'blister their bottom red,' to 'brainwash' them, to spank weeks-old babies, and reassure them that 'little blue bruises' are a positive sign from the Lord (Freadhoff, 1982, p. 9).

An Indiana man, believing that Scripture-based child rearing demanded that a child should be whipped "until his will was broken," beat his three-year-old son to death. The beating that killed Bradley Lonadier "was only one of many and only part of the torture that the Lonadiers inflicted on the boy," allegedly at the urging of Steven Jackson, the head of Covenant Community Fellowship (Harms, 1982).

In 1986 fifteen members of the Yahweh Temple of the Black Hebrew Israelites were charged with ritualistic beatings and child torture. Five children placed under protective custody by authorities told how they were hit with switches, rods, and religious statues in bizarre ritualistic beatings ("Hebrew Israelites," 1986).

In 1990 the United States District Court in Fort Smith, Arkansas, awarded over $1 million to Robert Miller and his family, all formerly associated with "evangelist" Tony Alamo. A key charge in the suit involved the assertion that Tony Alamo put on "public exhibitions of corporal punishment, in the form of paddling, upon minor children; and the proof amply showed that Kody Miller, while being restrained by four adult men, was struck vigorously 140 times with a large wooden paddle by a grown man. The evidence further showed that this punishment was inflicted in a room filled with adults and children and was not only painful (Kody's buttocks were bleeding) but humiliating in the extreme. One of the adult witnesses [to the event], indeed one of the principal participants, was Kody's mother" ("Judgment against," 1990).

In 1984 Ariel Ben Sherman, leader of the Good Shepherd Tabernacle in Salem, Oregon, was charged with five counts related to child abuse. He was accused of having children from the religious commune tied up and handcuffed, confined in dark areas, suspended by ropes from ceiling hooks, and deprived of food, water, and sanitary facilities ("Police seek," 1984).

Sometimes children are exploited economically as well as physically abused. For example, Eldridge Broussard, the founder of the disbanded Ecclesia Athletic Association, and seven of his followers were indicted in 1991 in Portland, Oregon, on charges of enslaving children and denying them their civil rights. The government said that Broussard forced the group's children to be part of an exhibition team that participated in running and other athletics, and showcased them to gain corporate sponsorships and money, all the while systematically beating them, depriving them of food, and subjecting them to overcrowding and poor schooling ("Ecclesia 'slavery,'" 1992).

Reports of magazine sales organizations abusing children and controlling them through cultic techniques have surfaced from time to time. One case involved a 19-year-old girl who worked six days a week from 9:00 a.m. to as late as 2:00 in the morning, earning as little as $7.00 a day—less on days she failed to meet her quota. Such youngsters are typically discouraged from contacting their parents and threatened when they say they want to go home. Earlene Williams, of Parent Watch in New York City, estimates that as many as 30,000 children may be lured into such organizations ("Teens allege," 1992).

Sexual Abuse and Murder

It is not surprising that sexual abuse will sometimes accompany physical abuse. The Swiss periodical *Sonntagsblick* told of 20 Children of God youngsters living isolated from other people, without schooling, in a house due to be demolished in a rural Zurich parish. There had been claims that sect girls were sometimes driven across the border to Germany to solicit on the street. A Bern children's news agency reported the case of a 12-year-old girl from the group who was admitted to a hospital suffering severely from venereal disease. The child was said to be in a pitiable state, quite apathetic, and barely able to read or write ("Switzerland," 1991).

The sixty-one-year old, leader of a purportedly polygamist sect, pleaded guilty to sexually abusing four girls under the age of 14 in

Northern Utah ("Sect leader's," 1992). The 28-year-old son of Connecticut cult leader Julius Schacknow was accused of sexually assaulting children of families in the 100-member group, "The Work," for whom he baby-sat. The leader, who claims to be God and a "sinful Messiah," has himself been accused of sexual abuse in civil lawsuits, which he settled out of court, but has never faced criminal charges ("Cult leader's son," 1992).

Sometimes children are killed during attempts to "heal" them. A couple and two young, self-ordained preachers were indicted in 1985 in North Carolina for the choking death of a four-year-old during a "laying on of hands" healing service at a storefront church. This attempt to rid the boy of a demon resulted, according to a medical examiner's report, in abrasions and fingernail marks on the boy's throat and a crushed windpipe ("Parents and preachers," 1986). In Louisiana in 1987 an eight-year-old girl with Down's syndrome was strangled to death, while her mother was present, in an attempt to exorcise evil spirits from her body ("Five held," 1987). In 1986 a ten-year-old boy was starved and beaten with sticks by a fundamentalist Christian cult, His Rest Christian Fellowship, that believed the youngster was possessed by demons. Police said that the malnourished and abused child, who has never been to school, is probably only one of many victims of the group's exorcism rites. Authorities also reported that the 19-year-old son of another member of the church was beaten and cut with knives in a purification ritual by other members when he tried unsuccessfully to run away ("Beatings, mutilations," 1986).

Sometimes children are murdered in cultic groups. Six members of a polygamous sect notorious for a doctrine calling for the deaths of apostates were indicted in federal court in the 1988 slayings of three men and an eight-year-old girl in Texas. The group's founder, Ervil LeBaron, died in 1981 while serving a sentence in Utah for the 1977 murder of rival polygamist leader Rulon Allred ("Church of First Born," 1992). In 1990 Daniel Kraft, Jr., admitted in a Cleveland court to assisting in the slayings of a family of five and told of the scriptural plan that drove a band of religious zealots to commit murder. Dennis and Cheryl Avery and their three daughters were killed on a rural Ohio farm under the orders of "prophet" Carl Lundgren, with whom they had become disenchanted. Kraft testified that the killings were a required religious sacrifice, made necessary because of the Avery's disbelief in Lundgren as a prophet. Lundgren was sentenced to death in the case ("Guilty plea," 1990).

TREATMENT ISSUES

We know very little about the psychological treatment of children who have left cults. No systematic study of children's post-cult psychological picture has been conducted. Very little clinical work has been reported on. The suggestions that follow are based more on reasoning than experience. Essentially we are saying: "We know A about cults; we know B about child development; we would expect, based on our knowledge of A and B, that children leaving cults would exhibit C and require treatment D." Therefore, we urge the reader to be very cautious in applying the following approach to the treatment of children who have left cults. Heed the dictum, "Treat each case individually."

Adult or young-adult cult joiners have a more or less mature personality before they enter the cult. As noted in the introduction to this book, cultists may develop a cult "pseudopersonality" in order to adapt to the intense and conflicting demands of the group. Leaving a cult and recovering from the experience requires, among other things, an "awakening" of the pre-cult personality and a need to integrate the pre-cult, in-cult, and post-cult experiences.

Children born in cults or brought into cults at an early age do not have a mature pre-cult personality to awaken. They are socialized into an environment that denigrates independent critical thinking, maintains members in a state of dependency, and fosters a private insecurity by attacking members while demanding that they not protest and show a positive front to the world. Thus, the cult environment can create an anxious dependent personality (Martin, Langone, Dole, & Wiltrout, 1992). In the case of adults, this is a pseudopersonality, ergo the rapid and large decline in dependency after cult rehabilitation (Martin et al., 1992). For children, however, anxious dependency may indeed be fundamental to the child's character.

People who join cults as adults learn a great deal about the mainstream world before they join. They may be indoctrinated into a bizarre belief system with bizarre practices. But if they leave, they can call upon their pre-cult knowledge about the world in their attempts to adjust to mainstream society.

Children raised in cults have little knowledge about the world, especially if their group was isolated. Therefore, when they leave a cult, even if its practices and beliefs were highly deviant, they will take the cult's worldview with them because they know no other. Hence, their capacity to think critically and act independently may be deficient, not merely "blocked" as may be the case with ex-cultists who joined as adults. Ironically, those children who were most uncooperative in the cult, those who rebelled, may be most likely to make an effective transition into mainstream society, because they will not have imbibed the group's worldview so completely as others. However, those children who rebelled, and even many who didn't, may tend to express natural impulses inappropriately, that is, they may "act out," when they are freed from the severely controlling cult environment. Such children may, as a consequence, have significant difficulty adapting to rules in school and dealing with community expectations.

The picture painted above suggests that persons raised in a cult will experience culture shock upon leaving (whatever the reason). Moreover, their capacity to negotiate the transition successfully is likely to be hampered because the society they are entering places a premium on critical thinking and independence, both of which were stifled in the cult. If they have also been physically abused or neglected, they may have medical problems and the residuals of psychological trauma. Moreover, the family—the normal primary support system of children—may be unavailable, or even part of the problem picture rather than part of the solution. How does one help such persons?

First of all, medical attention may be needed. A complete physical examination should be performed as a precaution. The medical exam should include a thorough history, especially in regard to abuse and neglect. Because of the high probability of abuse and neglect, specialists should be brought in to examine the ex-cultist. These specialists should keep in mind that experiences that we would readily identify as abusive may be perceived as the normal course of events to the former cultist, especially if he or she is still a child and has had little exposure to the noncult world. Thus, standard questions used to evaluate whether there has been child abuse and neglect (e.g., Has anyone touched you in a way that made you feel uncomfortable?) may not elicit the expected responses—for example, a child may have been raised to believe that having oral sex with adults is normal and accepted (personal communication, A. Markowitz, Feb., 1993).

Second, a long-term psychotherapeutic relationship will probably be advisable. The magnitude of adjustment confronting such ex-cultists, their limited capacities, and the likely lack of a social support system beyond the immediate family (if that) suggest that much time and psychological support will be needed. Psychotherapy is not likely to be traditional. They will probably need immense educational effort, not only about how cults work, but about how the mainstream world works as well. Their education will have to include skill building, especially social skills, as well as cognitive learning. Many things that we take for granted may be alien to these former cult members.

Third, these persons will also probably need socialization experiences. Socialization is different from education because it involves much more than systematic learning. It consists of a myriad of experiences through which people learn the unwritten rules and expectations of a culture. It is difficult to "teach" someone about thousands of minor rules such as, to take an extreme example, the inappropriateness of asking a bus driver where one should sit. Individuals accustomed to years of totalism may be inclined to ask just such a question of someone they may perceive to be an authority figure. To a great extent ex-cultists born in cults must learn these types of rules and expectations through guided experience.

Therapy can help with the guiding, but it cannot provide the real-life experiences. Furthermore, unlike in traditional therapy, the therapist may not be able to assume that the ex-member client will necessarily encounter experiences from which to learn. Unless the therapist actively encourages the client to seek out experiences that will contribute to socialization, the ex-member client may be likely to fall into a safe routine that limits his or her growth. Or, on the other hand, he or she may attempt to deal with uncertainty and lack of confidence by breaking social rules and projecting an overdriven and specious independence. Therapists will probably have to deal with many internal issues related to trust, self-esteem, and the appropriate expression of natural impulses.

The suggestions above apply more to adults or young adults who were born in a cult. Young children will not only need therapeutic, educational, and socialization experiences, but will need management as well. Someone will have to make sure that the various remedial interventions are coordinated and make sense to the child. Parents may be able to do this, although they may also be struggling with post-cult issues. Therefore, the therapist, or some other helper, may be called upon to function as an ombudsman, as the child's advocate.

CONCLUSIONS

Our investigation of this field has at times been upsetting. The abuses to which children have been subjected can be horrendous. The degree to which cult leaders can escape accountability by hiding behind the First Amendment is troubling. And the lack of concern and action about this problem is shameful.

In this chapter we have tried to shed light on this problem so as to make psychotherapists and other helpers more effective when they encounter children or adults born in cults. Because of the number of adults and young adults who joined cults in the 1980s, the number of such persons will probably increase dramatically during the next 5 to 10 years as people born in cults leave.

Our suggestions, however, are very preliminary. Consequently, if the helping professions are to deal effectively with this problem, we must learn more. As a minimum we need well-articulated case studies. But we especially need to research this problem systematically. We need to survey child care workers, physicians, and others. We need to interview and survey former cult members. And we need to examine adults and children born in cults in a systematic, scientific manner. We hope that some of our readers will be inspired to take on some of these important tasks.

REFERENCES

Beatings, mutilations, in cultish church. (1986, October 19). *Cult Observer*, p. 9. From *The Toronto Sun*, July 11, 1986.

Bellefeuille, R. (1986, February 14). Moise Theriault et ses disciples perdent la garde de leur enfants. *Le Soleil*, p. 1.

Church of First Born members indicted. (1992). *Cult Observer*, 9(8), p. 4. From *Mesa Tribune*, August 25, 1992.

Convicted in daughter's death. (1986, March/April). *Cult Observer*, p. 19. From *CHILD Newsletter*, Winter 1986.

Couple asks supreme court to review faith-healing conviction. (1988, May/June). *Cult Observer*, p. 6. From "U.S. Supreme Court Will Be Asked to Review Faith-death Conviction," *CHILD Newsletter*, Spring 1988, p. 4.

Cult leader's son charged with sexual abuse. (1992). *Cult Observer*, 9(1), p. 4. From *CAN News*, November 1991, p. 6.

Ecclesia 'slavery' indictments. (1992). *Cult Observer*, 9(3), p. 4. From *The New York Times*, 2/10/91.

End Time couple charged. (1991). *Cult Observer*, 8(1), p. 6. From AP in *Miami Herald*, 12/20/90.

"End Time" reversals and convictions. (1992). *Cult Observer*, 9(6), p. 4. From *Lake City Reporter*, 7/3/92, pp. 1, 2; 7/6/92, pp. 1, 2.

Faith Assembly pleas. (1991). *Cult Observer*, 8(2), p. 5.

Faith-healing believers sentenced in child's pneumonia death. (1984, September 25). *Minneapolis Star and Tribune*, p. 8.

Faith healing in court. (1990). *Cult Observer*, 7(4), p. 9.

Five held in "exorcism" death of child. (1987, May/June). *Cult Observer*, p. 13. From "Five accused in child's death," *Daily Sentry-News*, January 11, 1987, p. 2A.

Freadhoff, C. (1982, January 28). Child discipline: Evangelist who advocates infant spanking, "breaking will" may promote abuse, experts say. *The Stars and Stripes*, p. 9.

Gaines, M. J., Wilson, M. A., Redican, K. J., & Baffi, C. R. (1984). The effects of cult membership on the health status of adults and children. *Health Values: Achieving High Level Wellness, 8*(2), pp. 13–17.

Gaspe cult leader gets two-year jail term. (1982, September 30). *Montreal Gazette.*

Grizzuti-Harrison, B. (1984, December). The children and the cult. *New England Monthly,* pp. 56–70.

Guilty plea to cult murders. (1990, November/December). *Cult Observer,* p. 6. From Martin Maggi, "Cult member pleads guilty, defends leader," Cleveland, Ohio *Plain Dealer,* November 6, 1990.

Harms, W. (1982, December 5). Cult members say "guru" made them beat boy. *Chicago Tribune.*

Hebrew Israelites charged with abuse. (1986, May/June). *Cult Observer,* p. 28. From UPI and the *Boston Globe,* April 6, 1986.

Helfer, R. (1983, August 5). *The children of the House of Judah.* Unpublished report. East Lansing: Michigan State University, Department of Pediatrics/Human Development.

House of Judah leader and members sentenced. (1987, March/April). *Cult Observer,* p. 11. From "Seven sect members get prison terms," *Minneapolis Star and Tribune,* December 20, 1986.

Island Pond commune. (1989, September/October). *Cult Observer,* p. 11. From New Bedford (MA) *Standard Times,* 8/27/89, p. A7.

Judgment against Alamo. (1990, September/October). *Cult Observer,* p. 3.

Landa, Shirley. (1984, September). *Child abuse in cults.* Paper presented at the International Congress on Child Abuse and Neglect, Montreal, Canada.

Landa, Susan. (1990/1991). Children and cults: A practical guide. *The University of Louisville Journal of Family Law, 29*(3), 591–634.

Markowitz, A., & Halperin, D. A. (1984). Cults and children. The abuse of the young. *Cultic Studies Journal, 1,* 143–155.

Martin, P., Langone, M. D., Dole, A., & Wiltrout, J. (1992). Post-cult symptoms as measured by the MCMI Before and After Residential Treatment. *Cultic Studies Journal, 9*(2), 219–250.

The measles epidemic. (1991). *Cult Observer, 8*(6), p. 6. From *CHILD Newsletter,* 1/91, pp. 1–4.

Michigan cult leader's new settlement. (1991). *Cult Observer, 8*(4) p. 3. From Reed Johnson, "Prophet & Loss," *Detroit News,* 3/9/91, pp. 3C, 4C.

Parents and preachers indicted in death. (1986, January/February). *Cult Observer,* p. 11. From *CHILD Newsletter,* Fall 1985.

Pediatricians urge exemption repeal. (1988, March/April). *Cult Observer,* p. 8. From "Pediatricians Fight Church Limit on Care," *Pediatrics,* January 6, 1988.

People v. Lybarger, 807 P.2d 570.

Police seek cult leader. (1984, November). *Cult Observer,* p. 3. From *The New York Times,* 11/23/84, p. A19 and the Middlesex (MA) *News,* 11/15/84, p. 13A.

Pre-natal and maternal mortality in a religious group in Indiana. (1984, June 1). *Morbidity and Mortality Weekly Report, 33,* pp. 297–298.

Sect leader's sexual abuse. (1992). *Cult Observer, 9*(2), p. 5. From *San Francisco Chronicle,* November 8, 1991, p. A10.

Sixty-two youths taken away from religious camp. (1983, July 9). *The New York Times*, p. 5.

Swan, R. (1990). *The law's response when religious beliefs against medical care impact on children.* Sioux City, IA: CHILD, Inc.

Switzerland. (1991). *Cult Observer, 8*(4), p. 9. From *FAIR News,* Winter 1990/91, p. 5.

Tabernacle couple charged in death. (1991). *Cult Observer, 8*(6), p. 6. From *CHILD Newsletter,* 1/91.

Teens allege magazine sales slavery. (1992). *Cult Observer, 9*(7), p. 5. From G. Weigel, "Teens say magazine sales jobs like slavery," *Seattle Times/ Seattle Post-Intelligencer,* 6/21/92, p. A7.

Wooden, K. (1981). *The children of Jonestown.* New York: McGraw-Hill.

Zlatos, B. (1984a, June 20). Grand jury hears sect child. *Fort Wayne News-Sentinel.*

Zlatos, B. (1984b, October 29). Faith couple gets 10 years. *Fort Wayne News-Sentinel,* pp. 1A, 3A.

18

RITUALISTIC ABUSE OF CHILDREN IN DAY-CARE CENTERS

Susan J. Kelley, Ph.D., R.N.

THERE ARE FEW ISSUES IN THE FIELD OF child maltreatment that evoke as strong emotions as that which has been termed *ritualistic abuse*. Unfortunately, professionals tend to take extreme positions on the prevalence of ritualistic abuse and the veracity of accounts by child victims and adult survivors. On one extreme are those who irresponsibly claim in the absence of corroborating evidence that tens of thousands of humans are sacrificed each year in ritualistic satanic cults. Such exaggerations and misinterpretations have destructive consequences. One consequence is the unnecessary fear and hysteria created by such allegations. Another result of these unsubstantiated claims is that some professionals, in reaction to extremists, automatically dismiss all allegations of ritualistic abuse as fallacious. These skeptics, who make up the other extreme, believe that alleged ritualistic-abuse victims are caught up in hysteria, group contagion, or have had the memories of ritual abuse implanted in their minds by therapists.

Ritualistic abuse has been reported to occur in a variety of milieus including day-care centers (Faller, 1990; Finkelhor, Williams, & Burns, 1988; Kelley, 1989; Waterman, Kelly, McCord, & Oliveri, 1990), neighborhood and community settings (Jonker & Jonker-Bakker, 1991; Snow & Sorensen, 1990), and within nuclear and extended families (Faller, 1990; Johnson, 1990; Young, Sachs, Braun, & Watkins, 1991).

Cases of ritualistic abuse typically involve multiple victims and multiple offenders (Finkelhor et al., 1988; Jonker & Jonker-Bakker, 1991; Kelley, 1989; Snow & Sorensen, 1990).

Reliable estimates of the extent of the problem are difficult to ascertain for several reasons. First of all, child protective agencies responsible for investigating cases of child abuse do not categorize them according to whether or not there was ritualistic involvement. Second, there is not an agreed-upon definition of ritualistic abuse, nor even agreement on whether or not the phenomenon warrants a special term or label such as *ritualistic*. Also, many professionals are unaware of this extreme form of maltreatment and fail to recognize indicators of ritualistic abuse in the histories of child and adult victims. Another factor that prevents reliable reporting is that usually children are too terrified to disclose the ritualistic components of the abuse. Often the ritualistic aspects are disclosed months or years after the child has revealed the sexually abusive acts and often after an investigation or therapy has ended. Another major obstacle to determining the extent of ritualistic abuse is the skepticism with which such allegations are met. The more horrible and bizarre the child's allegation, the less likely it is that the child victim will be believed.

In Finkelhor et al.'s (1988) national study of sexual abuse of children in day-care centers in the United States, 13% of the cases involved reports of ritualistic abuse.

DEFINITIONAL ISSUES

As with other types of abuse, there is no one accepted definition of what constitutes ritualistic abuse. Finkelhor et al. define it as

> abuse which occurs in a context linked to some symbols or group activity that have a religious, magical, or supernatural connotation, and where the invocation of these symbols or activities, repeated over time, is used to frighten or intimidate the children. (1988, p. 59)

Faller (1990) uses the term *ritualistic abuse* "in situations where the sexual abuse is part of some rite that appears to have significance related to a type of religion, satanism, witchcraft, or other cult practice" (p. 197). Lanning (1991) prefers the term *multidimensional sex ring* to *ritualistic abuse* because he believes the latter is "confusing, misleading, and counterproductive" (p. 171). Jones (1991) suggests that professionals should be concerned with the extent to which physical and psychological abuses accompany child sexual abuse without invoking the new term *ritualistic abuse*.

Finkelhor et al. (1988) proposed a three-fold typology of ritualistic abuse which is useful in clarifying different uses for the term.

Type I: cult-based ritualistic abuse involves an elaborate belief system and an attempt to create a particular spiritual or social system. The sexual abuse is not thought to be the ultimate goal of the perpetrator but rather a vehicle for inducing a religious or mystical experience in the adult perpetrators.

Type II: pseudoritualistic abuse involves ritualistic practices that are not part of a developed belief system. The primary motivation is not spiritual but rather the sexual exploitation of the child. Rituals, such as the use of costumes and killing of animals, are brought in primarily to intimidate children and are not part of an elaborate ideology.

Type III: psychopathological ritualism includes abuse of children in a ritualistic fashion that is not part of a developed ideology but rather part of an obsessive or delusional system of an individual or small group of perpetrators. In such cases the abuse may simply involve sexual preoccupations or sexual compulsions.

For the purposes of this chapter I will use the term *ritualistic abuse* to describe allegations of sexual and psychological abuse by perpetrators who engage in sexual activity as part of bizarre, sadistic, satanic, or pseudosatanic activities. The focus here is on what Finkelhor et al. (1988) have categorized as Type I and Type II. It is often difficult, however, if not impossible, to distinguish between Types I and II because the adult perpetrators' motivation for the abuse and whether or not it is part of an elaborate belief system are not always apparent from the children's disclosures.

DAY-CARE STUDY FINDINGS

The purpose of the study summarized here (which is reported elsewhere in greater detail [Burgess, Hartman, Kelley, Grant, & Gray, 1990; Kelley, 1989, 1990]) was to compare the characteristics and impact of two types of allegations by children abused in day-care settings: children who reported nonritualistic sexual abuse and children who reported ritualistic sexual abuse.

The sample was comprised of 134 subjects who were divided into three groups: sexual abuse ($n = 32$), ritualistic sexual abuse ($n = 35$), and nonabused children ($n = 67$). Group I (sexual abuse without rituals) consisted of 32 children aged 4 to 8 years at the time of the study; half were male. Group II (ritualistic sexual abuse) included 35 children aged 4 to 11 years at the time of the study; 40% were male. Subjects were assigned to this latter group if they reported involvement in satanic rituals. The satanic rituals reported involved worship of the Devil, participation in ceremonial acts where adults wore costumes or robes and used occult symbols, and threats of harm from supernatural powers.

The subjects were from 16 day-care centers, located in 12 different states, where sexual abuse occurred. Allegations of sexual abuse for all subjects in both abuse groups were substantiated by the child protective agency responsible for investigating the charges of sexual abuse. Criminal charges were brought against the abusers in 92% of the cases. When criminal charges were filed, 80% resulted in convictions of one or more offenders at the day-care center. There were no differences in conviction rates between the ritualistic-abuse cases and the nonritualistic-abuse cases. Of the remaining cases, approximately 5% resulted in innocent verdicts, 7% had charges dismissed, and 7% had trials in progress.

The comparison group was comprised of 67 nonabused children aged 4 to 11 years, with a mean age of 6.6 years, who had previously attended day care but with no known history of abuse. Comparison subjects were matched to children in the abuse groups on age, gender, socioeconomic status, and history of having attended day care.

Eighty-two percent of the subjects fell within the two highest social classes of the Hollingshead Index of Social Status. The parents in the study were generally well educated: 96% were high school graduates and 58% were college graduates.

Comparison of Ritualistic- and Sexual-abuse Disclosures

While children in both abuse groups experienced extensive sexual, physical, and psychological abuse, children in the ritualistic-abuse group suffered more types of abuse than children in the sexual-abuse group. The data reported in Table 1 were provided by the subjects' parents and are based on the children's disclosures to their parents, therapists, and law enforcement officials.

Sexual Abuse   Children in the ritualistic-abuse group experienced more types of sexual abuse than children in the sexual-abuse group (8.34 vs. 4.81). They also experienced more forms of penetration (vaginal, rectal, and oral) than children abused without rituals. In addition, children abused with rituals were more likely to report having pornographic pictures taken, being forced into sexual acts with other children, and having their breasts/chests fondled.

Table 1

Comparison of Sexual Abuse and Ritualistic Abuse Groups

	Group 1 Sexual abuse (*n* = 32)	Group 2 Ritualistic abuse (*n* = 35)	*p*
Type of sexual abuse			
Fondling of breasts/chest	21.9%	54.2%	.0065
Fondling of genitals	93.8	91.4	NS
Digital penetration	71.9	88.6	NS
Oral genital sex	59.4	88.6	.0061
Vaginal intercourse	31.3	71.4	.0151
Rectal intercourse	28.1	66.7	.0019
Object in vagina	56.3	60.9	NS
Object in rectum	56.3	80.0	.0363
Pornographic pictures taken	59.4	88.6	.0061
Satanic rituals	00.0	100.0	.0001
Sexual activity with other children	43.8	94.3	.0001
Type of physical abuse			
Physically abused	81.3%	97.1%	.0371
Given drugs	28.1	74.3	.0002
Deprived of meals	18.8	31.4	NS
Hit by abuser(s)	68.8	68.6	NS
Consumption of excrement	25.0	51.4	.0266
Physically restrained	37.5	71.4	.0053
Psychological abuse/threat			
Threatened with harm	96.9%	100.0%	NS
Would be killed	56.3	85.7	.0075
Parents would be killed	75.0	94.1	.0304
Sibling would be killed	31.3	31.4	NS
Dismemberment	15.6	37.1	.0472
Loss of parents' love	28.1	8.6	.037
Threatened with supernatural powers	39.3	100.0	.0001

From "Stress Responses of Children to Sexual Abuse and Ritualistic Abuse in Day-Care Centers" by S. J. Kelley, 1989, *Journal of Interpersonal Violence, 4*(4), 502–513. Adapted by permission.

Ritualistic abuse was associated with more victims per day-care center (43 vs. 34) and more offenders per child (5 vs. 2). Children in the ritualistic-abuse group also reported more episodes of sexual abuse per child than children in the sexual-abuse group.

Physical Abuse   Children in the ritualistic-abuse group were more likely than children in the sexual-abuse group to report being physically abused, physically restrained, forced to consume human excrement and body fluids (including urine, feces, and semen), and forced to take drugs or mind-altering substances. Seventy-four percent of the children in the ritualistic-abuse group and 28% in the sexual-abuse group were forced to ingest a substance or drug that made them drowsy, perhaps in an effort to make them less resistant to abusive acts and less likely to accurately recall details of the traumatic events.

Psychological Abuse   Severe intimidation was used to prevent victims in both groups from disclosing their abuse. Ninety-eight percent of the abused children were threatened with some form of physical harm; death threats were the most prevalent type used. Children in the ritualistic-abuse group were more likely to be threatened that either they or their parents would be killed if they ever disclosed the abuse. Also they were more likely to be threatened with harm from supernatural powers and with dismemberment. It appeared that the offenders in the ritualistic-abuse group used "overkill" to silence their victims; the level of intimidation used may have been intended to terrorize these young children.

Ritualistic Activities   Children in the ritualistic-abuse group reported participation in satanic or satanic-like rituals as well as threats with harm from supernatural powers. The satanic rituals described often involved the wearing of robes or costumes and the use of paraphernalia including candles, drugs or "magic potions," and satanic symbols such as inverted crucifixes and pentagrams. The satanic practices reported by these children are consistent with the satanic activities reported by Hill and Goodwin (1989) in their review of historical accounts of Satanism.

In the ritualistic-abuse group, 86% of the children described the use of chants and songs to invoke the power of Satan during the ceremonial abuse. The threats involving supernatural powers were most often related to Satan, evil spirits, or demons and included warnings such as, "Satan always knows where you are and what you are doing."

Comparison of Impact of Sexual
and Ritualistic Abuse

Children in the ritualistic-abuse group demonstrated significantly more behavior problems than subjects in the sexual-abuse and comparison groups as measured by the Child Behavior Checklist (p ≤ .05) (Achenbach & Edelbrock, 1983). In the ritualistic- abuse group, 48% of the children scored in the clinical range on the total behavior problem scale, compared to 32% of children in the sexual-abuse group. Scores ≥ 70 on the behavior problem total score are at the 98th percentile and are considered to be in the clinical range (Achenbach & Edelbrock, 1983). Only 2% of the general population would be expected to fall into the clinical range, indicating far greater behavior problems in both abuse groups than in a normative group.

Children in the ritualistic-abuse group had significantly higher mean scores than the sexual-abuse and comparison children on the internalizing dimension of the Child Behavior Checklist (p ≤ .05). In the ritualistic-abuse group, 57% scored in the clinical range on the internalizing dimension, compared to 38% in the sexual-abuse group. Although the children in the ritualistic-abuse group had a higher mean score on the externalizing dimension than children in the sexual-abuse group, the differences were not statistically significant.

Fears   Ritually abused children (91%) were more likely (p ≤ .05) to report persistent fears related to their victimization than children in the sexual-abuse group (72%) (Burgess, Hartman, & Kelley, 1990).

DISCUSSION

The findings of this study are consistent with findings of Waterman et al.'s (1990) study in which children who were ritually abused in day care and a group of sexually abused children were compared on behavioral functioning and emotional status utilizing extensive measures. Children in the ritualistic-abuse group reported sexual and physical abuse, satanic rituals, and terrorization by multiple perpetrators, while subjects in the sexual-abuse group reported sexual abuse by a single perpetrator, without ritualistic or terrorizing elements.

Waterman et al. (1990) used the Child Behavior Checklist (Achenbach & Edelbrock, 1983) as one of their outcome measures. Children in the ritualistic-abuse group scored significantly higher than children in the sexual-abuse group on total behavior problems and internalizing behaviors. There were no significant differences between the two abuse groups on externalizing behaviors or social competence. Those findings are remarkably similar to the ones in this study (Kelley, 1989): Ritually abused children scored significantly higher than sexually abused children on total behavior problems and internalizing behaviors. Forty-six percent of the children in Waterman et al.'s (1990) ritualistic-abuse group and 48% in Kelley's (1989) ritualistic-abuse group scored in the clinical range on the total behavior problem scale.

Waterman et al. (1990) found ritually abused children to be significantly more fearful than the control group, and the ritually abused children showed more fearfulness than phobic children on the Louisville Fear Survey. Again, those findings are consistent with the findings in this study (Kelley, 1989). Of particular interest is their finding that 37% of the children in the ritualistic-abuse group were reported to have excessive or unreasonable fear of the Devil and 27% had excessive fears of Hell.

A limitation of the study presented here is the use of parental reporting of children's behaviors to measure impact of abuse, since parents' reports of their children's behaviors could be biased by knowledge of their child's victimization and expectations of harm. However, this study's finding of increased impact in ritually abused children is consistent with therapists' reports of increased impact in ritually abused children as stated in the day-care studies of both Finkelhor et al. (1988) and Waterman et al. (1990). In Waterman et al.'s (1990) study, therapists using a modified version of the Child Behavior Checklist rated ritually abused children with increased total behavior problems and externalizing behavior problems. Therapists reported that 80% of ritually abused children met the criteria for Post-traumatic Stress Disorder (PTSD) compared to 36% of the sexual-abuse group. Increased impact of ritualistic abuse is also reported in the literature on adult survivors. Briere (1988) found that childhood history of ritualistic and bizarre abuse was associated with increased symptomatology in adulthood.

A major problem confronted by researchers and professionals when faced with children's allegations of ritualistic abuse is to attempt to determine the veracity of such allegations. When young children report what appears to be satanic practices it is difficult, and often impossible, to determine the perpetrators' motivation for use of satanic symbols and rituals. Most experts in the field of Satanism divide practitioners of Satanism into four categories:

1. Dabblers, often adolescents, who become attracted to Satanism on a superficial level and are not really committed to it
2. Self-styled or psychopathic Satanists who are attracted to violent forms of Satanism that are then grafted onto their preexisting pathology
3. Religious Satanists involved in well-organized, publicly acknowledged groups

4. Participants in Satanic cults, which are sophisticated, clandestine groups that may be engaged in criminal activities (Tucker, 1989, as cited in Langone & Blood, 1990)

Some perpetrators may actually be practicing a form of Satanism, while other adults who abuse children in conjunction with satanic-like practices may not actually be Satanists at all but instead use satanic-like rituals and symbols to scare children. In addition, it is often difficult to distinguish genuine satanic activity from activities that might be more accurately classified as bizarre sexual behavior, neo-Nazi rituals, and idiosyncratic mental aberrations (Langone & Blood, 1990).

Research on ritualistic abuse of children reported here and in other studies often contain many of the same characteristics as reported by Hill and Goodwin (1989) in their historical account of Satanism. Allegations of ritualistic abuse typically involve reports of

1. Forced sexual activity (Finkelhor et al., 1988; Jonker & Jonker-Bakker, 1991; Kelley, 1989; Snow & Sorensen, 1990; Waterman et al., 1990; Young et al., 1991)
2. Physical abuse or torture (Finkelhor et al., 1988; Jonker & Jonker-Bakker, 1991; Kelley, 1989; Snow & Sorensen, 1990; Young et al., 1991)
3. Ingestion of blood, semen, or excrements (Finkelhor et al., 1988; Jonker & Jonker-Bakker, 1991; Kelley, 1989; Snow & Sorensen, 1990; Young et al., 1991)
4. Ingestion of drugs (Kelley, 1989; Snow & Sorensen, 1990; Young et al., 1991)
5. Violent/death threats (Finkelhor et al., 1988; Kelley, 1989; Snow & Sorensen, 1990; Waterman et al., 1990; Young et al., 1991)
6. Threats with supernatural powers/spells (Finkelhor et al., 1988; Kelley, 1989; Snow & Sorensen, 1990; Waterman et al., 1990)
7. Satanic reference/paraphernalia (Finkelhor et al., 1988; Kelley, 1989; Snow & Sorensen, 1990; Waterman et al., 1990; Young et al., 1991)
8. Witnessing animal mutilations (Finkelhor et al., 1988; Kelley, 1989; Snow & Sorensen, 1990; Waterman et al., 1990; Young et al., 1991)
9. Killing of adults and children (Snow & Sorensen, 1990; Young et al., 1991)

While the striking similarities in the accounts of satanic and bizarre activities reported in these studies do not constitute proof that the subjects' accounts are entirely true, they do suggest that one of many possibilities to be considered and further explored is that the children did experience actual involvement in bizarre and abusive ritualistic activities. Other possibilities to be considered are: During the abusive episodes children may incorrectly perceive events and related details; children may later remember perceptions inaccurately; children are influenced by suggestion from therapists or parents that ritualistic activities occurred; children are disoriented at the time of abuse due to ingestion of drugs or alcohol which compromises future recall; and children are exaggerating or falsifying accounts. Terr (1988) suggested that some young children appear to cope with overwhelming, noxious past memories by elaborating upon them even further when they recall and relate them at a future date. Until further data are available, each of the possibilities needs to be considered feasible. It is unlikely that any single one of them explains all cases of alleged ritualistic abuse.

TREATMENT IMPLICATIONS

The treatment of ritually abused children will not differ significantly from the treatment of sexually abused children. Both groups have been traumatized and have limited capacities to understand what was done to them. Ritually abused children, however, are likely to exhibit more serious symptomatology. For both groups, where the abuse took place may be a significant factor. If family members were perpetrators, the treatment problem obviously is compounded because the child's primary psychological support persons are the cause of the problem. If the location was a day-care or neighborhood setting, the family's capacity to be supportive will probably be enhanced by intense family therapy. Sometimes family members appear to have as much difficulty dealing with the abuse as the child does. Family support, however, is crucial to the child's recovery. Waterman et al., for example, found that "by far the strongest predictors of outcome were family factors" (1990, p. 15), including perceiving the mother as responding more positively, fewer life stressors, more family closeness and cohesion, and the use of active coping measures, such as getting help from professionals.

Assessment of ritualistic abuse can be more difficult than with sexual abuse because the former engenders more skepticism among workers. Children often disclose ritualistic abuse after disclosing less threatening forms of abuse. It is vital that assessments be performed only by highly trained professionals with special expertise in the assessment and treatment of young children. A false negative judgment (i.e., concluding that no abuse occurred when in fact it did occur) can affect children for the rest of their lives and, indeed, may be decisive in determining whether a child recovers from abuse or develops a lifelong dysfunctional personality pattern. Waterman et al. (1990), for example, found that 17% of ritually abused children remained in the clinical range on the Child Behavior Checklist at a five-year follow-up. Although this reflected considerable improvement in the children's psychological status, normative data indicate that only 2.5% of children would be expected to fall in the clinical range.

A false positive judgment (i.e., concluding that abuse occurred when it really did not occur), on the other hand, can also profoundly affect the child's future. Consequently, professionals should make sure they know what they are doing before they present themselves as experts in such cases.

The psychological defenses children employ can complicate assessment. It is important to remember that disclosure is a process, not an event. Children may acknowledge, then recant, then reacknowledge that they were abused. One research study, for example, found that even in a group "where the perpetrator admitted sexually abusing children and was sentenced to life in prison, 23% of the children recanted their allegations at some time during the course of treatment" (Waterman et al., 1990, p. 23). In this same study 27% of the ritually abused children also recanted. But in both groups of recanters all but one child "subsequently redisclosed, and many revealed previously undisclosed acts" (p. 4).

The fact that ritually abused children exhibit much more posttraumatic stress than sexually abused children is, perhaps, the most significant factor differentiating the two groups with regard to treatment. Ritually abused children are much more likely to experience symptoms of Post-traumatic Stress Disorder (PTSD) — for example, fearfulness, flashbacks, hypervigilance. These fears must be explored and the children must be helped to feel safe and empowered. Waterman et al. (1990) describe some of the techniques that have been used:

> Role-playing, drawing fears, white magic rituals (utilizing forces of good rather than evil), relaxation training, and structured fantasy play about powerful figures. In dealing with manifestations of PTSD, relaxation exercises and self-hypnosis tapes were useful in treating nightmares, flashbacks and sleep disturbances, while hypervigilance and mistrust of others were often addressed by working directly with the child-therapist relationship. (pp. 20–21)

CONCLUSION

Ritualistic abuse of children continues to be an area with many more questions than answers. Researchers and professionals need to use a dispassionate approach in examining the complexities of these cases. Even those who are skeptical regarding the veracity of accounts of satanic and bizarre activities agree that the majority of these children have been traumatized and are in need of professional intervention. As the issues continue to be debated, let us not lose sight of the needs of these traumatized children and their families.

REFERENCES

Achenbach, T. M., & Edelbrock, C. S. (1983). *The Child Behavior Checklist manual.* Burlington: University of Vermont.

Briere, J. (1988). The long-term clinical correlates of childhood sexual victimization. *Annals of New York Academy of Sciences, 528,* 327–334.

Burgess, A. W., Hartman, C. R., & Kelley, S. J. (1990). Assessing child abuse: The TRIADS checklist. *Journal of Psychosocial Nursing, 28*(4), 7–14.

Burgess, A. W., Hartman, C. R., Kelley, S. J., Grant, C. A., & Gray, E. B. (1990). Parental response to child sexual abuse trials involving day-care settings. *Journal of Traumatic Stress, 3*(3), 395–405.

Faller, K. C. (1990). *Understanding child sexual maltreatment.* Newbury Park, CA: Sage.

Finkelhor, D., Williams, L., & Burns, N. (1988). *Sexual abuse in day care: A national study.* Durham: University of New Hampshire.

Hill, S., & Goodwin, J. (1989). Satanism: Similarities between patient accounts and pre-inquisition historical sources. *Dissociation, 2*(2), 39–43.

Johnson, C. F. (1990). Inflicted injury versus accidental injury. *Pediatric Clinics of North America, 37,* 791–814.

Jones, D. P. H. (1991). Ritualism and child sexual abuse. *Child Abuse and Neglect: The International Journal, 15,* 163–170.

Jonker, F., & Jonker-Bakker, P. (1991). Experiences with ritualistic child sexual abuse: A case study from the Netherlands. *Child Abuse and Neglect: The International Journal, 15,* 191–196.

Kelley, S. J. (1989). Stress responses of children to sexual abuse and ritualistic abuse in day-care centers. *Journal of Interpersonal Violence, 4,* 502–513.

Kelley, S. J. (1990). Parental stress response to sexual abuse and ritualistic abuse of children in day-care centers. *Nursing Research, 39*(1), 25–29.

Langone, M. D., & Blood, L. O. (1990). *Satanism and occult-related violence: What you should know.* Weston, MA: American Family Foundation.

Lanning, K. V. (1991). Ritual abuse: A law enforcement view or perspective. *Child Abuse and Neglect: The International Journal, 15,* 171–173.

Snow, B., & Sorensen, T. (1990). Ritualistic child abuse in a neighborhood setting. *Journal of Interpersonal Violence, 5*(4), 474–487.

Terr, L. (1988). What happens to early memories of trauma? A study of twenty children under age five at the time of documented traumatic events. *Journal of the American Academy of Child and Adolescent Psychiatry, 27,* 96–104.

Waterman, J., Kelly, R. J., McCord, J., & Oliveri, M. K. (1990). *Reported ritualistic and nonritualistic sexual abuse in preschoools: Effects and mediators.* Executive Summary submitted to National Center on Child Abuse and Neglect. Washington, DC.

Young, W. C., Sachs, R. G., Braun, B. G., & Watkins, R. T. (1991). Patients reporting ritual abuse in childhood: A clinical syndrome. Report of 37 cases. *Child Abuse and Neglect: The International Journal, 15,* 181–189.

19

TEEN SATANISM

Rob Tucker, M.Ed.*

SATANISM HAS BEEN THE SUBJECT OF much attention recently. Extreme cases tend to gain public focus through various media; the "Geraldo Rivera" television series in the fall of 1988 is one example. His two-hour special on Satanism was one of the highest rated "investigative" programs in the history of the network. Other television talk show hosts have followed with programs of their own. In April 1989 a gruesome cult performing human sacrifices was uncovered near Brownsville, Texas. A steady stream of horrendous acts apparently connected to Satanism have appeared in newspapers, magazines, and other popular media sources.

Reports on Satanism have also appeared in more responsible programs such as "60 Minutes." Satanism is no longer just a tabloid fringe topic. Two cases in Ontario, Canada, have involved allegations of ritual abuse with very young children. These children disclosed their apparent experiences with cannibalism, murder, animal mutilations, and other bizarre rituals in such a way as to inspire belief from many professionals. Television journalism on this subject tends to be relentlessly sensationalistic. Sensationalizing an already lurid subject tends to render the entire topic ridiculous. Hopefully, this will change in the near future.

*This chapter is based on a paper presented in 1989 at the Ontario Police Training College, Aylmer, Ontario.

Satanism is being taken more and more seriously by many professional groups, including the police, social service agencies, mental health workers, corrections personnel, and educators. Unfortunately, little is known about the phenomenon as a whole. This chapter outlines emergent concerns relating to one aspect of the problem – adolescent Satanism.

CLASSIFICATION OF LEVELS OF INVOLVEMENT IN SATANISM

Satanism is a religion. Unless illegal acts are committed, a Satanist is free to pursue this religion in a way free of government or police interference.

Satanism can be classified on four levels:

1. The first and least sophisticated is the "self-appointed/dabbler" level. This consists of individuals who become attracted to Satanism through popular books on the subject and through other available sources. The dabbler is not usually connected to a sophisticated group or cult, although small local "dabbler groups" are common.
2. The second level consists of "psychopathic Satanists." These are individuals who become attracted to Satanism because it seems to articulate and refine impulses that already exist within them. In other words, Satanism gets "wrapped around" an already existing pathology. This level and the dabbler category often overlap.
3. The third level, "religious Satanists," consists of publicly known groups such as the Church of Satan in California or the Temple of Set. These organizations openly advertise, have application forms, membership fees, and all the other attributes of small religious groups.
4. The fourth level, "satanic cults," are groups that act in secrecy, would appear to be responsible for some of the ritual abuse cases, and seem to act in profoundly sophisticated ways. Little direct evidence of these groups exists, but this may well change in the near future as ritual abuse itself is taken more seriously and as police devise ways to investigate the problem.

This four-level classification system seems to be widely accepted by experts in the field. Through personal discussions with these experts and through contacts at various professional gatherings, I have found that a general agreement about its utility seems to exist. It is, however, subject to change as more data becomes available. (The whole field itself is so new that just about everything at this stage is subject to change.)

Adolescent Satanists tend to fit into level one. *Adolescent* here refers to youths between the ages of 9 and 19. This group is unique, and so are the problems stemming from it.

Some cases are well known publicly. They are, of course, the more extreme and lurid accounts. Sean Sellers, for example, killed his family in Oklahoma and is now the youngest inmate on death row there. He claims to have killed for Satan. Sellers has appeared on "Geraldo"; his boyish good looks and innocent charm seem to deny the brutality of his crimes (killing a local store clerk and then killing his own parents). Sellers is profiled in *Devil Child* (Higgins, 1989), a sensationalized and somewhat confusing book, not unlike others of its type. Ricky Kasso, subject of the book *Say You Love Satan* (St. Clair, 1987), killed a friend in a satanic ceremony, was arrested, and then committed suicide. These and other cases are far more common than one would think, yet they bring little insight into the phenomenon itself. For example, was Satanism *causal*, or was it just an excuse wrapped around an already pathological individual? How widespread is the phenomenon? What attracts children to it?

ATTRACTIONS TO SATANISM

Satanism can be deeply attractive to adolescents for a number of reasons. Understanding this attraction is crucial, because without it, concrete interventions become difficult, if not impossible.

The *Satanic Bible* (LaVey, 1969) offers some real clues. Its author, Anton LaVey, runs the Church of Satan in California. The book is cheap and easily available to adolescents. It helps make the point that public images of the Satanist as a kind of babbling Mansonesque character are inaccurate: The *Satanic Bible* is a coherent, rational piece of work outlining a belief system that holds enormous interest for teens. Spokespeople for Satanism, including LaVey, tend to be powerful, articulate, and rational.

Another paperback often used by teens is the *Necronomicon*, apparently written by the "Mad Arab" Abdul Alhazared (1977). The book supposedly teaches readers how to invoke demons.

The Satanic Bible

The *Satanic Bible* may interest teens for a number of reasons. It advocates a kind of fierce independence that includes anarchy, rebellion, and radical self-sufficiency at a time in teens' lives when attitudes toward authority are being shaped. It advocates the rejection of any form of authority, whether religious, societal, or parental. Moral codes of any kind are simply impediments to be overcome. "Do What Thou Wilt Shall Be The Whole of The Law," a quote from Aleister Crowley (1976) in his *Book of the Law* expresses this well. Any individual who surrenders to laws or commands from outside sources (except, of course, from Satan) does so due to weakness. Since rebellion against authority generally runs through the teenage years (and can in fact be used to characterize those very difficult years), the satanic ideology can be enormously attractive, particularly for those already encountering difficulties with authority figures.

Thus, many of the signs and symbols of Satanism are utilized by youth to "get a reaction" from authority figures. The inverted crucifix, the inverted pentagram (five-pointed star), the numerals 666, and so on are used because of their power to offend adults and cause concern (this is not the only reason—the symbols have other occult meanings as well). Obviously not all youth displaying these signs are Satanists; the majority are simply doing what adolescents love to do—upset Mom and Dad. But by utilizing this theme of rebellion, satanic ideology clearly sends out a message to youth that compromise with *any* authority is weak.

Aleister Crowley is the intellectual source of much modern-day Satanism; he called himself the "Great Beast 666." He was a showman who delighted in public outrage. LaVey knew Crowley's work well, and the *Necronomicon* is dedicated to Crowley. Crowley was probably not a Satanist in terms of present images, but he did articulate the belief system outlined in this chapter.

LaVey's *Satanic Bible* also advocates the release of instincts, especially those contained by social moral codes. The appeal is for a kind of "here/now" indulgence of natural drives, especially aggressive and sexual drives, with a complete absence of respect for other considerations. Repression of any form is wrong; release of any desire is correct. Since the sexual and aggressive drives are intense during the teen years, it is easy to see why this philosophy might appeal to youth. If followed to its logical conclusion, the philosophy advocates one long never-ending party of self-indulgence.

The religious philosophy of Satanism offers, in fact, what would appear to be a "teenage dream": "Satan represents indulgence, instead of abstinence" "Satan represents all of the so-called sins, as they all lead to physical, mental, or emotional gratification!" (LaVey, 1969, p. 25). The sophisticated reader could easily interpret this in a broader context; the young teenager might not be as capable.

Egotism, the inflation of the self at the expense of others, is the core message delivered here. Given the fact that teenagers struggle with self-definition, the message can distort this already difficult process of self-growth.

Satanism vs. Mainstream Religion

Apart from its appeal to adolescent rebellion and the unfettered release of instinctual drives, the *Satanic Bible* speaks to the all-too-common smugness, hypocrisy, and self-delusion of mainstream religion. Teens need only go to one more meaningless Sunday service to observe their parents' Sunday-only holiness, and from there to read LaVey's book. After observing this hypocrisy day in and day out, LaVey concluded, "I knew then that the Christian Church thrives on hypocrisy, and that man's carnal nature will out!"

Young people only have to watch types like "Jim and Tammy" at work, or the manipulative fund-raising antics of Oral Roberts, or the loud hypocrisy of Jimmy Swaggart, to agree with LaVey. The obnoxious antics of certain televangelists have no doubt had a huge impact on public perceptions of Christianity in general. They clearly represent only one aspect of the religion; yet many kids unfamiliar with Christianity except through televised versions tend to feel they represent all of Christianity. LaVey's message therefore has a widely receptive younger audience.

Now, whether or not this assessment of Christianity is fair or true, it is commonly stated by young people to be one of the main factors attracting them to Satanism. Sean Sellers certainly felt this way. All of the youth I have counseled have stated that this is one of the major attractions Satanism held for them. Satanism, they say, at least admits the truth. "Satanism represents undefiled wisdom, instead of hypocritical self-deceit!" "Satan represents vital existence, instead of spiritual pipe dreams!" (LaVey, 1969, p. 25).

But the attractions offered in the *Satanic Bible* run even deeper. LaVey offers a picture of reality in which humanity is portrayed as an advanced form of vicious animal, in which the weak are overwhelmed by the strong, and in which sentiments such as love, compassion, and warmth are the attributes of the weak. The vision is a mixture of Darwinism and a form of Machiavellianism combined with elements of the Nietzschean "will-to-power." The vision corresponds to many trends widely accepted in our culture today, and is consistent with some aspects of scientific materialism. This does not mean that our society is "satanic" or that science is the "tool of the devil." It simply means that the satanic philosophy will seem strangely familiar to our children and not as weird or foreign as outsiders might anticipate.

Power is the thread running through the satanic religion—power to be free of any limitation (including moral codes), free of any restriction or impulse. It is a celebration of the self in such a way that the self becomes the center of the universe. The "self," in short, is God. "Man, the animal, is the godhead to the Satanist" (LaVey, 1969, p. 89); "Every man is a god if he chooses to recognize himself as one" (p. 96). Satanism, in other words, is clearly not just a bizarre religion without coherence.

The host of a national radio show once directed a question to me. We were discussing Satanism, and I had just outlined some of the attractions: the rebellion, the release of desires so that immediate gratification is achieved, the distrust of mainline religion, the elevation of self (narcissism) to an almost godlike stature, the worship of power and success. The host's question was obvious: How is Satanism different from values already accepted in our society? Wasn't I simply describing the average corporate boardroom?

The question struck me because, despite platitudes to the contrary, much of modern conduct *does* seem to be regulated by beliefs not unlike those promoted by LaVey, a point LaVey agrees with emphatically. In fact, he states outright that Satanism simply recognizes what is already out there, and that it is the real (if unrecognized) religion of our society. He obviously stretches the point for effect—modern society is not "satanic." The point here is that LaVey has articulated a belief system amazingly familiar to the everyday experience of many youth.

No wonder it attracts adolescents. When looked at this way, the surprise is that it doesn't attract more.

Group Formation

There is of course more to Satanism than just its worldview. Other elements may draw young people as well. For example, should a group form around a local satanic leader, then promises of excitement, group identity, bonding, and other forms of affiliation can become pronounced. Some groups develop around a charismatic youth, others around an older leader who may exploit the group for illegal purposes (drugs, prostitution, pornography), and still others around more serious attempts to act out the satanic worldview.

Heavy Metal Music

In the subculture of satanic youth and dabbler groups, certain forms of heavy metal music predominate. Music by rock groups such as

Slayer, Celtic Frost, and Ozzy Osbourne can be distinguished by its overt promotion of satanic ideology. It is actually religious music, if one accepts the premise that Satanism is a religion. Even a superficial reading of some of the songs will reveal this. Space prevents full disclosure of these songs, but the titles should be revealing enough: "Sabbath Bloody Sabbath," "Looking Down the Cross," "The Number of the Beast." Look closely at these lyrics during the next visit to the record store; this music may be just a commercial scam, but its content speaks directly to Satanism, and its thrust is much more than just entertainment.

Two themes, for example, emerge clearly in this "dark metal." The first is suicide, the second, ritual killing and mutilation.

Suicide is promoted as an answer to life's problems, as a kind of ritual or religious act of courage and devotion. Songs such as "Suicide Solution," "Mandatory Suicide," "Killing Yourself to Live," "Suicidal Winds," extol the virtues of this "solution." A case was launched in the United States by parents who feel their son's suicide occurred as a result of the influence of heavy metal music.

Killing and mutilating others is also promoted as an act of catharsis. Again, here are a few titles: "Spill the Blood," "Bodily Dismemberment," "Killing Is My Business . . . And Business Is Good!"—the list goes on.

One can only guess what effect these kinds of lyrics can have on youth who listen to them daily, relentlessly, obsessively. The music seems to cement some satanic youth groups together, and is often a strong influence on "solitary" Satanists as well. Certainly, music like this could heavily interest children already tending toward pathological fantasies, but it is apparently attractive to "normal" kids as well.

The contrast between the more intellectual brand of Satanism offered by LaVey, and the more grotesque extremes depicted in the music and in lurid newspaper accounts, may point toward two different kinds of adolescent Satanists. It should be clear that the dropping of prohibitions advertised by the first could lead to the second. But both types seem united by their love of dark metal music and by the systematically pathological content in it. The music may not cause pathological outbursts, but it certainly seems to be heavily correlated with the more overtly twisted behavior of some Satanists.

Paranormal and Occult Experiences

One final attraction can be listed here. This is the fascination with strange "powers" and experiences apparently offered through Satanism. Young people today seem fascinated and intrigued by the claims of the paranormal and the occult. These may include everything from channeling (inviting discarnate entities to take possession of one's body) to spiritualism, out-of-body experiences, beliefs in the power of ritual magic, and so on. Now, it should be stated that belief in these powers *does not* constitute adherence to Satanism. The "occult" simply means that which is hidden. Satanism can be seen as one extreme aspect of the occult. Some teens *may* be drawn to it through their involvement in the occult, but that is the only real connection. Most occultists abhor the extreme forms of "black magic" such as Satanism. Wicca, or witchcraft, refers to a pre-Christian or pagan form of worship, and most Wiccans are upset at being lumped together with Satanists. This should always be kept in mind when books such as *Cults That Kill* (Kahaner, 1988), an otherwise very good book, speak of "occult crime." The term is unfair; by comparison, one could speak of "Catholic crime" when priests molest youngsters in their care, or "Moslem crime" when fundamentalists order killings in the name of all Islam. This is clearly inflammatory and unfair. *Theologically*, the occult may be seen as suspect by certain religious groups, but this is, and should remain, a theological concern.

The strange experiences sometimes reported by young people attracted to Satanism are not well understood by professionals generally, and these experiences may overwhelm and fascinate youth who receive them. There is no space to detail these experiences here. Some children claim they actually observe discarnate entities, hear discarnate voices speak to them, "see" visions of various types, and actually commune with various spiritual satanic agents. Mental illness accounts for some of these cases, but therapists may have trouble "hanging" convenient labels on every case of this nature.

Indeed, all of this can be dismissed as nonsense, as mental illness, as manipulations, as false reality; it may in fact be all of this and more. The point to remember, however, is that these experiences are real to the child, and may form a pool of experience that the child draws on to decide conduct and behavior. A rough parallel can be made with the born-again experience in Christianity; most born-again Christians can point to the exact moment of time that they felt Jesus come into them. The experience is not observable to the outsider, yet intensely real and rich to the person who is experiencing it. (No insult is meant here toward Christianity; no theological comparisons are intended.) Unless this kind of experience is recognized, the full range of attractions to Satanism will be overlooked.

Adolescents today are deeply fascinated by these kinds of experiences. A quick look in any bookstore reveals titles that explain "how to" channel discarnate entities, astral travel, become clairvoyant, and so on. Authors such as Shirley MacLaine produce bestsellers based on these experiences. In my opinion, this is not a passing fad. An entire tradition in psychology purports to study such "transpersonal" experiences through the works of men like Maslow, Grof, and so on. These "strange experiences" are apparently not as rare as one might think. However, there is a difference when the examination of these matters is in the hands of responsible investigators rather than "fringe elements." Of particular interest is Andrew Weil's (1986) book, *The Natural Mind*, in which he postulates the idea that "altered" or "extended" states of consciousness are absolutely necessary for overall health, and that searching for them is a normal and natural part of human growth. In that light, Satanism can be seen as a pathological "dark side" of the altered state. Thus, true spiritual liberation may accompany these paranormal experiences; on the other hand, when they occur in murky settings replete with satanic imagery and themes, they tend to exert a profound influence in a more negative direction.

"Thrill Highs"

One other type of experience should be mentioned—the apparent euphoria sometimes achieved in certain satanic ceremonies. The euphoria, or "high," is often linked to destructive acts against others. Some youths report it as a very powerful urge to harm; they can achieve it by systematically torturing and killing animals. The "power rush," it should be recalled, is celebrated throughout dark metal music. The "wilding" attack in New York in May 1989 and the Matamoros (Mexico) ritual killings speak directly to the apparent pleasure, lack of remorse, and lack of guilt characterizing this kind of "thrill kill."

That human beings are capable of finding pleasure through inflicting pain on others is known; that some teens drawn deeply into Satanism appear to actually *learn* this kind of "pleasure" is perhaps less well known.

Summary

Adolescents may find themselves involved because of the promise of "freedom" through rebellion and instinctual release; because of the perception of rampant hypocrisy elsewhere; because of the elevation of the self to the status of godhood and the infatuation with power; because of the promise of identity through group belonging; because of the fascination with various "powers" and other paranormal experiences; and because of the "thrill high." Satanism promises a good "rush" and instant gratification. Professionals who take its influence too lightly may be in danger of serious oversights: When the extreme manifestations of Satanism take over – the infatuation with death (suicide and killing) and the lust for absolute power over others – professionals should know the signs to look for.

If a Satanist is successful in the quest for power, and succeeds in destroying the weaknesses that limit power (love, compassion, and warmth on the one hand, and adherence to any moral code or impulse of conscience on the other), then a state very similar to the old categories termed "psychopathic" or "sociopathic" emerges. In other words, the deeply committed Satanist would be incapable of real human attachment to another, unable to feel remorse or guilt. An individual in this condition might well come to the attention of various professionals. This state *is* the problem, not odd religious practices. We are faced here with the chilling thought that the "sociopathic" state may evolve from commitment to the satanic belief system. Surely this possibility deserves urgent attention and consideration by police and by various children's support agencies.

MEASURING THE INCIDENCE OF SATANISM

The question of prevalence now emerges. How widespread is the problem?

Because awareness of Satanism is a recent phenomenon, and because it has attracted little professional attention until now, few objective measures exist. We are forced to rely on media coverage of particularly lurid cases, and are forced to rely, as well, on impressions by practitioners in the field. Parallels with the rise of awareness of child sexual abuse itself can be drawn here. Cases were seen, eventually collated, and then, over time, woven into a somewhat coherent whole through systematic studies. We are now at the precollation stage in terms of Satanism. Some information is available, however.

For example, calls to the Council on Mind Abuse in Toronto, Canada (where I worked as Director), escalated during 1990; about 10 serious calls per month came in 1989, but in 1990 the figure was closer to 50. Given the fact that our agency is not well known to the general public, that it is restricted to Toronto, and that the majority of these cases are referred from professional sources, one might expect the actual incidence levels to be much higher. Professionals *are* seeing a problem; some adolescents in their care are manifesting an apparent attachment to Satanism. Once again, statistics are not directly available, but professional interest appears intense and growing.

Some indirect statistics may have some bearing here. Andrew Greeley, of the University of Chicago National Opinion Research Center, found that 42% of adults surveyed believe they have contacted a deceased friend or relative, and 67% feel they have had psychic experiences. Once again, this has little to do with Satanism directly, but does point to a fascination with the occult generally. These statistics may underestimate teenage fascination with these matters. In a 1984 Gallup poll it was found that 59% of teenagers believe in paranormal experiences.

Reginald Bibby (1987) surveyed the state of Canadian religion and found that 25% believe it is possible to speak to the dead, while 60% believe that people have psychic powers. These statistics may reflect the teenage population as well. They certainly express my own experiences with groups of teenagers in various high schools around lower Ontario.

Other statistics seem to support belief in the devil as a distinct being. A recent survey by Gallup International lists belief in the devil at 66% of those polled in Northern Ireland, 66% in the United States, 30% in Great Britain, and down to 12% in Sweden.

To fall back on impressions once again, teen Satanism seems to be neither a rural nor an urban phenomenon specifically. Due to the easy availability of satanic source material, this should come as no surprise.

SATANISM AS RELIGION

The troubling question of Satanism as a religion may cause some concern. I will address this briefly, and then proceed with an overview of cases, suggested intervention strategies, a discussion of reasons why teen Satanism may be on the rise, and, finally, a summary and forecast for the next decade.

Satanism has not emerged from a vacuum. It has a history. The image of Satan has evolved over time, as have our perceptions of evil itself. (For an excellent scholarly, objective study of Satan, I suggest J. B. Russell's [1988] book, *The Prince of Darkness*.)

Because the image of Satan still horrifies people today, it is hard to think of Satanism as a religion. Religions, after all, are supposed to offer hope, love, and positive visions of beauty and transcendence. Yet why can't a religion form around the opposite or "dark" end of the human spectrum? Satanic groups have apparently been active in one form or another from the fifteenth century on, and perhaps even earlier. Religion has always attempted to deal with profound issues such as death, eternity, the hereafter, and so on. Yet, in its own way, Satanism does, as well.

Indeed, any member of the U.S. armed forces can be married, buried, or serviced by a satanic priest. Dr. Michael Aquino, a Lt-Colonel in the U.S. army, leads the Temple of Set, the second best-known satanic religious group (level 3). Like it or not, the current tone of tolerance for *all* religious minorities includes Satanism. It should only be a matter of time before Satanists call for equal rights and paid holiday leave on satanic days of worship.

From the law enforcement perspective, therefore, Satanism is not illegal. Certain acts committed by individuals apparently under the influence of Satanism, however, may be illegal. Social service agencies, in a like manner, may have to recognize the rights of children in care to worship Satan and to display satanic symbolism.

But note the problem here: When followed to its logical extreme, Satanism moves against the stated goals of every known therapeutic intervention. Therapy seeks to connect the client to healthy human feelings such as love, warmth, and trust. Satanism seeks the opposite. Therapy attempts to connect the client to wider social realities, whereas Satanism mocks connections of any form. So just what *are* we going to do with a religion clearly promoting destructive ideals undermining real therapeutic gains?

The answer is clear: We may have to examine religion in the same way we have had to examine the family. That is, 20 years ago, the family was a sacrosanct institution beyond criticism; we have since learned that criticizing dysfunctional families (for example, for child abuse) need not mean the destruction of our confidence in, or reverence of, the family itself. In the same way, we may have to consider examining "dysfunctional" religions in order to understand and deal with their impact. The phenomena of destructive cults generally, and Satanism specifically, may leave us little choice—unless, of course, we decide to ignore the problem and pretend it doesn't exist.

Allowing Satanism to obtain the status of a religion in no way implies acceptance of its beliefs, but just as most religious beliefs have specific consequences and problems affecting individuals in different ways, so too does Satanism. And these problems, as has been pointed out, can be extreme.

PROFILES OF TEENS

I turn now to some cases that have emerged in Toronto. All of these cases involved teens, all are real; few are widely known. Readers wishing to pursue widely known cases can read *Cults That Kill, The Ulti-mate Evil*, and other material.

Before outlining these cases, I'd like to draw two different profiles of teens attracted to Satanism.

Profile 1

The first profile will be familiar to police, youth workers, and other professionals who work with "marginalized" children. Typically, these youth have a history of problems with socialization, sometimes stemming back to preschool. They are often described as "loners," are underachievers, and generally present as "problem" kids. They are usually of above-average intelligence; are stimulated by images and themes of power and violence (there may be a history involving torture of animals, for example); and may have a history of aggression, disruption, and even criminal activity at an early age. They usually come from difficult, if not pathological, home backgrounds and may have been "cycled" through many different group homes. Their ability to trust, to bond, and to share with others is profoundly limited. They will often appear to others as manipulative and deceptive, and will usually earn the dislike of most people they meet.

It should be clear why youths with this profile might be attracted to Satanism. The satanic philosophy states what they already "know": that no one should be trusted, that love and trust end in pain and disillusionment, that everyone is hypocritical and will hurt others if they can, and that in the end no one will ever really care. They know that power is everything; the appeal of power is the ability to control a world over which they have had no control. Satanism, when openly displayed, also has the advantage of frightening others. With that comes attention, and with attention comes power. Furthermore, if a group is involved, the offer of actually *belonging* to something (even if the bonding is only for convenience), of finding some kind of acceptance, and of controlling others in the group can be overwhelming. The attraction of unrestricted violence, the acting out of ritual aggression – all of this clearly sends an appealing invitation to this type of adolescent.

When deeply involved, these individuals can become extremely dangerous to themselves and others. Without any previously developed sense of self (that is, without a positive identity or self-image), the line between fantasy and reality can easily be crossed. Having crossed that line, the youths may then identify themselves *at a core level* as Satanist. Prognosis for this type and depth of involvement is probably not good: Satanism has "answered" all the individual's needs. They know who they are, they know where they belong, they know the "truth" about love and conscience, and they know their God.

Profile 2

The second profile departs radically. Here we find youth who are outwardly well-adjusted, popular with classmates, and from home backgrounds that appear to be loving and stable. These individuals are usually highly intelligent, extremely curious, and driven to search for meaning and purpose. They will usually explore world religions at an early age and will demonstrate acute awareness of the problems facing our world. This awareness is sometimes so acute that anxiety and even depression may develop.

Previously, I mentioned that there are two poles of Satanism: the first revolving around intellectual adherence (such as outlined by LaVey or Aquino), the second around the more brutal, violent extremes. It should be clear that Profile 1 is attracted to be the latter pole and, equally clear, Profile 2 is attracted to the former. These distinctions are extremely important, especially when interventions are considered.

That both poles may lead to similar conclusions and outcomes is a frightening aspect of the problem. Profile 2 individuals, however, are often easier to work with, in that they usually have an intact self-image prior to involvement, which can be reactivated and redirected. They also have an intact sense of intellectual curiosity, and can therefore be approached from that perspective. Usually they have a very deep sense of outrage about hypocrisy, and an extremely intense desire to find the truth, no matter how hard it might be. Hence the appeal of Satanism. To think that Profile 2 kids are "weird" or "sick" or otherwise displaying hidden pathologies is to completely miss the point. These kids are just as likely to diagnose the clinician as suffering from spiritual and personal confusion, and may actually overwhelm clinical investigators. A "just say no" approach with these teenagers will garner only their derision.

CASE STUDIES

Two cases are presented here based on the two profiles. The profiles, of course, are not absolute — sometimes the "good middle class kid" *is* hiding family or personal pathology, and sometimes the "marginalized" child comes from a good home and is actually struggling to find personal meaning. Generalizations always distort reality, but, having said this, I think the profiles are still useful.

The following have been drawn from real cases, but some details have been changed to protect confidentiality. I sincerely hope that my own efforts to understand and help these kids will inspire better qualified professionals to take a closer look.

Case #1

Jason is 14. He is in the custody of the Children's Aid Society. His mother is an alcoholic single parent. His father left the family when Jason was two. Jason has a history of abuse and neglect. His school records reflect a history of underachievement, and his peer interactions have always been difficult. Toward adults, he is aggressive and often violent. His older brother is apparently involved with various forms of crime, including drugs.

Jason was recently sent to a psychiatric facility for assessment. His behavior had deteriorated rapidly over the past few months. Aggressive incidents had increased in seriousness and frequency. In particular, group-home staff were concerned about Jason's behavior during the incidents. He appeared completely out of control. His expressions seemed to reflect a rather bizarre quality, as if he was no longer *connected* to himself. The effect on staff was immediate – everyone was afraid of Jason, afraid of his unpredictable outbursts.

Prior to this sudden downturn in behavior, Jason had become infatuated by certain forms of heavy metal music. He listened to this music obsessively. Its themes of violence apparently enthralled him. These themes came out in his drawings, his writings, and his conversations with others. His clothing gradually changed to reflect images he found on some of the album covers. At first, the group-home staff thought little of it since his peers generally were reflecting the same styles.

But Jason seemed to take it further. He purchased a copy of the *Satanic Bible* and took it with him everywhere. Satanic images, such as the inverted pentagram, inverted crosses, and the numerals 666 appeared on all of his school notebooks. He wrote small articles outlining the philosophy of Satanism, and began calling himself by a new name. Staff found special knives, candles, goblets, and other odd items in his room. Other residents suggested that he had ritually killed small animals. From time to time he could be heard chanting.

His peers were frightened. He clearly enjoyed their fear, often embellishing his stories. He claimed that he had special powers to harm his enemies, a claim taken seriously by other residents. Tensions in the group-home rose. Staff were not immune from the tensions. Most had seen the "Geraldo" two-hour special on Satanism and weren't sure how to proceed. As the levels of tension and fear rose, Jason's behavior deteriorated further. Despite staff attempts to limit his interest in Satanism, his involvement grew. He claimed he was "possessed" from time to time by an entity which he had named and drawn repeatedly. He felt that the entity was more powerful and capable than he could ever be. He said he welcomed its presence.

Initial psychiatric evaluations found little. His behavior in assessment settings was exemplary. Staff frustration grew because of the shared sense that, sooner or later, he was going to seriously harm someone. His violent episodes, although explosive, had a sense of organization or purpose behind them — he seemed to be taking extreme pleasure from them.

Case #2

Sharon, on the other hand, came from an apparently normal and loving home. She was an excellent student, had many good friends, was on the student council, and seemed happy. Her parents were well off and happy with their relationship with Sharon and each other.

Sharon's behavior and appearance transformed suddenly. Being 15, she had generally been acutely aware of her appearance. This changed. She dropped her friends, dressed exclusively in black, and wore various amulets and jewelry with satanic symbolism. She dropped out of family life. Her parents became increasingly concerned, although they thought it might just be a "phase."

Her notebooks at school, and her bedroom at home, all reflected her fascination with images of horror and killing. In particular, she became infatuated with suicide. Communication with others ceased. She appeared robotic and cold to her parents. At times they felt that she was just "not there," although physically present.

One evening, she had a "vision." The vision told her that she would have to kill her teacher in order to achieve a higher state of consciousness and higher powers generally. The next day she actually took a knife to school and attempted to assault her teacher. She failed. After the attempt she ran from the school, went home, and drank some duplicating fluid. Her suicide attempt was unsuccessful. She was taken into custody and hospitalized.

Assessment

Both these examples are real and both occurred in the Toronto area. Cases similar in nature have been reported across the country. Some are more extreme, others less so. But, regardless of extremity, it would appear to make sense that we take a closer look at the phenomenon. Examining assessment and intervention strategies is one way of doing this. This examination is directed toward professionals facing therapeutic issues more than toward law enforcement. Hopefully, police officers and other legal professionals can still benefit from some of the insights offered here; moreover, multidisciplinary teamwork is often essential – when Satanism takes its full course, both police and social services tend to get involved together.

Assessment is extremely important. The following questions and strategies might be useful:

Determine the Client's Background   This determination should be conducted like any other. Family history, psychological/psychiatric workups, and so on, can all be useful. The client's preinvolvement ego structure is especially important. In other words, a poor self-image and pathological tendencies before involvement with Satanism may mean that the primary problem is not Satanism at all. The satanic imagery and themes may simply be "wrapped around" an already destructive persona.

Determine the Behavioral Problems   Are the problems behavioral? If so, exactly what are they? Is criminal activity involved? Is the client acting out? If so, how and in what circumstances? How do others see the client? If they suspect Satanism is involved, what exactly do they mean? Any supporting evidence should be gathered (such as notebooks, stories, drawings). Just because the client is involved with Satanism does not mean that other behavioral problems are present. They almost always are, but should be determined first.

Determine Group Involvement   Until now, the assessment has been routine. At this point, however, the type and depth of involvement must be explored. Recall that three basic attractions are available:

- The belief system itself (that is, attractions to the themes of anarchy/rebelliousness, unfettered instincts, hatred of perceived hypocrisy, celebration of the Machiavellian/Nietzschean power urge)
- The presence of a group (offering belonging, identity, even "family")
- Various experiences (paranormal and "thrill high")

If a group is involved, then the problem is more difficult. Basically, this information can be obtained in a number of ways, including asking the client directly. However obtained, the information will tend to expose one of three known forms of group organization:

"Dabbler" groups formed by a charismatic teen and usually unconnected to other groups. These groups may be well-known in the local community and may be known to police as well. Such groups often practice various rituals found in commercially available books, although the rituals are usually altered to suit the group's taste. Dabbler groups may be responsible for animal mutilations and satanic graffiti appearing in the local area. Often these groups have a secret location. When found by outsiders, these locations tend to cause extreme public alarm. Rumors of a "satanic cult" will spread; according to earlier definitions, dabbler groups are not "cults" at all.

Criminal groups usually run by an adult. These groups are made up of teenagers but run for profit by older adults. Criminal activities often include drugs, prostitution, theft, and pornography. The teens' attraction to Satanism is used as a control mechanism. One young girl in Toronto, for example, thought she had found a real satanic "priest." In fact, she had found a pimp who then prostituted her on the street. The older adults may themselves be involved in Satanism, but tend to use it cynically in order to maintain control over the teenagers in the group.

Teen gangs that merge various racist, Nazi, and ideological concerns with Satanism or satanic practices. The gangs seem to be a rising urban problem worldwide. Skinhead gangs in particular may be a concern here. Nazi themes blend extremely well with the darker side of the occult generally. (For links between destructive occultism, Nazism, and racism, read Goodrick-Clarke's [1992] book, *The Occult Roots of Nazism*.) Certain gangs seem to utilize various satanic rituals as initiation rites.

Correctly assessing the presence and type of group is important.

Determine Attachments to the Belief System   This obviously requires knowledge of the belief system itself. For example, if the client is aware of the works of Aleister Crowley, then chances are good that attachment is strong. If the client is unable to establish the meaning of various symbols and signs, then probably involvement is superficial and/or strongly tied to other attachments (group or experience). Outside expertise may have to be called in at this point, but the basic information is available to those seeking to develop expertise themselves.

Determine Attachments to Various Experiences   This is even more difficult than point 4. Clients have to trust the investigator implicitly. This trust usually rests on their understanding that (a) they won't be ridiculed, (b) they won't be judged "insane," and (c) the investigator or therapist has some personal knowledge of the power and attraction of these kinds of experiences. In many cases these children have journeyed to the far ends of human experience, sometimes with the aid of various psychoactive drugs. Easy explanations just don't work in that realm. The power of these experiences to shape and determine the client's behavior should not be underestimated – the teenager who has "encountered" a demonic entity that has threatened to kill him or her will act on that *perceived* reality despite what the outside world might think.

To summarize, assessment is designed to determine:

- Preinvolvement data
- Presenting problems
- Type(s) of attachment (group, belief system, experiences)
- Depth of involvement in each type of attachment

Teenagers typically do not become involved in higher levels of Satanism (psychopathic, religious Satanism, satanic cults), although this is not always the case.

Overall, the determination of *causality* is important. Is the client's behavior driven primarily by the first two concerns listed above (as is usually the case with Profile 1 teenagers)? If so, then the Satanism will likely make already underlying problems much worse. Ignoring these problems to focus exclusively on the Satanism would therefore be a mistake. On the other hand, preinvolvement problems may not be present. In this case, a form of voluntary counseling would make the most sense. Clients of this type can respond remarkably well in a short period of time, especially if they have a strong ego structure to work with. Profile 2 teens come to mind here. Finally, satanic involvement may be driven by neither Profile 1 nor Profile 2 concerns – it may be driven by simple attention-seeking. This can usually be determined fairly easily, especially by staff who know the client well.

TREATMENT AND INTERVENTION

Treatment issues stem from clear assessment procedures. Intervention is designed for one purpose: to sever the bonds connecting the child to destructive aspects of Satanism. These bonds, or attachments, as outlined above, are considered here in terms of the two profiles.

Before examining the profiles, a short note about teens using Satanism as an attention-seeking device is important. This often occurs in group-homes where a serious case has been uncovered, where staff have reacted strongly, and where other residents also want a "piece of the action." It may also occur in homes where the child is determined to shock the parents in order to get attention. Like other forms of attention-seeking behavior, it can either be ignored or refocused (for example, by providing positive attention). Usually the "Satanism" will fall away as the child's needs are met. To overreact here is to simply make the problem worse by driving the child deeper into Satanism. Correct assessment is clearly important in this regard.

Profile 1 Clients

The Profile 1 client is not necessarily driven by attention-seeking needs alone. Usual strategies will, therefore, not work. Profile 1 kids are extremely difficult to work with. Once Satanism takes hold, and once clients identify themselves at fundamental levels as Satanists, intervention becomes problematic at best. Underlying problems and pathologies may become amplified no matter what interventions are undertaken.

Nevertheless, the following might prove useful. First of all, if group involvement exists, then immediate action should be taken. For example, if a local dabbler group is active, then steps should be taken to identify the leader and to separate the client from the group and from the leader. This is obviously not possible in all circumstances and depends on the child's age (the older the harder). Unrestricted access to such a group will deepen the client's attachment through pseudoaffiliation and group bonding. This will make therapeutic interventions extremely difficult, particularly if the client sees the group frequently and finds identity there.

If the group is criminal or if it demonstrates a higher-order organization, then the problem is that much more difficult. The client may be under real fear of retaliation for disclosing information or for leaving the group. Police involvement is absolutely essential here. These groups can be dealt with effectively, but not as a therapeutic issue. It is therefore extremely important to determine what *type* of group, if any, is involved. Mistaking a dabbler group for a criminal organization tends only to create an unnecessary climate of fear and confusion.

Profile 1 teens are vulnerable to group attractions. They tend to find a sense of power and identity existing nowhere else in their lives. The group can function as a surrogate family where the client finds a distorted kind of acceptance, meaning, and belonging. When this attachment becomes solidified it is difficult, if not impossible, to break. In other words, what other bonding mechanisms can be offered as a replacement?

Profile 1 individuals tend to be less attached, however, to the belief system of Satanism itself. They may read the *Satanic Bible* and may appear to have more than a passing understanding of the phenomenon, but their attachments tend to rest more with group affiliation or with various experiences. If group involvement has been ruled out, and the client is apparently acting alone, then attachments to the belief system may be deeper. Knowing clients' overall intellectual capabilities can help: Usually, the more capable they are, the more attached to the belief system they will be. Interactions with these young people can be astonishing. Attempts at "therapy" can often shift to considerations of metaphysics, the general idea being that the therapist is an idiot and the client truly aware of reality. Pretending that this is irrelevant or nonexistent will just frustrate the client. In order to respond, the therapist should be prepared to explore the worldview articulated by the client. Again, this is only necessary when attachments are deep, when the client is being driven by the destructive aspects of the belief system. Clearly, awareness of the belief system is essential.

If the Profile 1 client has experienced paranormal or "thrill high" aspects of Satanism, and if these experiences have been integrated into his or her preexisting pathologies, then the problem becomes even more difficult. Cutting the bonds attaching the client to these experiences is extremely difficult. If the client's reality orientation is already marginal, then his or her perception of entities commanding certain behaviors may be irresistible. Several cases of this type have already occurred in Ontario. One example concerns a 25-year-old Brantford, Ontario, youth who slit the throat of his 12-year-old sister. He had apparently been involved in Satanism for a number of years. He said he was instructed to kill before October 31, 1988. In his mind, apparently, this killing would bring a new form of life and power. He was found to be legally sane, although he had a definite Profile 1 background, which included everything from alcohol and drug abuse to acts of sexual sadism.

If underlying sadistic pathologies are also present, and if the client has experienced the "thrill kill" feeling, then intervention may have to move into a containment/monitoring mode. It would appear, in other words, that the underlying core message of Satanism — the destruction of human capacities of love, warmth, and trust, and the destruction of adherence to any moral code — when actually achieved, may leave the client in a state of desensitization or even derealization. The level of danger presented by such clients can be acute.

Profile 1 clients are extremely difficult to work with. Even if the various attachments are severed, then previous problems emerge once again, and the therapist must face finding something to replace the bonding to Satanism. Anyone working in the field knows how difficult this can be. Success would seem to depend on having alternatives available for the client to choose from. This, of course, is an ongoing problem facing therapists everywhere.

Profile 2 Clients

Profile 2 clients are somewhat easier, in that they often have a pre-involvement persona to turn to. They may also be lucky enough to have a supportive family. Often they have become attached to Satanism as a consequence of their own appropriate search for personal and religious meaning. Intervention frequently involves helping the client to determine just what it is they actually want. For example, one young girl was deeply attracted to the core message in Satanism as outlined by LaVey. She felt that he was telling the truth. She felt that all other religions were a sham and that through Satanism she could achieve enormous power. She had never actually looked at the "hidden agenda," and was unaware of the meaning behind many of the rituals she conducted. In other words, her involvement in Satanism was more accidental than purposeful.

This is not always the case with Profile 2 individuals. Some of them become very deeply involved, and may arrive at the same endpoint as Profile 1 kids: They become depersonalized and may become involved in various criminal activities. But the cutting of bonding to the group, to the belief system, and to the experience is not as difficult, and reorientation following intervention is much more likely.

THERAPY VS. THE PRACTICE
OF A RELIGION

The actual techniques used to "cut the bonds" with either profile are too detailed to mention here. But an important question remains: What right do therapists have to interfere with clients' religion by cutting their bonds to it?

If we accept that Satanism is a religion (and I believe we have no choice in this regard), then we come to the very uncomfortable position that Satanism may be a destructive religion. As demonstrated previously, the core themes of Satanism revolve around desensitization, depersonalization, and aggression (inward or outward). Any legitimate therapy moves in opposite directions, toward the enhancement of emotional life, toward a healthy attitude to others, toward an opening and acceptance of both the pleasure and pain of human existence. By proceeding with therapy, then, the client's human rights may be violated.

This may seem absurd. But it is not absurd to the child-care worker in a group-home who sees the very worst aspects of a resident's pathologies amplified and deepened through Satanism, and who feels powerless to intervene. It is not absurd to the psychiatrist who cannot find any category in the *Diagnostic & Statistical Manual of Mental Disorders* to describe clinically destructive behavior associated with Satanism. It is not absurd to the mother who looks in the eyes of her child to find only a deadened, lifeless expression devoid of the memory of any human warmth.

My own solution is to leave aside the religious issue and to examine the content of the belief system in a way that makes sense for each individual situation. If the courts decide, however, that Satanism cannot be challenged in government-sponsored therapeutic settings (group homes, correctional facilities), then interventions will be impossible.

This issue clearly has the potential to explode. More than 10 years ago, a report on cults in Ontario was commissioned. The Hill Report (Hill, 1980) concluded that the government should under no circumstances become involved in the "cult issue." Hill was fully aware of problems faced by individual citizens in this regard but felt that, in balance, the problem should be left alone. It was determined that the cult issue was a "political mine field." Like it or not, however, the issue is apparently here to stay. Destructive religion would appear to be all too much with us. Easy answers are, of course, impossible, We don't want another inquisition. On the other hand, we don't want to stand aside and watch helplessly as people are hurt in the name of "religion." Clearly, this issue deserves attention and study.

Focusing on the Belief System

Readers may also note that I have not dwelt on the "lurid" aspects of Satanism (the ritual killings, the animal mutilations, the details of specific ceremonies and how they are conducted). This information is available elsewhere; moreover, the lurid aspects themselves are only the outward expression of the belief system itself. For example, the killing of an animal in a ritual setting serves to (1) bond the individual to the group, (2) transform any reaction of empathy or pity for the animal's pain into pleasure, and (3) provide a means of obtaining personal/magical power. Almost every aspect of Satanism can be distilled in this manner. The apparently bewildering, frightening, and bizarre qualities associated with it can therefore be translated into a rational framework. This translation can, in turn bring the phenomenon down to manageable levels. Most investigators new to the issue look for lists of special dates, symbols, ceremonial artifacts, and so on. Although these are important, they only represent outward manifestations of the belief system itself, and frequently only confuse everything—most groups and individuals develop their own symbolic systems, and outsiders can spend useless hours trying to "interpret" their meaning. Understanding the belief system and the attractions it offers will be more effective in the long run for police and for therapists alike.

Law enforcement issues clearly do not come into play unless specific laws have been broken, yet they are still related to the above comments. As has been pointed out, breaking laws *is* the core message of Satanism. These laws may be moral, social, or legal. Not all adolescents involved in Satanism break legal laws, but most begin an escalating spiral of defiance and cruelty that can often lead to the breaking of these laws. This spiral can be frustrating for police, because Satanism itself is not illegal, nor is the possession of black robes, candles, and symbolic items. Even ritually killing an animal leads to minimal consequences for the child, especially in today's climate of permissiveness toward youth. When serious crimes are actually perpetrated by a youth, and when these crimes occur within the context of Satanism, then police officers should be aware of the significance of this context even though it may not have direct bearing on enforcing the law. The problem is somewhat parallel to that faced by therapists: Just as therapists may have to consider Satanism as a causal force behind some pathological behavior, so police officers and the legal system, in general, may have to examine Satanism as a possible motivation behind certain crimes. These and other related issues will very likely emerge in the next decade.

CONCLUSION

I'd like to examine two final issues: the impact on staff, therapists, and others; and predictions for the next decade.

Impact

There is no training available for therapists encountering Satanism. ("Possession 101" is not a required subject for the average psychology student.) Encountering Satanism can be quite a shock. Levels of fear, confusion, and even terror frequently surround these cases, as most therapists will openly admit. Some staff may be driven to the religion of their youth, some may forsake religion completely, some may become convinced that a satanic group is after them. In most cases, this effect wears off once staff understand the core nature of Satanism and once they are permitted to express and vent their fear openly in a safe environment with other staff or supervisors. Moreover, staff can begin to grasp that they don't have to believe in Satan to accept that others do, and that this belief in Satan may direct individuals to perform acts that would otherwise appear irrational, if not insane. The religious aspect can never be completely removed, however, and I strongly suggest that this aspect of the problem not be overlooked. It is part of the presenting clinical picture and deserves sensitive, professional attention.

The Next Decade

The coming years will probably bring more, not less of the kinds of problems associated with Satanism today. When all three bonding mechanisms are at work, it is clear that basic needs are being met: the need to belong, to believe, to find identity, meaning, and power. These needs are powerful, especially in teenagers, and cannot be denied. It would appear that society as a whole is actually moving away from meeting these needs: Family units are deteriorating, community life offers little for kids who move frequently, churches seem to be attracting fewer and fewer young people. Moreover, young people are inheriting a world rife with the possibilities of imminent destruction through environmental disaster, nuclear war, and other destructive possibilities. Any organization or belief system offering a sense of identity, meaning, and purpose should therefore prosper in this climate. Satanic youth gangs, particularly those that are well organized, offer all of this and more.

One final comment—our society at this time is overflowing with images of violence, killing, and horror. A quick glance at local movie fare will confirm this. I have the opportunity occasionally to speak to Grade 13 students; they cheer when Charles Manson is mentioned (see, for example, Schreck, 1988). Freddy Kruger, the serial killer in the *Nightmare on Elm Street* series, is the hero, not the villain. We might want to begin examining the impact of this kind of material on the lives of our children. When horror becomes daily fare, and when "thrill killing" becomes the stuff not only of fantasy but also of reality, then we may be allowing forms of desensitization and dehumanization to run free with our children. And Satanism, after all is said and done, *is* the religion of the desensitized, the disconnected, the "inhuman." Ignoring it should no longer be an option.

REFERENCES

Alhazred, A. (1977). *Necronomicon.* New York: Avon Books.

Bibby, R. (1987). *Fragmental gods.* Concord, Ontario, Canada: Irwin.

Crowley, A. (1976). *Book of the law.* York Beach, ME: Samuel Weiser.

Goldenthal, H. (1989, Feb. 25–Mar. 2). Venting skinhead violence. *NOW Magazine* (Toronto).

Goodrick-Clarke, N. (1992). *The occult roots of Nazism: Secret Aryan cults and their influence on Nazi ideology.* New York: New York University Press.

Grof, S. (1985). *Beyond the brain: Birth, death, and transcendence in psychotherapy.* Albany: State University of New York Press.

Herrington, A. (1972). *Psychopaths.* New York: Touchstone.

Higgins, N. D. (1989). *Devil child.* New York: St. Martin's Press.

Hill, D. G. (1980, June). *Study of mind development groups, sects and cults in Ontario.* A Report to the Ontario Government.

Kahaner, L. (1988). *Cults that kill.* New York: Warner.

Katz, J. (1989). *Seductions of crime.* New York: Basic Books.

King, F. (1977). *The magical world of Aleister Crowley.* London: Weidenfeld & Nicolson.

Langone, M. D., & Blood, L. O. (1990). *Satanism and occult-related violence: What you should know.* Weston, MA: American Family Foundation.

LaVey, A. (1969). *Satanic bible.* New York: Avon Books.

LaVey, A. (1976). *The satanic rituals.* New York: Avon Books.

Magid, K., & McKelvey, C.A. (1989). *High risk: Children without a conscience.* New York: Bantam Books.

Marron, K. (1988). *Ritual abuse.* Toronto: McClelland-Bantam.

Maslow, A. (1976). *Religions, values, and peak experiences.* New York: Penguin.

Norris, J. (1989). *Serial killers.* New York: Doubleday.

Ornstein, R. E. (1972). *The psychology of consciousness.* New York: W. H. Freeman.

Power Metal magazine. (1989, June). p. 56.

Raschke, C. (1990). *Painted black: From drug killings to heavy metal — The epidemic of satanic crime terrorizing our communities.* San Francisco: HarperSanFrancisco.

Russell, J. B. (1988). *The prince of darkness.* Ithaca, NY: Cornell University Press.

Schreck, N. (Ed.). (1988). *The Manson file.* New York: Amok Press.

St. Clair, D. (1987). *Say you love Satan.* New York: Dell.

Symond, J. (1971). *The great beast: The life and magic of Aleister Crowley.* London: Macdonald.

Tart, C. (1972). *Altered states of consciousness.* Garden City, NY: Doubleday.

Terry, M. (1987). *The ultimate evil: An investigation into America's most dangerous satanic cult.* Garden City, NY: Doubleday.

Weil, A. (1986). *The natural mind: An investigation of drugs and higher consciousness.* Boston: Houghton Mifflin.

Wilson, C. (1988). *Aleister Crowley: The nature of the beast.* San Francisco: Thorsons.

20

LEGAL CONSIDERATIONS: REGAINING INDEPENDENCE AND INITIATIVE

Herbert L. Rosedale, Esq.

CONTROVERSIES BETWEEN ZEALOTS AND SOCIETY are not new. They go back to the establishment of the social contract and relate to many of its subsequent implications. Aspects of the controversies surfaced during the period of accommodation between ideological monarchies and the middle classes and during the period of division between secular and ecclesiastical authority with divergent claims to fealty. The controversies renew from time to time when beliefs of individuals or groups are so strong that they lead them to ignore or violate secular law. These conflicts arise over a wide range of legal issues that arouse strong passions and, consequently, particularly stimulate zealots of many different stripes. Examples include the injustice of racially discriminatory laws, conflicts over right-to-lifers' attacking abortion clinics, and orchestrated efforts to nullify laws offensive to a particular group for ideological or economic reasons. In contemporary society, controversies relating to destructive, totalistic cults have expanded markedly during the past 15 years.

When I first started to speak out about cults approximately 10 years ago, I was one of an extremely small group of lawyers who were willing to address cultic groups' broad range of challenges to individual freedom and personal liberty. The podium had in fact been largely forfeited to a strident, well-organized clique of "civil libertarian" experts who discoursed at length upon the inviolability of the First Amendment and the rights, vulnerabilities, and vitality of so-called new religious movements.

Those who challenged totalistic groups were concerned with the deception and manipulation of recruits and members and the existence of psychological, financial, and sometimes even physical abuse within the groups without informed consent. The critics' priorities were education and deterrence. Critics believed that individuals could be quickly and decisively deprived of their ability to think critically and to make independent judgments and that the process of deprogramming could restore cultists' ability to independently choose a general course of conduct that could either involve return to the group or to their pre-group life-style and values.

Early debates focused on a number of questions: Did these groups obtain membership through volitional though nontraditional religious conversions or through coercive manipulation or fraudulent tactics that deprived the new member of his or her freedom of choice? Could totalistic groups, in claiming members' complete allegiance and obedience, demand and enforce termination of all familial communications? Could such a group require a member to isolate children and grandchildren from family members outside the organization? Was action initiated by perceived emotional and physical risk of a new member justified by necessity in the face of criminal charges of kidnapping when a group member was involuntarily removed from the group? Did counseling of any kind, whether consensual or nonconsensual, violate civil rights of members of totalistic groups, who claimed they were being subjected to faith-breaking presentations? Did religious motivation immunize noncriminal injurious activities? In short, legal analysis and discussion addressed at length questions of irrational conversion, the nature of free will and volition, and the extent of protection that should be afforded to bizarre religious groups. These questions were addressed by, among others, Delgado (1977, 1979, 1982), Dressler (1979), Lucksted and Martell (1982), and Shapiro (1983).

Recently, however, using the First Amendment as an absolute icon has become more difficult. It is now generally accepted that the right to religious freedom does not confer upon anyone the concomitant right to injure another or deprive persons of freedom under the guise of religious motivation. Indeed, recent decisions appear to have given more weight to the primacy of other socially validated concerns, such as monogamy, family structure, and the prohibition of mind-altering drugs, over the desire to engage in a religious practice.

In recent years it has become far more evident that destructive cultic groups are not limited to those who claim religious bonds. The same issues arise and must be dealt with when a leader exercising power and control over members requires politically correct ideas, dictates behaviors for achieving psychological or physical well-being, or prescribes an absolute course of subordinate conduct in order to become wealthy, healthy, or wise.

As the field has broadened so has its perspective lengthened so as to consider legal problems arising after a person emerges from a cult and struggles to regain independence and a sense of self-worth. I have personally dealt with several dozen such people for whom such concerns were primary. A person's ability to help former cult members deal with the legal issues that arise is necessarily predicated on an understanding of the process to which they were subjected. In this chapter I examine such legal issues rather than look back to the older debates in this area.

ROLE OF LAW IN
THE RECOVERY PROCESS

After a person leaves a totalistic group, he or she often turns first to the question of how to restore the essential legal trappings of individual independence. First and foremost, the person addresses changes that occurred in his or her family during the period of group involvement.

Marriage

Dissolving a marriage entered into while a member of a group to someone who has remained in the group is frequently a first order of business. This is not always easy, because sometimes the spouse is physically inaccessible (geographically or otherwise) to the one who left the group. On the other hand, the spouse who remains in the group may not wish to stay married either since retention of ties to someone outside the group poses a potential danger to the group, as it may provide a source of outside information and disruption encroaching upon the leader's ability to control the member remaining in the group. Continuation of the marriage may also prevent a new union with another group member.

First, the ex-member should determine whether the marriage was legally contracted or merely ceremonial. If the marriage was legal, there are various ways to dissolve it, usually by divorce or annulment. No-fault consensual divorce is the most common method, but annulment is sometimes available when it can be proved that the marriage was not entered into knowingly or voluntarily or that there was fraud in its inducement. Since some ex-members will want an annulment rather than a divorce because of religious values and moral precepts, the possibility of annulment should be fully explored. In a recent case, an annulment was granted based on a professional's testimony that the marriage had been ordered by the cult leader, and therefore the marriage had not been entered into with the couple's free will and consent.

Children

A second aspect of family structure that often must be addressed deals with children. Child custody, visitation rights, education, and religious practices are among issues that may arise (Greene, 1989; Kandel, 1987/1988). Cases dealing with the dissolution of marriages of persons with mixed religious faiths offer guidance and legal precedent.

If the ex-member seeks legal custody, visitation rights, or restrictions on the cult member's activities, much will hinge on expert testimony about the practices of the group and their effects on the child. Depending on a child's age and circumstances, it may be shown that the group's practices may be harmful to the child's best interest. With proper use of expert testimony, decisions have been made in which the parent emerging from the group has been granted sole custody and, in some instances, limitations have been placed upon the child's contacts with the parent remaining in the destructive group, or participation in the group's activities.

It is necessary to carefully document actual and prospective harm before going into a judicial hearing (Greene, 1989; Kandel, 1987/1988). Sometimes agreements are able to be reached between spouses when there is a cooperative willingness to deal with the best interests of the children. I am aware of many cases in which membership in a group has not so dominated the views of parents that they are unable to perceive the jeopardy to their children's welfare posed by the children's continued participation in certain of the group's practices.

A difficult issue receiving current attention is how to treat children who have spent major developmental portions of their lives in a group that restricted their ability to interact with people in the outside world. Very little study has been done to document this problem (see Chapter 17). Further study is needed, and comparisons to other groups living in separate communities may be helpful.

The law is on the edge of establishing the rights of grandparents to have communication with their grandchild. The thrust and pace of this development in the law differs from state to state, in some instances relying on statutes, in others being a matter of case-by-case decisions. These issues arise most frequently when parents are members of a group and grandparents, who are not members, seek communication or contact with their grandchild and enrichment of their grandchild's life through exposure to extended families. Issues also arise when grandparents discover serious deficiencies in the medical treatment or education their grandchild receives in or because of the practices of the group.

The decisive legal issue is the welfare of the grandchild. What is important is the development of the law and its recognition of the value of communication between children and all members of their families, including grandparents, even in the face of parental opposition. While much is left uncertain, this recognition should give great hope to the grandparent in this situation who is hoping to gain access to the grandchild. I also believe, although I know of no legal authority, that one should not reject out of hand a potential assertion of aunts' and uncles' rights asserted by a sibling of a parent in a cult.

Severing Contractual Commitments

It is usually necessary to sever cult-related contractual commitments made while the person was a cult member. For example, the member's lawyer may have been chosen by the group as a way of subordinating that person's rights to group control. This lawyer may primarily represent the group's best interests. Termination of that lawyer-client relationship as soon as possible is essential, for it places shackles upon the will of the emerged person.

While this may seem self-evident, I offer as an example a bizarre case in suburban New York. The judge in that case asserted that by the act of discharging a group-chosen lawyer, a former cult member may have evidenced a lack of independence of will. During this contest the group-chosen lawyer, against the expressed intent of the ex-member, sought to stir up claims against the ex-member's parents and interfered with her relationship with her newly chosen lawyer. The judge ordered her to have a psychiatric examination to determine her mental capacity. Despite arguments that firing one's lawyer is not a sign of insanity, the woman was compelled to undergo a psychiatric examination. Luckily it all worked out, but it was a humiliation the ex-member should never have been subjected to.

Another area of concern may be contracts that the person signed as a group member, some of which by their terms last millions of years. An objective reading will show that it is absurd to think that these contracts are legally enforceable documents. However, when a person emerges from a totalistic commitment, he or she needs to be assured that these contracts are legally unenforceable. In order to free the person from the oppressive fear that the contracts constitute morally or legally binding obligations, it is also important to explain to the ex-member why the contracts are not legally valid, so the person can view them in a newly independent rational context, restoring his or her respect for the legal system and deepening the person's understanding of his or her exploitation by the group.

It is very important that all contracts made as a group member be reviewed by a lawyer before the ex-member continues to honor them. Some contracts may be voidable because the person was fraudulently induced to sign them, or because the contract requires the person to perform illegal acts or unenforceably restricts the person from taking desired action. Sometimes the group will seek to pressure a former member to ratify a contract by asking the ex-member to honor a commitment as a demonstration of goodwill. If a former member, after leaving a group, continues to carry out his or her duties under a contract, a court might rule that the contract has been ratified, even though it could have been avoided. This might occur, for example, when the group bills the former member for "unpaid" donations and the person pays these bills after leaving the group. Contracts may also require unenforceable donations of services or agreements to commit or refrain from certain activities.

It is essential that ex-members be able to turn to a lawyer and supporter of their own choosing. Nothing should be done between the ex-member and the group without consulting counsel.

Recoupment of Financial Losses

After severing their contractual burdens, former cult members often try to recoup the financial losses they incurred during membership. For example, a member may have been underpaid as an employee of one of the group's businesses, may have been swindled out of money, or may have paid money for services that were not completely used.

Group businesses must comply with applicable regulations and labor laws. Groups operate gas stations, fur shops, newspapers, restaurants, printing plants, publishing houses, and sell flowers and books. These businesses must observe minimum wage laws and laws governing hours and conditions of employment.

Numerous former members have won legal redress based on the group's noncompliance with these laws, but claims must be made promptly because of short statutes of limitations. In this area government agencies, such as state and federal Departments of Labor, will frequently aid in the formulation of a claim and effect a recovery; in such an instance, a lawyer is needed only to guide the complainant through the appropriate state agencies. Additionally, an injury that may have been incurred as a result of unsafe conditions of employment may provide grounds for appropriate recourse and may likewise be enforced by state agencies. Losses may have been incurred through job exploitation, such as fraudulently induced donations or investments in a cult-related enterprise based on sales representatives.

Alternatively, the member may have paid money to be set up in a business franchise using the name of the group or a name owned by the group. In such circumstances, the ex-member may be legally entitled to full reimbursement if the group failed to comply with applicable laws at the inception of the arrangement. Additionally, if a legally required "cooling-off" period was not granted to allow the member to change his or her mind, certain types of contracts may be void. In cases where the member was given a "license" to use some of the trappings of the group or its "technologies," failure to comply with state laws may invalidate the agreement. In other cases, where the ex-member prepaid for services never received, the ex-member may be able to recoup part of the money attributable to the unused portion of the services.

In no circumstances should financial losses be abandoned; a lawyer should review the matter to see if legal recourse exists. However, the law does not provide a right to the recoupment of all losses. An honest case assessment should be made before an ex-member heads down the ofttimes costly road of litigation, seeking a large recovery for real but nonrecoverable loss. There are some losses that are simply too hard to prove or too remotely connected to a wrongful act to be able to be recovered through the courts. That does not mean the injury and pain of loss is not real. It merely means that the law's reach does not extend as far as the greedy grasp of a destructive group.

Emotional or Consequential Loss

In many instances the most severe loss that a member has suffered is an emotional damage incurred as a consequence of abuse. In such cases recovery of damages is extremely difficult and often speculative. Again, this does not mean that the injury is not real. What it means is that these cases may not readily be settled by the group, and the time from inception to financial recovery may stretch out over many, many years. Lawyers will be very reluctant to take on such litigation because of the expense in prosecuting it. While some lawyers do accept cases based upon sharing in a recovery, most will reject such an arrangement where the recovery is long deferred or requires too much time and expense to achieve. Also, during the process of litigation cult groups seek to make recovery of a judgment extremely difficult so that even a victory may not be translated into dollar recoupment. In recent periods we have seen a number of significant recoveries against cult groups go up and down on appeal in the highest courts of the Supreme Court, while a plaintiff who has won verdicts remains uncompensated.

An additional factor in undertaking such litigation is the emotional stress and strain upon the former cult member. The cult, in their defense, will not hesitate to assert that the group was not the cause of the plaintiff's pain and loss. In doing so, the cult will use – to its benefit and to the detriment of the former member – whatever private and confidential information it has regarding the ex-member and his or her families, friends, and acquaintances.

The time necessary for the ex-member's participation in the litigation, as we know, can often be substantial and dragged out over long periods of time, providing yet another impediment to the process of recovery and the ability of the former member to reorganize his or her life.

I do not unqualifiedly discourage litigation, and note that a few people made it work for them by achieving appropriate legal redress for harm done, and others have gained a significant degree of self-esteem by having the opportunity to confront their oppressor in the legal arena.

BROADER SOCIETAL ISSUES

In addition to the immediate legal issues that arise when a member leaves a destructive group, there are larger social questions as well.

Abuse of Women and Children

Within totalistic groups there is a pattern of victimization of the weak by the strong. Most prevalent is the systematic abuse of women and children (see Chapters 17 and 18) through the exercise of arbitrary power and the demand for perfect performance. The very first resolution unanimously adopted by the Interfaith Coalition of Concern about Cults in the New York metropolitan area was the condemnation of the abuse of women and children by destructive totalistic groups.

It has become clear that the perpetration of such abuse is not limited to religious groups. Exploitation of the weak, the naive, the credible, and the vulnerable is an issue troubling our society and other societies worldwide. Groups working to protect victims of destructive cults are working more closely with groups representing those victimized by other forms of familial or societal abuse.

In a number of states, governmental action has been successful in extricating children from abusive groups to save them from further injury. In some instances, courts have supported the government's interest in the health and welfare of minors over the opposition of a parent who submits to the group leader's unquestioned authority with unconditional obedience. Other cases, unfortunately, have not succeeded in rescuing these children. Significant controversy still remains concerning the denial of medical treatment to children (see Chapter 17).

Progress with respect to sexual abuse and victimization of women has been slow. More and more evidence of this type of abuse has surfaced, much of it related to abuses of power and destructive rituals.

Many Varieties of Abusive Groups

The years of public education undertaken by critics of totalistic groups have increased public awareness of the destructive consequences for those who surrender their own independent judgment to cultic groups. Education and publicity have also increased awareness of the risk in abusive psychological groups that are not full-fledged cults. Indeed, such abusive practices may occur in groups that seek a good purpose, such as a cure for drug abuse or weight reduction. Similarly, we have become more aware of abusive techniques in psychological well-being groups, "sport clubs," and certain masters or "Svengalis" in the arts. Nothing more graphically illustrates the irrelevance of the cults' professed purposes than the examination of the variety of subject matters covered by them. Power and profit are the sole unifying common elements.

Political Threats

A flickering of awareness of the political threat to our society posed by totalistic and cult-controlled groups is developing. Activities of the New Alliance Party, Lyndon LaRouche's political parties and front groups, and Transcendental Meditation's Natural Law Party have recently sparked meaningful debate. All these groups siphon support from federal sources. The Unification Church has come under scrutiny for its politically active front groups and its funding of ultraconservative political organizations here and abroad. Additionally, attention has been directed toward the practices of a number of groups that seek to create or cleanse society on religious or ethnic grounds, and seek to coopt and corrupt with cash offers in exchange for power and control.

Religious Groups

During this period of time many conventional religions have become aware and concerned about groups that have become abusive. Concern about them and the harm they foist upon their members frequently has become a subject of discussion among mainline religious leaders (see Chapter 12). Hopefully, this concern evidences a trend away from using religious motivation as an immunity toward a recognition of civic responsibility regardless of religious motivation.

Economic Power and the Legal System

Totalistic groups wield economic power and use it for social and legal leverage. There is no counting the number of people who have discovered that holding a valid legal right is worthless against a group that can make it economically impractical to enforce. As a lawyer, I am keenly aware of the deficiency in our legal system when one side has a "deep pocket" of economic resources. An opponent with fewer resources may be prevented from obtaining justice because of a seemingly limitless horde of opposing lawyers imposing overwhelming costs and obtaining interminable delays.

I have been approached by many people who possess written acknowledgment that sums are due them from certain groups, yet they cannot enforce their rights because the legal fees would cost more than the amount involved. Sometimes groups are willing to spend far more than is at issue to defeat and delay recovery on a claim, just to deter others.

It is not that a new set of laws is needed. Totalistic groups can be brought within the legal system rather than allowed to remain outside or above it. Totalistic groups are not entitled to special treatment or protection. They should become responsible members of our community.

THE PRESENT AND THE FUTURE

The role of the legal system in addressing problems arising out of the presence of destructive cults in our society has gone through a period of slow evolution. Existing legal modalities have been adapted to deal with the problems created by destructive cults (Rosedale, 1989). In reaching these conclusions significant controversies remain concerning the following: relationships among family members, the balance between church and state, the preservation of individual liberty and freedom of thought, and the application of laws governing fraud and misrepresentation without regard to the motive of the person or group committing these acts.

In many instances the legal system comes up short of being just. It is hobbled by the economic cost of enforcing legal rights. It is limited by the effort required to cut through the use of myth and the perversion of language common to totalistic groups. An example of this appeared in an exchange of letters (Rosedale, 1992; Small, 1992) in *The American Lawyer* after its publication of an article (Horne, 1992) about the Church of Scientology's legal representation. A lawyer who had represented the church pointed out that in his view the differences between the Church of Scientology and ordinary litigants was that the church made decisions "as a matter of principle" and was willing to litigate over principle more vigorously than other citizens. His statement is morally neutral until you determine what the principle is. If the "principle" is to crush dissent or financially punish critics by using the legal system as a weapon, then the morally neutral statement becomes a road map for oppression. When I confronted a lawyer about his tolerance of his client's criminal conduct in a Scientology-related case, he told me, "You do what you have to do to win." So much for "principle."

I understand all too well that the decisions of totalistic groups to fight their critics to the death may be a matter of principle. That principle is anathema in our pluralistic society and in an adversarial legal system which still requires commitment to the survival of the disenfranchised.

The legal system provides some aid to those in the process of recovery and disengagement from totalistic groups. It does not provide emotional satisfaction in redressing a wrong, nor does it adequately compensate for harm done. However, over a period of time it has enabled people who left totalistic groups to at least partly pull themselves out of the morass that they have entered into, to readjust their family relationships, to complete their severance, and to impose upon the totalistic groups a degree of accountability previously unknown. In this, the system has performed a useful function, provided its limitations are acknowledged and understood. As we move forward, I hope that the law will continue to address the wrongs that have occurred and that it will be an instrument of private redress and a vehicle for the reformation of behavior through accountability.

CHECKLIST FOR POST-CULT LEGAL ISSUES

Family Issues

Marriage

- ✓ Does the ex-member want to dissolve a marriage to someone still in the cult?
- ✓ Was the marriage legally binding or just ceremonial?
- ✓ If legal marriage, can it be annulled because it was induced by fraud or coercion?
- ✓ If not, is it possible to obtain a divorce?

Children

- ✓ Are there or does the ex-member anticipate child custody conflicts with a spouse in the group?
- ✓ What custody arrangement is in the best interest of a child who has one parent in a cult and one parent who has left the group?
- ✓ Would custody or visitation by the parent in the group be harmful to the child because of the group's practices? If so, testimony by expert witnesses is crucial for success in court.
- ✓ Do the grandparents wish to have contact with a grandchild, one or both of whose parents are in a restrictive group?

Financial Issues

Contracts

- ✓ Are there loans, obligations, or contracts that ought to be reviewed, either to avoid further obligations or to recover past payments? This should be done as soon as possible by a lawyer

of the ex-member's choosing. The ex-member should be advised
how to respond to pressure from the group to fulfill a contract.

✔ Did the former member enter into damaging contracts with
the group that are legally unenforceable?

Financial Losses

✔ If the ex-member worked in a group business, has the group
violated wage and hour laws? Was the ex-member appropriately paid for services rendered to the group? Because legal
deadlines for pursuing these types of claims are short, the ex-
member must act rapidly.

✔ If the former member signed a contract giving the group
money or property, were state laws regulating contracts (such
as the required "cooling-off" period) violated so that the contract is void?

✔ Does the ex-member believe he or she might have been misled,
defrauded, or otherwise exploited in business dealings with the
group or its leader?

✔ Is the group interfering with contractual arrangements between the ex-member and persons remaining in the group?

Physical and Psychological Abuse

✔ Is the group violating laws that protect children and adults
from physical abuse?

✔ Is the government empowered to remove children from abusive
groups?

✔ Does the ex-member have reason to believe that he or she suffered unusually severe emotional distress or residual physical
injuries as a result of the group involvement?

REFERENCES

Delgado, R. (1977). Religious totalism: Gentle and ungentle persuasion under
the First Amendment. *Southern California Law Review, 5*(1), 1–97.

Delgado, R. (1979). A response to professor Dressler. *Minnesota Law Review,
63,* 361–365.

Delgado, R. (1982). Cults and conversion: The case for informed consent. *Geor-
gia Law Review, 16*(3), 533–574.

Dressler, J. (1979). Professor Delgado's "brainwashing" defense: Courting a
determinist legal system. *Minnesota Law Review, 63,* 335–360.

Greene, F. (1989). Litigating child custody with religious cults. *Cultic Studies
Journal 6*(1), 69–75.

Horne, W. W. (1992, July/August). The two faces of Scientology. *The American Lawyer*, pp. 74–82.

Kandel, R. F. (1987/1988). Litigating the cult-related child custody case. *Cultic Studies Journal*, 4/5(1), 123–131.

Lucksted, O. D., & Martell, D. F. (1982, April, May, & June). Cults: A conflict between religious liberty and involuntary servitude? *FBI Law Enforcement Bulletin*, 51(4, 5, 6), pp. 16–20, 16–23, 16–21.

Rosedale, H. L. (1989). Legal analysis of intent as a continuum emphasizing social context of volition. *Cultic Studies Journal*, 6(1), 25–31.

Rosedale, H. L. (1992, September). Letter to the editor. *The American Lawyer*, pp. 17–18.

Shapiro, R. (1983). Of robots, persons, and the protection of religious beliefs. *Southern California Law Review*, 56(6), 1277–1318.

Small, T. (1992, September). Letter to the editor. *The American Lawyer*, pp. 17–18.

INDEX